CONTEMPORARY
POLITICAL IDEOLOGIES

Contemporary
Political Ideologies

A Comparative Analysis

Tenth Edition

LYMAN TOWER SARGENT
University of Missouri–St. Louis

WADSWORTH PUBLISHING COMPANY
I(T)P® An International Thomson Publishing Company

Belmont • Albany • Bonn • Boston • Cincinnati • Detroit • London • Madrid
Melbourne • Mexico City • New York • Paris • San Francisco • Singapore
Tokyo • Toronto • Washington

Political Science Editor: Tammy Goldfeld
Editorial Assistant: Heide Chavez
Production Services Coordinator: Gary Mcdonald
Production: Mary Douglas/Rogue Valley Publications
Print Buyer: Karen Hunt
Permissions Editor: Jeanne Bosschart
Designer: Stephen Rapley
Copy Editor: Adrienne Armstrong
Cover Designer: Ross Carron Design
Compositor: Kachina Typesetting Inc.
Printer: Quebecor Printing/Fairfield

I(T)P   A Division of International Thomson Publishing Inc.
The ITP logo is a registered trademark under license.

For more information, contact Wadsworth Publishing Company:

Wadsworth Publishing Company
10 Davis Drive
Belmont, California 94002, USA

International Thomson Editores
Campos Eliseos 385, Piso 7
Col. Polanco
11560 México D.F. México

International Thomson Publishing Europe
Berkshire House 168-173
High Holborn
London, WC1V 7AA, England

International Thomson Publishing GmbH
Königswinterer Strasse 418
53227 Bonn, Germany

Thomas Nelson Australia
102 Dodds Street
South Melbourne 3205
Victoria, Australia

International Thomson Publishing Asia
221 Henderson Road
#05-10 Henderson Building
Singapore 0315

Nelson Canada
1120 Birchmount Road
Scarborough, Ontario
Canada M1K 5G4

International Thomson Publishing Japan
Hirakawacho Kyowa Building, 3F
2-2-1 Hirakawacho
Chiyoda-ku, Tokyo 102, Japan

1 2 3 4 5 6 7 8 9 10—01 00 99 98 97 96

Library of Congress Cataloging-in-Publication Data

Sargent, Lyman Tower, 1940-
    Contemporary political ideologies : a comparative analysis / Lyman
    Tower Sargent. — Ed. 10.
        p. cm.
    Includes bibliographical references and index.
    ISBN 0-534-50694-1
    1. Political science—History. I. Title.
    JA83.S34 1996   95-4848
    320.5'09—dc20

To Evan

About the Author

Lyman Tower Sargent is Professor of Political Science and Chair of the Department of Political Science at the University of Missouri–St. Louis. He has been a visiting professor at the University of Exeter, England, an academic visitor at the London School of Economics and Political Science, and a fellow at the Institute for Advanced Study, Princeton. He is the author of *Contemporary Political Ideologies: A Reader* (Wadsworth, 1990); *New Left Thought: An Introduction* (Dorsey, 1972); *Techniques of Political Analysis: An Introduction* (with Thomas A. Zant, Wadsworth, 1970); *British and American Utopian Literature 1516–1985: An Annotated, Chronological Bibliography* (Garland, 1988); *Extremism in America: A Reader* (New York University Press, 1995); and numerous articles in political theory.

Preface

According to Feliks Gross, political ideologies in this century have replaced religion as the focus of both human liberation and human fanaticism.[1] Ideologies like *Marxism, democracy*, and *nationalism*, whose names are well recognized but whose contents are not well known, form the focus of this study. The essential features of certain ideologies in the world today are presented in a way that can be readily understood. To the extent possible, the ideologies are shown as they are understood by their believers, along with some of the criticisms made by their opponents. My goal is to help readers draw their own conclusions about each ideology based on a reasonably balanced picture of that ideology.

The world is currently continuing the period of rapid change that began with the collapse of the former Soviet Union as a world power. Many of the ideologies that constitute important parts of the way people understand what is happening around them have been deeply affected by these changes. The long-term results of these changes are not yet clear, but for many people significant changes are taking place in the way they view the world.

Most notably, nationalism has become one of the most obvious aspects of the contemporary political scene. Newspapers and television are full of pictures and stories from the former Yugoslavia, Rwanda, and other countries where people are daily killing each other in the name of identity and political advantage. These conflicts are deeply rooted in the past histories of the areas involved, histories that helped create the identities in conflict. More than ever it is essential to understand the characteristics of nationalism to understand the daily news.

Communists are having to reassess their entire belief system. Many have not

---

[1]Feliks Gross, *Ideologies, Goals, and Values* (Westport, CT: Greenwood Press, 1985), p. xxiii.

changed significantly. For some the failure of capitalism to bring the instant prosperity that they had hoped for has led to a nostalgia for the previous system; for others the fact that many people are actually worse off now than they had been under the previous system has led them to return to those earlier beliefs. As a result, under various labels former Communists are being elected to office in the countries of the former Soviet Union and Eastern Europe. At the other extreme, some Communists have become instant converts to capitalism, and former Communists are among the leading entrepreneurs of the new market economy and the owners and managers of the now privatized state industries.

Democratic capitalists, who generally believe that they won the Cold War, are growing worried about what they see to be the naivete of the former Communists and their expectations for rapid change. The growth of serious poverty and the emergence of powerful criminal organizations in the former communist countries indicate that the tranformation from centralized, state controlled economies to market economies will not be easy.

In addition to the changes taking place in the economies of the former communist countries, there is a worldwide movement of democratization. Countries in Africa, South America, and Latin America as well as in Eastern Europe and the former Soviet Union are in the process of trying to establish political institutions that are responsive to the wishes of the people to replace or reform institutions that were under the control of elites, a single political party, or the military.

Islam continues to be a growing force in world politics and remains generally little understood in the United States. Environmentalism is becoming an international social movement and is slowly becoming more clearly an ideology. Feminism is also becoming an international ideology and, in doing so, is becoming more complex.

Since the first edition was published over 30 years ago, this book has remained the leading text in the field. I have maintained the essential character of the book as a comparative introduction to the dominant and some minor ideologies of the modern world. Most chapters conclude with a summary of current trends and an extensive list of suggested readings. I have tried to maintain the usefulness and flexibility of the work as a teaching tool. The inclusion of updated material makes this edition the most current text on the market.

Acknowledgments

I wish to thank the following people for help in preparing this edition. The office staff of the Department of Political Science, Lana Vierdag, Jan Frantzen, and Kristine Brooks, have put up with my ever-increasing demands. I thank manuscript reviewers Joan Davison, Rollins College, and Lawrence Hough, East Carolina University, for their helpful suggestions. I also wish to thank Deborah Altus for her comments on the ninth edition; I have incorporated them into my discussion of the cooperative movement.

Lyman Tower Sargent

Contents

1

Ideologies: What Are They and Why Study Them?

At the world population conference in Cairo, Egypt, in 1994, a debate took place over the reproductive rights of women. This debate could not have taken place even twenty years ago. One of the reasons it could take place in 1994 is that feminism has become a global social movement that has a number of central beliefs, one of which is that women should have greater control over their own bodies. An ideology has influenced public policy.

In 1994 the United States threatened to invade Haiti in the name of democracy. Countries all over the world are going through a process called *democratization*. Eritrea is trying to create a democratic system of government where none existed. Democracy seems to have become a belief system accepted by most of the world. An ideology is changing the face of world politics.

In April 1995, individuals who identify with the radical right in the United States bombed a federal building in Oklahoma City. Not since the urban terrorism of the 1960s has the United States witnessed a home-grown, ideologically based terrorism that has justified bombing on the basis of belief. Also, the sixties bombers typically targeted unoccupied buildings and did not generally attack people who were not directly involved in the activities they opposed. The radical right has been involved in a number of individual murders, mostly based on race, but a terrorist act such as the Oklahoma City bombing has been a possibility for some time.

Over the past few years we have seen people in the former Yugoslavia killing each other because of their religious, ethnic, and national differences and we have seen a civil war in Rwanda in which two peoples slaughtered each other for similar reasons. In each case the hatreds that led to the killing go deeply into the past and, in both cases, result in part because outsiders combined in one country peoples with histories of conflict. The belief in an ideology justifies mass murder.

The leader of one country contends that industries must be taken away from their private owners and operated under government supervision; the leader of another country contends that industries must be taken away from those that operate them under government supervision and sold to private owners. Each is convinced that this position is economically and morally correct. Why the difference? The answer is ideology.

These are but a few examples of the ways in which ideology affects people's behavior. Obviously, ideology is important if we are to understand what happens in the world. In addition, understanding the various ideologies of the world will help us understand our own beliefs and the beliefs of our friends and associates.

Whether we are aware of it or not, most of us are influenced by ideology. Every television program, newspaper, book, or film, directly or indirectly, intentionally or unintentionally, presents an ideology. Some of these presentations are simple; others are complex. All of them influence us. As we grow up, our families, teachers, and friends help shape our personalities and beliefs by pushing us to do or believe what they do or believe. At times we also make conscious choices among beliefs and attitudes, either because we weigh one position against another and conclude that one is better or worse according to some standard, or perhaps simply because we do or do not respect a person who holds that belief.

We gradually come to the set of beliefs and attitudes with which we will live. This set of beliefs may change, but it changes less as we grow older. This is true not simply because we get "set in our ways" as we get older, although that does happen. It is also true because our entire view of the world and our explanations for both social and personal happenings depend on our particular understanding of the past. It is extraordinarily difficult to set aside a lifetime's experience and accept that we have been wrong.

Most of us are not aware of all aspects of what we believe. We do not examine our beliefs very often, if at all. We may rethink one position or change another without really thinking about it, but we rarely look carefully or thoroughly at our beliefs. We simply accept them.

In the development of our own beliefs and attitudes, we are affected by a variety of belief systems—religious and/or political views of the world that are, or are believed to be, internally consistent and consciously held by many people; we call these belief systems *ideologies*. At times each of us reacts on the basis of an ideology; at such times we are acting as though we accepted the ideology, even if we don't accept all of the attitudes and beliefs that make up that ideology. We may accept parts of these ideologies simply because we have been taught to react positively or negatively to words that represent them. For example, people growing up in the United States are likely to be certain that capitalism is right and communism wrong. We react to words because they have emotional content, even if they do not have intellectual content for us. Most people, of course, find some emotional and some intellectual content in important words.

How do we identify an ideology? The most obvious way is through the use of language in general or through the use of particular words that are identified with an ideology. For example, someone influenced by capitalism will usually speak favorably of the free market, and someone influenced by Marxism will use the word *class* in specific ways. This does not necessarily mean that the person accepts all the positions taken by a committed believer in the ideology, but paying attention to language is a good way of identifying ideological influences. Becoming aware of the ideological loading of words and the ways beliefs and attitudes fit together to constitute an ideology should also help us better understand our own beliefs. Readers will probably recognize themselves somewhere in this book and may also encounter serious questions about their beliefs.

IDEOLOGY DEFINED

Much controversy exists among scholars about the meaning and effect of ideology.[1] One scholar has even written that "ideology is the most elusive concept in the whole of social science."[2] This section constructs a definition of ideology and shows how ideology relates to political philosophy and political theory. The section then illustrates the relationship between ideologies and beliefs, noting how ideologies and ideological conflicts affect people. Finally, a few of the most important theorists of ideology are presented, and the current controversies among theorists are described.

An ideology is a value system or belief system accepted as fact or truth by some group. It is composed of sets of attitudes toward the various institutions and processes of society. An ideology provides the believer with a picture of the world both as it is and as it should be, and, in doing so, organizes the tremendous complexity of the world into something fairly simple and understandable. Ideologies are organized or patterned beliefs. The degree of organization and the simplicity of the resulting picture vary considerably from ideology to ideology, and the ever-increasing complexity of the

---

[1]An excellent introductory discussion of the concept of ideology can be found in Raymond Williams, *Keywords: A Vocabulary of Culture and Society*, rev. ed. (New York: Oxford University Press, 1983), pp. 153–157. See also Mostafa Rejai, "Ideology," in *Dictionary of the History of Ideas*, 4 vols., ed. Philip P. Wiener (New York: Scribner's, 1973, vol. 2, pp. 552–559.

[2]David McLellan, *Ideology* (Minneapolis: University of Minnesota Press, 1986), p. 1.

world tends to blur the pictures. At the same time, however, the fundamental pattern of each ideology remains fairly constant.

Political Philosophy, Political Theory, and Political Ideology

In order to understand ideologies, we must comprehend their theoretical or philosophical bases. Scholars use various terms to discuss political ideas, and it is desirable to distinguish among the most important of those terms. Unfortunately, these terms are often used loosely, and some of the time the uses are interchangeable. Still, the terms *political ideology, political theory,* and *political philosophy* are frequently used to refer to different ways of thinking about political ideas. The first term, *political ideology,* relates, as we have seen, to the beliefs of a group. That term should never be used in place of either of the other two. The other two terms are often used interchangeably, and much of the time nothing is wrong with that. But at other times, it is important to distinguish between the two.

When used specifically, *political theory* refers to scientific theory or generalizations about politics and society that are based on data, just like any generalization in any science. There is a debate in the social sciences about whether such generalizations should or can be free of evaluative or normative content— "value-free," as the phrase goes. There is a growing consensus today that such "value-free" social science is extremely rare if not impossible. *Political philosophy* is, on the other hand, explicitly evaluative or normative. It is a set of ideas about how governments and people should behave.

The terms are connected because every political philosophy is based in part on a political theory. In other words, every statement about how people and governments should behave contains a statement about how they do behave. In addition, every political ideology contains both political theory and political philosophy, generalizations about how people and governments do behave and how they should behave. But in a political ideology, these generalizations become belief systems rather than empirical or normative analyses of behavior.

BELIEFS AND IDEOLOGIES

We all have beliefs; we are all influenced by ideologies, but we do not all have a coherent system of beliefs. And even those of us who do have such a system of beliefs are not all influenced by it in the same way or to the same extent.

In the United States the general assumption has been that very few people have ideologies. This assumption was based on the tendency to equate ideologies with the extremes and is harder to maintain today with so much of American political debate clearly based on belief rather than reasoned argument. In much of the rest of the world it has been assumed that in some ways everyone has an ideology because the argument is widely accepted that ideology permeates culture.

American scholars tend to assume that people who hold ideologies are aware that they do, whereas European writers contend that ideology is important just because most people aren't aware that they hold one. To some extent this lack of awareness reflects a tendency to think that "only other people have ideologies—I don't." If an ideology is dominant in an area, it is unlikely to be recognized except by someone outside the area. For example, during all the years that Americans tended to see themselves as nonideological, Europeans argued for the existence of an ideology that was shared by most Americans.

As an example of ideology in current usage, let us take an oversimplified and extreme case that will illustrate both the nature of ideology and the process of change within an ideology. In the past, movies presented viewers with a simple, clearly defined view of the clash of good and evil in the American West. The good guy and the bad guy were even identified by white clothes and a white horse for the hero and black clothes and a black horse for the villain. The good guys always won. All ideologies include definitions of who are the good guys and who are the bad guys, and sometimes these definitions are as simple as in the old Westerns.

Although much of the basic pattern has not changed and the identical pattern can be found in some science fiction movies, today's Westerns show the two sides dressed the same and riding the same color horses. In addition, many present the bad guy as not entirely evil and the good guy as not always entirely good.

These differences illustrate some of the problems in analyzing ideologies as they change over time. Some ideologies retain the old rigid good–bad division. In others, such a complexity of factors is at work that it is difficult, or even impossible, to tell the good guys from the bad guys. In this situation a believer is often affected by more than one set of beliefs. She or he is influenced by, for example, the positions of a political party, a church, and a corporation or union. Each of these stands can constitute a partially or fully developed ideology. Although some parts of these systems may coincide perfectly or closely enough to not cause conflict within the individual, other parts may differ greatly.

SOCIAL MOVEMENTS AND THE DEVELOPMENT OF IDEOLOGY

In the past half century a number of new or revitalized ideologies have emerged, such as feminism, Liberation Theology, and environmentalism. But where do ideologies come from? The answer appears simple at first glance: ideologies emerge as social movements grow and mature. While this answer applies to most cases—environmentalism is the best example, with feminism complicated only by its long, neglected history and the changes it has undergone as it matured—there are exceptions. Liberation Theology, for example, developed first as an intellectual movement, initially in Europe, and only later as a social movement, primarily in South America. Liberation Theology was created by theologians and philosophers.

If we look back at older ideologies, we can see that some clearly emerge as the result of developing social movements—nationalism is the clearest example as it emerged during the development of the nation-state—and others are created by thinkers responding to changing conditions. To a non-Marxist, Marxism is a clear example of this, although a Marxist would see its development as a response to social changes. Most ideologies appear to develop as means of trying to understand social change and then, filling needs for people, become systems of belief.

IDEOLOGICAL CONFLICTS

Some people may not even notice the differences between the various sets of beliefs that influence them, but others will be so torn apart by the conflict that they develop serious mental problems. Most of us muddle through, aware that we are not really consistent in our beliefs and behavior but not terribly bothered by that fact.

Similar situations occur within countries. In most open societies where many ideologies are recognized and accepted, conflict within the individual is unlikely to become important. But conflicts among ideologies may become obvious, and, if the numbers of adherents of conflicting ideologies are large enough and close enough in size, a country's stability can be affected. On the other hand, in a closed system with only one official ideology, if an individual holds beliefs counter to that ideology he or she will probably be intensely aware of the difference and be affected by it. The same thing is true for the country as a whole. Ideological differences, particularly differences within the official ideology, become more important and can cause serious conflict.

The phenomenon apparent in American movies about the Old West occurs in all societies. As a society grows more complex, it becomes harder to present a simple division between good and bad, between the white and black hats. Black and white are mixed and become gray. We have discovered that the world is not as simple as the older movies would have us believe; the new Western reflects this recognition.

Even with this change in the pattern of some ideologies, all ideologies attempt to organize our complex world into a pattern that will at least give some signposts to help the believer distinguish good from bad. Finally, in none of them do the ideal and reality meet, and there is a struggle to bring the two together through changes in either the ideal or the reality.

In any society, different segments of the population will hold different ideologies. For example, within the United States today, the overwhelming majority, if asked, would call themselves believers in democracy. But some would call themselves anarchists, Fascists, and so forth. Every society exhibits a variety of ideologies. In no case will a given society be so completely dominated by a single ideology as to have no ideological alternatives available within the system, even though those alternatives may be actively suppressed by the regime.

Many of those willing to label themselves as democrats or as adherents of some other ideology do not act in the way the ideology would be expected to lead them to act. But most people build up a pattern of behavior, some aspects of which come directly from the dominant political ideology of the country in which they live. For example, it is a bit surprising that people accept the outcome of elections rather than fighting for their side when they lose. But most people in countries with established democracies are so conditioned to accept loss in elections that they do so without ever thinking about revolt. This acceptance is not always the rule, though. There are countries in most parts of the world in which elections produce violent attempts, sometimes successful, to change the results. Such violence occurs even in democratic countries. There are recent cases in both Haiti and Nigeria where elected presidents were overthrown by the military. In Nigeria the president was never even allowed to assume office; the military dictator, who had agreed to the elections, simply threw out the results and kept office.

Differences Within Ideologies

Differences exist within each ideology that make each a cluster of ideologies. Democracy is the most obvious example, being composed of at least two major categories—democratic capitalism and democratic socialism. All who place themselves in either of these categories believe themselves to be democrats and often see themselves as the only true democrats. In addition to this major division, there are numerous disagreements over the emphasis placed on certain aspects of democracy and over the tactics used in achieving desired goals. No ideology is completely free from this sort of disagreement. A variety of differing positions and disagreements together make up the ideology and allow it to change to meet changing conditions. Only a dead ideology is free from such differences.

To reiterate, individuals may hold a variety of beliefs that may be in conflict. Normally, people do not recognize the conflicting nature of their beliefs, and they apply their beliefs to different situations without ever looking at their values as a whole. A person either fails to see the problem, argues that the positions are not irreconcilable, or gradually rejects one position. This conflict presents one of the most serious obstacles to a clear understanding of ideologies; it will remain a theme in the consideration of each ideology.

IDEOLOGY AND PRACTICE

A central concern of all students of ideology is the extent to which and the ways in which ideology affects practice. Evidence is limited by the very nature of the question, and there used to be a widespread attitude in the United States that belief does not affect the practice of politicians. Today that effect is obvious.

Political leaders use the language of the dominant ideology of their country to justify their actions. But do their actions derive from ideology or expediency?

In addition, contradictions are often apparent between the actions of adherents of some ideologies when out of power and their actions when in power. At the same time, ideological language has come to permeate politics in the last quarter of the twentieth century; it is not all facade with no reality behind it.

The most likely effect of ideology is in the limiting of options. Except in extraordinary circumstances, political leaders will not perceive as options policies that fall outside their ideology. In this way ideology limits but does not determine practice. However, we have had the opportunity to witness just such an extraordinary breakout from ideology in Eastern Europe and the former Soviet Union. Political leaders in various countries have been struggling to free themselves from the preconceptions of communism. Some have simply accepted an alternative ideology, while others have not changed significantly.

THEORIES OF IDEOLOGY

The word *ideology* was first used in the early 1800s by a group of French thinkers called the Ideologues to describe an approach to understanding how ideas are formed. The word was picked up by others and used mostly as a label for ways in which people block out messages that threaten them. For all these thinkers, ideologies keep people from understanding the truth about their situations. It is only recently that theories of ideology have ceased to generally treat ideology negatively, as an escape from or a way to hide reality. Today both social scientists and political theorists are searching for neutral definitions. The following section briefly discusses theorists and a debate over the end of ideology in the West.

Karl Marx

Karl Marx (1818–1883) argued that ideologies blind people to facts about their place in society. He described as ideological any set of political *illusions* produced by the social experiences of a *class* (i.e., a social group defined by its economic role; for example, owners or workers). Marx called ideology *false consciousness*. For Marx, a person's membership in a particular class produced a picture of the world shaped by the experiences of that class. Thus it would be almost impossible for an individual class member to form an accurate conception of the world. Marx argued that *socialization* (i.e., the process by which an individual comes to accept the values of the society) is strongly shaped by one's place in the class system of that society. In other words, he contended that the social setting in which each of us lives determines the broad outlines of the way we think. The members of different classes are both directly and indirectly taught to think and behave in ways "appropriate" for their own class. This pattern is often called the *social construction of reality*. In other words, what we perceive as reality is created by the social world we inhabit; living in a different society, we would perceive a different reality.

Georges Sorel

A different approach to ideology, using the word *myth* rather than *ideology*, was proposed by Georges Sorel (1847–1922). Sorel argued that mass movements develop visions of the future that their members don't quite believe in, but that are an essential part of what motivates them. He called these visions *myths*. Sorel focused on fairly specific myths, like the belief in the general strike prevalent among syndicalists, rather than the broader belief systems that this text calls *ideologies*. Also, as the word *myth* implies, the depth of belief in a myth is not the same as for an ideology. But myths can galvanize people and are clearly part of all ideologies.

Sigmund Freud

Sigmund Freud (1856–1939) made one point that must be noted about beliefs such as ideologies. Freud was specifically concerned with religious belief, but his comments apply equally well to political ideologies. Freud argued that although belief systems are illusions based on the distortion or repression of our psychological needs, they still provide an organized framework for explaining the world and its ills. An accepted explanation, even one that is demonstrably wrong, can be comforting. Thus Freud, like Marx, saw ideologies as illusions that keep us deluded and content with a difficult, if not intolerable, condition. Freud prescribed psychoanalysis if the illusion becomes sufficiently pathological; Marx prescribed revolution.

Antonio Gramsci

A political activist and social theorist influenced by both Marx and Sorel, Antonio Gramsci (1891–1937) developed most of his contributions while imprisoned by the Italian Fascists during the last eleven years of his life. Gramsci argued that the ruling classes dominate the means of socialization (education, religion, the media, and even the family) to such an extent that an intellectual, cultural, and social *hegemony* is created that conditions the way all people in that society perceive the world.[3]

Karl Mannheim

Karl Mannheim (1893–1947) gave a description of ideology close to Marx's, except Mannheim attempted to avoid the negative connotations that Marx intended in his definition. For Marx, ideologies were illusions that kept members of a class from understanding their true place in society. Mannheim attempted to deal with the same phenomenon scientifically. He argued that ideology should be treated from two perspectives, which he labeled "the total conception" and "the particular conception" of ideology.[4]

---

[3]An excellent discussion of hegemony may be found in Williams, *Keywords*, pp. 144–146.

[4]Karl Mannheim, *Ideology and Utopia: An Introduction to the Sociology of Knowledge*, trans. Louis Wirth and Edward Shils (New York: Harcourt Brace Jovanovich, 1936), pp. 55–56.

The "total conception" is a general description of the beliefs held in common by a group, such as a social class or an age group. These beliefs are similar to the blinders on a horse, limiting the believer's view of the world to what is acceptable to the ideology. A person whose mind has been sufficiently formed by his or her membership in a group either simply does not perceive information that conflicts with the belief system or is provided by that belief system with a convenient explanation that allows the problem to be shunted aside without being recognized as a threat. For Mannheim, an ideology is produced by a failing ruling class to protect itself from the realization of its coming extinction.

The "particular conception" is a description of the situation in which people recognize the beliefs of opponents as "more or less conscious disguises of the real nature of a situation, a true recognition of which would not be in accord with his interest."[5] This is the belief that the other person's ideas, but not our own, are false representations of the world, illusions or masks that hide the truth from the believer.

Mannheim believed that intellectuals who were not frozen into a class would be capable of recognizing ideologies. Influenced by both Marx and Freud, Mannheim used a class analysis, but he prescribed education and psychoanalysis as the solution.

Clifford Geertz

One of the most influential recent commentators on ideology is the anthropologist and social theorist Clifford Geertz (1926–).[6] For Geertz, ideologies are systems of symbols that bring order to the world. These symbols derive from culture, are psychologically satisfying, and provide a mechanism through which we can understand the world around us. An ideology, then, is a coherent set of such symbols. Geertz, like Mannheim, is searching for a relatively neutral definition of ideology.

The End of Ideology Debate

In the 1950s and 1960s a debate started, particularly in the United States, about whether or not ideological politics had ended in the West.[7] In a few cases this argument went so far as to suggest that ideological politics had never existed in the United States. However, even if this were once true, it no longer is, and the roots of the contemporary situation go back precisely to the time when the debate over the end of ideology was raging.

---

[5]Mannheim, *Ideology and Utopia*, p. 55.

[6]See Clifford Geertz, "Ideology as a Cultural System," in *Ideology and Discontent*, ed. David E. Apter (New York: Free Press of Glencoe, 1964), pp. 47–76.

[7]For the debate, see Mostafa Rejai, ed., *Decline of Ideology?* (Chicago: Aldine-Atherton, 1971); and Chaim I. Waxman, ed., *The End of Ideology Debate* (New York: Funk & Wagnalls, 1968). The book that gave rise to the debate in the United States was Daniel Bell, *The End of Ideology: On the Exhaustion of Political Ideas in the Fifties* (New York: Free Press of Glencoe, 1960).

Today we see ideological politics throughout the world. How could anyone believe that ideology was ending only thirty to forty years ago? Part of the answer is definitional. For some people the word *ideological* simply meant *extremist*, and U.S. politics were perceived as based on compromises that assumed a fundamental agreement. This perception of the U.S. political system was possible only if the focus was on the political center, where such agreement used to exist. But even in the 1950s the agreement was unraveling.

Perhaps it is best to say that the end of ideology, to the extent it existed at all, could better be labeled *the exhaustion with ideology*. By the late 1950s the twentieth century had seen two world wars; numerous minor wars; the full development of two major ideologies, communism and fascism; and, in the United States, two major anti-left campaigns (in the 1920s and 1950s) and a major anti-Fascist campaign during World War II. One of the responses to all this was an attempt to escape from ideology into objectivity. Particularly in the social sciences, attempts were made to eliminate value judgments from research. While the social sciences are more objective than they were prior to World War II, scholars rapidly discovered that there are limits to objectivity where human beings are concerned. Also, the development of important political movements, such as the civil rights movement in the United States, which demanded that people take a stand, taught social scientists and others that understanding a situation as objectively and thoroughly as possible and taking a position about it can be complementary actions rather than contradictory ones. And then came Vietnam, and the need to take a position shattered whatever remained of objectivity.

Some writers argued that not only had ideology ended in the West, but that its demise was a good thing because ideology was a bad thing. Ideological politics were seen as divisive politics—politics that made compromise impossible, that drove people apart. Ideology also hindered Western progress toward the "good society." Had ideology not gotten in the way, a better society might have been possible in the near future through the usual practices of compromise politics.

The participants in the debate differed both over what they were talking about and to some extent over whether the end of ideology was a good thing. Some people suggested ideology was ending in communist as well as Western countries. Again, this was generally seen as favorable. The single point on which the debaters came closest to agreeing was that ideology is bad for us and if it hadn't ended, it should.

In the years since the 1960s, thinking has moved a long way in the opposite direction, back toward objectivity but with a much greater recognition of the difficulties involved. With the collapse of communist regimes, the end of ideology debate has been revived to some extent, but what is actually happening is that the adherents of one ideology—democratic capitalism—are celebrating what is perceived as victory over that ideology's main opponent. Ideology has certainly not come to an end.

The Situation Today

The overwhelming tradition has been that ideology hides truth. Thus it has been considered dangerous by most commentators. Today, influenced by postmodernism, scholars focus on competing ideologies and their "truths" without worrying too much about whether or not these ideologies are hiding a truth. To each set of believers, it is the other ideologies that are hiding the truth.

As a result, these days ideology is itself what we have come to call an *essentially contested concept* or a concept about which there is such fundamental disagreement that no resolution is possible.[8] Most political debate swirls around such contested concepts. Ideology is at one and the same time a mechanism of social or psychological compensation for an individual or social group, a cultural artifact, and a self-contained logic that explains the world. Today, ideologies almost always contain a scientific explanation of the world, because science is today's most pervasive ideology.

Some of the fundamental differences over what constitutes an ideology are the result of differences between the two major ideologies influencing Western scholars on the subject—Marxism and liberalism.[9] But today these differences have fragmented, and we are faced with interpretations of ideology that, while still generally based on either Marxism or liberalism, present ideology in cultural, philosophical, psychoanalytic, and sociological terms. A recent study of the concept, Terry Eagleton's *Ideology* (1991), lists sixteen contemporary definitions, which he contends can be reduced to six, some of which are mutually exclusive.[10]

In addition, in the recent past we have witnessed the emergence of numerous new or, more accurately, newly labeled views of the world that are sometimes called ideologies. We have also seen the advocates of certain well-established ideologies, such as capitalism, gain an intellectual self-confidence that was not apparent earlier, while adherents of other ideologies, most notably communism, have lost confidence. In addition, as groups become aware of themselves as groups with ideological ties, they seem to become more aware of the roots of their ideologies, and forerunners who were hitherto not considered very important become more significant.

The competition among ideologies appears to have become more clearly both political *and* intellectual. The battle is for both the hearts and the minds of adherents and political converts, and within ideologies there is a quest for coherence and grounding that contradicts many of the theories we use to understand ideology. The result is that the ideological map is more complex than ever, and it is even more necessary to understand the theoretical roots of ideologies than it was in the past.

---

[8]See W. B. Gallie, "Essentially Contested Concepts," *Proceedings of the Aristotelian Society*, n.s. 56 (1955–1956): 167–198; and William E. Connolly, *The Terms of Political Discourse*, 2d ed. (Oxford, England: Martin Robertson, 1983).

[9]For a discussion of these differences, see Ian Adams, *The Logic of Political Belief: A Philosophical Analysis of Ideology* (Savage, MD: Barnes & Noble Books, 1989), pp. 1–23.

[10]Terry Eagleton, *Ideology: An Introduction* (London: Verso, 1991), pp. 1–30.

A redevelopment of the end of ideology theory greeted the publication in 1989 of "Have We Reached the End of History?" by Francis Fukuyama.[11] In this essay, Fukuyama argued that liberalism—his name for democratic capitalism—had obviously won the day and that no other ideology was a serious contender for dominance. For Fukuyama, fundamental contradictions no longer exist in the world, either in ideology or practice.

Fukuyama suggests that nationalism and Muslim fundamentalism are minor alternatives but will pose no threat to democratic capitalism. He fails to recognize that much of the Islamic world that is not fundamentalist also rejects democratic capitalism; and, of course, in the brief time since his essay was published, the world has witnessed the tremendous power of nationalism. He does not seem to be aware of the alternatives posed by feminism or environmentalism, all or most of whose adherents reject democratic capitalism.

Even if democratic capitalism is currently dominant, fundamental contradictions still exist between rich and poor, ethnic groups, religions, the genders, the races, and between the human race and the natural world that can produce new ideologies or developments within old ones. Fukuyama's article is best viewed as reflecting the celebration at the ending of communism in much of the world rather than as a serious statement about the current situation.

IDEOLOGIES TO BE CONSIDERED

The ideologies selected for consideration in this book have been chosen on the basis of two main criteria: their importance in the world today and the author's desire to present a broad range of political beliefs. Nationalism; democracy and its two major forms, democratic capitalism and democratic socialism; Marxism; and Islam clearly fall into the first category. Each must be understood before the news of the day can be intelligently grasped. Anarchism clearly belongs in the second category. Although anarchism never has been dominant in any area for long, it still has many adherents and a continuing popularity. A survey of political ideology would be incomplete without anarchism. The other ideologies included fall somewhere between these two categories. Each is important for an understanding of recent history and current events but not to the same degree as nationalism, democracy, Marxism, and Islam. In addition, each represents a point on the spectrum of political beliefs that is not clearly occupied by any of the others.

One belief system, nationalism, is different from all the others because it affects all the others. Nationalism is important because it is part of the other ideologies; therefore, it will be discussed first to make it possible to see its effects on the other ideologies. The placement and order of the other ideologies are

---

[11]Francis Fukuyama, "Have We Reached the End of History?" (Santa Monica, CA: The RAND Corporation, February 1989).

not arbitrary, but other arrangements are possible. Feminism is placed in its own section, between democracy and Marxism, because it has developed so much internationally that it no longer fits anywhere else.

METHOD OF ANALYSIS

The wide variety of ideologies raises a problem for the analyst. Since each ideology differs significantly from the others, no single approach is appropriate to all of them. Each ideology emphasizes different aspects of society and ignores other aspects that are stressed by another ideology. Therefore, it is not possible to treat each ideology in exactly the same way. It is necessary to present ideologies as they exist in the world rather than on the basis of a formal model. Thus each one will be analyzed as its nature dictates.

Reasons for Comparing Ideologies

It is nevertheless desirable to compare ideologies. Why compare? Political scientists compare political systems and political ideologies for a number of reasons. At the simplest level, we compare in order to remind ourselves and others that there are different ways of doing things; in the context of ideologies, differing beliefs exist in the world. It is important to realize that people who hold these beliefs are as sure that they are right as we are that we are right. On a more complicated level, we compare things because it helps us better understand other people and ourselves—to see what both they and we do and believe. Understanding something better is (according to what might be called a teacher's ideology) always good. Understanding is also important because we can't change anything unless we understand it. Comparing helps us both to understand better what we do and believe and to recognize that there are other ways of doing and believing that might be useful to us.

How we compare can also help illuminate why we compare. We could just study other political systems or political beliefs without ever comparing them. But through comparison, we discover both great differences and great similarities. At the same time, we discover that differences often hide similarities. We find, for example, that most belief systems have a means of ranking people in some sort of hierarchy, but we also find that the bases for those rankings differ. Thus we conclude that people disagree over what is most important about the differences among people but that people agree that some basis for making distinctions exists. In other words, we find that a difference is the result of a similarity.

This example shows us that our complex world can be understood. In a world that is so often in conflict, it is essential that we strive to understand both ourselves and others. Comparing political systems and beliefs is one small step toward that understanding.

Questions

Any analysis of any part of society, including the value system, is an attempt to answer a series of questions regarding the various institutions and processes mentioned above. This series of questions can be divided into two parts: (1) How should society function? and (2) How does society actually function? The answers to the first question give us a picture of the value system. The answers to the second question give us an image of the social system in operation.

The following is a set of questions designed to provide a fairly complete analysis of the assumptions of an ideology. Using questions like these, it is possible to compare ideologies.

1. Human nature
    a. What are the basic characteristics of human beings as human beings?
    b. What effect does human nature have on the political system?

2. The origin of society and government or the state
    a. What is the origin of society? Why does it develop?
    b. What is the origin of government or the state? Why does it develop?

3. Political obligation (duty, responsibility, law)
    a. Why do people obey the government?
    b. Why should people obey the government, or should they obey it at all?
    c. Is disobedience ever justifiable?
    d. Is revolution ever justifiable?

4. Law
    a. What are the nature and function of law?
    b. Should the regulation of society depend on the immediate decisions of individuals or on sets of rules and regulations that place limitations on all members of society, including political leaders—in other words, the rule of law?
    c. Should there be sets of fundamental laws or constitutions that cannot be changed by the ordinary processes of legislation?

5. Freedom and liberty (rights—substantive and procedural)
    a. Are men and women free in any way vis-à-vis the government?
    b. Should they be free vis-à-vis the government?
    c. Assuming that some type or types of freedom are both possible and desirable, what should these be? Should they be limited or unlimited? Who places the limits?

6. Equality
    a. Are individuals in any way "naturally" equal?
    b. Should they be in any way equal?
    c. Assuming that some type or types of equality are both possible and desirable, what should these be? Should they be absolute or

relative? If relative, what criteria should be used to establish them? Who establishes them? Who establishes the criteria? Who enforces the criteria?

7. Community (fraternity)
   a. Should ties among individuals composing a group form a bond that takes precedence over the needs and wishes of the individual members of the group?
   b. If this is desirable, how can it be encouraged? If this is undesirable, how can it be discouraged? Who decides?

8. Power (authority)
   a. Should any individual or group of individuals be able to control, determine, or direct the actions of others?
   b. If this is desirable, what form or forms should it take? Should it be limited or unlimited? Who limits it and how?

9. Justice
   a. It is usually assumed that justice is desirable, but what is it? Is it individual or social?
   b. Who decides the characteristics of justice? Who enforces these characteristics?

10. The end of society or government
    a. For what purpose or purposes does society or government exist?
    b. Who decides what these purposes are, or are they consciously chosen?

11. Structural characteristics of government
    a. What is the best or best possible form of government? Why?
    b. Are there alternative forms of government that are equally good? What is the standard of judgment? Who decides?

The Social System

To compare differing ideologies, some way must be devised so similar information is made available for each ideology. In order to achieve some sort of comparability, the complex of interactions among individuals, groups, and institutions that we call society has been divided into five segments:

1. The value system,
2. The socialization system,
3. The social stratification and social mobility system,
4. The economic system, and
5. The political system.

This breakdown is simply a very loose set of categories designed to provide some minimal order to the analysis. These categories allow the attitudes found in the various ideologies to be described.

Each chapter will attempt to explain the attitudes found in each ideology toward the various institutions and processes of society. As a result, it will be possible to see what questions are important within each ideology and therefore to establish a basis for comparing them. Before this can be done, it is necessary to understand a bit more about each of these institutions and processes.

Values. The value system is determined by the answers given to the above questions, which show the hierarchy of values in each society and each ideology. One aspect of each value system that is particularly important is that the value system provides us with the basis for evaluating each ideology.

But is there, as Mannheim thought, some way of standing completely outside all ideologies, thus making it possible to evaluate them from the standpoint of something at least approaching objectivity? There is a growing consensus that this may not be possible or, at the minimum, is extremely difficult. At the same time it is essential that we do in fact evaluate ideologies and differentiate among them and that we need to do it on some basis that is more reliable than the belief in an ideology. Some people find their answers in religion, but evaluation is still necessary for those who can't find their answers there. For most such people the answer is found in trying, as objectively as possible, to measure the effects of actions based on ideologies on human beings or, to include the most radical environmentalists, on the natural order as a whole.

Socialization. The socialization system is the process by which individuals accept the values of the society as their own. The most important institutions affecting the ways in which and the degree to which individuals gain these values are (1) the family system, (2) the educational system, (3) the religious sytem, and (4) a variety of other influences, such as the mass media and the peer group. We are not always sure of the mechanisms by which the various institutions of socialization operate. It is obvious that a child is strongly influenced in her or his whole outlook on life by family environment and by early school years. It is, perhaps, less clear how the other institutions of socialization influence an individual's outlook on life. We can assume that the same messages repeated over and over again in institutions that the individual has been taught to respect, such as the religious and educational systems, may have a cumulative effect and thereby become part of the individual's value system. The mass media operate in the same way.

Social Stratification. The social stratification system is the way in which a society ranks groups within it. This ranking may be a very clearly defined class system or it may be very loose, with the lines between classes or status groups somewhat hazy. Social stratification is usually summed up within a political ideology by the question of equality. Some ideologies contain the idea that everyone within the society should be equal in specified ways. For example, some people talk about equality of opportunity and political equality; others believe in economic and social equality. Only if there were no economic, social, political, or any other inequalities would there be no social stratification system. Almost no one has ever suggested such complete equality, but each of these more limited types of equality has been suggested or tried at various times.

Social Mobility. One of these types of equality—equality of opportunity—is particularly important in any society. *Equality of opportunity* means that no artificial obstacles or barriers keep any individual or group from moving from one class to another. Equality of opportunity defines certain parts of the social mobility system within a society. Every society has a mobility system determining the ease or difficulty with which an individual can move among classes or other strata in the society. The system also determines the basis for such movement. For example, in traditional China an individual could move into the upper classes of society by successfully completing a series of examinations. Many contemporary societies have no such formal system but base mobility on standards such as wealth.

The Economic System. The economic system is concerned with the production, distribution, and consumption of wealth. The major parts of the economic system that will concern us relate to (1) production, (2) distribution and consumption, and (3) the relationship of the economic system to the political system. We shall be particularly concerned with questions about the desired degree of economic equality and the means for achieving this goal. Most ideologies reject extremes of wealth and poverty; therefore, each contains means of correcting the imbalance, such as, for example, the graduated income tax or the nationalization of industries. But each ideology also differs from others as to what constitute extremes of wealth and poverty.

These days it is generally accepted that the economic and political systems are closely intertwined. This has not always been the case, and some ideologies still stress the separation of the two systems. Therefore, it is particularly important to understand each ideology's position on the appropriate relationship between the economic system and the political system

The Political System. Most of the economic questions discussed will relate to more purely political questions. The political system is that segment of society that draws together or integrates all the others. Within the political system decisions are made that are binding on the whole society; thus the political system holds the key to any understanding of the whole ideological and social system. A *political ideology* does not concern itself only with narrowly defined governmental activity but rather touches on all aspects of the social system; therefore, a political ideology provides answers, in one form or another, to all of the questions outlined earlier.

SUGGESTED READINGS

ADAMS, IAN.,*The Logic of Political Belief: A Philosophical Analysis of Ideology.* Savage, MD: Barnes & Noble Books, 1989.

BARADAT, LEON P. *Political Ideologies: Their Origins and Impact.* 4th ed. Englewood Cliffs, NJ: Prentice-Hall, 1991.

BARRETT, MICHÈLE. *The Politics of Truth: From Marx to Foucault.* London: Polity, 1991.

BARTH, HANS. *Truth and Ideology.* Trans. Frederic Lilge. Berkeley: University of California Press, 1976.

BELL, DANIEL. *The End of Ideology: On the Exhaustion of Political Ideas in the Fifties with a New Afterword.* Cambridge, MA: Harvard University Press, 1988.

BOUDON, RAYMOND. *The Analysis of Ideology.* Trans. Malcolm Slater. Chicago: University of Chicago Press, 1989.

CONNOLLY, WILLIAM E. *Political Science & Ideology.* New York: Atherton, 1967.

DUNCAN, GRAEME. "Understanding Ideology." *Political Studies* 35, no. 4 (December 1987): 649–659.

EAGLETON, TERRY. *Ideology: An Introduction.* London: Verso, 1991.

ECCLESHALL, ROBERT, VINCENT GEOGHEGAN, RICHARD JAY, and RICK WILFORD. *Political Ideologies: An Introduction.* London: Hutchinson, 1984.

EDELMAN, MURRAY. *Constructing the Political Spectacle.* Chicago: University of Chicago Press, 1988.

FREUD, SIGMUND. *The Future of an Illusion.* Trans. and ed. James Strachey. New York: Norton, 1961.

GEERTZ, CLIFFORD. "Ideology as a Cultural System." In *Ideology and Discontent,* edited by David E. Apter, pp. 47–76. New York: Free Press of Glencoe, 1964.

GEORGE, VIC, and PAUL WILDING. *Ideology and Social Welfare.* London: Routledge & Kegan Paul, 1976.

GOODWIN, BARBARA. *Using Political Ideas.* Rev. ed. London: Wiley, 1987.

GOULDNER, ALVIN W. *The Dialectic of Ideology and Technology: The Origins, Grammar, and Future of Ideology.* New York: Seabury Press, 1976.

GROSS, FELIKS. *Ideologies, Goals, and Values.* Westport, CT: Greenwood Press, 1985.

HAMILTON, MALCOLM B. "The Elements of the Concept of Ideology." *Political Studies* 35, no. 1 (March 1987): 18–38.

HEYWOOD, ANDREW. *Political Ideologies: An Introduction.* New York: St. Martin's Press, 1992.

LANE, ROBERT E. *Political Ideology: Why the American Common Man Believes What He Does.* New York: Free Press of Glencoe, 1962.

LARRAIN, JORGE. *The Concept of Ideology.* London: Hutchinson, 1979.

LICHTHEIM, GEORGE. *The Concept of Ideology and Other Essays.* New York: Random House, 1967.

MACRIDIS, ROY C. *Contemporary Political Ideologies: Movements and Regimes.* 5th ed. New York: Harper Collins, 1992.

MANNHEIM, KARL. *Ideology and Utopia: An Introduction to the Sociology of Knowledge.* Trans. Louis Wirth and Edward Shils. New York: Harcourt Brace Jovanovich, 1936.

MANNING, D. J., and T. J. ROBINSON. *The Place of Ideology in Political Life.* London: Croom Helm, 1985.

MCCARNEY, JOE. *The Real World of Ideology.* Brighton, England/Atlantic Highlands, NJ: Harvester Press/Humanities Press, 1980.

MCLELLAN, DAVID. *Ideology.* Minneapolis: University of Minnesota Press, 1986.

MÉSZAROS, ISTVAN. *The Power of Ideology.* New York: New York University Press, 1989.

MINOGUE, KENNETH. *Alien Powers: The Pure Theory of Ideology.* New York: St. Martin's, 1985.

MULLINS, WILLARD A. "On the Concept of Ideology in Political Science." *American Political Science Review* 66 (June 1972): 498–510.

PAREKH, BHIKHU. *Marx's Theory of Ideology*. Baltimore, MD: Johns Hopkins University Press, 1982.

PLAMENATZ, JOHN. *Ideology*. London: Pall Mall Press, 1970.

REJAI, MOSTAFA. "Ideology." In *Dictionary of the History of Ideas*, edited by Philip P. Wiener, Vol. 2, pp. 552–559. New York: Scribner's, 1973.

———, ed. *Decline of Ideology?* Chicago: Aldine-Atherton, 1971.

ROSENBERG, SHAWN W. *Reason, Ideology and Politics*. Princeton, NJ: Princeton University Press, 1988.

ROSSI-LANDI, FERRUCCIO. *Marxism and Ideology*. Trans. Roger Griffin. Oxford, England: Clarendon Press, 1990.

RUDE, GEORGE. *Ideology and Popular Protest*. London: Lawrence and Wishart, 1980.

SCOTT, ALAN. *Ideology and the New Social Movements*. London: Unwin Hyman, 1990.

SKIDMORE, MAX J. *Ideologies: Politics in Action*. San Diego, CA: Harcourt Brace Jovanovich, 1989.

SUSSER, BERNARD. *The Grammar of Modern Ideology*. London: Routledge, 1988.

THERBORN, GORAN. *The Ideology of Power and the Power of Ideology*. London: NLB, 1980.

THOMPSON, JOHN B. *Ideology and Modern Culture: Critical Social Theory in the Era of Mass Communications*. Stanford, CA: Stanford University Press, 1990.

TODD, EMMANUEL. *The Explanation of Ideology: Family Structure and Social Systems*. Trans. David Garrioch. Oxford, England: Basil Blackwell, 1985.

WALFORD, GEORGE. *Beyond Politics: An Outline of Systematic Ideology*. London: Calabria Press, 1990.

WAXMAN, CHAIM I., ed. *The End of Ideology Debate*. New York: Funk & Wagnalls, 1968.

WODAK, RUTH, ed. *Language, Power and Ideology: Studies in Political Discourse*. Amsterdam: John Benjamins Publishing Co., 1989.

WOLIN, SHELDON S. *Politics and Vision: Continuity and Innovation in Western Political Thought*. Boston: Little, Brown, 1960.

ZIZEK, SLAVOJ. *The Sublime Object of Ideology*. London: Verso, 1989.

2

Nationalism

Nationalism today is one of the central concerns for anyone interested in questions of war and peace throughout the world. In Eastern Europe and the former Soviet Union, nationalism has produced bloody conflicts amounting to genocide and many lesser conflicts. In many other parts of the world, peoples identifying themselves as nations are at war with others who are identified as the national enemy. At the same time, countries like Eritrea, which fought Ethiopia for twenty years for the right to be an independent nation, are, having won, in the process of creating the institutions of a new state brought about by that same nationalism.

Although nationalism has a particularly bad name today, it is important not to forget that it can be a positive as well as a negative force. In particular, people in the Third World tend to view nationalism positively because they associate it with their liberation from colonial oppression. But this is not just a Third World phenomenon. For example, the people of Québec, a province of Canada, are considering breaking away from Canada and forming an independent country, and there are separatist movements in a number of European countries, such as the Flemish separatist movement in Belgium and the Basque separatist movement in Spain. For such groups nationalism is clearly a positive force.

At the same time that nationalism is proving so divisive in so much of the world, some areas appear to be in the early stages of overcoming that divisiveness. For example, the Republic of Ireland and the United Kingdom may be in the process of bringing peace to Northern Ireland because the Irish Republican Army (IRA) has called a truce in the decades-long war. In addition, Israel and the Palestine Liberation Organization (PLO) have signed a peace treaty in which Israel has given up control over some territory; Israel and Jordan have also signed a peace treaty. Finally, North and South Korea are beginning to have serious contact for the first time since the Korean War of the 1950s.

The impact of nationalism can be seen at any international sporting event such as the Olympics and the World Cup. The television coverage of these events varies tremendously from country to country depending on the success or failure of the athletes from each country, and the emotions generated by national success or failure in an event like the World Cup have to be seen to be believed.

In many instances in the past, ideologies either were clearly connected with certain countries or particular countries were symbols of an ideology. The United States and democratic capitalism and the Soviet Union and Marxism are examples. This connection no longer holds true. All ideologies are transnational, and this has happened just as nations have become more important in other ways.

Nationalism has not changed its characteristics nor, as I have argued since the first edition of this book in 1969, its importance. What have changed are our awareness of nationalism and our intense concern over the economic and political instability brought about by divisive nationalist movements.

In the West we seldom use the word *nationalist* to describe ourselves. If we think in these terms, we call ourselves *patriotic*. Americans prefer to be called patriotic rather than nationalist, but patriotism and nationalism are similar phenomena. The root word of *nationalism* is *nation*; it means a people with a common culture and history that produces an identity. Nations sometimes occur as small, identifiable units within the political boundaries of a country, or sometimes they cross over those boundaries. Black Nationalists in the United States perceive themselves to be a nation of the first sort, one contained within the borders of a country. They appeal to their presumed identity as a nation to argue for cultural, economic, and, in some cases, political separation from the United States. The Romany or Gypsies are an example of a nation of the second sort, because they exist in many countries while having certain traditions in common and many of them share a common language.

As an ideology, nationalism is unusual in that it affects all other ideologies, and, as a result, nationalism may be the most important of the ideologies. For example, Robert Coles, an authority on the political beliefs of children, wrote, "Nowhere on the five continents I've visited in this study has nationalism failed to become an important element in the developing conscience of young people. . . ."[1] As a result of this pervasiveness, the modern world simply cannot be understood without nationalism.

But many people reject nationalism, in large part because they see its connection to war and revolution, and advocate *internationalism* or an identification with the world as a whole rather than with one part of it. Without overdoing the analogy, we can compare the difference between nationalism and interna-

---

[1]Robert Coles, *The Political Life of Children* (Boston: The Atlantic Monthly Press, 1986), p. 66.

tionalism to the differing, but strong, feelings a person may feel toward the state, region, or locality in which they live and the country as a whole. Most U.S. citizens have some sense of loyalty to both their home state and the United States. Many do not have a sense of loyalty to the world as a whole, but this is not to say that the feelings of those who do are different from those of a person who feels strongly about both a particular state and the United States. Internationalism is the same type of phenomenon as patriotism and nationalism; by looking at all three, we should be able to understand each one more thoroughly.

DEFINING NATIONALISM

Nationalism is a complex word, and there are disagreements about how to define it, but most definitions include the following:

1. National consciousness or awareness of oneself as part of a group,
2. National identity or identification with the group,
3. Geographical identification or a geographical dimension to the group (there are some exceptions to this element),
4. Patriotism or love of the group, and
5. Demands for action to enhance the group.

Nationalism came on the political map of the Western world with World War I when the first group of European states split from one of the monarchies that then dominated Europe. At the end of the war the Treaty of Versailles established a right of "national self-determination," and the boundaries of states were redrawn based on this principle. The treatment of Germany in this treaty was one of the causes for the development of dissatisfaction in Germany and, ultimately, the rise of Adolf Hitler, the development of fascism and national socialism with their intense nationalism, and the coming of World War II. After World War II, the focus of nationalism became the Third World, anticolonialism, and the wars that developed as the colonies freed themselves from their European rulers. Today nationalism is most apparent in the conflicts in parts of Eastern Europe and the former Soviet Union.

Nationalism, therefore, is equated with trouble and probably could not have been kept free from the negative connotations it has in the West. *Patriotism*, which is best defined as and commonly used to mean love of country, has a more positive tone, at least in the United States. But it also refers to people who are so patriotic that they cannot see anything good anywhere in the world except in their own country. Thus *patriotism* sometimes means an unrealistic isolation and unreasoning devotion to country. *Internationalism* is the most neutral of the three terms.

Symbols of nationality such as the flag and the national anthem are supposed to produce a feeling akin to patriotism. It is probably true that even the most unpatriotic of us has felt the effect of such symbols at one time or another. This effect is hard to characterize. Perhaps it is a thrill of recognition at belonging to something larger and more important than ourselves. Phrased another way, it might be the recognition that our lives and destinies are wrapped up in the lives and destinies of many others. Such recognition comes through symbols. We cannot see in others the same thing we see and feel in a symbol. We respond emotionally; we do not think about what a poor piece of music the national anthem may be or that the flag is colored pieces of cloth sewn together. We see and feel in these symbols an emotion that makes us one of a community.

In this way, nationalism can act upon an individual more powerfully than any other ideology. All ideologies can affect individuals emotionally, and each ideology has certain "sacred" symbols that produce a reaction in the believer. But nationalism sometimes produces the reaction even in the nonbeliever. It affects individuals more deeply and needs less reinforcement than any other ideology does. Other ideologies may become this rooted, but they seem to do so less often.

The feelings nationalism arouses have been presented and defended in many ways. Teutonic or German nationalism reached heights of emotion in the operas of Richard Wagner, which appeal to and are built upon deeply held feelings. In the same way, but on a less emotional level, Edmund Burke referred to this feeling as he talked about society as a pact between the living, the dead, and those yet to be born. For Burke, the nation is a union of all generations that must not be lightly changed or broken; the nation is for all eternity. Wagner was more emotional; in his operas he presented the basic folk tales and myths that, to him, were the roots of a great German nation. It is not surprising that Hitler was a great lover of the operas of Wagner. Hitler built national socialism on the same feelings and some of the same ideas Wagner presented musically.

As a word, *nationalism* is similar to other words such as *community* or phrases like *public* or *national interest*. Such words and phrases refer to groups of people who have some bond (strong or weak) that they believe gives them an identity as part of something larger than themselves. The most obvious cases are small, intimate groups of individuals, such as the family, which is made up of individuals with different interests and, to some extent, different outlooks on life, but with a common factor that forms a unit. The family continues over generations and has an emotional unity that provides a basis for identification. But there is considerable difference between the ties of a family and something as distant or abstract as a nation or the public. Nevertheless, there is at least one fundamental similarity; the recognition of both the family and the nation as a unit presupposes some sort of recognition of groups of people forming something more lasting than the individuals composing it.

The English language makes it difficult for us to speak of group identity without using hybrid terms. For example, when we speak of national interest, we want to imply that the nation is something separate from, and perhaps more than, the sum of the individuals composing it. We can say we are conscious of or recognize the nation or the public, but the words do not have an emotional content that makes it possible to readily express a feeling of unity or identity. In addition, people vary in the extent to which they feel this group consciousness. Some people hardly feel it at all. Some identify completely with a group. The latter seldom think of themselves as anything but members of a particular group. But since no phrase in English can really evoke the feeling of group unity or identity, we find it difficult to express this feeling.

But despite the problems, all this leads to a fairly simple means of understanding nationalism. Nationalism is one way in which individuals identify themselves with groups. The most obvious example of this identification is the nuclear family of parents and children. A slightly more complex level is the larger or extended family that includes grandparents, aunts and uncles, cousins, and so forth. Some people also include identification with ancestors and, to a growing extent, future generations.

At the next step, this identification changes slightly in character because, for most groups, location is added, but even these days when so many people move so often, there is a strong tendency to identify with a locality. Either by birth or long residence, a certain place becomes important to an individual, and criticism of that place is resented. This feeling can be extended, sometimes in weakened form but often as strongly, to a region, such as a state or a part of the country like the South in the United States.

The step to national consciousness is a small one and for many people is easier than regional identification. It is a fact that people identify with their country, and national consciousness or awareness and national identity are the basic ingredients of what we call patriotism and nationalism.

When we say someone is a patriot, we are saying that she or he is aware of being part of a country (national consciousness), identifies with the country (national identity), and feels a positive love of country. Patriotism can be totally unquestioning, as in the famous slogan "My country right or wrong," or it can be a love aware of imperfections. There are degrees of patriotism.

As commonly used, *nationalism* means the same thing, although to most people nationalism implies demands made, action rather than feelings. In developed countries nationalism means trouble and is a bad thing; patriotism is a good thing; therefore, we tend to think of them as significantly different. They are not. At most, nationalism is a stronger expression of feeling than patriotism.

Nationalism includes demands for action intended to strengthen the country, but the feeling we call nationalism is also aroused by nations that are not modern countries or states. The existence of different languages in a country usually means different groupings of peoples existed or still exist there with differing traditions, including sometimes different religions as well as distinct languages. For example, presently in many countries a variety of languages are spoken representing earlier nations that now share one country. For example, the country that was known as Czechoslovakia was formed after World War I from two ethnic groups, the Czechs and the Slovaks. After the overthrow of communism it became the Czech and Slovak Federative Republic, which on

January 1, 1993, became two separate countries, the Czech Republic and Slovakia. What was Yugoslavia was formed after World War I from five ethnic groups, and what will result from the chaos is still unclear.

All this means that the people, or at least the nationalists, identify with a particular group having its own history, culture, and tradition. In order to understand how these attitudes were formed, it will be useful to examine the development of nationalism.

THE DEVELOPMENT OF NATIONALISM

Nationalism has been most prominent in the twentieth century, although it is not an invention of this century, and some of its forms have changed dramatically. The major parts of the mix of ideas that come together to become nationalism originated as early as the fourteenth through the sixteenth centuries.[2] Although some of the elements can undoubtedly be traced back further, as Isaiah Berlin wrote, "consciousness of national identity may be as old as consciousness itself. But nationalism, unlike tribal feeling or xenophobia, to which it is related but with which it is not identical, seems scarcely to have existed in ancient or classical times."[3]

Something like nationalism originated as a defense of the locality, region, or nation against an external power. The first likely examples come from conflicts in the late Middle Ages between various cities and nations and the papacy. But it wasn't until the eighteenth century, first in Germany and later in France, that a coherent doctrine of nationalism developed. One of the earliest theorists of nationalism, Johann Gottfried von Herder (1744–1803), argued that it is a basic human need to belong to a group; at least at one level that group is the nation. Being part of a nation gives us a part of our identity. We have a past, a history, ancestors—"roots"—that place us in a tradition. We are born in a "stream of tradition" that helps to define us as individuals.[4]

This "stream of tradition" creates a national identity. It is composed in most cases of a geography, a history, usually a language, and often a religion. The process of becoming a nation, or *nation building* as it is sometimes called, is the process of welding together or integrating these things into a whole, which creates a people or a nation.[5]

The history of most countries illustrates this process, and in the Third World today it is a conscious undertaking. It will be interesting to see how reemerging

---

[2] The best discussion can be found in Quentin Skinner, *The Foundations of Modern Political Thought*, 2 vols. (Cambridge, England: Cambridge University Press, 1978).

[3] Isaiah Berlin, "The Bent Twig: A Note on Nationalism," *Foreign Affairs* 51, no. 1 (October 1972): 15. The next paragraphs are based on Berlin's article.

[4] Ibid., p. 16.

[5] See, for example, Karl W. Deutsch and William J. Foltz, eds., *Nation-Building* (New York: Atherton Press, 1963).

nations, like the Baltic states of Estonia, Latvia, and Lithuania, deal with the problems involved. Nations are being born or reborn; peoples are being created. Some of the attempts will fail.

It is clear now that no new nation was formed with either the Soviet Union or Yugoslavia, but the reborn countries that were temporarily part of these larger countries are having difficulties creating clear identities for themselves and, in the former Yugoslavia, the conflicts have reached such proportions that it is difficult to imagine a successful reestablishment of ties among whatever nations are created at the end of the fighting. But this situation is not new. In 1947, after what amounted to a religious war, Pakistan was formed out of what had been parts of India; in 1971 Bangladesh broke free from Pakistan and became an independent country. The relations among Bangladesh, India, and Pakistan remain tense today, and it is unclear whether any *nation* exists. Each of the three countries is deeply divided internally by language, tribal, and class differences, and India, in addition, is fractured by religious conflicts.

Nationalism and New Nations

Nationalism is a central concern in the Third World, where there are literally new nations with which the people have no identification. Even in those nations that are at least similar in territory to the colonial or precolonial period and have a long-standing identification as a unit, such as India, various loyalties, such as to caste or common language, adversely affect attempts to solve or even identify national problems. In many of the new African countries, tribal loyalties are historically more important than national loyalties; in some cases tribal boundaries are not the same as national ones. In such cases conflicting loyalties are likely to cause difficulties for many years. An obvious case is Rwanda. There is no simple solution. It is difficult to know how to develop an identification with the nation without destroying earlier identification with other groups, such as tribal units or religious or language groupings.

Japan is an interesting case of the problems of conflicting loyalties in a non-tribal nation. Japan has a long tradition of rule by one family, but in reality it was almost always ruled by someone called the *shogun* rather than by the emperor. In the nineteenth century, Japanese scholars rediscovered the historical role of the emperor as a strong ruler. This discovery, combined with a rediscovery of the traditional culture, helped pave the way for a revolution to give back to the emperor the powers he had once held. The emperor was technically given back his power, while the tradition of dualistic rule was maintained. At the same time, the revolution helped develop a reidentification with Japan on the part of many people. This reidentification with Japan helped create the conditions that led to the development of fascism in Japan that, in turn, led to the war in the Pacific during World War II.

Nationalism is at the center of both fascism and national socialism; therefore, we should not be surprised at the development of regimes in newly developing countries that are similar to past Fascist countries. A. James Gregor called fascism "the first revolutionary mass movement regime which aspired to commit the totality of human and natural resources of an historic community to national development."[6] Hence, the parallels between fascism and some of the recent modernization movements may not be accidental.

The first new nation that succeeded in developing a national identity among its people was the United States,[7] and it faced few of the problems of the new nations of the twentieth century. On the other hand, while many South American countries have succeeded in establishing national identities in the minds of their people, they are beset with all the other economic and political problems that the new nations of Africa and Asia have. Therefore, while national identity is clearly important, it is only part of the solution to the problems of these countries, and it can be hard to achieve.

One of the major difficulties facing many of the new nations is lack of knowledge of their histories and cultures. In African countries, for example, the histories or cultures that are known are often tribal rather than national. The attempt to revitalize indigenous cultures is characteristic of most of the new nations, but it can pose serious problems when certain parts of the culture impede development. In India, for example, caste works against cooperation across caste lines, religious proscriptions restrict the foods available to people with limited food resources, and language and religious differences fragment the society as a whole. Thus a concern for culture and tradition can both help and impede the process of modernization. Max Weber argued that the religious system of Puritanism helped greatly in the development of capitalism and hence industrialization in the United States.[8] Likewise, there may be elements of the religious systems of Africa and Asia that will either help or impede industrialization.

A central problem for many developing and developed countries is that they are multinational. This means that two or more groups of people with different identities, traditions, languages, and/or religions are trying to live within the same geographical boundaries and political system. Not surprisingly, this can cause considerable tension.

A national tradition cannot be manufactured overnight. But at least one factor can be used to help develop a national identity—the colonial experience. The movement to rid the country of a colonial power is usually a nationalist movement that helps to form some identity. But this is not enough to maintain that identity after the movement has succeeded. The nationalist movement may help to tie a particular nation together for a while, but such an identity cannot last indefinitely.

---

[6]A. James Gregor, *The Ideology of Fascism: The Rationale of Totalitarianism* (New York: Free Press, 1969), p. xii. For a counterargument, see Arnold Hughes and Martin Kolinsky, " 'Paradigmatic Fascism' and Modernization: A Critique," *Political Studies* 24 (December 1976): 371–396.

[7]See Seymour M. Lipset, *First New Nation: The United States in Historical and Comparative Perspective* (New York: Basic Books, 1963).

[8]See Max Weber, *The Protestant Ethic and the Spirit of Capitalism*, trans. Talcott Parsons (New York: Scribner's, 1930).

TIES AMONG NATIONS

While one side of nation building is the assertion of independence from other nations, the realities of the world economy and the relative strength and weakness of states mean that nations also seek ties with other nations.

Regionalism

One means of doing that is to form economic and/or political ties with other countries. But while countries no longer propose joining together formally to establish a new country, as Tanganyika and Zanzibar did in 1964 to become the United Republic of Tanzania, other ties are still being created.

The single most successful effort at regionalism is among developed nations. The EU or European Union originated as the ECSC or the European Coal and Steel Community; became the EEC or European Economic Community, popularly known as the Common Market; and then became the EC or European Community. The ECSC originated with France, West Germany, Italy, Belgium, Luxembourg, and the Netherlands as members. In 1958 the Treaty of Rome established the EEC, and in 1967 it became the European Community. In 1973 the United Kingdom, Ireland, and Denmark joined; in 1981 Greece was added; and Spain and Portugal joined in 1986. Recently the name has been changed again, to the European Union. Austria, Finland, and Sweden have voted to join; Norway rejected membership. The Eastern European countries of Bulgaria, the Czech Republic, Hungary, Poland, Romania, and Slovakia and the Baltic countries of Estonia, Latvia, and Lithuania are all interested in joining and have begun to develop working relations with the EU with a view to joining in the near future. Turkey has expressed interest in joining, but poor relations with member-state Greece and concerns about Turkish immigration into EU counties has kept it from doing so.

As the EU has grown, it has also been changing from an almost purely economic union to an economic and political union. The European Court of Justice acts as an appeals court for cases brought against national laws, and the European Parliament, composed of directly elected members, has begun to act as an independent political forum, even though its powers are severely limited. The parliament is not a lawmaking body, but it must be consulted on all bills being discussed by the ruling body, the Council of Ministers, and it has tried to limit the powers of the council.

The EU is a very powerful economic bloc, and its expansion into Scandinavia and Eastern Europe will make it even stronger. Officially all internal barriers were dropped in 1992 to establish one large economic unit. While the changes have not been as dramatic as hoped by some and feared by others and plans for a single currency and a single central bank have been blocked, immense progress has been made to forming one large economic unit.

Political unity, the goal of many, is progressing much more slowly, but more and more people identify themselves as Europeans as much as or more than citizens of one of the member countries. This is the necessary first step toward real political unity in the future. Still, the elections for the European Parliament get mixed reactions from the peoples of the various countries. For example, in the 1989 election 91 percent voted in Belgium, where voting is compulsory, 63.4 percent in Germany, and 80 percent in Greece, but only 36 percent voted in the United Kingdom.

Internationalism

The emphasis on there being a whole within which differing peoples and cultures can be accepted is the heart of internationalism. Space exploration has produced pictures of earth hanging in space surrounded by absolutely nothing. Many people have found in these photographs a realization that we human beings live together with no place else to go. This realization has led many to believe that some way must be found for all of us to get along peacefully. But generally, internationalism does not produce the same emotional fervor as nationalism. Internationalism seems to be more a matter of reason than of emotion. People who support internationalism oppose the feelings aroused by nationalism, believing that they are divisive and lead to dangerous confrontations among nations.

Internationalists believe that the world should be united in some way. They do not all agree on what this way should be. Some, for example, argue for a world government with very strong powers. Others argue for some sort of loose confederation. Still others argue for a federal system of government similar to that of the United States, with powers divided between a world government and the government of each country belonging to the federation. Others are unsure what form unity might take but believe strongly that unity is essential.

In a general sense, internationalism is similar to nationalism. It requires a recognition of ties among all individuals in the world, in the same sense that nationalism requires a recognition of ties among those living in a country. We noted the symbols that can help give rise to the feeling of nationalism. Internationalism does not have many such symbols, and it is likely that an individual will have less of an emotional identification with the world as a whole than with a nation or region, even though he or she may intellectually recognize ties to others around the world. Thus internationalism is not likely to be as strong a force as nationalism unless some crisis produces the need for these ties to be recognized and the emotional fervor that would bring about an identification of the individual with a world community. A science fiction cliché has an invasion from outer space acting as the crisis that produces the recognition that we are all human beings living together on a fragile planet that is our common home.

Today, recognition that actions in one country affect the health and safety of people in another country through pollution such as acid rain, the destruction of the ozone layer, changes in weather patterns, and other impacts on the global environment has brought a new urgency and prominence to internationalism. Although it is too early to point to specific policy changes, there is a growing sense that nations must find ways of cooperating on environmental issues. The agreement of all concerned nations to a treaty to protect Antarctica (the United States was the only country to refuse to sign) may be the first step toward a new internationalism.

In addition, the world seems near to recognizing that conflict in one place is dangerous for other places, and the United Nations is involved in a number of "peacekeeping" missions. Part of the reason for internationalizing peacekeeping through the United Nations is that nationalism produces resentment at the involvement of powerful countries like the United States; the use of troops from smaller countries, particularly countries from the same general area of the world, helps reduce this resentment. Thus nationalism is helping the creation of at least one instance of internationalism.

CURRENT TRENDS

The most obvious political effect of nationalism is divisiveness in the international community. We see this in Eastern Europe and the former Soviet Union, where nations with long traditions that are currently part of states containing various other nations and ethnic groups are trying to become independent. We also see it in the Americas, where many people resent the United States' traditional domination of the area. The second effect of nationalism, which can be seen as a second level of divisiveness, is found in the emerging nations of Africa, Asia, and the Middle East. These nations have recognized that there would be advantages to agreement among themselves, but nationalism has made it difficult for them to work together effectively. In addition, feelings of nationalism have put wedges between newly emerging nations and the colonial powers. But as a third effect, nationalism has provided a means of unifying emerging countries, thereby producing the opposite of divisions. The rejection of the previously dominant power acts as a means of developing a national identity, cohesiveness, and purpose. Thus nationalism presents a mixed picture. From the perspective of the developed world, it is a dangerous phenomenon. From the perspective of the developing world and the ethnic groups of the former USSR and Eastern Europe, it is both a liberating and a unifying force.

In the recent past, significant changes have taken place in crucial areas of national conflict, but the central issues remain much the same. The two major areas of conflict are religion and language.

Religion and Nationalism

Nationalism seems to create the greatest problems when combined with religious differences. This can be seen clearly in three areas where great changes have taken place recently: the Middle East, Northern Ireland, and the former Yugoslavia, which is still an area of armed conflict based in part on religious differences.

The Middle East. The Middle East is the center of one of the greatest complexities of nationalisms. The area includes most of the countries where Islam is the dominant religion, plus Israel and Ethiopia. This means it stretches across the whole of northern Africa all the way to the Pakistan-India border, north to the southern border of Russia, and south to the middle of Africa. Within those borders are a huge population; intense national loyalties and hatreds; immense natural wealth together with appalling poverty; and a number of sects of Islam, Coptic Ethiopia, and Jewish Isreal.

One continuing conflict is that between Israel and the Palestinians. The Palestinians are the descendants of inhabitants of the territory that is now Israel who either chose to leave or were forced to leave when Israel was established. Since then they have lived in refugee camps in the countries surrounding Israel, in various Middle Eastern countries, or, more recently, in designated areas within Israel. They have recently gained a territory in the Gaza area that was formerly part of Israel. That Israel would cede territory to its longtime enemy had seemed impossible until it actually happened, and it has caused considerable conflict within Israel. Gaining a territory has been a mixed blessing for Palestinian leaders because it has brought into focus conflicts among the Palestinians, particularly between the followers of Yasir Arafat (1929–), the leader of the PLO (Palestine Liberation Organization), who became the de facto ruler of Gaza, and the adherents of Hamas, a more radical group that opposes any peace with Israel. But most Palestinians living in the Gaza area were overjoyed to gain a territorial base, one of their long-term goals. For these Palestinians, they were a nation without a land; now they are a nation with a land.

The treaties between Israel and the Palestinians and between Israel and Jordan are the first steps toward a wider peace in the Middle East, but many problems still remain. Israel and Syria must forge a treaty. Iraq remains an international outcast that clearly still has designs on Kuwait. Lebanon, Saudi Arabia, and the other states on the Arabian peninsula must also still come to terms with Israel.

Northern Ireland. Another area where dramatic change has taken place is Northern Ireland, which is composed of the six northernmost counties of Ireland that voted to become part of the United Kingdom of Great Britain and Northern Ireland (Great Britain is composed of the three once-independent countries of England, Scotland, and Wales) when the Irish Free State (later Eire or the Republic of Ireland) was formed in 1922. Eire is predominantly Roman Catholic; Northern Ireland is predominantly Protestant (Protestants tend to call the area Ulster). Recently the IRA (Irish Republican Army) has called a cease-fire in their long-term struggle to bring about a united Ireland. The various Ulster groups trying to maintain the connection with Great Britain have generally chosen to abide by the cease-fire, although both sides have violated it from time to time.

This cease-fire is the first step toward a treaty between the Eire and the United Kingdom regarding the status of Northern Ireland. As of early 1995, very few specific proposals are available.

The Former Yugoslavia. The area that was Yugoslavia is an interesting example of chickens coming home to roost. Once central authority collapsed,
Yugoslavia effectively disappeared as a country to be replaced, at last count, with
the countries of Bosnia and Herzegovina (generally known as Bosnia), Croatia,
Macedonia, Slovenia, and what is still officially Yugoslavia (composed of Serbia,
which dominates Kosovo, Vojvodina, and Montenegro) with continuing wars
based on religious differences (Christianity and Islam) and the desire for more
territory. Macedonia, which is also the name of the adjoining region of Greece,
is an area of potential future conflict as is Kosovo, inhabited mostly by ethnic
Albanians and bordering Albania.

In all these areas, religious differences combine with nationalism to make
the problems particularly difficult to solve. But the limited advances made in
Northern Ireland and in Israel's relations with its neighbors suggest that solutions may not be impossible.

Language and Nationalism

In the other major focus of nationalism, language, conflict results from a dominant group trying to eliminate the minority by absorbing it into the dominant
culture. Usually, this effort includes providing education only in the language
of the majority.

Europe. In Spain there is a long-term conflict between the Spanish-speaking
majority and a Basque minority that wants self-rule. The Spanish government
has not yet come up with a formula acceptable to the more radical fringes of the
Basque separatists. That may be impossible to do, but a process of giving some
autonomy to the Basque region has the support of moderate Basques, is working, and has isolated the radicals. In Belgium, a similar but less violent dispute
has been growing in intensity between the French-speaking Walloons of the
south and the Flemish-speaking people of the north. Each area now has its
official language, but the dispute continues around the capital, Brussels (the
Flemish spelling) or Bruxelles (the French spelling), and in the border regions.

Canada. One of the Canadian provinces, Québec, is French-speaking, while
the rest of the country is overwhelmingly English-speaking. Since the French-
speaking minority is the majority in one province, certain compromises have
been possible, and French is the only official language in Québec. Still, the
solutions that have been found thus far are not entirely acceptable to either the
French- or English-speaking populations. In recent years the dispute has only
very rarely produced violence, but many Québécois believe that only independence from Canada will allow them their own culture, language, and control
of their future.

As of early 1995 the political party advocating independence for Québec,
the Parti Québécois, won the most recent election. It proposes to hold a referendum on independence in the near future and, if independence wins, negotiate
the establishment of a new nation-state.

Another problem facing Canada is with its Inuit population. The Inuit, previously known by non-Inuits as Eskimos, are insisting on greater recognition of their identity as a separate nation within Canada. Some argue for separation from Canada.

Nationalism is also a focus of concern in Canada in a different sense. Many Canadians resent the political and economic dominance of their country by the United States. The North American Free Trade Agreement (NAFTA) was the extension to Mexico of an agreement between the United States and Canada, and the leaders of the three countries have agreed to further extend it to include Chile. Its effects are still unclear. The initial agreement between Canada and the United States has certainly removed some trade barriers, but each country has accused the other of violating the treaty. The same situation exists with Mexico; some trade barriers have been removed, but Mexico's economy has been badly damaged. Some jobs have been created and some jobs lost, fulfilling the predictions of both the proponents and opponents of NAFTA.

Another free trade treaty, the General Agreement on Tariffs and Trade or GATT, has raised the same issues as NAFTA but has also specifically raised the issue of political control over the national economy because GATT establishes an international body that can judge whether or not a country's trade policies violate the treaty. A third free trade treaty, among the thirty-three countries of the Americas excluding Cuba, is also in the works.

Free trade treaties are comparable to the first step in Europe following World War II that created the Common Market. Even at the very beginning there were those in Europe who saw the Common Market as the first step toward political union. None of the three recent free trade agreements envision anything beyond freeing trade; political union has never been mentioned and is, at present, inconceivable.

Other Issues

Immigration. A major issue that reflects the current influence of nationalism and a variety of other concerns is immigration and the position of the immigrant in society. A number of European countries, most notably France and Germany, have erected barriers against immigration from outside the European Union. Germany has experienced a number of physical attacks on immigrants, including attacks that resulted in the deaths of the immigrants.

The United States, which has historically prided itself on being a nation of immigrants (all U.S. citizens except those of direct and unmixed Native American heritage are the descendants of immigrants), is now deeply concerned about limiting the number of immigrants admitted. While this is a central political concern today, it is not new. In the past, immigration has been restricted on the basis of country of origin with particularly severe restrictions on those immigrants originating outside of Europe.

Nationalism and the Extreme Right. In the United States those on the extreme right see themselves as the only true defenders of America. These groups include those traditionally expressing such a position, the various Nazi and neo-Nazi parties, and newer groups that see America as a land set aside by God for the white race, such as the Aryan Nation. All such groups see the United States as under threat both internally and externally. The internal threat is from racial minorities and immigrants as well as from those of the left who do not have the best interests of the country at heart. The external threat is more complicated than it used to be. Some believe that the demise of communism is not real or that Russia will become the next threat or have shifted their concern from the former Soviet Union to China.[9]

SUGGESTED READINGS

Bibliographies

DEUTSCH, KARL W. *Interdisciplinary Bibliography on Nationalism 1935–1953.* Cambridge, MA: Technology Press, 1955.

PINSON, KOPPEL S. *A Bibliographic Introduc-*tion to Nationalism. New York: Columbia University Press, 1953.

SMITH, ANTHONY D. *Nationalism: A Trend Report and Bibliography.* Vol. 21, no. 3 of *Current Sociology.* The Hague: Mouton, 1973.

General Works

ALTER, PETER. *Nationalism.* Trans. Stuart McKinnon-Evans. London: Edward Arnold, 1989.

ANDERSON, BENEDICT. *Imagined Communities: Reflections on the Origin and Spread of Nationalism.* London: Verso, 1983.

BEER, WILLIAM R., and JAMES E. JACOB, eds. *Language Policy and National Unity.* Totowa, NJ: Rowman and Allanheld, 1985.

BERLIN, ISAIAH. "The Bent Twig: A Note on Nationalism." *Foreign Affairs* 51, no. 1 (October 1972): 11–30.

———. "Nationalism: Past Neglect and Present Power." *Partisan Review* 46, no. 3 (1979): 337–358.

BRASS, PAUL R. *Ethnicity and Nationalism: Theory and Comparison.* Newbury Park, CA: Sage, 1991.

BREUILLY, JOHN. *Nationalism and the State.* Manchester, England: Manchester University Press, 1982.

CARR, EDWARD HALLETT. *Nationalism and After.* London: Macmillan, 1945.

COMMITTEE ON INTERNATIONAL RELATIONS, GROUP FOR THE ADVANCEMENT OF PSYCHIATRY. *Us and Them: The Psychology of Ethnonationalism.* New York: Brunner/Mazel, 1987.

CONNOR, WALKER. *Ethnonationalism: The Quests for Understanding.* Princeton, NJ: Princeton University Press, 1994.

COOK, RAMSAY, ed. *French-Canadian Nationalism: An Anthology.* Toronto: Macmillan, 1969.

DEUTSCH, KARL W. "The Trend of European Nationalism—the Language Aspects." *American Political Science Review* 36, no. 2 (June 1942): 533–541.

———. *Nationalism and Social Communication: An Inquiry into the Foundations of*

---

[9]For more information, see Lyman Tower Sargent, ed. *Extremism in America: A Reader* (New York: New York University Press, 1995).

Nationality. 2d ed. Cambridge, MA: MIT Press, 1966.

————. *Nationalism and Its Alternatives.* New York: Knopf, 1969.

————. *Tides Among Nations.* New York: Free Press, 1979.

————, and WILLIAM J. FOLTZ, eds. *Nation-Building.* New York: Atherton Press, 1963.

DIUK, NADIA, and ADRIAN KARATNYCKY. *The Hidden Nations: The People Challenge the Soviet Union.* New York: William Morrow, 1990.

DOOB, LEONARD W. *Patriotism and Nationalism: Their Psychological Foundations.* New Haven, CT: Yale University Press, 1954.

EDWARDS, JOHN. *Language, Society and Identity.* Oxford, England: Basil Blackwell, 1985.

FARAH, TAWFIC E., ed. *Pan-Arabism and Arab Nationalism: The Continuing Debate.* Boulder, CO: Westview Press, 1987.

GELLNER, ERNEST. *Nations and Nationalism.* Oxford, England: Basil Blackwell, 1983.

GREENFIELD, LIAH. *Nationalism: Five Roads to Modernity.* Cambridge, MA: Harvard University Press, 1992.

HAJDA, LUBOMYR, and MARK BEISSINGER, eds. *The Nationalities Factor in Soviet Politics and Society.* Boulder, CO: Westview Press, 1990.

HAYES, CARLTON J. H. *The Historical Evolution of Modern Nationalism.* New York: Macmillan, 1931.

————. *Essays on Nationalism.* New York: Russell & Russell, 1966. Originally published in 1926.

————. *Nationalism: A Religion.* New York: Macmillan, 1960.

HERTZ, FRIEDRICH O. *Nationality in History and Politics: A Psychology and Sociology of National Sentiment and Nationalism.* London: Routledge & Kegan Paul, 1944.

HOBSBAWM, E. J. *Nations and Nationalism Since 1780: Programme, Myth, Reality.*
Cambridge, England: Cambridge University Press, 1990.

IGNATIEFF, MICHAEL. *Blood and Belonging: Journeys into the New Nationalism.* New York: Farrar, Straus and Giroux, 1993.

KAMENKA, EUGENE, ed. *Nationalism: The Nature and Evolution of an Idea.* Canberra: Australian National University Press, 1973.

KEDOURIE, ELIE. *Nationalism.* Rev. ed. London: Hutchinson University Library, 1951.

KELLAS, JAMES G. *The Politics of Nationalism and Ethnicity.* New York: St. Martin's Press, 1991.

KOHN, HANS. *Prophets and Peoples: Studies in Nineteenth Century Nationalism.* New York: Macmillan, 1946.

————. *American Nationalism: An Interpretive Essay.* New York: Macmillan, 1957.

————. *The Age of Nationalism: The First Era of Global History,* New York: Harper & Row, 1962.

————. *Nationalism, Its Meaning and History,* Rev. ed. Princeton, NJ: Van Nostrand, 1965.

————. *The Idea of Nationalism: A Study in Its Origins and Background.* New York: Collier, 1967. Originally published in 1944.

KRISTEVA, JULIA. *Nations Without Nationalism.* Trans. Leon S. Roudiez. New York: Columbia University Press, 1993.

MAYALL, JAMES. *Nationalism and International Society.* Cambridge, England: Cambridge University Press, 1990.

MINOGUE, K. R. *Nationalism.* New York: Basic Books, 1967.

MITCHISON, ROSALIND, ed. *The Roots of Nationalism: Studies in Northern Europe.* Edinburgh, Scotland: John Donald Publishers, 1980.

MOSTOV, JULIE. "Democracy and the Politics of National Identity." *Studies in East European Thought* 46 (1994): 9–31.

MOYNIHAN, DANIEL PATRICK. *Pandaemonium: Ethnicity in International*

Politics. Oxford, England: Oxford University Press, 1993.

MUNCK, RONALDO. *The Difficult Dialogue: Marxism and Nationalism*. London: Zed Books, 1986.

NORBU, DAWA. *Culture and the Politics of Third World Nationalism*. London: Routledge, 1992.

O'BRIEN, CONOR CRUISE. *God Land: Reflections on Religion and Nationalism*. Cambridge, MA: Harvard University Press, 1988.

PALUMBO, MICHAEL, and WILLIAM O. SHANAHAN, eds. *Nationalism: Essays in Honor of Louis L. Snyder*. Westport, CT: Greenwood Press, 1981.

PFAFF, WILLIAM. *The Wrath of Nations: Civilization and the Furies of Nationalism*. New York: Simon & Schuster, 1993.

RA'ANAN, URI, ed. *The Soviet Empire: The Challenge of National and Democratic Movements*. Lexington, MA: Lexington Books, 1990.

ROYAL INSTITUTE OF INTERNATIONAL AFFAIRS. *Nationalism*. Oxford, England: Oxford University Press, 1939.

SEE, KATHERINE O'SULLIVAN. *First World Nationalisms: Class and Ethnic Politics in Northern Ireland and Quebec*. Chicago: University of Chicago Press, 1986.

SEERS, DUDLEY. *The Political Economy of Nationalism*. Oxford, England: Oxford University Press, 1983.

SETON-WATSON, HUGH. *Nations and States: An Enquiry into the Origins of Nations and the Politics of Nationalism*. London: Methuen, 1977.

SHAFER, BOYD C. *Nationalism, Myth and Reality*. New York: Harcourt Brace Jovanovich, 1955.

———. *Faces of Nationalism: New Realities and Old Myths*. New York: Harcourt Brace Jovanovich, 1972.

SMITH, ANTHONY D., ed. *Nationalist Movements*. London: Macmillan, 1976.

———. *Nationalism in the Twentieth Century*. Oxford, England: Martin Robertson, 1979.

———. *The Ethnic Revival*. Cambridge,

England: Cambridge University Press, 1981.

———. *Theories of Nationalism*. 2d ed. New York: Holmes & Meier, 1983.

———. *The Ethnic Origins of Nations*. Oxford, England: Basil Blackwell, 1986.

———. *National Identity*. Reno, NV: University of Nevada Press, 1991.

SNYDER, LOUIS L. *The Meaning of Nationalism*. New Brunswick, NJ: Rutgers University Press, 1954.

———, ed. *Dynamics of Nationalism: Readings in Its Meanings and Development*. New York: Van Nostrand Reinhold, 1955.

———. *New Nationalism*. Ithaca, NY: Cornell University Press, 1968.

———. *Global Mini-Nationalisms: Autonomy or Independence*. Westport, CT: Greenwood Press, 1982.

———. *Macro-Nationalisms: A History of the Pan-Movements*. Westport, CT: Greenwood Press, 1984.

———. *Encyclopedia of Nationalism*. New York: Paragon House, 1990.

STACK, JOHN F. *The Primordial Challenge: Ethnicity in the Contemporary World*. Westport, CT: Greenwood Press, 1986.

TAGORE, SIR RABINDRANATH. *Nationalism*. New York: Macmillan, 1917.

TAMIR, YAEL. *Liberal Nationalism*. Princeton, NJ: Princeton University Press, 1993.

TIBI, BASSAM. *Arab Nationalism: A Critical Inquiry*. Ed. and trans. Marion Farouk-Sluglett and Peter Sluglett. New York: St. Martin's Press, 1990.

TIRYAKIAN, EDWARD A., and RONALD ROGOWSKI, eds. *New Nationalisms of the Developed West*. Boston, MA: Allen & Unwin, 1985.

TIVEY, LEONARD, ed. *The Nation-State: The Formation of Modern Politics*. Oxford, England: Martin Robertson, 1981.

TURKI, FAWAZ. *The Disinherited Journal of a Palestinian Exile*. New York: Monthly Review Press, 1972.

VALLIÈRES, PIERRE. *White Niggers of America: The Precocious Autobiography of a Quebec "Terrorist."* Trans. Joan Pinkham. New York: Monthly Review Press, 1971.

YOUNG, CRAWFORD, ed. *The Rising Tide of Cultural Pluralism: The Nation-State at Bay?* Madison, WI: University of Wisconsin Press, 1993.

ZELINSKY, WILBUR. *Nation into State: The Shifting Symbolic Foundations of American Nationalism.* Chapel Hill, NC: University of North Carolina Press, 1988.

PART I

Democracy

3

The Principles of
Democracy

Democracy has evolved over many centuries through modifications in certain theories called *democratic* and in practices of countries called *democratic*. There have been and continue to be substantial differences among these countries and theories; therefore, there are a variety of meanings of the word "democratic," depending on both the political persuasion of the speaker and the form of democracy being considered.

Some writers argue that the word *democracy* should be used to refer to one type of democracy, known as direct democracy, in which citizens take part directly in the making of political decisions. These people want to replace most uses of the word *democratic* with the word *republican*, which they feel refers more accurately to a system of government by elected representatives. Other writers prefer to see the term *democracy* modified by some word such as *participatory* to emphasize the role of citizens in decision making and to suggest that the role be strengthened.

The word *democracy* comes from two Greek words, *demos* = people and *kratos* = rule. Therefore, the word means *rule by the people* and can refer to direct, participatory, and representative forms of rule by the people. Today the word has a positive meaning throughout most of the world, so much so that even some political systems with very little or no rule by the people are called democratic.[1]

---

[1]See C. B. Macpherson, *The Real World of Democracy* (Oxford, England: Clarendon Press, 1966) for a discussion of democracy and an argument that the various uses of the word are legitimate.

The following analysis uses a simple model of the key elements of democracy as it exists today, or at least of those elements most often considered significant. They are:

1. Citizen involvement in decision making,
2. A system of representation,
3. The rule of law,
4. An electoral system—majority rule,
5. Some degree of equality among citizens,
6. Some degree of liberty or freedom granted to or retained by citizens, and
7. Education.

CITIZEN INVOLVEMENT

The most fundamental characteristic of any democratic system, truly its defining characteristic, is the idea that citizens should be involved in the making of political decisions, either directly or through representatives of their choosing. These two approaches can be characterized as:

1. *Direct democracy*—Citizens take part personally in deliberations and vote on issues. Citizens debate and pass on all laws.
2. *Representative democracy*—Citizens choose (elect) other citizens to debate and pass on laws.

Direct democracy has only rarely been practiced as a means of governing a country, but most people have experienced such involvement at a lower level. Almost everyone in the West has, at some time, had a chance to discuss and vote on an issue. This may have taken place at a school or university, in a church or synagogue, in a union meeting or at a club, or in one of the hundreds of other groups that allow voting members to decide at least some of the questions that concern the membership. Voting on issues personally is the defining activity of a citizen in a direct democracy.

In addition, most people have voted in an election in some such organization, thereby taking part in one of the basic steps of choosing a representative; fewer people, but still a substantial number, have cast their vote in the election of a public official. These are the activities of representative democracy.

Other forms of citizen involvement include actively participating in a political party or interest group, attending and participating in political meetings or public hearings, simply discussing politics, or contacting a public official about an issue. A growing area of involvement is for citizens to work for or against issues that will be voted on during an election. This area is growing because interest groups or groups of citizens are bringing more issues directly to the electorate through initiative petitions or referenda.

In a representative system, citizen involvement should help ensure that public officials are responsive to the people. Candidates for public office must convince voters that there are good reasons to vote for them rather than their opponents. In particular, elected officials are expected to show that they are responsive to the changing needs and demands of their constituents. Of course, no system can guarantee responsive public officials, but having to run for reelection certainly helps.

In addition, involvement is thought to be good for the citizen. Defenders of democracy believe that being involved in decision making (even if this means simply casting a vote at an election) will expand the horizons of voters and make them more aware of current issues. Involvement brings about a feeling of responsibility, a sense of belonging to a community, and knowledge. Involved citizens become better, more complete people.

This is particularly true for those whose involvement goes beyond the vote to more active participation. Citizens who choose to get directly involved in the political life of their community will benefit more than the more passive citizens who limit their participation to the vote.

Defenders of democracy ask a simple question, Who else should make political decisions? A monarch? A political boss? Bureaucrats? The rich? Who better knows the interests of the average citizen than the average citizen?

In some countries, including the United States, few people even bother to vote. (Figure 3-1 illustrates the turnout in recent national elections in selected countries.) Not voting does not mean that decisions won't be made; someone will still make them. Do high levels of not voting undermine democracy? Does it matter? These questions have produced a number of approaches to either justify the system that exists or propose changes in it. These approaches include elitism, pluralism, corporatism or neo-corporatism, and participatory theories of democracy. The first three all assume that democracy is working fairly well with low levels of participation. Participatory theories argue that democracy is not working and that ways must be found to increase participation.

Elitism

The elitist approach asserts that democracy is "a method of making decisions which ensures efficiency in administration and policy making and yet requires some measure of responsiveness to popular opinion on the part of the ruling elites."[2] In this view, citizen involvement is primarily a check on political leaders while maintaining competition among rival elites. The arguments for elitist theories center on efficiency and the perceived inability of the voter to make informed decisions. The citizen casting his or her vote is, in this view, simply a mechanism for deciding among competing elites. Given the complexity of the modern world and the issues involved, so the argument goes, it is impossible for the average citizen to know enough to participate intelligently in decision mak-

---

[2]Jack L. Walker, "A Critique of the Elitist Theory of Democracy," *American Political Science Review* 60 (June 1966): 286.

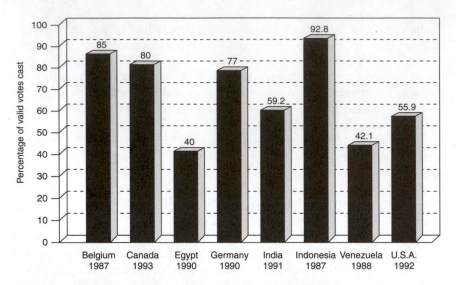

FIGURE 3.1　Percentage of the population voting in selected countries.

SOURCE: Figures for Belgium, Canada, Egypt, India, and Indonesia supplied by their embassies; figures for Germany and Venezuela from the New York Times; figures for the United States from the Federal Election Commission. Note: Voting is compulsory in Belgium.

ing. But since competition is still thought desirable, the vote is used to choose the group that will be given temporary power.

The classic response to elitist theories is to argue that efficiency is not as important as the positive influence of participation on the citizen and that the average citizen is probably capable of understanding most issues. As democratic theory developed, the problem of the informed citizen was recognized, and it became common for such theories to include an emphasis on education so that citizens would have the knowledge required to be effective participants.

The elitist theorists argue, in effect, that classical representative democracy does not—even cannot—work in the modern world. Their opponents argue that it can work even though new problems make a truly informed citizenry even more important than in the past as well as more difficult to achieve.[3]

Pluralism

Closely related to this argument is a controversy over pluralism.[4] In pluralism, the political system is seen as composed of interest groups competing for power with none strong enough to dominate. As long as competition exists and is fair, no single interest can gain too much power; that interest will always be held in

---

[3]For various positions, see, for example, Lane Davis, "The Costs of Realism: Contemporary Re-statements of Democracy," *Western Political Quarterly* 17 (March 1964): 37–46; and Peter Bachrach, *The Theory of Democratic Elitism: A Critique* (Boston: Little, Brown, 1967).

[4]On the controversy, see David Nicholls, *Three Varieties of Pluralism* (New York: St. Martin's, 1974); Henry S. Kariel, *The Decline of American Pluralism* (Stanford, CA: Stanford University Press, 1961); Marvin E. Olsen, "Social Pluralism as a Basis for Democracy," in *Power in Societies*, ed. Marvin E.

check by the other interests. Advocates contend that pluralism is the best system for a representative democracy, because pluralism protects citizens from too great a centralization of power and allows all the diverse interests within a society to be expressed.

Most modern societies are plural in that they are composed of a variety of groups based on characteristics such as wealth, race, gender, ethnic or national origin, profession, and religion. Defenders of pluralism argue that this diversity should be recognized and protected. Thus pluralism includes both a positive awareness of the group basis of most contemporary societies and an attitude toward democracy.

Critics of pluralism make two major points. First, they argue that pluralism represents a cynical disregard of all values except the manipulation of power. According to the antipluralists, the only thing of interest to the competing elites is staying in office. All democratic and human values are secondary to this overriding goal. Thus the suggestion that pluralism protects freedom is false. Pluralism is a protection for freedom, or any other value, only as long as that value is to the political benefit of the competing groups. Second, antipluralists note that the supposedly competing groups cooperate to maintain the present system and their positions of power within it. Thus pluralism and the groups that compete within it are obstacles to change. Alternatively, pluralists in the United States argue that pluralism supplements the system of checks and balances enshrined in the U.S. Constitution with additional checks on power. Outside the United States, pluralists argue that the competition among groups is often the major means of limiting centralized power.

Corporatism

An approach has developed that views pluralism as a partial misunderstanding of the complexity of modern society. Corporatism (or neo-corporatism, as some of its proponents prefer to call it to distinguish it from a similar idea found in fascism) rejects pluralism because the pluralist analysis contains no role for government agencies. Corporatists contend that interest groups both compete and cooperate with each other and effectively share power with government bureaucracies. Interest groups do not merely consult with government but have become fully integrated into the process of policy making and policy implementation. As one writer put it, *corporatism* means the "negotiation of policy between state agencies and interest organisations arising from the division of labour in society, where policy agreements are implemented through the collaboration of the interest organisations and their willingness and ability to secure the compliance of their members."[5]

Olsen (New York: Macmillan, 1970), pp. 182–188; Reginald J. Harrison, *Pluralism and Corporatism: The Political Evolution of Modern Democracies* (London: George Allen & Unwin, 1980); William Alton Keslo, *American Democratic Theory: Pluralism and Its Critics* (Westport, CT: Greenwood Press, 1978); Arend Liphart, *Democracy in Plural Societies: A Comparative Exploration* (New Haven, CT: Yale University Press, 1977); and Stanislaw Ehrlich and Graham Wootten, eds., *Three Faces of Pluralism: Political, Ethnic and Religious* (Westmead, England: Gower Publishing, 1980).

[5]Wyn Grant, "Introduction," to *The Political Economy of Corporatism*, ed. Wyn Grant (London: Macmillan, 1985), pp. 3–4.

The theory of corporatism has had a great impact on the way in which interest organizations, particularly in the economy, perceive their relations with one another and with government. Although corporatism has not significantly reduced competition among interest groups, it has provided the basis for their taking a more active role in the actual development of policy in cooperation with government bureaucracies.

Critics of corporatism argue that it simply justifies greater power on the part of unelected people, that the similarity of the concept in fascism is no accident, and that corporatism constitutes an explicit denial of the power of citizens to control their own lives in a democracy. Critics of elitism, pluralism, and corporatism often suggest that more, not less, direct participation on the part of the citizens is the best approach to democracy.

Participatory Democracy

The most direct challenge to previous approaches is found among those who argue that the low level of citizen involvement is a problem that should not be rationalized away but solved. Advocates of participatory democracy regard elitism, pluralism, and corporatism as disregarding the most fundamental principle of democracy, and they contend that the principle can be saved by shifting power away from elected officials to citizens. In other words, they propose moving the system away from representative democracy in the direction of direct democracy.[6]

The participatory democrat argues that individuals should not be bound by laws they did not help make or participate in making. In other words, the individual, all individuals, must be consulted in the making of laws that will affect them. If they are not consulted, the law is invalid. The law is also invalid if the individual believes it is unjust. This idea is again an attempt to make the representative more responsive to the wishes of constituents and, in a broader sense, to bring the whole representative system more in line with the ideals of direct democracy.

In addition to asserting that a more participatory democracy can work, advocates of this position argue that only with greater participation can the other principles of democracy be fulfilled. According to this argument, people will never be truly politically equal or really free unless they become active and involved citizens committed to making the system work by making representative democracy more like direct democracy. At the same time, contemporary defenders of participatory democracy are not opponents of representation; they just believe that voters should keep their representatives on a shorter leash.

Opponents of participatory democracy generally argue that it simply goes too far and as a result is impractical. Many opponents take the position that

---

[6]See, for example, Carole Pateman, *Participation and Democratic Theory* (Cambridge, England: Cambridge University Press, 1970).

participatory democracy would be fine if it were possible but contend that it cannot be achieved in our complex world. These critics assert that contemporary political decisions require both an expertise and an amount of time not available to the average citizen. As a result, they argue, a system of representative democracy is necessary.

REPRESENTATION

If direct participation is difficult to achieve or, for some, not a good idea, then it is necessary to develop a way for people to participate indirectly. The primary means has been through representatives or people chosen by citizens to act for them. In other words, citizens delegate to one of their number the responsibility for making certain decisions. The person chosen may be a delegate from a geographical area or of a certain number of people (representation by area or population). The citizens represented are called the *constituents* or the representative's *constituency*.

The word *represent* is used in a number of different ways that help provide an understanding of the situation:

1. Something *represents* something else when it is a faithful reproduction or exact copy of the original.

2. Something that symbolizes something else is said to *represent* it.

3. A lawyer *represents* a client when he or she acts in place of or for the client.

Clearly, the third use of the word *represent* is closest to the way we think of a representative in democracy, but it isn't quite that simple because no constituency is composed of citizens whose interests are identical. As a result, there are two main approaches to the relationship between the representative and her or his constituency with most actual representatives fitting somewhere between the two extremes. First, some representatives try to reflect the varied interests of his or her constituents as precisely as possible. Second, in a famous speech, Edmund Burke made a further distinction important to theorists of representation and practical politicians alike:

> To deliver an opinion is the right of all men; that of constituents is a weighty and respectable opinion, which a representative ought always rejoice to hear, and which he ought always most seriously to consider. But *authoritative* instructions, *mandates* issued, which the member is bound blindly and implicitly to obey, to vote for, and to argue for, though contrary to the dearest conviction of his judgment and conscience—these are things utterly unknown to the laws of this land, and which arise from a fundamental mistake of the whole order and tenor of our Constitution.
>
> Parliament is not a *congress* of ambassadors from different and hostile interests, which each must maintain, as an agent and advocate, against other agents and advocates; but Parliament is a *deliberative* assembly of *one* nation, with one interest,

that of the whole; where, not local purposes, not local prejudices, ought to guide, but the general good, resulting from the general reason of the whole. You choose a member, indeed; but when you have chosen him, he is not a member of Bristol, he is a member of *Parliament*. If the local constituent should form a hasty opinion evidently opposite to the real good of the rest of the community, the member for that place ought to be as far as any other from an endeavor to give it effect.[7]

Here Burke presents a case for the representative as an independent agent who is a representative solely in the sense that she or he is elected by the people in a particular area. In doing this, Burke specifically rejects representation in the third sense outlined above, the representative as agent for some individual or group.

Seldom, if ever, will an elected official fit exactly one and only one of the roles assigned by the theories of representation. Even the most Burkean representative will act as a constituency agent at times or on certain issues.[8] The typical representative is likely to act as an agent for her or his constituents whenever they are actively concerned with a particular issue or to assist individuals or groups of constituents when they are dealing with the bureaucracy and need assistance. At the same time, the typical representative is likely to act as the Burkean representative on issues that do not directly concern the constituency (and thus about which little or no pressure is received from the constituency).

As we have already seen in the discussion of participatory theories, an issue that concerns some theorists is how to give representative democracy some of the attributes of direct democracy. In the United States such practices as the initiative, referendum, and recall were developed as devices to allow the people as a whole to play a direct role in political decision making, and they are again being used extensively.

This problem can be seen most clearly in the thinking of Jean-Jacques Rousseau (1712–1778). At one point he said, "Thus deputies of the people are not, and cannot be, its representatives; they are merely its agents, and can make no final decisions. Any law which the people have not ratified in person is null, it is not a law."[9] Here Rousseau has used two of our definitions of *represent*. For him a representative was not an agent but one who acts only with constituent approval. Rousseau realized that within a large country direct democracy was impractical, even impossible, and although he maintained the ideal of direct democracy, he did discuss representation in a more favorable light. He said:

> I have just shown that government weakens as the number of magistrates [elected officials] increases; and I have already shown that the more numerous the people

---

[7]Speech to the Electors of Bristol (1774) in *The Works of the Right Honorable Edmund Burke*, 7th ed. (Boston: Little, Brown, 1881), vol. 11, p. 96 (emphasis in original).

[8]See David H. Davidson, *The Role of the Congressman* (New York: Pegasus, 1969), pp. 114–142; Donald R. Matthews, *U.S. Senators and Their World* (New York: Vintage Books, 1960), pp. 217–242; Charles L. Clapp, *The Congressman: His Work as He Sees It* (Washington, DC: Brookings Institution, 1963), pp. 50–103; and John R. Johannes, *To Serve the People: Congress and Constituency Service* (Lincoln: University of Nebraska Press, 1984).

[9]Jean-Jacques Rousseau, *Du contrat social* (Paris: Le Renaissance de Livre, 1762), p. 86.

Jean-Jacques Rousseau (1712–1778) is best known as a political philosopher. His works *Discours sur les sciences et les arts (Discourse on the Arts and Sciences*, 1750), *Discours sur l'origine et les fondements de l'inégalité (Discourse on the Origin and Foundations of Inequality*, 1755), *Émile* (1762), a treatise on education, *Du contrat social (Of the Social Contract*, 1762), and others placed him in the forefront among critics of contemporary society. He argued that civilization was corrupting and that a return to a simpler society in which each individual could fully participate was the remedy for the current social ills. His arguments were used as justifications for the French Revolution. The meaning, intent, and effect of Rousseau's ideas are still widely debated; interpretations of his thought range from the belief that he was one of the founders of modern totalitarianism to the belief that he was an important defender of democracy. (*Library of Congress*)

is, the more repressive force is needed. From which it follows that the ratio of magistrates to government should be in inverse proportions to the ratio of subjects to sovereign; which means that the more the state expands, the more the government ought to contract; and thus that the number of rulers should diminish in proportion to the increases of the population.[10]

Rousseau would have liked to see a country small enough so every person could be his[11] own representative, but as a population rises this becomes more and more difficult. Thus the number of rulers must of necessity diminish through the establishment of some type of representative system. But Rousseau strongly believed that the closer a system can come to a direct democracy

---

[10] Rousseau, *Du contrat social*, p. 59.

[11] In Rousseau's case it is fairly clear that he would not extend direct political involvement to women. On Rousseau's treatment of women, see Susan Moller Okin, "Rousseau," in her *Women in Western Political Thought* (Princeton: Princeton University Press, 1979), pp. 99–194.

through an increase in the number of magistrates, the better the system will be.[12] Rousseau's approach to representation has gained favor in recent years in movements in support of *participatory democracy* and what is being called *communitarianism*.

THE RULE OF LAW

In a democracy an elected representative participates in the making of laws but is still bound by the law. Once passed, the law is supreme, not those who made the law. Representatives can participate in changing a law, but until it is changed they, along with everyone else, must obey it.

This apparently simple notion came about only after a long struggle. It was one of the basic principles demanded in the early conflicts that led to the establishment of democratic institutions. Before that, monarchs claimed that they had been appointed by God to rule—the divine right of kings—and were, therefore, above the law. The principle involved is that a society should be able to bind itself to the rules it collectively has chosen and that no individual or institution should be outside the rules so chosen.

THE ELECTORAL SYSTEM—
MAJORITY RULE

Therefore, the means of choosing representatives is central to making democracy work, and there has been considerable conflict over the electoral system or other procedures put in place to do this. What might appear to be simple questions prove to raise serious issues. For example,

1. For what period of time should someone be elected?

2. Should elected representatives be allowed to be reelected to the same office? If yes, how many times? If no, can they be elected again after not holding the office for a period of time? How long?

3. What percentage of the vote does a person need to be chosen? Fifty percent + 1 works nicely if there are only two candidates, but not if there are more than two.

4. If there are more than two candidates, should there be a second election (called a runoff) to choose between the two highest vote-getters in the first election?

---

[12]See Rousseau's discussion of such a system in *Projet de constitution pour la Corse* ("Constitutional Project for Corsica"), in Jean-Jacques Rousseau, *Political Writings*, trans. and ed. Frederick Watkins (London: Thomas Nelson & Sons, 1953), pp. 227–330.

5. Are there any circumstances where more than a majority (more than fifty percent + 1) should be required?

6. How many representatives should be chosen to a representative assembly?

7. How many representatives should be chosen from each area?

At times all of these questions have been in dispute and most still are. Also, many countries are currently going through a process of what is being called *democratization* in which these questions *must* be answered in the process of establishing representative institutions where none had existed.

The electoral process begins with the selection of candidates. The means by which this takes place varies from country to country and even within countries. In some cases, the system is entirely under the control of political parties, and the citizen must become active in a party to influence the choice of candidates. In other cases, while the political party is still important, an election (in the United States called a primary) is held to reduce the number of candidates. In this situation citizens can influence the final list of candidates by voting. Obviously, donating money to or working actively for a candidate can also influence the outcome.

For the citizen who simply wants to vote intelligently, deciding whom to vote for will depend largely on the available information. For many offices a high percentage of voters vote on the basis of party identification alone, while those who don't depend on information provided by the candidate's campaign and the media. Reliable information is not always easy to come by, and voters often feel they are forced to make choices without the information necessary to make a fully informed decision. This may be one of the reasons for the low voter turnout in some countries. Getting adequate information can take more effort than some voters are willing to expend.

With a few exceptions, specific institutional arrangements for elections are not of much importance, but the exceptions are noteworthy. The normal rule of elections is that the side with the most votes wins, but it is always important to remember that this does not mean that those with the most votes are right; it just means that since more people voted for A rather than B, A must be accepted until the next election gives people the chance to change to B if they wish.

Majority rule tends to be based on the assumption that any issue has only two sides. If, for example, there are three candidates in an election, majority rule becomes more complicated, since it is harder to determine what the majority wants. In addition, in many elections relatively few potential voters actually cast their ballots; therefore, the majority may not be represented in the result. (Some countries, therefore, *require* their citizens to vote.) This objection can, of course, be answered by saying that those who do not vote do not care, but it can also be answered by saying that perhaps some of the people who do not vote do not feel that any candidate sufficiently reflects their position. This difficulty indicates the advantage of having more than two candidates in an election, but we have already seen the disadvantage of such an arrangement—if no one receives a clear majority, does this constitute majority rule?

At times various governments have made it difficult or even impossible for more than two sides to be represented on the ballot. On the other hand, various governments have used a system called *proportional representation* (PR) to solve this problem. In a system using proportional representation, the seats in the legislature are won on the basis of the percentage of the votes cast for a party. In a very simple example of PR, using a one-hundred-seat legislature like the U.S. Senate, if a minor party got 10 percent of the vote it would get ten seats, whereas in the usual system where only the party that gets the majority of votes in a district is seated, it would almost certainly get no seats.

Another way to make the representative system more representative is to change from single- to multiple-member districts. In the usual system, one person is elected for each district, but at times various governments have tried electing two or more people from a district. This means minorities are more likely to elect a representative.

A final institutional arrangement designed to protect minorities is the common practice in the United States of requiring more than a simple majority on certain issues, particularly money issues. This is almost always the approach used in amending basic sets of rules, such as constitutions. The purpose is to protect the rights of the minority, it being felt that a minority with strongly held opinions should not be dictated to by the majority, at least on some issues.

This again raises the whole problem of participation in the political system. The electoral system, although seemingly only a mechanism for determining the composition of the government over the next few years, actually provides the major and sometimes the sole means of political participation for individuals living in a large, complex, modern society. The electoral system, therefore, takes on peculiar importance for democratic theory; since it often provides a significant or the only means of political participation, the electoral system is the key to whether or not the system is democratic. Individuals, when entering the voting booth, must be sure that their vote will be counted; that the election provides some choice; and that the choice is meaningful in that voters are actually free to vote for any of the options. It is also important to remember the most obvious point; that is, that an individual is allowed to vote in the first place. Finally, each vote should be equal to any other vote.[13]

These questions of electoral procedure bring into focus other important problems. The electoral system, in addition to providing a means of political participation, is designed to guarantee the peaceful change of political power from one individual or group to another. This purpose in turn raises the whole problem of leadership within a democracy, a question confronting democratic theorists since ancient Athens. The importance of leadership in democratic the-

---

[13]The need for equality of votes in a democracy is disputed by some who, believing themselves to be democratic, argue that since some individuals are worth more to the community than the normal run-of-the-mill citizen, these individuals should be provided with more votes on the basis of some formula such as the amount of taxes they pay. Two examples are Mark Twain's short story "The Curious Republic of Gondour," *Atlantic Monthly* 36 (October 1875): 461–463; and H. L. Hunt's *Alpaca* (Dallas: H. L. Hunt, 1960) and *Alpaca Revisited* (Dallas: H.L.H. Products, 1967). In the nineteenth century, proposals for plural votes based on some principle such as education were fairly common. See, for example, John Stuart Mill, *Considerations on Representative Government*, ed. Currin V. Shields (New York: Liberal Arts Press, 1958), pp. 136–143.

ory is particularly significant in representative democracy. Whatever theory of representation is accepted, the elected official is given some political power not directly held by constituents. This power can be removed through the electoral process, but in the meantime it is held by an individual who can directly participate in political decision making to the extent of the power vested in the office. In addition, the official may exercise political leadership by helping form or inform the opinions of constituents and others by defining the political issues he or she believes significant and by propagandizing for particular positions.[14]

Historically, most democratic theorists have been concerned with limiting the political power held by any one individual or group within the society while at the same time providing intelligent and capable leadership. For example, James Madison (1751–1836), an important figure in the framing of the U.S. Constitution and fourth president of the United States, was greatly worried about the possibility of some faction, including a "majority faction," gaining political power and exercising it in its own interest.

In the tenth number of *The Federalist Papers* (1787–1788), Madison suggested that the best protectors of freedom are the division of powers between the states and the national government; the separation of powers among the executive, legislative, and judicial branches of government found in the U.S. Constitution; and the diversity of a large country. Others involved in the writing and defense of the Constitution advocated an enlightened aristocracy exercising political power but periodically checked through election, rather than rule by the people. In other words, they accepted Burke's theory of representation and made it the essence of their theory of government.

A central problem with majority rule and the purpose of all these proposals to limit it is the tendency of majorities to suppress minorities. Systems like proportional representation, requirements for a higher percentage than fifty percent of the vote, and Madison's proposals regarding the U.S. Constitution are attempts to ensure that minorities are protected from the majority.

EQUALITY

Although equality has been discussed for centuries, only during this century has it taken on central importance in democratic theory and practice. Today equality is one of those concepts that produces fundamental disagreement.[15] For some people the achievement of some form of equality is absolutely essential; for

---

[14]On the problem of leadership, see James MacGregor Burns, *Leadership* (New York: Harper & Row, 1978); Barbara Kellerman, ed. *Political Leadership: A Source Book*, (Pittsburgh, PA: University of Pittsburgh Press, 1986); Robert C. Tucker, *Politics as Leadership* (Columbia: University of Missouri Press, 1981); Ann Ruth Willner, *The Spellbinders: Charismatic Political Leadership* (New Haven, CT: Yale University Press, 1984); Jean Blondel, *Political Leadership: Towards a General Analysis* (London: Sage, 1987); and Bryan D. Jones, ed., *Leadership and Politics: New Perspectives in Political Science* (Lawrence: University Press of Kansas, 1989).

[15]A number of concepts produce such fundamental disagreement. See W. B. Gallie, "Essentially Contested Concepts," *Proceedings of the Aristotelian Society*, ns 56 (1956), pp. 167–198; and William E. Connolly, "Essentially Contested Concepts," in his *The Terms of Political Discourse*, 2d ed. (Princeton, NJ: Princeton University Press, 1983), pp. 10 – 44.

James Madison (1751–1836) was secretary of state (1801–1809) during the presidency of Thomas Jefferson and then was the fourth president of the United States (1809–1817). Madison is now mostly remembered as one of the authors of *The Federalist Papers* (1787–1788) and as a major contributor to the drafting of the U.S. Constitution. Madison was concerned with the problem of minority rights and argued that the Constitution as written would provide adequate protection for minorities. (*Library of Congress*)

others the achievement of any form of equality is impossible; for still others, even if some form of equality were possible, it would not be desirable. Part of this disagreement comes from lumping together very different types of equality in one concept. Equality as a general concept includes five separate types of equality: political equality, equality before the law, equality of opportunity, economic equality, and equality of respect or social equality.

If there is a strict sense of equality applicable to human beings, it is sameness in relevant aspects.[16] But the phrase "in relevant aspects" modifying "sameness" shows that we have to define carefully what is relevant and what is not relevant in talking about equality; failure to do this is another reason for the disagreements over the meaning and importance of equality.

Political Equality

The importance of defining *relevant aspects* can be seen even in what would appear to be the simplest form of equality, political equality. If we assume the existence of some form of representative democracy, political equality refers to

---

[16]See the discussion in *Nomos IX: Equality*, ed. J. Roland Pennock and John W. Chapman (New York: Atherton Press, 1967), particularly the article "Egalitarianism and the Idea of Equality," by Hugo Adam Bedau, pp. 3–27.

equality at the ballot box, equality in the ability to be elected to public office, and equality of political influence.

Voting. Equality at the ballot box entails the following:

1. Each individual must have reasonably easy access to the place of voting.

2. Each person must be free to cast his or her own vote as he or she wishes.

3. Each vote must be given exactly the same weight when counted.

These conditions constitute an ideal and are much harder to fulfill than they at first appear to be.

There are a number of reasons for this difficulty. First, there is the question of citizenship. To vote one must be a citizen. Each country has its own regulations about who is a citizen and how citizenship is acquired. For example, in most countries, if you are born in that country you are a citizen. But if your parents are citizens of another country, you will probably have the right to be a citizen of their country. Some countries also allow their citizens to be simultaneously citizens of another country; others do not. In addition to birth, citizenship can be gained by being *naturalized* or granted citizenship by a country. Naturalization usually requires a formal process culminating in a ceremony in which allegiance is sworn to the new country.

Citizenship can also be lost. In many, though not all, countries, swearing allegiance to another country will result in the loss of citizenship. In the United States, serving in the military of another country is supposed to result in the loss of U.S. citizenship. Each country has its own rules on the loss of citizenship; in some countries it is virtually impossible to lose citizenship, whereas in others many different actions can result in such loss.

Second, there is an age requirement for voting. Each country has an established age at which citizens are first allowed to vote. At present the most common voting age is eighteen, although there are exceptions (for example, the voting age in Indonesia is seventeen and in India, twenty-one). No one under that age can vote.

Third, various people may have had the right to vote taken away from them. In the United States, for example, people convicted of certain crimes lose the right to vote. Also, at times and in various countries other formal limitations have been placed on the right to vote. Examples of such limitations are requirements that a voter own a specified amount of property or belong to a particular religion; race and gender have also served as limitations and, in some places, still do.

In addition, there are many informal avenues of inequality. First, and perhaps most obvious, are racial and sexual discrimination. Even with legal limitations on voting removed, women and minorities in most countries have been so discouraged from political participation that they still vote at a much lower rate than white males. Second, some older and many handicapped voters may have difficulty getting to the polling place. For example, the polling place in my area formerly required voters to negotiate two sets of stairs, and although arrangements could be made to vote without having to use the stairs, some voters didn't know this or felt that the effort required was too great and chose not to vote. The situation has been corrected, but this example illustrates that the right to vote can be taken away simply by not thinking through what is required to actually vote.

Also, a person who cannot influence what names are printed on the ballot—that is, choose the candidates—is not equal to those who can. There are two ways to influence the choice of who becomes a candidate: money and active participation in the political system. For many people the lack of money makes it very difficult to participate actively, but most people who don't participate simply choose not to.

Finally, each voter votes in a district, which should be roughly equal in population to other districts. If one district has a much larger population than another district, each vote is diluted in that it does not have the same strength in determining the outcome as a vote in a smaller district. The closer the districts are in population size, the closer the votes will be in strength. For example, to take an extreme case, if voter A lives in a district of 50,000 voters and voter B lives in one with only 10,000, B's vote will be worth five of A's. Some countries, such as the United States, require that district boundaries be changed regularly (usually after each census) to achieve this form of equality. The process is called *reapportionment*.

Running for Office. Equality in the ability to be elected to public office means that everyone who has the vote can be elected to public office, although particular offices usually have age qualifications and other specific requirements, such as residence in a specified area. In many countries it has become very expensive to run for public office; hence, equality in the ability to be elected to public office has been seriously eroded. Most countries have seen attempts to limit the effect of wealth by legally controlling campaign spending. Some countries, such as Great Britain, place very strict limitations on the amount that candidates can spend.

In addition, there are social constraints on running for office. Traditionally in the United States, it has been difficult or even impossible for African Americans, women, Hispanics, and other ethnic minorities, to name just a few groups, to become serious candidates for office. Similar situations, although with different groups, exist in most countries. While members of such groups may have the legal right to run for office, that right has frequently been meaningless because there was no chance they could be elected. The situation is slowly improving in most countries.

Political Influence. Political equality also refers to an equality of political influence among citizens. Such equality means that all who choose to participate can do so without any formal limitations based on their membership in any religious, racial, ethnic, gender, or economic category. Of course, all these categories have at times both formally affected political influence and informally affected people's ability to participate and the likelihood that they will choose to participate.

Equality Before the Law

Equality before the law resembles the definition of equality as sameness in relevant aspects because it means that all people will be treated in the same way by the legal system, and it is not hedged about by so many formal definitions of relevant aspects. Depictions of justice usually show a blindfolded woman holding a scale. The scale is an indication that the issues will be weighed; the blindfold indicates that they will be weighed fairly, taking into account nothing beyond the issues of the case.

Since a major function of law and legal procedures is to establish general rules that all people are expected to accept, law, by its very nature, is an equalizing force in society if it is enforced fairly. Clearly, equality before the law in practice is undermined by the socioeconomic inequalities that exist in all societies. But equality before the law is one of democracy's clearest goals.

Equality of Opportunity

The third type of equality is related to social stratification and mobility systems. Equality of opportunity means, first, that every individual in society will be able to move up or down within the class or status system depending on that individual's ability and application of that ability. Second, it means that no artificial barrier will keep any person from achieving what she or he can through ability and hard work. The key problem in the definition of equality of opportunity is the word *artificial*, which refers to individual characteristics such as race or religion that do not affect inherent abilities. Today much of the argument about equality centers on the definition of *artificial*. Race, gender, religion, ethnic or national origin, and sexual orientation are most often cited as such artificial barriers.

Social stratification and mobility systems vary greatly from society to society. We tend to think of social status and mobility as easy to measure because we link them to an easily quantifiable object—money. In most Western societies today, that measure is a fairly accurate guide to status (except at the level of the traditional aristocracy) and the major means of gaining or losing status. But even in the West it is not quite that simple because status depends on the respect a position in society is given as well as the income that goes with the position. For example, clergy are not generally very well paid but are accorded a status higher than their income. In a society according status on the basis of some other value (such as education), money would not automatically bring status. Equality of opportunity depends on the value accorded status.

Economic Equality

The fourth aspect of equality, economic equality, is very bothersome. Few political philosophers have advocated sameness in this regard, but a complete discussion cannot ignore this definition of economic equality. Economic equality could mean that every individual within a society should have the same income, and such a definition was proposed by Edward Bellamy in his popular novel *Looking Backward* (1888). This definition is normally avoided because most advocates of economic equality are more concerned with the political and legal aspects of equality and with equality of opportunity than with strict financial equality. In addition, complete equality of income could be unfair to everyone since it would not take into account the differing needs of different individuals. Of course, if income levels were sufficiently high, differences in need would be irrelevant, because all individuals would have enough no matter what their needs were. But very few exponents of economic equality expect such high income levels; therefore, what constitutes basic or fundamental human needs is a matter of considerable concern.

The usual argument for economic equality is that every individual within society must be guaranteed a minimum level of economic *security*. Such security will allow the individual the scope to become a fully active citizen. The stress is on security, not equality. The major contention, the key to the argument, is that without some degree of security the individual citizen will not be in a position to participate effectively even in the limited role of a voter.

Extreme levels of poverty effectively bar an individual from participation in the life of the community. This effect is particularly significant in education. It has been found that a child in a typical middle-class or lower middle-class home has had toys and other objects that help teach many of the skills essential to learning. A simple thing such as having a book read aloud a number of times shows the child the turning of the pages and will indicate that the English language is read from left to right and, thus, will set up a pattern the eyes will follow.

The child who has not had any of this preparation will start out a year or two, or even more, behind the child who has. There are also certain skills essential even for relatively unskilled jobs that a child learns by playing with toys. A child who has simple toys to play with is learning these skills; a child who does not have such toys will not gain these skills and will have to find a way of learning them later or be barred from even those unskilled jobs. The effect of such deprivation on a child's life can be profound, and we are unsure whether some of these effects can be reversed for children who are already in our school systems. Thus children at five or six may already have handicaps they will never be able to overcome. They may already have lost the possibility of developing their full potentials. There are exceptions: some children brought up in families that have suffered generations of extreme poverty do make it. However, the overwhelming majority do not, because they have simply lost out to the children of parents who can afford simple toys and books and the time to spend with their children.

Does a great inequality in income eliminate equality of opportunity? How great an inequality is permissible? How can the extremes be brought closer together? We shall look at these problems in greater detail as we discuss the differences between democratic capitalism and democratic socialism.

Equality of Respect or Social Equality

The fifth type of equality, equality of respect or social equality, is in some ways the most difficult to define. At its base is the belief that all human beings are due equal respect just because they are human; we are all equal in our fundamental humanity. Social equality is derived from this fundamental belief. Equality of respect refers to a level of individual interpersonal relations not covered by any of the other aspects of equality. The civil rights movement in the United States once developed a slogan, "Black is Beautiful," which illustrates the point. In Western society, the color black has had connotations of evil, as in the black clothes of the villain in early movies about the Old West. Advertising on television and in magazines used to reinforce this connotation by never using black models. The slogan "Black is Beautiful" was directed particularly at African American children to give them the idea that it could be good, not bad, to be black and that they could be black and still respect themselves and be respected by others. In a narrow sense, social equality means that no public or private association may erect barriers to activity within the association. Again, there is the problem of defining *artificial*, but generally we use it in the same sense as above, that is, denoting characteristics, such as gender, sexual orientation, race, ethnic or national origin, or religion, that do not affect an individual's inherent abilities. Examples of this type of equality might be the lack of artificial barriers to membership in a country club or in the use of a public park. Thus social equality refers to the absence of the class and status distinctions that raise such artificial barriers and that have been and still are recognized in every society. In this sense, it includes aspects of equality of opportunity.

As such, social equality is a fairly intangible thing. It means that a wide variety of people with different backgrounds, positions, and incomes can all be accepted. Again, we encounter the problem of what barriers are artificial and what might be meaningful barriers to this type of equality. Poverty may become a meaningful barrier even though it started as an artificial one. A poverty-stricken individual and an individual from the middle or lower middle class, let alone from the upper class, would have a very difficult time associating effectively with each other because they come from radically different cultures. But this barrier is really an artificial one. Complete social equality would mean that the gap could be bridged, that the cultural differences could be overcome and made unimportant or accepted as valuable diversity.

Education is believed to be one of the main mechanisms for overcoming inequality, but in many countries education is also a means of preserving inequalities. For example, in Britain large numbers of students are educated privately in what are called public schools. These students then proceed to the best universities and generally into the best jobs. (The same process takes place in most countries but on a smaller scale.) At the same time, these students are cut off from the broader society, and thus privilege, antagonism, and ignorance establish the basis for significant social inequality. In some countries efforts have

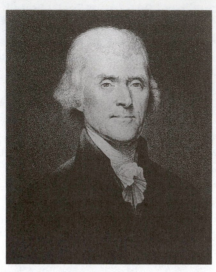

Thomas Jefferson (1743–1826), the third president of the United States, was involved in almost all the issues that dominated American political life during his lifetime. Of all the things he accomplished, Jefferson thought his three most important actions were writing the Declaration of Independence and the Virginia Act for Establishing Religious Freedom and founding the University of Virginia. (*Library of Congress*)

been made to overcome such patterns by establishing schools that bring together people from a wide variety of backgrounds in an attempt to eliminate class or racial ignorance and animosity.

FREEDOM, LIBERTY, AND RIGHTS

Historically, the desire for equality has often been expressed as an aspect of liberty. When Thomas Jefferson (1743–1826), drafting the Declaration of Independence, spoke of equality, he meant that people were equal in the rights they had. Equality of opportunity is often thought of as a right. On the other hand, many people believe attempts to achieve a degree of economic equality are directly in conflict with attempts to maintain economic liberty.

The words *liberty*, *freedom*, and *right* are most often used interchangeably. Although some scholars prefer to make careful distinctions among the meanings, it is not necessary to do so. All three refer to the ability to act without restrictions or with restrictions that are themselves limited in specified or specifiable ways. *Freedom* is the most general term. *Liberty* usually refers to social and political freedom. *Right* usually refers to specific legally guaranteed freedoms. Also, *right* has been broadened to include basic human or natural rights. Finally,

John Locke (1632–1704) was an important British philosopher and political thinker of
the seventeenth century. His most important works were *Essay Concerning Human Understanding* (1689) and, in political thought, *Two Treatises of Government* (published in
1690 but written much earlier). The first of the two treatises is an attack on the divine
right of kings as put forth by Robert Filmer. The second treatise is an argument for rule
by consent of the governed, a defense of private property and majority rule, and a justification for revolution. The U.S. Declaration of Independence was based on the second
treatise, and Locke was a major influence on a number of thinkers in the United States
at the time of the revolution and the drafting of the U.S. Constitution. (*Library of Congress*)

rights have become the focus of those in the United States who wish to expand
constitutional guarantees and protections. As a result such questions as "Does
the U.S. Constitution provide for a right of privacy?" have become the center
of legal, political, and philosophic debate.

There is no such thing as complete freedom. In the first place, one must
maintain life and perform a number of essential bodily functions. It is possible
to choose the times one eats, drinks, sleeps, and so on, but one cannot
choose not to eat, drink, sleep, and so forth for very long. In the second
place, there are other people. Although they are essential for a complete life,
they are restricting. An old adage states, "Your freedom to swing your arm
stops at my nose." Although superficial, it does point out that the existence
of others must be taken into account and that other people can be a limit
on free action.

A democratic society should be fairly free and open rather than controlled.
It is the general assumption of democratic theory that whatever does no damage
to the society as a whole or to the individuals within it should be the concern
of no one but the individual or individuals involved.

Natural Rights and Civil Rights

The most influential approach to liberty is found in the distinction between the rights a person has or should have as a human being and the rights derived from government. The former are often called natural rights; the latter are called civil rights. Although the trend today is either to reject the concept of natural rights altogether and call all rights civil rights or to replace the word *natural* with *human*, the traditional distinction is still useful.

Many democratic theorists, such as John Locke, argued that human beings as human beings, separate from all government or society, have certain rights that should never be given up or taken away. People do not give up these rights on joining a society or government, and the society or government should not attempt to take these rights away. If a government does try to take them away, the people are justified in revolting to change the government. Not all theorists make this last argument. The most important point is that natural rights establish limits. The Bill of Rights in the U.S. Constitution is a good example. Many of the amendments in the Bill of Rights begin, "Congress shall make no law regarding . . . " The wording clearly indicates a limit on governmental activity. Isaiah Berlin calls this approach *negative liberty*. By this term he describes the area of life within which one "is or should be left to do or be what he is able to do or be, without interference by other persons."[17]

In the United States, tradition emphasizes the danger of possible interference from government. Certain areas of life, such as speech, religion, press, and assembly, have been defined as areas of "negative liberty" where each person is left to do, on the whole, what she or he wants. Negative liberty as practiced illustrates the complexity of democracy. Government is seen as the most likely agent to attempt to restrict liberty. Government is also the major protector of liberty, and it must protect people even against itself. This is one reason many Western democracies have established what we call a system of checks and balances within the government. No segment of government should be able to rule unchecked by any other segment; as a result, the rights of citizens are protected.

Berlin also developed a concept that he called *positive liberty*. As used by Berlin, this refers to the possibility of individuals controlling their own destiny or their ability to choose among options. For Berlin, positive liberty is the area of rational self-control or "self-mastery." For others, positive liberty means that the government should ensure conditions in which the full development of each individual is possible.[18] On the whole, as will be seen in the next chapter, democratic capitalists stress negative liberty, and democratic socialists stress positive liberty while trying to maintain most of the negative liberties.

---

[17]Isaiah Berlin, "Two Concepts of Liberty," in his *Four Essays on Liberty* (London: Oxford University Press, 1969), pp. 121–122.

[18]See, for example, the argument in Christian Bay, *The Structure of Freedom* (Stanford, CA: Stanford University Press, 1958); and Bay, *Strategies of Political Emancipation* (Notre Dame, IN: University of Notre Dame Press, 1981).

The most important natural right—the right to self-preservation—is basic to this understanding of positive liberty. This right can be interpreted to mean that every person has a right to the necessary minimum of food, clothing, and shelter needed to live in a given society. Since standards vary considerably from society to society, the necessary minimum might vary a great deal.

From this perspective, positive liberty might include the right to an education equal to one's ability and the right to a job. This approach to positive liberty logically extends to establishing as a right anything that can be shown to be essential to the development, and perhaps even the expression, of each person's potential as a human being.

Thus, positive liberty can include as rights a wide variety of economic and social practices in addition to the political rights that usually come to mind when speaking of rights. "The Universal Declaration of Human Rights"[19] includes such rights in its definition of the rights all human beings should have, such as that found in Article 22, which states that "everyone, as a member of society, has the right to social security and is entitled to realization, through national effort and in accordance with the organization and resources of each State, of the economic, social and cultural rights indispensable for his dignity and the free development of his personality." Positive liberty is not usually extended this far, but these examples illustrate the complexity of the questions involved.

Other so-called natural rights have also been widely debated.[20] One of the most controversial is the right to property.[21] Some contend that there must be a nearly absolute right to acquire and accumulate private property because ownership of property is an avenue to the full development and expression of the human personality. Others argue that private property must be limited because the control of such property gives additional power to those who own it. (Additional arguments for and against the institution of private property will be considered in chapter 4.)

Although there is widespread disagreement on the specific natural rights, it is generally agreed that after the formation of government, these rights must become civil rights or rights specifically guaranteed and protected by the government, even—or particularly—against itself. This formulation of liberty raises many problems. The most basic difficulty is the assumption that a government will be willing to guarantee rights against itself. Many thinkers have assumed

---

[19]"The Universal Declaration of Human Rights" was adopted by the United Nations in 1948.

[20]See Ronald Dworkin, *Taking Rights Seriously*, rev. ed. (London: Duckworth, 1978); Richard Flathman, *The Practice of Rights* (Cambridge, England: Cambridge University Press, 1976); and *Nomos XXIII: Human Rights*, ed. J. Roland Pennock and John W. Chapman (New York: New York University Press, 1981).

[21]For the debate on the question of property, see Lawrence C. Becker, *Property Rights: Philosophic Foundations* (Boston: Routledge & Kegan Paul, 1977); *Property, Profits, and Economic Justice*, ed. Virginia Held (Belmont, CA: Wadsworth, 1980); *Property: Mainstream and Critical Positions*, ed. C. B. Macpherson (Oxford, England: Basil Blackwell, 1978); *Nomos XXII: Property*, ed. J. Roland Pennock and John W. Chapman (New York: New York University Press, 1980); and Alan Ryan, *Property and Political Theory* (Oxford, England: Basil Blackwell, 1984).

that representative democracy with fairly frequent elections will solve the problem. Any such government should recognize that an infringement of people's civil rights would ensure its defeat in the next election. Experience has shown this is not necessarily true, and the result has been apathy,[22] civil disobedience,[23] and revolution,[24] with apathy currently the greatest concern in most developed democracies. At the same time, the protection of liberties is still considered one of the primary duties of a democratic political system and a central part of democratic theory.

Types of Liberty

It is more difficult to define types of liberty than to discuss types of equality but, loosely, civil rights include the following specific liberties or freedoms:

1. The right to vote,

2. Freedom of speech,

3. Freedom of the press,

4. Freedom of assembly,

5. Freedom of religion,

6. Freedom of movement, and

7. Freedom from arbitrary treatment by the political and legal system.

The first six of these are areas of life that the democratic argument says should be left, within very broad limits, to the discretion of the individual. Of these six, freedom of movement is the least commonly discussed among theorists of democracy. The seventh item, freedom from arbitrary treatment, is simply a way of stating positively the belief that government must protect the citizen from

---

[22]See Everett Carl Ladd, Jr., *Where Have All the Voters Gone? The Fracturing of America's Political Parties* (New York: Norton, 1978); Arthur H. Miller, "Political Issues and Trust in Government: 1964–1970," *American Political Science Review* 68, no. 3 (September 1974): 951–972; G. Bingham Powell, "American Voter Turnout in Comparative Perspective," *American Political Science Review* 80, no. 1 (March 1986): 17–43; and Stephen Bennett, *Apathy in America 1960–1984: Causes and Consequences of Citizen Political Indifference* (Dobbs Ferry, NY: Transnational Publishers, 1986).

[23]See, for example, Mohandas K. Gandhi, *Non-Violent Resistance (Satyagraha)* (New York: Schocken Books, 1951); *Political Obligation and Civil Disobedience: Readings*, ed. Michael P. Smith and Kenneth L. Deutsch (New York: Thomas Y. Crowell, 1972); and the various works of Martin Luther King, Jr., such as *Strength to Love* (New York: Harper & Row, 1963), *Stride Toward Freedom* (New York: Harper & Row, 1953), *Where Do We Go from Here?* (New York: Harper & Row, 1967), and *Why We Can't Wait* (New York: Harper & Row, 1963).

[24]See, for example, John Dunn, *Modern Revolutions: An Introduction to the Analysis of a Political Phenomenon* (Cambridge, England: Cambridge University Press, 1972). See also Mostafa Rejai, *The Strategy of Political Revolution* (Garden City, NY: Doubleday, 1973); Peter Calvert, *Revolution* (London: Macmillan, 1970); Jack Woddis, *New Theories of Revolution: A Commentary on the Views of Frantz Fanon, Regis Debray, and Herbert Marcuse* (New York: International Publishers, 1972); Mark N. Hagopian, *The Moral Meaning of Revolution* (New Haven, CT: Yale University Press, 1979); A. S. Cohan, *Theories of Revolution: An Introduction* (London: Nelson, 1975); and James H. Billington, *Fire in the Minds of Men: Origins of the Revolutionary Faith* (New York: Basic Books, 1980).

government. The various freedoms—particularly those of speech, press, assembly, and religion—are closely related.

The Right to Vote. The right to vote without interference is, of course, the key to the ability to change the system. It is the ultimate check on government and the true guarantor of any freedom.

Freedom of Speech. With some minimal disagreement, most thinkers consider freedom of speech the most important freedom. Within democracy freedom of speech has a special place. The right to vote does not mean much if it is impossible to hear opposing points of view and to express one's own opinion. The same reasoning is behind the freedoms of press and assembly. The rights to publish opinion and to meet together to discuss political issues are fundamental rights if people are to vote intelligently. The right to vote implies, even requires, a right to information and the free expression of opinion both orally and in writing. Freedom of speech requires freedom of assembly; freedom to speak is meaningless without the possibility of an audience.

John Stuart Mill (1806–1873) explained the importance of freedom of speech and press in a slightly different way in his classic work *On Liberty* (1859).

> This, then, is the appropriate region of human liberty. It comprises, first, the inward domain of consciousness; demanding liberty of conscience in the most comprehensive sense; liberty of thought and feeling; absolute freedom of opinion and sentiment on all subjects, practical or speculative, scientific, moral, or theological. The liberty of expressing and publishing opinions may seem to fall under a different principle, since it belongs to that part of the conduct of an individual which concerns other people; but, being almost of as much importance as the liberty of thought itself and resting in great part on the same reasons, is practically inseparable from it.[25]

For Mill, thought requires the freedom to express oneself orally and in writing. The search for truth requires that challenge, debate, and disagreement be possible. Mill argued this from four different perspectives.

> First, if any opinion is compelled to silence, that opinion may, for aught we can certainly know, be true. To deny this is to assume our own infallibility.
>
> Secondly, though the silenced opinion be an error, it may, and very commonly does, contain a portion of truth; and since the general or prevailing opinion on any subject is rarely or never the whole truth, it is only by the collision of adverse opinions that the remainder of the truth has any chance of being supplied.
>
> Thirdly, even if the received opinion be not only true, but the whole truth; unless it is suffered to be, and actually is, vigorously and earnestly contested, it will, by most of those who receive it, be held in the manner of a prejudice, with little comprehension or feeling of its rational grounds. And not only this, but, fourthly, the meaning of the doctrine itself will be in danger of being lost or enfeebled, and deprived of its vital effect on the character and conduct; the dogma

---

[25]John Stuart Mill, *On Liberty*, 4th ed. (London: Longman, Reader & Dyer, 1869), p. 26.

becoming a mere formal profession, inefficacious for good, but cumbering the ground and preventing the growth of any real and heartfelt conviction, from reason or personal experience.[26]

Without freedom of expression truth is lost, is never found, becomes mere prejudice, or is enfeebled. Assuming that there is truth to be found, freedom of expression is essential; if there is no truth to be found, freedom of expression is even more important as the only device available to sort out the better opinion from the worse.

Freedom of the Press. Mill joined speech and press closely together and, for political concerns, the argument that a generally free press is essential in a democracy is almost noncontroversial. But there are areas of concern outside the strictly political realm, most obviously related to the publication of pornography, and there are even concerns about some more narrowly political issues.

If freedom of the press is taken to be an absolute, there should be no restrictions on the publication of pornography. With some exceptions, most pornography depicts individuals of one of two groups—women or children—as objects to be used, often violently, by another group—men. Viewed this way pornography is an issue with strong political overtones and illustrates a central concern of contemporary students of democracy, the conflict of rights. Whose rights should be protected, the publishers and consumers of pornography or the women and children who are turned into consumer goods?

A more narrowly political issue involves the publication of material designed to incite the overthrow of a government by violence. An absolute version of freedom of the press would require the government to ensure that those trying to overthrow it have the right to publish calls for its overthrow and even manuals on how to produce bombs and directions on where and how to place them. Many people find such a position ludicrous; an equal number find it perfectly reasonable.

A third issue is governmental secrecy. Some, particularly those working for the press, contend that the press should have free access to the whole government decision-making process. Others, particularly those working in government, argue that government should be free to choose what the press is allowed to know and publish. Most people fall somewhere in between, believing that some governmental actions must be secret and that others, ranging from a few to most, should not be secret. The problem is that governments decide what must be secret, and this leads to distrust. There is no way around this problem, and the press and government will inevitably be at odds about the extent of permissible secrecy.

Tension between the press and government is unavoidable and probably healthy. Western democracies justly criticize countries with a controlled press while trying to keep their own press from publishing things they want kept

---

[26]Mill, *On Liberty*, p. 95.

secret. The degree of press freedom varies among democracies; there is no such thing as a completely free press, but a fairly high degree of such freedom is essential in a democracy since in the modern world the communication of political ideas requires the right to publish those ideas.

Freedom of Assembly. The freedom to speak requires the freedom to have an audience. Although broadcasting means that the audience need not be gathered in one place, the ability to meet together to discuss political issues, make decisions on those issues, and choose candidates is clearly still fundamental to a functioning democracy.

The political issues related to the freedom of assembly are issues of public order. Should parades and demonstrations that may produce violence be allowed? What limitations on assembly should be permissible to keep traffic moving or to prevent violence? All governments, from the local to the national, in all democracies are constantly faced with the problem of how to regulate assembly without making it politically ineffective.

Freedom of Religion. Freedom of religion is usually supported on precisely the same grounds Mill used to defend freedom of speech and press, and worshiping together requires the freedom of assembly. Even if we are certain that we have the whole truth—perhaps particularly if we are certain—we should always distrust our own presumed infallibility and welcome the continuation of the search. Freedom of religion has, particularly in North America, come to be identified with the separation of church and state. The search for religious truth, in this view, requires that government be a neutral bystander neither favoring nor suppressing any aspect of that search.[27]

In many countries this issue takes a more complex form. In the first place, many countries have an established church or a church that is officially recognized by the government and may receive financial and other public support. Secondly, many countries have political parties that are tied (directly or indirectly) to religious bodies. In Europe most of these parties are labeled Christian Democrats or some variant thereof. These parties are most often conservative. In such circumstances the quest for freedom of religion becomes more problematic, although in modern Europe all such political parties support freedom of religion. But every religion has had at some time or other to face the question of its relationship to political power. This issue is particularly important today in the Third World, and it deeply divides the Roman Catholic Church.

Freedom of Movement. Freedom of movement is less commonly included among the basic freedoms, but it is as important as the others since the ability to move freely is a major protection for other freedoms. Some restrictions are

---

[27]On this debate, see Loren Beth, *The American Theory of Church and State* (Gainesville: University of Florida Press, 1958); Gerald V. Bradley, *Church-State Relationships in America* (Westport, CT: Greenwood Press, 1987); and Leo Pfeffer, *Church, State and Freedom*, rev. ed. (Boston: Beacon Press, 1967).

already in effect. Many democratic countries, particularly in Western Europe, require their citizens to carry identity papers and require hotels, for example, to record the number on these papers when someone registers in the hotel. All countries require passports for travel to some foreign countries. And the growth of government programs means that most countries have records of the location and changes of permanent address for a growing number of citizens. But in no democracy is it necessary to get prior approval from a government to travel within its borders, and, most important, within a democracy people can freely move from place to place for political activity.

Freedom from Arbitrary Treatment. The last freedom, freedom from arbitrary treatment by the political and legal system, is also a major protection for the other freedoms. All democratic societies have clearly established procedural rights designed to guarantee that every individual will be treated fairly by the system. Without these procedural rights, the substantive rights of freedom of speech, press, and so on would not be as secure.

Basic guarantees include those found in the U.S. Bill of Rights, such as freedom from cruel and unusual punishment (designed to prohibit torture; now an issue in the debate over capital punishment); the right to a writ of habeas corpus (Latin meaning "[that] you have the body"), or the right to demand that a prisoner be brought before an officer of the court so that the lawfulness of the imprisonment can be determined; and the right to a trial by a jury of one's peers.

Most recently, the notion of freedom in the United States and a number of other democracies has developed in the context of legally defined and enforceable rights. Many court decisions, often highly controversial, have gradually changed—sometimes expanded, sometimes reduced—the areas in which an individual citizen or group of citizens can expect the legal system to be concerned with their rights. Most of these changes have centered on the extent to which it is possible for all citizens to have equal rights and to have those rights enforced equally.

Toleration. Another way in which the idea of freedom has been expressed is through toleration of diverse beliefs and ways of life. Toleration means that one accepts another person believing or doing something that one believes to be wrong. Religious toleration is the most obvious case, and in some ways it is the most difficult case. If I am certain that my way is the only one that leads to salvation, I am unlikely to tolerate an opposing belief that I am convinced is dangerous to my and your salvation. That is why most religious believers want to convert people to their beliefs. Religious tolerance is, in fact, a relatively recent phenomenon. Many people reject it, believing that they have found the one true road to salvation. As late as the seventeenth century the word *tolerance* had a negative meaning and *intolerance* a positive one.

Within a relatively short time, though, the connotation of the words shifted: tolerance became a virtue and intolerance a vice. Today we tend to extend the idea of tolerance beyond religion to questions of political and other beliefs and ways of life. Freedom comes to include a large area in which we accept other people even though we disagree with them.[28]

Tolerance is basic to modern democracy because one of the keys to democracy is the recognition of very basic disagreements among citizens and, more important, the acceptance of these disagreements. The diversity of the population and the protection of that diversity through tolerance are extremely important. Tolerance must exist or democracy cannot work.

Two other areas of freedom should be noted briefly: the silence of the law and unenforceability. It is part of the Anglo–American tradition that unless there is a law prohibiting an action, that action is within the area of individual discretion until such a law is written. In the United States, when the law is written, it cannot affect actions that preceded it. In many other countries, newly passed laws can be used to find past acts illegal. Also, the experience of Prohibition in the United States indicated that there are unenforceable laws, laws people simply won't accept. Thus, unenforceability can also be seen as an aspect of freedom.

Liberty is limited to some extent by all political systems. The democratic system has built into it certain safeguards that tend to protect individuals from having their freedoms too severely restricted. Of course, these safeguards do not always work. The most fundamental of these safeguards is the basic characteristic of a democracy—the people have some control over their government. Democratic theorists have never adequately dealt with the problem of severe restrictions of rights that are desired or acquiesced in by the majority. Thus a problem for democracy is how to achieve sufficient tolerance of differences so that the majority is willing to protect the rights of the minority. For many the answer is education.

EDUCATION

Education as a fundamental principle of democracy may be mildly controversial, but it should not be. Democratic theorists such as John Locke, Jean-Jacques Rousseau, and John Stuart Mill wrote treatises on education that tied their political theories loosely or tightly to the need for an educated populace. In the United States the founders of the democracy believed in the essential role of education in developing an effective democracy. In fact, the statement that an educated citizenry is necessary in a democracy is commonplace. What might make it appear controversial is that contemporary commentators no longer make the connection clearly, and there is argument over the nature of the education needed.

The argument regarding the need for education is fairly simple. A citizen is required to make choices among candidates and issues. In order to do so he or

---

[28]See Preston King, *Toleration* (New York: St. Martin's, 1976); and Glenn Tinder, *Tolerance: Toward a New Civility* (Amherst: University of Massachusetts Press, 1975).

she must have the basic skills of reading, writing, and arithmetic (rather illiterately known as the three Rs) since the information provided is often communicated in print, numbers are used extensively, and it may be necessary for the citizen to communicate in writing. Equally important, the citizen must be able to evaluate the information, weigh pros and cons, and decide what positions best correspond to her or his interests. Of course, the citizen must also be able to correctly identify those interests. In the modern world the knowledge and evaluative skills necessary to judge the issues might appear to require considerable formal education, and that is where part of the current controversy lies.

A democracy can operate without an educated populace. India is a functioning democracy with a very high level of illiteracy; all democracies have faced this problem at times. But a democracy of illiterates is very limited unless the culture actively encourages oral dissemination of information and discussion of issues. The elitist model of democracy would have no trouble with a high level of illiteracy, but every other approach to democracy would find it an issue that required solution. Thus it is fair to say that an educated populace is one of the prerequisites of a fully functioning democracy.

But what constitutes an educated populace? On this question there are basic divisions. Some people believe that knowledge of how the government functions is sufficient. Others believe that formal education in the principles of democracy and how to evaluate arguments is necessary. Many positions between these are taken, with about the only agreement in most democracies being that the educational system isn't doing what it should.

CONCLUSION

The principles of democracy all relate to one another and all stem from the most fundamental democratic principle: citizen involvement. Politically, equality and freedom both characterize and protect citizen involvement. They characterize citizen involvement in that democracy demands the freedom to vote and equality of the vote; they protect citizen involvement because a free and equal electorate can insist on the maintenance of that freedom and equality. A free and equal electorate needs education to ensure that that freedom and equality are meaningful and to make informed choices as citizens. Today the electoral system is the major avenue for the expression of citizen involvement, and of course the system of representation is the purpose and result of the electoral system and the way in which citizens are involved.

CURRENT TRENDS

The principles of democracy do not change; even many of the issues and debates they raise remain much the same over the years. In any given year in any democracy particular issues will be prominent, but for about the last decade certain issues have been of concern in most democracies.

One concern strikes at the very roots of democracy—the power of interest groups. Many people believe that legislators and bureaucrats are not making decisions based on the best interests of their constituents or the country or region as a whole. They believe that decisions are being based on the desires of interest groups that are able to influence these decisions through various means including direct payments (bribery) at one extreme to providing biased information at the other. The central issue of democracy is whether or not groups of citizens who organize for their own benefit should have more power in the system than citizens who are not specifically concerned with the issues but have no way of being heard without joining or forming such a group. What does citizen involvement mean when some groups have immense power? This concern has a long history, but it has come back to center stage because people are aware of the issue in a way they haven't been for some time.

Another issue that has arisen recently is term limits. The question of whether or not people in the United States can limit the number of terms that an office-holder can serve in Congress without a constitutional amendment has a much longer history than most people know. Radical democrats at the time of the American Revolution wanted a system of severely restricted term limits; many wanted the limit to be one term. The president of the United States is limited to two terms by constitutional amendment. In many states, governors are restricted to a specified number of terms, and it is clear that the people in a state can limit the terms of office of state officeholders. But the U.S. Supreme Court has decided that the people of states cannot restrict the number of terms that members of the House and Senate from their state can serve. A constitutional amendment will be needed to do that. The question for democracy is not the specific constitutional requirements, but whether the fact that incumbents have clear advantages over nonincumbents in running for office should be modified by forcing incumbents out on a regular basis even though they could probably win reelection.

The development of computer and television technology has opened up the possibility of greater political participation. It is now possible for citizens to view debates and immediately register their vote. Although such systems are likely to be adopted only in local politics, their potential is enormous for changing the way democracy works. Some people believe that such technology can make participatory democracy possible. In many areas it is now possible to watch debates but not participate in them before local governing bodies; in a few areas it is possible to electronically vote from home while watching such a debate. These votes are only expressions of opinion, not binding, but the procedure shows that binding direct votes are technically if not politically possible.

In a number of areas, the basic principles of democracy are being rethought and reexamined. For example, a central issue today is the question of privacy: how large is the area of negative liberty where the individual should simply be left alone? The debate includes questions ranging from wiretapping to sexual morality and so-called victimless crimes such as prostitution.

Another set of issues centers around who should control the application of potentially dangerous but also potentially valuable new areas of science and technology, such as nuclear power, psychosurgery, research in recombinant DNA, and techniques of behavior modification. The fundamental problem is who should make decisions and how, when our knowledge is uncertain, experts disagree, and the effects could be extremely far-reaching.

A related issue is the problem of how to make bureaucracies more accountable both to the governments they supposedly serve and to the citizenry at large. This raises the slightly older question of elite rule in a new guise, because proponents of democratic elitism have always argued that the elite could be changed by the people at any election. The bureaucratic elites cannot be changed this way, and many argue that the next major development of democratic theory should focus on providing some form of citizen control of non-elected elites.

A whole range of problems centers on access to data in computers. A skilled hacker can gain access to data in banks, the military, research institutes, credit unions, and universities. It is possible to steal, erase, or change the data in computers. Most of the time experts can trace such tampering back to its source, and both hackers and those trying to counter them are becoming more sophisticated. Examples include the famous program that jammed computers all over the country and entry into defense computers and into computers at the Lawrence Livermore National Laboratories.

The nonprint media pose a range of problems for freedom of the press that do not currently affect the print media. It is possible to publish on a low budget and without government approval. It is even possible to make and distribute some nonprint material on a low budget and without government approval. It is possible to do radio and television broadcasts the same way, but it is illegal. But video cameras are readily obtainable, videos can be made inexpensively and reproduced cheaply, and people are in the process of establishing distribution mechanisms that avoid regulations for both political and pornographic videos. Clearly the meaning of *press* in *freedom of the press* has already changed, and the law has begun to change with it. But the law has not really kept up with technology, and a series of legal issues is likely to be raised in the near future.

The means by which it is possible for computers in various places to communicate with each other and the growing sophistication of those means make it possible to send words, pictures, and music in any combination any place there is a computer capable of receiving the material. So far this method of communication has escaped most government regulation and is open to anyone who can arrange a connection, which is simple and inexpensive or free. Governments are moving to regulate the system, and the private sector is moving to replace the free communication with paid communication. However, at present computer communications is an area of free press that is almost completely free from individual cost or government regulation.

Examples of the problems that have already occurred are the availability of pornography, the use of the system for advertising, and what might be called "hate speech" ("flaming," in the jargon). It is clear that the system is being used for various criminal activities from gaining restricted information about individuals, companies, or institutions to planning racial intimidation. Many people want the system simply left alone; others feel that it needs regulation.

Another area of concern over freedom of the press has arisen because many people perceive the press to have lost whatever claims to objectivity it once had. The press (including here all the communications media) is perceived as lacking balance, hyping "news" that will attract an audience rather than presenting information of long-term importance (in the United States the O. J. Simpson case is seen as the primary recent example), and, in many cases, reporting dishonestly to support one side or another on an issue. This loss of confidence in the media has gone a long way toward undermining the effectiveness of the media as a means of providing the information citizens need to make reasoned choices in a democracy.

A major contemporary issue is whether depictions of violence cause violence, and if they do, what to do about it. (An offshoot of this question is whether pornography encourages violence against women and children, and if so, what to do about it.) The first question has produced many studies, but so far it is impossible to answer with certainty. In some well-attested cases, people have copied violent actions that they have seen broadcast, so the answer would seem to be yes, but did the broadcast cause the violence or just the specific form of the violence? We don't know. If the answer is that depictions of violence can cause violence, what should be done? Can depictions of violence be regulated without destroying the freedom of the press necessary for a fully functioning democracy? The likely answer is, "Probably, but only with difficulty." The same answer applies to the regulation of pornography.

All these issues raise again the potential conflict, to be discussed further in the next chapter, among the rights of an individual to express her- or himself, the market that distributes some of the products of that expression, and the right of a society to protect its members from the perceived damage of certain forms of expression. Whose rights are paramount?

A number of other important issues have recently arisen around the problem of equality. In the United States in the recent past, equality has mostly been discussed as a question of civil rights for African Americans and women. But the most serious issues concern not the general position that women and minorities have rights equal to those of white men but rather how to overcome years of discrimination. For example, a significant concern has been in employment— does discriminating in favor of groups who are not represented in the labor force to the extent one would expect, given their proportions in the population, discriminate against the people who might otherwise have expected to fill those jobs? Specifically, does the establishment of quotas for the hiring of groups that have been discriminated against produce unwarranted discrimination (called reverse discrimination) against others?

One debate among theorists is over the meaning of equality. Some theorists suggest that the goal of equality should be an equality of results, whereas others emphasize equality of opportunity. Those arguing for equality of results contend that, in practice, equality of opportunity is a sham that allows people to blame those who fail for their failures. These theorists contend that only by looking at what happens is it possible to judge the success of programs to eliminate discrimination.

Other issues have also arisen. What, for example, is the basis for the fact that African Americans are executed in the United States at a much higher rate than whites accused of the same or similar crimes? Or, why do African Americans make up such a high proportion of the inmates of prisons? Are African Americans being treated equally in the legal system? Is this even a racial question? Some argue that the issue is class rather than race. Others argue that there is no problem; the system is working fairly. Evidence has been produced for all these positions.

Another issue that deeply divides people is abortion and particularly the problem of public funding for abortions. Should government take a moral stance for or against abortion? What are the appropriate rights of the women (and men) involved?

In the United States today the relationship of church and state has reemerged as a central issue. The tradition is complex. North America was originally colonized by groups desiring to practice their own religious beliefs but with no notion of toleration for other beliefs. The existence of a variety of churches and the loss of faith common in the eighteenth-century Enlightenment led to the establishment of the freedom of religion clause in the U.S. Bill of Rights. But in practice the United States was overwhelmingly Protestant until well into the twentieth century and not very tolerant of non–Protestants. Most recently the growing diversity of American religious belief and the development of evangelical Christianity, combined with a number of Supreme Court decisions supporting a fairly rigid barrier between church and state, have led to a developing conflict over prayer in schools, government aid to parochial schools (also a major issue in France), and, in general, the place of the church in political life. In addition, the growth of non-Christian religions in most Western countries has begun to stretch the limits of toleration. Jews have been faced with anti-Semitism for generations. Today, Muslims are becoming a major target of discrimination.

Multiculturalism

One of the growing concerns with democratic pluralism is multiculturalism, particularly in education. To what extent should a society with a dominant culture or cultures teach children about the dominant cultures rather than the minority cultures? Put another way, don't children have a right to learn about *their* heritage rather than being forced to learn about the dominant culture? These two ways of putting what is essentially the same question illustrate the problem. Those in the dominant culture have as much a right to value their culture as those in the minority cultures, but do they have a right to impose it? In the past this right was never questioned. Today people in minority cultures are demanding that their cultures be taught as well as the majority culture. Multiculturalism raises questions of majority versus minority rights and how to make a plural society genuinely pluralistic.

Difference

How can individual and group difference be recognized and valued in a society that believes in equality, or should it? In a development that has changed the focus of debate, a shift has occurred, stemming primarily from debates within feminism, from a concern with the *sameness* component of equality to the recognition that *difference* is important and valuable and should be protected, even fostered. The argument does not depend on whether the differences are based on biology or are socially constructed.

While the definition of equality as "sameness in relevant aspects" does not prohibit a focus on difference, the emphasis since the beginning of the civil rights movement has been on sameness. The change is to move the focus to what is a *relevant* difference. Thirty years ago such an emphasis was used as an excuse to take rights from minorities; the assumption now is that such rights are so well established that it is now safe to again recognize relevant differences.

The issue comes back to one of the fundamental questions of democracy: How do we balance the interests of the majority and the minority? Or, what may be a more accurate reflection of the current situation in the United States: How do we balance the interests of various minorities given that there is no longer an overall or general minority—only temporary majorities and minorities on specific issues?

For example, what does equality mean to someone who is disabled? Immediately after World War II various European countries tried to compensate for war injuries by providing those physically disabled in the war easier access to certain jobs and transportation and established other programs that clearly recognized that society needed to act to integrate them into the postwar society as much as possible. The United States had much more limited programs. With time these programs gradually disappeared, but recently, and now beginning in the United States, people with disabilities have been gaining recognition by stressing that society must compensate for their disabilities so they are able to fully participate in society. This has been done by establishing legally protected rights that will provide them with equal opportunity. Again, it is important to note the connection between rights and equality.

Another method used by groups advocating for people with disabilities has been in attempting to change the language used to describe them. The earlier usage was "handicapped." Later usage has included "disabled," "people with disabilities," and "differently abled."

I teach at a public university that happens to be located on fairly hilly terrain. Some years ago, well before there were advocacy groups for the disabled, some faculty and students decided to demonstrate the difficulties faced by students in wheelchairs by spending a few days trying to get around the campus in wheelchairs. In many places it was virtually impossible to get between buildings, into buildings, or from parking lots to buildings. On the whole, the university responded positively by removing certain barriers, replacing steps with ramps, and providing a parking area that was close to and on the same level as the center of the campus. But it was not until laws requiring access were passed that other barriers disappeared. Problems remain.

Most efforts to bring about equality of opportunity for the disabled have focused on those with observable physical disabilities; those with less obvious problems have had difficulty getting the help they need. For example, a student with severe heart problems that restricted the distance she could walk was regularly chastised by other disabled students for using handicapped parking because she had no outward signs of a disability.

How does democracy deal with subjects when one side is absolutely convinced that they are right and the other side is wrong? How does democracy deal with a situation where a temporary majority is willing to impose its version of the truth on a sizeable minority? How does democracy deal with a situation in which "informing" voters becomes "manipulating" voters with half-truths and outright lies?

Democratization

Perhaps the most important political phenomenon in the world today is the process called *democratization*. Countries ranging from Germany, which is trying to incorporate the former East Germany into the political and economic system of the former West Germany, to Eritrea on the Horn of Africa, which is trying to establish democratic institutions after years of revolutionary warfare. Russia and the now independent states of the former Soviet Union and various countries of South America that have recently removed dictators are all trying to establish democratic procedures and institutions and change the lifelong habits of their citizens.

The establishment of new political institutions is relatively easy; getting those institutions accepted by the citizenry and creating democratic citizens is much more difficult. This problem is forcing citizens to go back to the essential meaning of *democracy* and ask what fundamental principles they must make part of their lives. Democratic decision making, for example, requires the acceptance of the fact that one may lose, that one may be part of a minority. Many citizens of the former East Germany, for example, believe that because they are a minority in the German population, their interests are not being considered. They argue that it is not the case that they reject democracy, but that the German democracy has no place for minority rights. Is majority rule without minority rights democracy?

How can people who have rightly feared government officials become active participants in democratic debate and be willing to dissent from the positions of government leaders? Not very long ago such activity resulted in death or detention in a prison or a mental hospital. How can people from such backgrounds come to trust government or, since many people in well-established democracies don't trust government, at least accept the fact that political dissent is normal and is extremely unlikely to be punished?

The greatest issues for democracy today are modifications of the basic questions: To what extent can meaningful participation be provided in our complex modern civilization? And, how can we foster both freedom and equality and make them realities that are achieved rather than goals that are always slightly out of reach?

SUGGESTED READINGS

Some Classics of Democracy

BENTHAM, JEREMY. *An Introduction to the Principles of Morals and Legislation.*

BURKE, EDMUND. *Reflections on the Revolution in France.*

The Constitution of the United States of America.

Declaration of Independence of the United States.

The Federalist Papers.

LOCKE, JOHN. *Two Treatises of Government.*

MILL, JOHN STUART. *On Liberty.*

MONTESQUIEU, CHARLES-LOUIS DE SECONDAT. *De l'esprit des lois (The Spirit of the Laws).*

ROUSSEAU, JEAN-JACQUES. *Du contrat social (Of the Social Contract).*

WOLLSTONECRAFT, MARY. *A Vindication of the Rights of Woman.*

Works About Democracy

ANTCZAK, FREDERICK J. *Thought and Character: The Rhetoric of Democratic Education.* Ames: Iowa State University Press, 1985.

ARBLASTER, ANTHONY. *Democracy.* Minneapolis: University of Minnesota Press, 1987.

ARTERTON, F. CHRISTOPHER. *Teledemocracy: Can Technology Protect Democracy?* Newbury Park, CA: Sage Publications, 1987.

BACHRACH, PETER, and ARYEH BOTWINICK. *Power and Empowerment: A Radical Theory of Participatory Democracy.* Philadelphia: Temple University Press, 1992.

BARBER, BENJAMIN R. *Strong Democracy: Participatory Politics for a New Age.* Berkeley: University of California Press, 1984.

BAUMANN, ZYGMUNT. *Freedom.* Minneapolis: University of Minnesota Press, 1988.

BAY, CHRISTIAN. *The Structure of Freedom.* Stanford, CA: Stanford University Press, 1958.

BEITZ, CHARLES R. *Political Equality: An Essay in Democratic Theory.* Princeton, NJ: Princeton University Press, 1989.

BIRCH, ANTHONY H. *The Concepts and Theories of Modern Democracy.* London: Routledge, 1993.

BOBBIO, NORBERTO. *The Future of Democracy: A Defence of the Rules of the Game.* Trans. Roger Griffin. Minneapolis: University of Minnesota Press, 1987.

BOYTE, HARRY C. *CommonWealth: A Return to Citizen Politics.* New York: Free Press, 1989.

BRESSEA, PEREIRA, LUIZ CARLOS, JOSÉ MARÍA MARAVALL, and ADAM PRZEWORSKI. *Economic Reforms in New Democracies: A Social-Democratic Approach.* Cambridge, England: Cambridge University Press, 1993.

BURNHEIM, JOHN. *Is Democracy Possible? The Alternative to Electoral Politics.* London: Polity Press, 1985.

BURNS, JAMES MACGREGOR. *Cobblestone Leadership: Majority Rule, Minority Power.* Norman: University of Oklahoma Press, 1990.

CAWSON, ALAN. *Corporatism and Welfare: Social Policy and State Intervention in Britain.* London: Heinemann Educational, 1982.

CHAPMAN, JOHN W., and IAN SHAPIRO, eds. *Democratic Community.* New York: New York University Press, 1993.

CHRISTOPHERSEN, JENS A. *The Meaning of Democracy as Used in European Ideologies: An Historical Study in Political Language.* Oslo: Universitetsforlaget, 1966.

COHEN, CARL. *Democracy.* Athens: University of Georgia Press, 1971.

DAHL, ROBERT A. *Polyarchy: Participation and Opposition.* New Haven, CT: Yale University Press, 1971.

———. *Dilemmas of Pluralist Democracy: Autonomy vs. Control.* New Haven, CT: Yale University Press, 1982.

———. *Democracy and Its Critics.* New Haven, CT: Yale University Press, 1989.

———. *After the Revolution: Authority in a Good Society.* New Haven, CT: Yale University Press, 1990.

DAHRENDORF, RALF. *Law and Order.* Boulder, CO: Westview Press, 1985.

DI PALMA, GIUSEPPE, *To Craft Democracies: An Essay on Democratic Transitions.* Berkeley: University of California Press, 1990.

DRYZEK, JOHN S. *Discursive Democracy: Politics, Policy, and Political Science.* Cambridge, England: Cambridge University Press, 1990.

DUNN, JOHN, ed. *Democracy: The Unfinished Journey. 508 BC to AD 1993.* Oxford, England: Oxford University Press, 1992.

DURNHEIM, JOHN. *Is Democracy Possible? The Alternative to Electoral Politics.* Cambridge, England: Polity Press, 1985.

DYSON, A. E., and JULIAN LOVELOCK, eds. *Education and Democracy.* London: Routledge & Kegan Paul, 1984.

ENTEMAN, WILLARD F. *Managerialism: The Emergence of a New Ideology.* Madison: University of Wisconsin Press, 1993.

ETZIONI-HALEVY, EVA. *Bureaucracy and Democracy: A Political Dilemma.* London: Routledge & Kegan Paul, 1983.

EVANS, SARA M., and HARRY C. BOYTE. *Free Spaces: The Sources of Democratic Change in America.* [New edition.] Chicago: University of Chicago Press, 1992. Originally published 1986.

EZRAHI, YARON. *The Descent of Icarus: Science and the Transformation of Contemporary Democracy.* Cambridge, MA: Harvard University Press, 1990.

FRIED, CHARLES. *Right and Wrong.* Cambridge, MA: Harvard University Press, 1978.

GILBERT, ALAN. *Democratic Individuality.* Cambridge, England: Cambridge University Press, 1990.

GOULD, CAROL C. *Rethinking Democracy: Freedom and Social Cooperation in Politics, Economy, and Society.* Cambridge, England: Cambridge University Press, 1988.

GRANT, WYN, ed. *The Political Economy of Corporatism.* London: Macmillan, 1985.

GREEN, PHILIP. *The Pursuit of Inequality.* New York: Pantheon Books, 1981.

———. *Retrieving Democracy: In Search of Civic Equality.* Totowa, NJ: Rowman & Allanheld, 1985.

GREENBERG, EDWARD S. *Workplace Democracy: The Political Effects of Participation.* Ithaca, NY: Cornell University Press, 1986.

GRUBAR, JUDITH E. *Controlling Bureaucracies: Dilemmas in Democratic Governance.* Berkeley: University of California Press, 1987.

HADENIUS, AXEL. *Democracy and Development.* Cambridge, England: Cambridge University Press, 1992.

HARRISON, REGINALD J. *Pluralism and Corporatism: The Political Evolution of Modern Democracies.* London: George Allen & Unwin, 1980.

HART, VIVIEN. *Distrust and Democracy: Political Distrust in Britain and America.* Cambridge, England: Cambridge University Press, 1978.

HELLINGER, DANIEL, and DENNIS JUDD. *The Democratic Facade.* Pacific Grove, CA: Brooks/Cole, 1991.

HONIG, BONNIE. *Political Theory and the Displacement of Politics.* Ithaca, NY: Cornell University Press, 1993.

HORTON, JOHN, and SUSAN MENDUS, eds. *Aspects of Toleration: Philosophical Studies.* New York: Methuen, 1985.

HUNTINGTON, SAMUEL P. *The Third*

Wave: Democratization in the Late Twentieth Century. Norman: University of Oklahoma Press, 1991.

JORDAN, BILL. *Freedom and the Welfare State.* London: Routledge & Kegan Paul, 1976.

KAINZ, HOWARD P. *Democracy East and West: A Philosophical Overview.* New York: St. Martin's, 1984.

KELSO, WILLIAM ALTON. *American Democratic Theory: Pluralism and Its Critics.* Westport, CT: Greenwood Press, 1978.

LAUDEN, KENNETH C. *Communications Technology and Democratic Participation.* New York: Praeger, 1977.

LINDBLOM, CHARLES E. *Democracy and Market System.* Oslo: Norwegian University Press, 1988.

McCLOSKY, HERBERT, and ALIDA BRILL. *Dimensions of Tolerance: What Americans Believe About Civil Liberties.* New York: Russell Sage Foundation/Basic Books, 1984.

MACPHERSON, C. B. *The Real World of Democracy.* Oxford, England: Clarendon Press, 1966.

————. *Democratic Theory: Essays in Retrieval.* Oxford, England: Clarendon Press, 1973.

————. *The Life and Times of Liberal Democracy.* New York: Oxford University Press, 1977.

MANSBRIDGE, JANE J. *Beyond Adversary Democracy.* New York: Basic Books, 1980.

MAYO, HENRY B. *An Introduction to Democratic Theory.* New York: Oxford University Press, 1960.

MOUFFE, CHANTAL, ed. *Dimensions of Radical Democracy: Pluralism, Citizenship, Community.* London: Verso, 1992.

————. *The Return of the Political.* London: Verso, 1993.

NELSON, WILLIAM N. *On Justifying Democracy.* London: Routledge & Kegan Paul, 1980.

NIELSEN, KAI. *Equality and Liberty: A Defense of Radical Egalitarianism.* Totowa, NJ: Rowman and Allanheld, 1985.

O'DONNELL, GUILLERMO, PHILLIPPE SCHMITTER, and LAURENCE WHITEHEAD, eds. *Transitions from Authoritarian Rule: Prospects for Democracy.* Baltimore, MD: Johns Hopkins University Press, 1986.

OPPENHEIM, FELIX E. *Dimensions of Freedom: An Analysis.* New York: St. Martin's, 1961.

PARRY, GERAINT, and MICHAEL MORAN, eds. *Democracy and Democratization.* London: Routledge, 1994.

PAUL, ELLEN FRANKEL, FRED D. MILLER, JR., and JEFFREY PAUL, eds. *Liberty and Equality.* Oxford, England: Basil Blackwell for the Social Philosophy and Policy Center, Bowling Green State University, 1985.

PENNOCK, J. ROLAND. *Democratic Political Theory.* Princeton, NJ: Princeton University Press, 1979.

PENNOCK, J. ROLAND, and JOHN W. CHAPMAN, eds. *Liberal Democracy. Nomos XXV: Yearbook of the American Society for Political and Legal Philosophy.* New York: New York University Press, 1983.

RAE, DOUGLAS, DOUGLAS YATES, JENNIFER HOCHSCHILD, JOSEPH MORONE, and CAROL FESSLER. *Equalities.* Cambridge, MA: Harvard University Press, 1981.

RAWLS, JOHN. *A Theory of Justice.* Oxford, England: Clarendon Press, 1972.

RAZ, JOSEPH. *The Morality of Freedom.* Oxford, England: Clarendon Press, 1986.

ROTHSCHILD, JOYCE, and J. ALLEN WHITT. *The Cooperative Workplace: Potentials and Dilemmas of Organizational Democracy and Participation.* Cambridge, England: Cambridge University Press, 1986.

SARTORI, GIOVANNI. *The Theory of Democracy Revisited.* 2 vols. Chatham, NY: Chatham House, 1987.

SEN, AMARTYA. *On Economic Inequality: The Radcliffe Lectures Delivered in the University of Warwick 1972.* Oxford, England: Clarendon Press, 1973.

TREADGOLD, DONALD W. *Freedom: A History.* New York: New York University Press, 1990.

VANHANEN, TATU. *The Process of Democratization: A Comparative Study of 147 States, 1980–88*. New York: Taylor & Francis, 1990.

———, ed. *Strategies of Democratization*. Washington, DC: Crane & Russak, 1992.

WALZER, MICHAEL. *Radical Principles: Reflections of an Unreconstructed Democrat.* New York: Basic Books, 1980.

———. *Spheres of Justice: A Defense of Pluralism and Equality*. New York: Basic Books, 1983.

WHITE, PATRICIA. *Beyond Domination: An Essay in the Political Philosophy of Education*. London: Routledge & Kegan Paul, 1983.

WILLIAMSON, PETER J. *Corporatism in Perspective: An Introductory Guide to Corporatist Theory*. London: Sage, 1989.

———. *Varieties of Corporatism: A Conceptual Discussion*. Cambridge, England: Cambridge University Press, 1985.

WRINGE, COLIN. *Democracy, Schooling and Political Education*. London: George Allen & Unwin, 1984.

ZIMMERMAN, JOSEPH F. *Participatory Democracy: Populism Revived*. New York: Praeger, 1986.

4

❦

Capitalism, Socialism, and Democracy

To most citizens of North America, democracy and capitalism are so closely tied that the idea there might be an alternative seems foolish. To many citizens of some countries in Europe and the Third World, it is self-evident that democracy and socialism are the only possible partners. In the United States the word *socialist* is so negative that it causes rejection of an idea without further discussion; in many countries *capitalist* has the same effect. To put it mildly, there is a lot of disagreement and misunderstanding concerning these two economic systems.

The discussion that follows is intended to clarify the meaning of capitalism and socialism and show why adherents of each claim to be the only true democrats. Thus the emphasis will be on the arguments for and against capitalism and socialism as being supportive of democracy. Both the positive and the negative arguments must be presented, because in each case much of the argument for one alternative is based on the argument against the other.

Both capitalism and socialism are economic systems that can be combined with different political systems. Capitalism fits well with both authoritarian political systems (for example, South Korea and Singapore) and democratic ones (for example, the United States and Canada). Equally, socialism fits well with authoritarian regimes (for example, Libya and China) and democratic ones (for example, Egypt and Tanzania). There are many more authoritarian capitalist regimes than democratic capitalist ones and far more authoritarian socialist regimes than democratic socialist ones, and although authoritarian regimes are clearly under pressure today, they are still the most common form.[1]

DEMOCRATIC CAPITALISM

Today democratic capitalism is perceived as having won the argument with socialism. With the collapse of the authoritarian socialism that we call communism, capitalists have a renewed confidence in their beliefs. Capitalism has returned to its roots in the free market, and many of its defenders contend that the problems capitalism encountered were due to a loss of faith in the free market. In one sense, this resurrected belief in the free market makes the whole argument much simpler, but it also simplifies and focuses the attack on capitalism since the operations of the free market are the traditional point of attack.

The Principles of Democratic Capitalism

Traditional capitalism, often called *free market* or *laissez-faire capitalism*, is characterized by:

1. Private ownership of property,
2. No legal limit on the accumulation of property,
3. The free market—no government intervention in the economy,
4. The profit motive as the driving force of capitalism, and
5. Profit as the measure of efficiency.

The fundamental position as stated by Adam Smith (1723–1790), the Scottish economist and moral philosopher who is generally thought of as the intellectual father of capitalism, is that human beings are most effectively motivated by self-interest.[2] In economic terms, this means that individuals should be free (the free market) to pursue their interests (profit). The result should be the most efficient economic system, and everyone will benefit. Goods will be produced that sell as cheaply as possible since, if they aren't, someone else will step in and replace the current manufacturer. Jobs will be created by entrepreneurs searching for a way to make a profit. The entire economy will be stimulated and grow, thus producing a higher standard of living for everyone, as long as the entrepreneur is free to operate and can make a sufficient profit to make it worth her or his while. Workers can choose to spend their money on consumer goods or, by

---

[1] There have been many studies of authoritarianism, going back to Theodor W. Adorno et al., *The Authoritarian Personality* (New York: Harper & Row, 1950).

[2] For an extensive history of the development of capitalism, see Fernand Braudel, *Civilization and Capitalism 15th–18th Century*, 3 vols.: vol. 1 trans. Miriam Kochand, trans. revised by Siân Reynolds; vols. 2–3 trans. Siân Reynolds (New York: Harper & Row, 1981–1984).

Adam Smith (1723 –1790) is best known as the author of *An Inquiry into the Nature and Causes of the Wealth of Nations* (1776 —better known under the short title *The Wealth of Nations*), in which he presented a history of economics in Europe, a description of manufacturing in his day, and most important, a set of recommendations. Smith argued that the greatest social benefit would be produced by each individual pursuing his or her own self-interest. He applied this idea to the operations of the economic system and, thereby, he became famous for providing the moral justification and part of the intellectual foundation of capitalism. (*Library of Congress*)

saving, enter the competition by going into business for themselves. Some will fail, and some will succeed extraordinarily.

In the twentieth century some changes, possibly temporary, were made in capitalism. First, in the culmination of a trend that had begun in the late nineteenth century, government regulation of the economy was accepted. Regulation came about because the English economist John Maynard Keynes (1883–1946) had argued, and generally convinced other economists, that depressions could be avoided by regulating the economy, specifically by using public expenditures to pump money into the economy and soak up excess unemployment. Prosperity for all without serious fluctuations—the so-called boom-and-bust cycle—could be virtually guaranteed. Thus Keynes provided for direct governmental intervention in the economy.

Second, in the Great Depression banks closed, causing the loss of people's life savings, and pensions disappeared along with the companies that had provided them. These events left many people without the financial support they had counted on for their old age. As a direct result, government-administered retirement systems were established in most Western countries. In the United States this was the beginning of the social security system, which was initially designed to be self-supporting (monies paid in by employees and employers would accumulate and be paid out on retirement). The expansion of the program to most of the population, the expansion of benefits, and the rapid increase in the number of persons who not only lived long enough to retire but then lived a long time after retirement combined to undermine the financial base of the system.

On the same principle—that people should be protected from radical shifts in economic fortune—other programs were added. Countries varied in the speed and extent of expansion of such governmental intervention in the economy. The United States was probably the slowest of the economically developed democracies to add programs, and it added far fewer than most. In the United States most of the programs were established during the so-called War on Poverty of the presidency of Lyndon Johnson.[3] These programs were then greatly expanded during the presidency of Richard Nixon. This resulted in capitalism—called "the mixed economy"—having extensive government regulation and publicly financed assistance and pension programs.

As has already been mentioned, capitalists have turned against their recent past and reasserted the primacy of the free market. During the 1980s, most Western countries dismantled at least some government regulation, cut back assistance and pension programs, and privatized parts of the economy that had been publicly owned or operated.

Capitalism and Democracy

For capitalists, democracy requires capitalism because they believe capitalism supports the central democratic value of freedom. Capitalists believe that freedom is based on private property, and capitalism, by stressing private property, makes economic freedom central. Capitalists also believe that economic freedom is a primary support for political liberty. Economic freedom means that everyone is free to enter the marketplace, accumulate property without limit, and use that property as they choose. Capitalists see two potential sources of control that must be blocked—monopolies and government. Monopolies, they belileve, will always be temporary if the free market is allowed to operate; therefore, the real problem is government.

The amount of property and money held by individuals directly affects the amount of money they spend. The amount individuals spend directly affects the amount any industry can produce; the amount industry can produce affects the number of people it can hire; the number of people industry can hire again affects the amount of money available to be spent by individuals for the products of industry; the amount of products industry can produce then affects its profit. In this way, some limitation on the amount of property or money that can be

---

[3]The War on Poverty came about as a result of the publication of *The Other America: Poverty in the United States* (New York: Macmillan, 1962) by Michael Harrington, which graphically recounted the extent of poverty in the United States.

held by any individual helps rather than deters the entire capitalist system because it forces the money to circulate more widely.

A stronger approach views any government regulation as destroying the basis for the capitalist system and, hence, individualism and liberty. The defenders of some government regulation (but not control) of the economy say that the absence of government regulation itself destroys the democratic capitalistic system because a few people can control the economy, and even the government, through monopolies. Other bad effects of a lack of government regulation are sometimes mentioned, but the development of monopolies is the most important politically.

Democratic capitalism is not practiced solely in the industrialized nations of the West. Democratic capitalism originated in the West, and it is the area that has provided the model for many countries, but alternative models are available.

The best known alternative is Japan. In Japan an attempt has been made to avoid the continual conflict between owners or managers and workers that has characterized the West and that still exists in some countries. The largest Japanese corporations avoid such conflict by providing what are, in essence, lifetime contracts for workers. In return they expect the workers to have a real identification with the corporation.

A number of Western countries are trying to replace the conflict or adversary model of industrial relations that has dominated democratic capitalism with a model that sees management and labor as dependent on each other for success. Germany, the most successful Western industrial democratic capitalist country, has a system that gives a great deal of power to unions as a means of avoiding conflict. Avoiding conflict is also one goal of the corporatist or neo-corporatist theory of democracy described in the previous chapter. Corporatists want workers and employers to join with government in ensuring the smooth running of the economy.

Monopolies. The problem of monopolies was illustrated in the United States during the period of the first growth of industrialism and particularly the great expansion of the railroads. Such men as J. P. Morgan (1837–1913), James J. Hill (1838–1916), and John D. Rockefeller (1839–1937) virtually controlled the American economy and thereby the American government. This monopolistic tendency, some capitalists argue, destroys the capitalist system by radically limiting the number of companies or individuals who can adequately compete within the system. The system is not competitive when only a few companies can set prices. Under such circumstances few people with new ideas or approaches are able to try them out. It is not talent that succeeds in such a system but the monopolist's will. This situation does not fit the traditional myth of the capitalist system in which the clerk becomes corporation president by hard work. The clerk of a monopolist might become a business president someday, but not necessarily by hard work. The key to success would be the whim of the monopolist.

The most important effect of monopoly, viewed from the perspective of democracy, is the control of the government that the monopolist can exercise. Such control severely restricts the degree to which democracy can exist because it might even negate the effect of popular participation in political decision making.[4]

President Dwight D. Eisenhower (1890–1969), in his farewell address, warned the American people about a military-industrial complex that he contended was close to ruling the United States through informal channels. Eisenhower was concerned about the close relationship between the military and the large industries that produced military goods under contract to the Pentagon. He was also concerned with the fact that many high-ranking officers "retired" after twenty years in the military to take jobs with the industries with which they had negotiated contracts and with whom their former colleagues would be negotiating future contracts. He believed that these relationships and the growth of the sector of the economy providing goods to the military were leading to a dangerous concentration of economic and political power. This could happen even more readily under a monopolistic system.[5]

Many capitalists believe that the competitive pressures of a truly free market will prevent the development of monopolies. They also believe that any monopoly that does develop will not last long because of the same pressures.

Economic Freedom. Thus even within capitalism the desired extent of economic freedom is the subject of debate. The basic premise is that capitalism allows more freedom for the individual than does any other economic system. Any individual with sufficient interest and funds can buy stock in any number of companies. Stock owners become part owners of a company or companies and can, if time and money permit, participate in some decisions of the company at the annual meetings, although this opportunity is limited for the small shareholder.

In addition, there are those like Milton Friedman (1912–) who argue that capitalism provides greater political freedom than any other system. "The kind of economic organization that provides economic freedom directly, namely, competitive capitalism, also promotes political freedom because it separates economic power from political power and in this way enables the one to offset the other."[6] This separation can be compared to a checks-and-balances system such as that in the U.S. Constitution. Government power is limited by centers of economic power that also limit one another. These centers of economic power are in turn limited by government, which is also subject to regular elections. If both economic and political power are

---

[4]For a different view, see Gabriel Kolko, *The Triumph of Conservatism: A Reinterpretation of American History, 1900–1916* (New York: Free Press, 1963).

[5]Some critics argue that this happened some time ago. See, for example, Paul A. Baran and Paul M. Sweezy, *Monopoly Capital: An Essay on the American Economic and Social Order* (New York: Monthly Review Press, 1966).

[6]Milton Friedman, *Capitalism and Freedom* (Chicago: University of Chicago Press, 1962), p. 9.

centralized in government, there is no check on the activities of government except through the vote.

The individual is free to enter the economic system subject to some government regulation and some limitation due to the existence of many large corporations. The individual succeeds or fails depending on his or her willingness to work hard and the desire of the consumer, manipulated to some extent by advertising, to buy the product. This is economic freedom and shows the relationship of capitalism to equality of opportunity. Every person should be able to become a capitalist and have the potential to get rich.

Equality of Opportunity. This concern with equality of opportunity was one of the motivations behind the development of a welfare system designed to ensure that everyone within the society will actually have such opportunity. This concern is not based solely on humanitarian ends but also on the recognition that people who cannot provide for themselves can be a burden on society and a waste of potential human resources. In addition, welfare programs have been concerned with the aged, who have contributed to society but who need help to provide for retirement when many costs, such as medical bills, tend to rise while incomes decline.

Welfare. Welfare systems include two types of public assistance, one based on need and one not so based. The need-based programs are those, like food stamps or Aid to Families with Dependent Children, that are triggered by income level. Non-need programs are those, like Social Security or federal and military pension programs, that are paid regardless of other income received. Some non-need programs are partially funded by earlier contributions by the recipients; others are noncontributory.

Welfare systems around the world are criticized for doing exactly what they were designed to do—that is, giving money away rather than providing an individual with the means of earning it. This criticism is particularly common and appropriate in the capitalist system because the point of the criticism is that the welfare system is not providing equality of opportunity. Instead, the welfare system is actually removing people from the mainstream of economic life, giving them a subsistence on which to live and not allowing them to enter the capitalist system even at the most minimal level of wage earner.

The system is also criticized on similar grounds by some welfare recipients, who have recognized that they are being kept in poverty. They have also been treated poorly by the bureaucracies that distribute the funds. Too often these bureaucracies have not even attempted to understand the human problems they are supposedly solving. This failing is to some extent understandable because the bureaucracies have been tremendously overburdened with work. The people staffing them have been poorly paid and have enjoyed little status in their jobs. Many who live day by day with human misery establish a mechanism of self-defense. They reject personal involvement in their casework, fearing they will be overwhelmed and unable to function.

Recently the word *welfare* has returned to the political vocabulary in the

United States as an almost entirely negative term. For a while the word *welfare* was replaced with the phrase *safety net*, a positive concept and a usage that returned the concept to the original intention of Depression-era liberals. For them *welfare* was a means of protecting the poor from the shifts of a free-market economy. Today, the strongest advocates of the free market argue that even a safety net may be an undesirable and dangerous restriction on the free market.

Criticisms of Democratic Capitalism

These criticisms come from within capitalism; other criticisms have a different character, coming, as they do, from noncapitalists and attacking the basic premises of capitalism. Most of these latter criticisms are based on what are perceived as the results of capitalism, particularly the extremes of wealth and poverty, the power over the political process that such wealth gives its owners, and the extreme inequality between employer and employee that exists under capitalism. As we have seen, some of these points have also bothered defenders of capitalism. Other criticisms attack the institution of private property, the free market, and the profit motive.

Results. There are two related issues in the criticism of capitalism's results—power and poverty. The economic and political power issue can be framed generally by asking how much power one person should have over another in a democratic society. Great wealth gives a person potential power in a political system, and critics argue that such wealth makes rule by the people impossible. Defenders of capitalism argue either that this is a non-issue (the rich are a minority, and the majority can always defeat them) or that limited regulation can solve the problem. But the essence of the argument is that the benefits of capitalism outweigh any danger.

Great wealth appears to go hand in hand with extreme poverty. Critics of capitalism argue that such extremes are inevitable in a capitalist system and wrong. No one should be condemned to a life of poverty so that a few individuals can be rich. Defenders of capitalism argue either that poverty is the fault of the poor (they have not worked hard enough) or that poverty will be overcome through the economic growth that capitalism makes possible.

Most defenders of capitalism, and in the United States most people, believe the power of an employer over an employee to be simply in the nature of things. But critics of capitalism see this exercise of power as undemocratic and demeaning to the worker.

Private Property. Critics of capitalism argue that the private control of property used in the manufacture and distribution of goods is wrong because it gives a great deal of power to a few people. Today, the power of private property is obvious as many companies relocate their operations for various reasons. Critics contend that such factors as the effect on a community, the well-being of the employees, the economic strength of a country should be taken into account in economic decision making. They usually argue that the creation of the value of property is social, not private, and therefore social effects should outweigh other factors in decision making. Capitalists respond that if wealth is to be produced, they must consider their competitive situation first and foremost in any decision. Giving social factors precedence would make capitalists uncompetitive and ultimately force them out of business to the detriment of all concerned.

The Profit Motive. Capitalists believe that the profit motive drives people to succeed and create wealth; their critics argue that even if that idea is true, it is wrong. They argue that the competition fostered is personally and socially unhealthy. Capitalists argue that competition is natural and healthy, both personally and socially, and that it is the major source of effort and excellence.

The Free Market. Critics of capitalism argue that there is no such thing as a free market and that the whole point of business activity is to control or dominate the market, not compete freely in it. They also argue that the free market, to the extent there is one, is inefficient. Capitalists, of course, argue that there either is a free market or could be one in most circumstances and that it is the only truly efficient mechanism for producing and distributing goods.

As can be seen, the disagreements are fundamental. They will come up frequently in succeeding pages, particularly since the same issues are often involved in the discussion of socialism.

DEMOCRATIC SOCIALISM

Socialism in all forms is currently under attack and many democratic socialists are dropping the label, particularly because many communists are now calling themselves democratic socialists. Particularly in Eastern Europe, it is difficult to know what a current political label really means. Democratic socialists are in this position because communism, which they criticized, is a form of socialism and has failed. Thus, democratic socialists, while not giving up their beliefs, do not want to be falsely identified with communism and are unsure what to call themselves. Social Democracy is the most common new label and allows for the incorporation of some elements of the market into democratic socialist theory.

The Principles of Democratic Socialism

Democratic socialism can be characterized as follows:

1. Much property held by the public through the democratically elected government, including most major industries, utilities, and the transportation system;

2. A limit on the accumulation of private property;

3. Governmental regulation of the economy;

4. Extensive publicly financed assistance and pension programs; and

5. Social costs and the provision of services added to purely financial considerations as the measure of efficiency.

Socialism has a long history, which some advocates like to trace back to biblical sources. It is more accurate to see socialism as originating as a response to the excesses of early industrial capitalism, but it should also be recognized that many socialists, particularly those calling themselves Christian socialists, found their inspiration in the New Testament.

Still, the origins of contemporary democratic socialism are best located in the early to mid-nineteenth century in the writings of the so-called utopian socialists, Robert Owen (1771–1858), Charles Fourier (1772–1837), Henri Saint-Simon (1760–1825), and Étienne Cabet (1798–1856). All these writers proposed village communities combining industrial and agricultural production and owned, in varying ways, by the inhabitants themselves. Thus, the essence of early socialism was the public ownership of the means of production. These theorists all also included varying forms of democratic political decision making, but they all distrusted the ability of people raised under capitalism to understand what was in their own best interests.

Karl Marx, discussed in detail in chapter 7, rejected these early socialists and developed his own version of socialism, which he called communism. There is considerable controversy among scholars regarding Marx's own attitude toward democracy, but two lines of thought developed from Marx, one emphasizing democracy and one, the dominant line, rejecting it. But other socialists rejected Marx, and later in the century two American writers, Edward Bellamy (1850–1898) and Henry George (1839–1897), produced versions of public ownership with what they saw as democratic control, although again both placed some limitations on democracy. In his last work, *Equality* (1897), Bellamy eliminated most of those limitations.

In the twentieth century in Britain a form of socialism developed, called Fabian Socialism (now embodied in the Fabian Society), that emphasizes the democratic elements of democratic socialism; electoral success, the rational presentation of their position (in innumerable publications), careful study of the current social situation, and an emphasis on gradualism.

Since that time many democratic socialist political parties, such as the Labour Party in the United Kingdom and the Social Democratic Party in Sweden, have been elected to office, been defeated and left office, and later been returned to office or remained in opposition. In Europe today democratic socialists often call themselves Social Democrats. This label is intended to stress the democratic nature of democratic socialism and to deemphasize links with other forms of socialism, particularly Marxian socialism. The best known adherents of this position have been Willy Brandt (1913–1992) of Germany, Olof Palme (1927–1986) of Sweden, and Michael Harrington (1928–1989) of the United States.

If one assumes citizens should control their political lives and contribute to political decision making, it is only a short step to the democratic socialist argument that citizens should have some say in economic decision making. There is no question that economic decisions in connection with, for example, an automobile manufacturing industry have a tremendous impact on an entire country. Therefore, democratic socialists argue, there must be some means for the people to check such economic decisions. However, what economic decisions are significant in this sense? What industries are key industries for a national economy? Democratic socialists argue that these questions should be answered by the elected representatives of the people and that the answers are likely to vary from country to country. In addition, the forms of governmental control and regulation and the extent of the public ownership of industy will vary depending on the decisions made by the elected representatives of the people, checked at the polls by the people themselves.

Another argument for democratic socialism, perhaps the most appealing one, is what might be called the humanitarian argument. Democratic socialists argue that only when the economic system is controlled by the people will solutions to basic social problems, like hunger and disease, be possible. Only under democratic socialism can the people demand solutions; therefore, democratic socialism is essential to overcome the most basic problems of society.

In practice democratic socialist systems vary considerably from country to country, particularly in the degree to which such things as industries, utilities, and transportation systems are directly owned by the government. In some countries most of these are governmentally owned, but in most, only specific parts of industrial complexes are owned by the government. For example, in Sweden, which most Americans think of as a socialist country, very few of the major industries are governmentally owned.

When we say much property is held by the public, this refers to property crucial to the functioning of the economic system. It does not mean there is no private property. Private property is still held by the individual in personal belongings, housing, most small businesses, and, in some cases, large corporations. Some democratic socialists, theorists, and systems do not limit the amount of private property that can be held by an individual, but most do. There is no necessity within democratic socialist theory for such limitations. On the other hand, most approaches suggest some degree of redistribution of income and thereby justify limited private property.

Socialism and Democracy

The fundamental assumption underlying democratic socialism is that participation in political decision making should be extended to include economic decision making. Democratic socialists argue that since the economy and politics are so closely intertwined, voters should be in a position to control their economic futures through the government they elect. Such voter control presupposes government's ability to control much of the economy through ownership of the most important parts of the economy.

The government of a democratic socialist system regulates that part of the

Michael Harrington (1928–1989) was co-chair of the Democratic Socialists of America, a Professor of Political Science at Queens College of the City University of New York, a public speaker, a commentator for National Public Radio, and a writer. He described himself as an "organizer, agitator, and activist." Harrington is best known for the book *The Other America: Poverty in the United States* (1962) that provided the basis for President Lyndon Johnson's War on Poverty. Harrington argued in *The New American Poverty* (1984) that the war on poverty had failed because politicians had never devoted the needed resources to it. Harrington's personal odyssey carried him through most of the major left-wing groups in the United States, and at his death he was respected as a critic of American policy by people from all parts of the political spectrum. (*Gretchen Donart/DSA*)

economy it does not own directly. This regulation is designed to ensure that the privately owned businesses are operated in the best interests of the society as a whole rather than simply for private profit. This point illuminates the ethos of democratic socialism. The word *socialism* refers to *social* theories rather than to theories oriented toward the individual. Democratic socialism is concerned with society as a whole.

In addition to the democratic proposition proclaimed in the basic assumption outlined above, democratic socialism suggests that liberty cannot be maintained without economic security. This argument resembles that of the democratic capitalist for welfare as a means of attaining equality of opportunity, but it is broader in that it demands more than equality of opportunity. The democratic socialist says neither the right to vote nor any other form of liberty is possible unless every person within the society is economically secure. If insecure, she or he will be incapable of exercising personal liberty. Such economic security is possible, it is argued, only with an extensive welfare system.

The democratic socialist welfare system has the same problems as the democratic capitalist welfare system, but there are two major differences: the welfare system of democratic socialism covers far more areas and sometimes has different financing. Of course, both systems are financed directly from taxes, but in the democratic socialist system profit from the nationalized industries (the industries owned by the government) can be used to help pay the costs of welfare.

The typical democratic socialist welfare system includes an extensive medical care system, which is provided either free or at minimal cost. The system usually includes prenatal care for expectant mothers, dental care, and eye examinations, in addition to the more typical health services. An obvious practical rationale for such a system is that a healthy individual can contribute more to society than a sick one. Therefore, it is to the advantage of society to ensure the health of all. This is the fundamental rationale of any welfare system—an individual who is maintained at the minimum level of life can contribute to society. The welfare system is also designed to take care of those who have already made a contribution to society and are now incapable of caring for themselves. Thus the welfare system provides money for food, housing, and the other minimum necessities.

The Problem of Bureaucracy. Bureaucracy presents one of the greatest problems for democratic socialism. Whether in business or government, it is difficult for a bureaucracy to be as well informed or as responsive to the needs of the people or industry it serves as would be ideal. Since bureaucracies are not directly responsible to the people, many argue that a large bureaucracy threatens the public control that the democratic socialist is trying to preserve. In democratic capitalism the economy is controlled privately, therefore, there are powerful people who aren't directly accountable to the electorate. In democratic socialism these people are replaced by bureaucrats who are not directly accountable to the electorate. In addition, since bureaucrats remain while politicians and governments change, it is not unusual for the bureaucrats to follow their own policies rather than those of the political leaders.

The problem is fundamental to the nature of a bureaucracy. Bureaucracies are established to administer laws (rules) established by the normal processes of legislation. These rules are applied equally (in the same way) to people even though people differ. Attempts to allow flexibility generally produce charges of favoritism, corruption, discrimination, and other forms of illegality. Quite simply, flexibility seems to undermine the equal application of rules even though that equal application may seem unfair.

Thus, bureaucracy raises a problem: how can rules be applied unequally but fairly? Laws are rules, and rules by their very nature are supposed to apply to everyone in the same way. People are different, and they have different needs. How can a bureaucracy ever do its job in these circumstances?

Therefore, at times democratic socialism faces the same problems for which it criticizes democratic capitalism. Still, the democratic socialist argues that people do have control over the bureaucracy through their elected representatives and that the government can immediately change the operations of the bureaucracy when it becomes cumbersome or ineffective. Democratic capitalists argue that under capitalism the people control the economic system through the market.

Many countries, both democratic socialist and democratic capitalist ones, have instituted an *ombudsman* (the word derives from a Swedish term for deputy or representative) who hears and investigates complaints about the bureaucracy. Sometimes the ombudsman is empowered to make sure the causes of the complaints are corrected. Such a person fills an obvious need because most bureaucracies are unwieldly, operate inefficiently, and find it hard to take individual differences into account. Of course, this role is also played by elected representatives, particularly in the United States.

Democratic countries have begun to recognize the problem of bureaucracy and have attempted to correct it. At the same time, the relatively independent nature of the bureaucracy may provide some protection for liberty. One agency may force another to respond better than it would on its own. Thus conflicts among parts of the bureaucracy may have a positive result.

Criticisms of Democratic Socialism

Antisocialist critics of democratic socialism have two basic arguments, focusing on the destruction of the free market and the centralization of power. Although many socialists now accept "market socialism," critics contend that the free market of competitive capitalism is essential for the efficient production and distribution of goods. Socialists have found that a limited market is more efficient and better able to respond to consumer demands than completely centralized regulation and, they argue, much more fair than a completely unregulated market.

In a related criticism, opponents of socialism argue that interference with the free market through government ownership and regulation puts too much power in the hands of government. This, they contend, leads inevitably to even greater centralization of power and the destruction of democracy. A more limited version of the same argument suggests that even if democracy is not destroyed, freedom will necessarily be limited in a democratic socialist regime. Democratic socialists respond that the electoral process is capable of checking any such tendency if it does occur, but they see no reason that it should occur.

Related to both criticisms is the question, what motivates the socialist bureaucrat? As we saw, the capitalist believes that human beings are motivated by self-interest—the profit motive. Self-interest, capitalists argue, will always make socialism unworkable. The socialist argues that the bureaucrat is motivated by the desire to serve. The capitalist laughs. The socialist responds that while the profit motive—the socialist might call it "greed"—may be necessary under capitalism, socialism makes it possible to be motivated by a desire to serve the public.

There is as much distance between socialism and its critics as between capitalism and its critics. But both socialists and capitalists are making the same claim—each group contending that it is the best for democracy.

CURRENT TRENDS

Today the most controversial issues within democracy are economic issues. The failure of the world economy to allow for continued economic growth and the need to control inflation without massive unemployment pose serious problems for both capitalism and socialism. One must wonder if any economic system is capable of dealing with the present situation because, in all fairness, both democratic socialist and democratic capitalist systems have failed to do so, although some capitalist and some socialist countries are doing better than they were a few years ago and some of each are doing worse.

For the democratic socialist, there are two problems. First, what changes need to be made to adjust to hard times and what changes are politically possible? For example, is it desirable and politically possible to close down government-owned factories? The second problem stems from the fact that many government-owned enterprises have been fairly inefficient (although so have many privately owned enterprises). Is it possible to nationalize a business and maintain its efficiency? The two problems are related; some enterprises might be made more efficient by closing some factories, but the rise in unemployment could be too high an economic and political cost to pay. Is it better to keep people employed in inefficient businesses than to have them added to the unemployment rolls and the lists of those receiving welfare?

Most democratic capitalist governments are choosing the opposite direction in the belief that hard times are caused by government involvement in the economy and that therefore the only solution will be found in a reversal of recent policies, particularly in the area of welfare programs.

Among democratic capitalists there have been some fairly minor disputes about how much government should be involved in the economy. Monetarists argue that the appropriate role of government is to control the supply of money in the economy, adjusting it to keep inflation low. This requires, they argue, a dramatic reduction in government spending because they believe that governmental borrowing is the main source of inflation. Government prints too much money simply because it must to fund its own borrowing.

Supporters of what used to be called supply-side economics include these points made by the monetarists but go one step further. A healthy economy, according to the supply-side argument, is one that encourages investment in enterprises that will produce goods, create jobs, and thus provide everyone with a better living. They say that welfare policies drain money from private investment that would create jobs, and thus welfare programs hurt everyone. They also argue that welfare reduces the incentive to work and that cutting the welfare system will put people into productive jobs. Thus they argue that the reduction in government spending must come from social programs.

In addition to the general policy questions, some narrower issues between socialism and capitalism are currently being debated. The most important of these is the problem of efficiency. Capitalists argue that the only efficient means of producing and distributing goods is the free market. Socialists argue that the free market neglects two subjects that should be included in considering what is or is not efficient—public service and social costs.

Including a public service factor would mean defining efficiency not as what is cost-effective or profitable but as the most cost-effective means of providing a particular service, such as transportation. Capitalists argue that even in those terms private competition will always be the best mechanism. Socialists respond that some services must be provided even if they produce losses, a condition that eliminates the possibility of private provision.

Including social costs means defining efficiency to include effects on the public, such as pollution, as a cost of doing business. Under this approach to efficient production, the cheapest way of doing something might not be the most efficient. Socialists argue that such costs are now borne by the public and should be recognized and built into the costs of production or distribution, wherever it would be most appropriate. Capitalists argue that such costs should be calculated separately, if at all, and should not be levied on the private sector.

These issues occur between conservatives and liberals as well as between capitalists and socialists, since many of the liberal-conservative conflicts today are economic ones. Disagreements within democracy can be looked at from a number of different perspectives, but the same questions keep recurring. Still, it is important to remember that the disagreements are within democracy and that the similarities between democratic capitalism and democratic socialism are much greater than the differences. The differences center on the point of governmental or public ownership of the majority of the important segments of the economy as opposed to private ownership. This central difference is the focus of the major disagreements between the democratic capitalists and the democratic socialists. Related to this central difference is another that should be emphasized—the conflicting concern with, on the one hand, economic freedom in democratic capitalism and, on the other hand, economic equality in democratic socialism. Other differences are of degree rather than of kind. The extent of the welfare system in democratic socialism is nowhere prohibited by democratic capitalist theory. The bureaucracies of the two are facing similar problems in the world today. Both democratic socialism and democratic capitalism have produced affluence, but poverty has remained in many countries. The governments of various countries are attempting to overcome poverty within the dictates of either the capitalist or the socialist system.

RECENT POLICY ISSUES

Deregulation

Deregulation means relinquishing government oversight of the economy. Many Western countries have deregulated their economies, but that effort has probably been most extensive in the United States. Regulation was supposedly introduced to protect the health and safety of consumers or to ensure that the free market was actually free—that is, not limited by the existence of monopolies or other practices that distorted the market. Most democratic capitalists accept the need for some regulation in these areas.

At the same time, however, most democratic capitalists in the United States contend that regulation went too far and caused more problems than it solved. The idea is that overregulation has forced inefficiencies on the economy and that the relaxation or elimination of regulations will allow for greater efficiency without compromising health and safety.

The result so far is not terribly encouraging. The corruption of the 1980s and early 1990s was often part of attempts to reduce competition and limit access to the market. Health and safety standards have been compromised in many industries, and the savings and loan collapse and the banking and insurance industry problems have hurt many consumers. Interestingly, many democratic capitalists blame the last two problems on a "failure" of regulation, and many have called for greater regulation. Therefore, both regulation and deregulation have their problems, and the needed balance is harder to find than had been expected.

Privatization

Privatization is the sale into private ownership of publicly owned enterprises. It also includes contracting with private firms for services, like refuse collection or the maintenance of public facilities like schools and hospitals, that had been performed by public employees. The United Kingdom has been particularly active in privatization.

The theory behind privatization is that competition will inevitably produce higher quality goods and services at a lower price than publicly produced goods and services. The result has been mixed. In some cases the result has been as expected; in other cases the quality and/or the price has been the opposite of the expectation.

Full Employment

One of the specific policy concerns of most democratic socialists is full employment, which does not usually mean that *everyone* is employed but instead that everyone defined by some standard as employable is employed. The definition allows democratic capitalists to sometimes argue that they favor full employment, but full employment eliminates a market in labor, and democratic capitalists want to keep that market.

A variety of means are used to achieve full employment, ranging from extensive, publicly funded retraining programs to wage supplements to guaranteed jobs in nationalized industries. Today, in order to provide greater economic flexibility, the means tend more toward retraining than wage supplements. The reason for full employment is that it is cheaper for a government to provide wage supplements and retraining and keep people in jobs and paying taxes than to pay the costs of unemployment, which include, in most countries, higher crime rates, more alcohol and drug abuse, and higher medical costs in addition to whatever direct welfare benefits might have to be paid out.

The Problem of Size

Democratic capitalists in the United States are beginning to argue that the consolidation of companies into larger and larger multinational corporations is desirable because these corporations will be better able to compete in the world market. This idea is a change from the past and particularly from the generally accepted argument that small businesses create jobs and large ones do not. The role of the multinationals in the U.S. economy has been a sore point for liberals for some time; in the past conservatives argued that the market would keep these corporations from becoming too big. Now the argument has changed. Democratic capitalists are defending the growth of the multinationals; democratic socialists are arguing for smallness.

Market Socialism

Market socialism, a phrase that democratic capitalists see as a contradiction in terms, is the most significant addition to the vocabulary of democratic socialism in many years. Its most significant theorist is David Miller (1946–) of Oxford University. Miller argues that democratic socialism needs to be rethought as a comprehensive political theory that advocates democratic political oversight of a decentralized economic system that still prevents the powerful from exploiting the weak.

Supporters of market socialism accept the democratic capitalist argument that centralized economic power is inefficient, and they argue, along with democratic capitalists, that markets promote greater freedom. But market socialists contend that democratic capitalism places power in the hands of the rich, that large corporations are as inefficient as large government, that such large corporations can function only by controllng the market, and, therefore, that regulated markets protect the weak, avoid monopolies, and produce markets at least as free as those under unregulated democratic capitalism.

In addition, market socialists insist that it is essential to have a functioning welfare system to protect people from the inevitable shifts of a market economy. Thus, market socialists have not abandoned the principles of democratic socialism but have moved in the direction of a mixed economy with variously owned enterprises (private, public, worker, and cooperative) competing within a regulated market.

Economic Democracy

Many people from different ideological perspectives have consistently raised the question of the degree to which democratic approaches can be applied to various aspects of the economy. At the most general level, democratic socialists argue for the radical reduction or elimination of private control of the major means of production. They wish to replace private control with some form of democratically accountable public control.

But more limited forms of public involvement in the economy have also been proposed and, in some cases, tried. For example, there have been many experiments—some successful, some not—in which companies have been owned and democratically operated by the workers in the company. This means that the workers set policy and hire and fire management. Such businesses are operating successfully in many Western countries including, most notably, Spain and the United States.

A growing trend is for workers in a company to own a substantial share of the stock, with the company run by a board of directors and managers in the same way as any other company. This is not an example of economic democracy unless the workers are actively involved in decision making that gives them significant authority.

The argument for economic democracy is the same as that for political democracy as was outlined in the previous chapter. The theoretical arguments for and against have been weighed in Robert A. Dahl's *A Preface to Economic Democracy* (1985) where he concludes, "A system of self-governing enterprises would be one part of a system of equalities and liberties in which both would, I believe, be stronger, on balance, than they can be in a system of competitive capitalism."[7]

Cooperation

A significant economic movement of long standing that many adherents relate to democratic socialism seems to be having something of a recent revival after a temporary decline in interest. Cooperation takes two forms—producer cooperatives and consumer cooperatives; both are generally well known and exist throughout the world, although today they are probably most common in the Third World. In all forms of cooperation, decision making is democratic, usually as direct involvement based on majority rule, although some cooperatives use consensual systems. Larger operations have representative systems with the representatives checked by regular meetings of the entire membership.

The consumer cooperative is a group of people who form a nonprofit organization to purchase goods in large quantities. Thus, they can pass on the savings from the bulk purchase, eliminate some levels of distribution, and not add a profit to the price. If goods are sold to nonmembers, any profit made by the cooperative is distributed to the members.

The producer cooperative is a group of people who form an organization to produce and distribute goods, usually under the management of the workers. Profits are then distributed among the workers. Agricultural cooperatives usually involve the processing and distribution of goods together with the joint purchase of expensive equipment but do not normally involve the joint own-

---

[7]Robert A. Dahl, *A Preface to Economic Democracy* (Berkeley: University of California Press, 1985), p. 162.

ership of land. Producer cooperatives frequently establish cooperative financial institutions such as banks, credit unions, and insurance agencies.

Consumer cooperation originated in 1844 with the Rochdale Society of Equitable Pioneers in England. The Rochdale Pioneers, as they are known, established a series of basic principles that cooperatives, with some updating, still follow. These principles include open membership; one member, one vote; limited rate of return on equity capital; surplus returned to the members or reinvested into the business; continuous education; and cooperation among cooperatives.

SUGGESTED READINGS

Democratic Capitalism

BAUMANN, FRED E., ed. *Democratic Capitalism? Essays in Search of a Concept.* Charlottesville: University of Virginia Press, 1986.

BELL, DANIEL. *The Cultural Contradictions of Capitalism.* New York: Basic Books, 1978.

BERGER, PETER L., ed. *Capitalism and Equality in America.* Lanham, MD: Hamilton Press and the Institute for Educational Affairs, 1987.

BOWLES, SAMUEL, and HERBERT GINTIS. *Democracy and Capitalism: Property, Community, and the Contradictions of Modern Social Thought.* New York: Basic Books, 1986.

BRAUDEL, FERNAND. *Civilization and Capitalism 15th–18th Century.* 3 vols: vol. 1 trans. Miriam Kochand, trans. revised by Siân Reynolds; vols. 2–3 trans. Siân Reynolds, New York: Harper & Row, 1981–1984.

BUCHANAN, ALLEN. *Ethics, Efficiency and the Market.* Totowa, NJ: Rowman & Allanheld, 1985.

CARENS, JOSEPH H. *Equality, Moral Incentives, and the Market: An Essay in Utopian Politico-Economic Thinking.* Chicago: University of Chicago Press, 1981.

CECIL, ANDREW R. *The Third Way: Enlightened Capitalism and the Search for a New Social Order.* Dallas: University of Texas at Dallas Press, 1980.

CHAPMAN, JOHN W., and J. ROLAND PENNOCK, eds. *Nomos XXXI: Markets and Justice.* New York: New York University Press, 1989.

CHASE, HAROLD W., and PAUL DOLAN. *The Case for Democratic Capitalism.* New York: Thomas Y. Crowell, 1964.

DAVIS, WILLIAM. *It's No Sin to Be Rich: A Defense of Capitalism.* Don Mills, Ontario, Canada: Musson, 1977.

DUNCAN, GRAEME, ed. *Democracy and the Capitalist State.* Cambridge, England: Cambridge University Press, 1989.

DWORKIN, GERALD, GORDON BERMANT, and PETER G. BROWN, eds. *Markets and Morals.* Washington, DC: Hemisphere Publishing, 1977.

FREEMAN, JOHN R. *Democracy and the Markets: The Politics of Mixed Economies.* Ithaca, NY: Cornell University Press, 1989.

FRIEDMAN, DAVID. *The Machinery of Freedom: Guide to Radical Capitalism.* 2d ed. La Salle, IL: Open Court, 1989.

FRIEDMAN, MILTON, *Capitalism and Freedom.* Chicago: University of Chicago Press, 1962.

——, and ROSE FRIEDMAN. *Free to Choose: A Personal Statement.* New York: Harcourt Brace Jovanovich, 1980.

GALBRAITH, JOHN KENNETH. *American*

Capitalism: The Concept of a Countervailing Power. White Plains, NY: M. E. Sharpe, 1980. Originally published 1952.

GILBERT, NEIL. *Capitalism and the Welfare State: Dilemmas of Social Benevolence.* New Haven, CT: Yale University Press, 1983.

GREEN, FRANCIS, and BOB SUTCLIFFE. *The Profit System.* London: Penguin, 1987.

HEILBRONER, ROBERT L. *Behind the Veil of Economics: Essays in the Worldly Philosophy.* New York: W. W. Norton, 1988.

HOOVER, KENNETH, and RAYMOND PLANT. *Conservative Capitalism in Britain and the United States: A Critical Appraisal.* London: Routledge, 1989.

IVENS, MICHAEL, ed. *Prophets of Freedom and Enterprise.* London: Kogan Page for Aims of Industry, 1975.

KELSO, LOUIS O., and MORTIMER J. ADLER. *The Capitalist Manifesto.* New York: Random House, 1958.

KEYNES, JOHN MAYNARD. *The Economic Consequences of the Peace.* New York: Harcourt, Brace and Howe, 1920.

———. *The General Theory of Employment Interest and Money.* New York: Harcourt Brace, 1936.

KRISTOL, IRVING. *Two Cheers for Capitalism.* New York: Basic Books, 1978.

MCCLOSKY, HERBERT, and JOHN TALLER. *The American Ethos: Public Attitudes Toward Capitalism and Democracy.* Cambridge, MA: Harvard University Press, 1984.

MILIBAND, RALPH. *Divided Societies: Class Struggle in Contemporary Capitalism.* Oxford, England: Clarendon Press, 1989.

NOVAK, MICHAEL. *The American Vision: An Essay on the Future of Democratic Capitalism.* Washington, DC: American Enterprise Institute for Public Policy Research, 1978.

———. *The Spirit of Democratic Capitalism.* New York: American Enterprise Institute for Public Policy Research/Simon & Schuster, 1982.

PEJOVICH, SVETOZAR, ed. *Philosophical and Economic Foundations of Capitalism.* Lexington, MA: Lexington Books, 1983.

SELDEN, RICHARD T., ed. *Capitalism and Freedom: Problems and Prospects. Proceedings of a Conference in Honor of Milton Friedman.* Charlottesville: University Press of Virginia, 1975.

SMITH, DENNIS. *Capitalist Democracy on Trial: The Transatlantic Debate from Tocqueville to the Present.* London: Routledge, 1990.

STEPELEVICH, LAWRENCE, ed. *The Capitalist Reader.* New Rochelle, NY: Arlington House, 1977.

VON MISES, LUDWIG. *Socialism: An Economic and Sociological Analysis.* 2d ed. Trans. J. Kahane. London: Jonathan Cape, 1951.

———. *The Anti-Capitalist Mentality.* Princeton, NJ: Van Nostrand, 1956.

———. *Bureaucracy.* New Haven: Yale University Press, 1944. Reprinted New Rochelle, NY: Arlington House, 1969.

———. *Liberalism: A Socio-Economic Exposition.* 2d ed. Trans. Ralph Raico. Kansas City, MO: Sheed Andrews and McMeel, 1978.

WALIGORSKI, CONRAD P. *The Political Theory of Conservative Economists.* Lawrence: University Press of Kansas, 1990.

WRIGHT, DAVID McCORD. *Democracy and Progress.* New York: Macmillan, 1948.

———. *Capitalism.* Chicago: Henry Regnery, 1962.

Democratic Socialism

BRONNER, STEPHEN ERIC. *Socialism Unbound.* New York: Routledge, 1990.

CRICK, BERNARD. *Socialism.* Minneapolis: University of Minnesota Press, 1987.

CROSSMAN, R. H. S., ed. *New Fabian Essays*. London: Turnstile Press, 1952.

CUNNINGHAM, FRANK. *Democratic Theory and Socialism*. Cambridge, England: Cambridge University Press, 1987.

DAHL, ROBERT A. *A Preface to Economic Democracy*. Berkeley: University of California Press, 1985.

DIXON, KEITH. *Freedom and Equality: The Moral Basis of Democratic Socialism*. London: Routledge & Kegan Paul, 1986.

DORRIEN, GARY J. *The Democratic Socialist Vision*. Totowa, NJ: Rowman & Littlefield, 1986.

GLASSMAN, RONALD M., WILLIAM H. SWATOS, JR., and PAUL L. ROSEN, eds. *Bureaucracy Against Democracy and Socialism*. Westport, CT: Greenwood Press, 1987.

GORZ, ANDRÉ. *Farewell to the Working Class: An Essay on Post-Industrial Socialism*. Trans. Michael Sonenscher. London: Pluto Press, 1982.

GOULD, BRYAN. *Socialism and Freedom*. London: Macmillan, 1985.

HAMILTON, MALCOLM B. *Democratic Socialism in Britain and Sweden*. New York: St. Martin's Press, 1989.

HARRINGTON, MICHAEL. *Socialism*. New York: Saturday Review Press, 1972.

———. *Socialism Past and Present*. New York: Arcade, 1989.

HIRST, PAUL Q. *Law, Socialism and Democracy*. London: Allen & Unwin, 1986.

HODGES, DONALD C. *The Bureaucratization of Socialism*. Amherst: University of Massachusetts Press, 1981.

KEANE, JOHN. *Public Life and Late Capitalism: Toward a Socialist Theory of Democracy*. Cambridge, England: Cambridge University Press, 1984.

KITCHING, GAVIN. *Rethinking Socialism: A Theory for a Better Practice*. London: Methuen, 1983.

LE GRAND, JULIAN, and SAUL ESTRIN, eds. *Market Socialism*. Oxford, England: Clarendon Press, 1989.

LEVINE, ANDREW. *Arguing for Socialism: Theoretical Considerations*. Boston: Routledge & Kegan Paul, 1984.

LUNTLEY, MICHAEL: *The Meaning of Socialism*. La Salle, IL: Open Court, 1989.

MILLER, DAVID. *Market, State, and Community: Theoretical Foundations of Market Socialism*. Oxford, England: Clarendon Press, 1989.

———. "A Vision of Market Socialism." *Dissent* (Summer 1991): 406–414.

NOVE, ALEC. *Efficiency Criteria for Nationalised Industries*. London: George Allen & Unwin, 1974.

POULANTZAS, NICOS. *State, Power, Socialism*. Trans. Patrick Camiller. London: NLB, 1978.

RAE, BOB. "A Socialist Credo." *Dissent* (Winter 1991): 42–44.

ROEMER, JOHN E. *A Future for Socialism*. Cambridge, MA: Harvard University Press, 1994.

RUSTIN, MICHAEL. *For a Pluralist Socialism*. London: Verso, 1985.

RYAN, ALAN. "Socialism for the Nineties: An Argument for This Time." *Dissent* (Fall 1990): 436–442.

SHAW, GEORGE BERNARD, ed. *Fabian Essays in Socialism*. London: Constable and Co., 1931. Originally published in 1889.

SIK, OTA. *For a Humane Economic Democracy*. Trans. Fred Eidlin and William Graf. New York: Praeger, 1985.

———, ed. *Socialism Today? The Changing Meaning of Socialism*. New York: St. Martin's Press, 1991.

WALTZER, MICHAEL. "A Day in the Life of a Socialist Citizen: Two Cheers for Participatory Democracy." (*Dissent* (May–June 1968): 243–247.

WRIGHT, ANTHONY. *Socialisms: Theories and Practices*. Oxford, England: Oxford University Press, 1986.

5

Conservatism, Liberalism, and Democracy

Conservatism and liberalism within democracy must be treated in three different ways because they are three different things. First, they are general sets of attitudes toward change, human nature, and tradition. Second, they are specific positions taken at a time and place by identifiable groups of people. Third, in particular countries they have histories, although these histories are so complex that the same individuals are sometimes included in the histories of both liberalism and conservatism. It is possible to trace the histories of Western conservative and liberal traditions, as currently seen by contemporary advocates, back to the seventeenth and eighteenth centuries. Despite some cross-fertilization, each country has its own histories. For North Americans, the histories are primarily connected with British political thought with limited French and German influences.

The general attitudes linked to the histories will be presented first, followed by the identifiable groups that exist in the United States in the mid-1990s—the new right, traditional conservatives, neoconservatives, neoliberals, and traditional liberals. Some of these groups exist in other countries, but not all of them do. The general attitudes labeled conservative and liberal have existed at most times, although not always under these labels; if the labels are made sufficiently vague, these attitudes exist in most or all countries today.

Some writers choose to treat conservatism and liberalism as separate ideologies rather than as tendencies within democracy, as they are presented here. Neither approach is perfect, but the approach used here captures the complexity of attitudes toward democracy by showing that, in addition to democrats who are capitalist and democrats who are socialist, there are democrats who are liberal and democrats who are conservative. In the United States almost all democrats are capitalists and either liberal or conservative. In some countries there are liberal and conservative democratic socialists as well as liberal and conservative democratic capitalists.

Conservatism and liberalism also differ from place to place and time to time. A Canadian conservative will emphasize something different from a Japanese or Swedish conservative. In addition, a conservative in the United States in the last half of the twentieth century does not believe the same thing that a U.S. conservative in 1890 did. In fact, the position taken by many conservatives today was called liberalism in the late nineteenth century, and many conservatives believe that they are the true liberals. Liberalism has also varied from time to time and place to place; but in both cases traditions identified by their adherents allow us to talk about conservatism and liberalism over time.

Even though conservatives often think of liberals as extremists and vice versa, both liberals and conservatives are found in the middle of the political spectrum. We call one extreme *reactionary*—one who wants to move dramatically in the direction of a past society (usually idealized) believed to be better than the present. The other extreme is usually called *radical*—one who wants dramatic change in the direction of a vision of a better society that has not yet existed. In both cases the differences center on the amount (and often the speed) of change desired. Both liberals and conservatives want to maintain the basic institutions and processes of the society in which they live. Radicals and reactionaries want to change those basic institutions and processes.

CONSERVATISM

Conservatives are interested in conserving something. Conservatism within democracy today has the following characteristcs:

1. Resistance to change;

2. Reverence for tradition and a distrust of human reason;

3. Rejection of the use of government to improve the human condition— ambivalence regarding governmental activity for other purposes;

4. Preference for individual freedom but willingness to limit freedom to maintain traditional values; and

5. Antiegalitarianism—distrust of human nature.

Modern conservatism is traceable to Edmund Burke (1729–1797), although he had precursors and a variety of alternative traditions existed in various countries. Burke is most noted for his emphasis on tradition. As he wrote in his most famous book, *Reflections on the Revolution in France* (1790),

> In states there are often more obscure and almost latent causes, things which appear at first view of little moment, on which a very great part of its prosperity or

adversity may most essentially depend. The science of government being therefore so practical in itself, and intended for such practical purposes, a matter which requires experience, and even more experience than any person can gain in his whole life, however sagacious and observing he may be, it is with infinite caution that any man ought to venture upon pulling down an edifice which has answered in any tolerable degree for ages the common purposes of society, or on building it up again, without models and patterns of approved utility before his eyes.[1]

Here we see both Burke's concern with the wisdom of the past and his concern with the complexity of social and political life. This latter concern leads to the conservative rejection of the liberal emphasis on rational planning;[2] life is too complicated for human beings to comprehend and control. In addition, some factors in society do not lend themselves to rational planning.

Burke also stressed another factor that is part of contemporary conservatism—private property. "Nothing is a due and adequate representation of a state that does not represent its ability, as well as its property."[3] And, Burke notes, both ability and property are inherited unequally.

What is generally called traditional conservatism is much the same as Burke's thinking. Neoconservatism is a reaction to particular conditions that exist today. The new right, while also responding to current issues, is similar to early conservative theories that developed parallel to Burke's conservatism, but there is no evidence that it has been influenced by those theories. While Burke emphasized the importance of religion, he wanted it completely separate from political life. Many Continental conservatives, on the other hand, did not want such a separation.

In an essay entitled "Why I Am Not a Conservative," F. A. Hayek (1899–1992), who called himself a liberal, wrote, "Conservatism proper is a legitimate, probably necessary, and certainly widespread attitude of opposition to drastic change."[4] Although his point is correct, it is too specific. Conservatives not only oppose "drastic change," as he says, but are hesitant about any change. As one writer put it, "the conservative does not oppose change, but he does resist it."[5] Conservatives do not unthinkingly oppose change; they resist it and question it because they are wary of social experimentation. They believe that something that has worked, even if not very well, is better than something untried and unknown.

The second characteristic of conservatism, a reverence for tradition, is composed of a number of subsidiary points including traditional moral standards,

---

[1]Edmund Burke. *The Works of the Right Honorable Edmund Burke*, rev. ed. (Boston: Little, Brown, 1865), 3: p. 312.

[2]See, for example, Michael Oakeshott, "Rationalism in Politics," in his *Rationalism in Politics and Other Essays* (New York: Basic Books, 1962), pp. 1–36.

[3]Burke, *Works*, 3: pp. 297–298.

[4]F. A. Hayek, "Why I Am Not a Conservative," in *The Constitution of Liberty* (London: Routledge & Kegan Paul, 1960), p. 397.

[5]Jay A. Sigler, "Introduction," in *The Conservative Tradition in American Thought*, ed. Jay A. Sigler

religion (with very few exceptions), and the assumption that the longer an institution has existed, the more likely it is to be worth preserving. Reverence for tradition springs from the conservative's basic distrust of reason as a means of improving humanity's lot. Conservatives do not reject reason completely, but they would rather trust tradition because they believe that tradition contains the accumulated wisdom of past generations. Note also how closely connected the first and second characteristics are—honoring tradition entails resistance to change.

This point is quite simple and clear-cut. The only really complicating factor is that conservatives (and liberals) change over time regarding the specifics they wish to preserve. The world changes, and conservatives change with it. They do not want to conserve all the past; they want to conserve what they believe is the best of the past.

The third characteristic presents the major dilemma in conservative thought. On the whole, conservatives believe governmental power should be reduced and individuals should make their own way in the world. (Note the similarity to traditional capitalism.) But there is an ambivalence here. Governmental power to support traditional moral standards and limit an individual's freedom regarding them is perfectly acceptable to some conservatives. Conservatives believe "genuinely ordered freedom is the only sort of liberty worth having: freedom made possible by order within the soul and order within the state."[6]

The case must not be overstated, however. Conservatives do reject the use of government to improve the human condition. They do so because (1) they are convinced the use of government does not necessarily improve the human condition and (2) they believe people left alone can do a better job. The first point is the key. It asserts that the use of government for social betterment will actually produce the opposite. People will, according to most conservatives, come to rely on government and lose the ability to help themselves.

Conservatives have held this position very consistently. Edmund Burke (1729–1797), writing in the eighteenth century, held it; Bernard Bosanquet (1848–1923), writing at the beginning of this century, held it; and modern conservatives, such as Russell Kirk (1918–1994), continued to hold it. Persons of the better sort will be hurt by governmental help; the poorer sort will not be helped.

Conservatives believe some people are better than other people and, therefore, should be honored more by society. "Aye, men are created different; and a government which ignores this law becomes an unjust government, for it sacrifices nobility to mediocrity; it pulls down the aspiring natures to gratify the inferior natures."[7] This is precisely the reason that conservatives are ambivalent about both government and individual freedom.

"The conservative accepts as natural the differences which separate men.

---

[6]Russell Kirk, "Prescription, Authority, and Ordered Freedom," in *What Is Conservatism?* ed. Frank S. Meyer (New York: Holt, Rinehart & Winston, 1964), p. 24.

[7]Kirk, "Prescription," p. 34.

Edmund Burke (1729–1797) is best known as the founder of modern conservatism. His *Reflections on the Revolution in France* (1790) is his most famous work, and in it he argued that society is a complex web of relationships among the past, present, and future that must not be lightly changed. He contended that social institutions slowly evolve over time to fit needs and conditions and that, therefore, tampering with tradition is likely to bring grief rather than improvement. He was an advocate of slow, gradual change; he did not reject change altogether nor argue for the return to some idealized past. *(Library of Congress)*

Class, intelligence, nationality, and race make men different."[8] This recognition of differences sometimes implies superiority or inferiority, but it does not necessarily do so. The recognition states that inferiority and superiority exist but does not necessarily tie them to race, class, or sex.

These are the defining characteristics of conservatism. These principles do not change much over time, and later in the chapter we will see how they are applied today in the United States.

LIBERALISM

Liberalism has a complex history, as does conservatism. Even dating the origins of liberalism is itself controversial. Some scholars purport to find liberalism in ancient Greece and Rome, but most commonly liberalism is traced to one of the seventeenth-century English revolutions. The two most likely origins are the revolution of the 1640s and the Levellers, particularly the Putney debates;

---

[8]Sigler, "Introduction," *The Conservative Tradition*, p. 13.

or the revolution of the 1680s and the writings of John Locke (1632–1704). The differences between these two origins are reflected in two different interpretations of liberalism. The Levellers were most concerned with greater equality, particularly the vote, as reflected in what is probably the most famous statement of the Levellers. In the Putney debates Colonel Thomas Rainsborough (d. 1648) said,

> I think that the poorest he that is in England hath a life to live, as the greatest he; and therefore truly, sir, I think it's clear, that every man that is to live under government ought first by his own consent to put himself under that government; and I do think that the poorest man in England is not at all bound in a strict sense to that government that he hath not had a voice to put himself under.[9]

Although Locke was also concerned with consent, he stressed rights, particularly property rights. Both the Levellers and Locke emphasized majority rule. Both recognized the likelihood of conflict between government and the people, and both sided with the people.

Today, most liberals argue that liberalism is primarily concerned with liberty and trace their roots to John Stuart Mill (1806–1873) and his little book *On Liberty* (1869), which stressed freedom of thought and speech. But the liberal emphasis on liberty has taken two differing routes from Mill to the present. One approach is really a continuation of Locke's concern with rights, including property rights. The other approach developed in the late nineteenth and early twentieth centuries in the writings of T. H. Green (1836–1882) and others, who argued that some people need help in order to be able to exercise their liberty. This argument was the beginning of what became known as *welfare liberalism*.

These varied strands brings us to a liberalism that today can be described as having the following characteristics:

1. A tendency to favor change;

2. Faith in human reason;

3. Willingness to use government to improve the human condition;

4. Preference for individual freedom but ambivalent about economic freedom; and

5. More optimistic about human nature than conservatives.

Hubert H. Humphrey (1911–1978) once wrote: "Liberals fully recognize that *change* is inevitable in the patterns of society and in the challenges which confront man."[10] Liberals generally believe people should keep trying to im-

---

[9] From A. S. P. Woodhouse, ed., *Puritanism and Liberty: Being the Army Debates (1647–9) from the Clarke Manuscripts with Supplementary Documents*, 2d ed. (London: J. M. Dent & Sons, 1974), p. 59.

[10] Hubert H. Humphrey, "Introduction," in Milton Viorst, *Liberalism: A Guide to Its Past, Present and Future in American Politics* (New York: Avon Books, 1963), p. vii (emphasis in original).

prove society. Somewhat less optimistic about progress than they once were, liberals still believe beneficial change is possible. Such change can come about through the conscious action of men and women, as unforeseen side effects of decisions, or through the operation of various social forces. But there will be change, and the liberal is convinced it can be directed and controlled for human benefit.

Liberals do not desire radical change that would do away with the basic structure of the current system. On this point, the difference between liberalism and conservatism is a matter of degree rather than kind. Liberals want more change and tend to favor social experimentation, but they want this only within the framework of the current political, legal, and economic system. Liberals are not radicals.

Change is welcomed because liberals trust human reason to devise solutions to human problems. This faith in the potential of reason is the key to the liberal credo—only with such faith can they accept the use of governmental power to improve the human condition. This faith is not a naive, unquestioning faith, but it assumes that social experimentation is valid and that it is better to use such powers as we have to control change than to allow change to control us.

Liberals contend some people must be helped to live better lives and fulfill their individual potentials, and they believe that such assistance can work. Conservatives believe just the opposite—helping people may make it impossible for them to fulfill their potentials as individuals. Liberals argue that people, though capable of reason and reasoned action, are often caught in situations where self-help, even if possible, is very difficult and that government should help. This assistance, far from injuring people, can (although it may not) give them the impetus to do more for themselves. The liberal assumption is that, although not everyone will respond, it is better to attempt to help than to do nothing. In contemporary society, liberals believe government is in the best position to provide help.

Liberals believe this help through governmental activity will lead to greater individual freedom. They argue that a person, once relieved of some basic problems, can enlarge his or her sphere of activity and improve both life and mind. Still, liberals are somewhat ambivalent about human nature. They contend that most problems derive from impersonal social and economic forces acting on humanity; human reason can solve the problems, but an unaided human being cannot. This is why liberals are ambivalent about economic freedom; they are afraid that one of the results of an unregulated economy would be great difference in power, which would be used to the detriment of the weaker members of society.

The tradition of liberalism most strongly stresses individual freedom. The term *liberalism* is closely related to liberty, and the emphasis on liberty has been a major thread in all liberal thought. The role of the government is limited—it cannot invade the rights and freedoms of the individual. Human beings will err, but liberals have always believed error is far better than the suppression of error. This belief follows from the belief in the value and

John Stuart Mill (1806–1873) was the most influential philosopher in the English-speaking world in the nineteenth century. His major political works were *On Liberty* (1859), *Considerations on Representative Government* (1861), *Utilitarianism* (1861), and *The Subjection of Women* (1869). Mill developed and modified the philosophy of utilitarianism of Jeremy Bentham (1748–1832), but Mill is best known today for his defense of freedom in *On Liberty* and for his defense of representative government. With his wife Harriet Taylor (1807–1858), Mill began to explore the subordinate role of women in contemporary society, and he became an advocate of women's rights. (*Library of Congress*)

inevitability of change. If change is good and will always occur, today's error may be tomorrow's truth.

As general tendencies, liberalism and conservatism are primarily attitudes toward change within the democratic tradition, resting uneasily between reaction and radicalism. Too often attempts are made to transform them into major ideologies with rigidly defined beliefs. Doing this is an error. Liberalism and conservatism do not have clear-cut belief systems except in response to current problems, but in such a response they can be identified.

CONTEMPORARY CONSERVATISM
IN THE UNITED STATES

Three groups of people share the label *conservative* in the United States today: the new right, the traditional conservative, and the neoconservative. At times they seem to disagree as much among themselves as with the liberals, and at other times the lines among them seem quite blurred. Still, they are defined by their positions on specific issues and therefore can usually be clearly identified.

Three sets of issues can be used to define contemporary conservatives (and liberals): social, fiscal, and foreign-policy issues. The mixture of positions on each of these and the emphasis placed on them define the differences among the three types of conservatives. Very briefly these positions can be characterized as follows:

> Social—a belief in traditional values centering on the home, family, and religion. At present this includes the belief that the appropriate place for women is in the home; a strong opposition to abortion; support for required prayer in schools; and opposition to the teaching of sex education and evolution, among other subjects.

> Fiscal—a belief in capitalism, opposition to most government regulation of the economy, and support for a balanced budget.

> Foreign policy—a belief in a strong military, an active opposition to communism (obviously now less important), and support for those who support us whatever their political position.

The New Right

What was then called the *radical right* developed in the 1950s and emphasized opposition to communism. At that time most radical right programs were negative and oppositional. Today, what is better called the *new right* is concerned with social issues, such as abortion, busing to integrate schools, pornography (shared with some feminists), prayer in schools, and local control of education, which are all seen as fundamentally moral questions.

The new right is primarily concerned with issues centering on the family, religion, and education. All these issues are, they argue, basically about morals. They generally believe that the proper place for women is in the home caring for and educating their children. They strongly oppose any position that can be seen as supporting nontraditional sexual relations, such as the movement for gay rights. The role of the schools is to teach parentally approved values and "the basics" (reading, writing, and arithmetic). Schools should have required, Christian prayer; creationism should be taught rather than evolution in biology classes (the new right does not believe in the separation of church and state).

These positions pose an apparent dilemma for the new right. They oppose government activity that imposes moral positions that they oppose, but they are willing to use government to impose their moral positions. But for the new right there is no dilemma because there is a simple division of right and wrong on moral questions, and government has an appropriate role to support the right morality and oppose the wrong morality. To them, tolerance of what they know to be the wrong positions is unacceptable.

The new right remains strongly conservative on foreign policy with anticommunism becoming support for a strong military. On fiscal policy, the new right argues for a free market and against government regulation because they see these positions as essential to political freedom.

Traditional Conservatism

What I call *traditional conservatism* is closest to the general characterization of conservatism outlined previously but has currently rather faded from view under pressure from the new right and neoconservatism. This does not mean that such conservatives don't exist; they have always been the mainstream of conservative thought, both in numbers and influence, and remain so. They are simply not getting the publicity that the other brands of conservatism are getting.

Traditional conservatives are more likely to support some government regulation of the economy than the new right is, but they are still fiscal conservatives. They are much less likely to be social conservatives than are members of the new right. While they support traditional moral values, they are not generally in favor of using government power to enforce them. Traditional conservatives are also foreign-policy conservatives, but in all three areas they emphasize gradual change and continuity rather than immediate, radical change.

Neoconservatism

Neoconservatives are ex-liberals who feel that liberalism lost its way in the 1960s and 1970s.[11] They are foreign-policy and fiscal conservatives and more liberal than other conservatives on social issues. Neoconservatives are close to traditional conservatives in their respect for religion and the family, and they want less government regulation and a greater reliance on the free market.

Neoconservatives do not reject the culture of the modern West—something they accuse the new right of doing. They believe that economic growth will allow more people to share in the benefits of that culture.[12]

The differences in these forms of conservatism are primarily ones of emphasis. The members of the new right stress social questions, neoconservatives stress the free market, and traditional conservatives take a moderately conservative position on those plus fiscal policy. All conservatives support free-market capitalism, want the United States to have a strong defense and foreign policy, and are concerned with traditional values.

---

[11] An excellent short statement of the neoconservative position is Richard T. Seager, *American Government and Politics: A Neoconservative Approach* (Glenview, IL: Scott, Foresman, 1982), pp. 39–48; also see Peter Steinfels, *The Neoconservatives: The Men Who Are Changing America's Politics* (New York: Simon & Schuster, 1979).

[12] See Irving Kristol, *Reflections of a Neoconservative: Looking Back, Looking Ahead* (New York: Basic Books, 1983), pp. 75–77.

CONTEMPORARY LIBERALISM
IN THE UNITED STATES

Liberals today come under two headings—neoliberals and traditional liberals. Liberalism is somewhat in disarray today. Liberals tend to be much less sure about their policies than they used to be. There has been a drift away from government regulation of the economy to the acceptance of the position that less regulation (not *no* regulation) might be a good idea. Liberals have also begun to believe that the welfare system needs to be redesigned but not scrapped. The old liberal faith that the government could help people to help themselves and the belief that recession and depression could be avoided by stimulating the economy have been challenged by a failing world economy. Liberalism has not yet found a new faith, but it has not yet entirely lost its old faith either. Liberals still stand for expanded personal freedom and therefore find themselves constantly at odds with the radical right. Liberals still believe that greater human equality is a desirable and achievable goal and thus are usually opposed to their traditional opposition, the conservatives, who reject the belief in equality as not reflecting the reality of the human race.

Liberals can also be characterized on the same three measures as conservatives, but there is much less agreement on the mix of the three than there is among conservatives. Social, fiscal, and foreign-policy liberals can be characterized very roughly as follows:

Social—a belief in freedom of choice. Today this tends to mean support for the pro-choice position on abortion, advocacy of the rights of women and minorities, and support for welfare programs.

Fiscal—a belief in the use of government intervention in the economy to regulate it and an acceptance, much reduced at present, of deficit spending.

Foreign policy—a belief in the need to work within the international community for the peaceful resolution of conflicts. Stress on cooperation and aid with a related reduction in emphasis on defense and the military.

Neoliberalism

Starting at the right of the liberal spectrum, the neoliberals have identified themselves as fiscal conservatives while remaining social and foreign-policy liberals, albeit with a slight shift to the conservative side in both cases.[13] Neoliberals stress that they are concerned with getting the system to work rather than with ideology.

---

[13]See Randall Rothenberg, *The Neoliberals: Creating the New American Politics* (New York: Simon & Schuster, 1984).

Neoliberals want to change the pattern of government spending because it is, they say, too high and inefficiently handled. They want a strong defense but more government oversight of military spending. They want efficient and effective welfare programs. They are particularly concerned with encouraging the development of new technology and controlling the changeover from the old technologies to avoid personal and regional damage. Generally they want what they consider to be a realistic liberalism that faces up to the rapid changes, particularly in the economy, that are currently taking place.

Traditional Liberalism

Although showing some resurgence, traditional liberalism (in this sense a tradition from the 1930s) is everybody's scapegoat. Described as advocating big government, deficit spending, and expensive welfare programs, traditional liberals, who believe that they have been misrepresented, are being blamed by conservatives and neoliberals alike for most of what is wrong with the United States today.

Traditional liberals see themselves as advocates of working people, the poor, and minorities against big business and as supporters of civil rights for African Americans, women, and ethnic minorities against the repression of government and business. Thus they see themselves as defenders of freedom and equality. They believe that only government is powerful enough to achieve these goals; therefore, they are in favor of strong government.

Today traditional liberals still believe in these goals, as do neoliberals, but they are no longer sure about how to achieve them. They believe that they were doing the right thing but have been told so often that the costs were too high that they have begun to question this themselves.

Liberalism is unified on goals but divided on means. Even traditional liberals are questioning deficit spending—spurred on by the fact that it has increased to its highest level under a conservative president. But all liberals believe in an egalitarian society with protection for civil rights; they are divided on how to achieve it.

CURRENT TRENDS

John Rawls

The most important contribution to liberalism in the last quarter century was the publication of *A Theory of Justice* (1971) by John Rawls (1921–). In *A Theory of Justice*, Rawls is concerned with establishing the fundamental principles of social justice. To do this he undertakes a thought experiment in which he imagines people in what he calls "the original position," in which people are assumed not to know what talents and abilities they have or what position they hold in society. They do not know their race or gender, whether they are rich or poor, powerful or weak. They are then asked to choose the principles on which to build a society. Rawls argues that the principles that would be chosen in such a situation are:

> First: Each person is to have an equal right to the most extensive basic liberty compatible with a similar liberty for others.
>
> Second: Social and economic inequalities are to be arranged so that they are both (a) reasonably expected to be to everyone's advantage, and (b) attached to positions that are open to all.[14]

These principles are intended to be applied in order. Thus, equality of rights has a higher priority than equality of opportunity.

Rawls contends that these are the fundamental principles of liberalism. The publication of *A Theory of Justice* set off a long debate among political theorists over all aspects of the book, but particularly about the thought experiment and the priorities that Rawls had assigned to the values he believed would result from it. In *Political Liberalism* (1993) Rawls has made explicit that he sees his arguments as contributions to contemporary political debate as well as contributions to a general theory of justice. He contends that we must recognize that our societies are composed of peoples with unreconcilable fundamental beliefs. As he puts it, "the problem of political liberalism is: How is it possible that there may exist over time a stable and just society of free and equal citizens profoundly divided by reasonable though incompatible religious, philosophical, and moral doctrines?[15] To answer the question, Rawls subtly modifies the two principles stated above, which now read as follows:

1. Each person has an equal claim to a fully adequate scheme of basic rights and liberties, which scheme is compatible with the same scheme for all; and in this scheme the equal political liberties, and only those liberties, are to be guaranteed their fair values.

2. Social and economic inequalities are to satisfy two conditions: first, they are to be attached to positions and offices open to all under conditions of fair equality of opportunity; and second, they are to be of the greatest benefit to the least advantaged members of society.[16]

This revision of his argument for "justice as fairness" puts Rawls squarely back in the middle of a recent debate that originated in arguments over *A Theory of Justice* but had moved into new territory, the debate between liberalism and communitarianism.

---

[14]John Rawls, *A Theory of Justice* (Cambridge, MA: Harvard University Press, 1971), p. 60.

[15]Rawls, *Political Liberalism* (New York: Columbia University Press, 1993), p. xviii.

[16]Ibid., pp. 5–6.

Liberalism and Communitarianism

In the last few years a major debate has erupted among democratic theorists between those who call themselves liberals and those who call themselves communitarians. According to the communitarian critique of liberalism, liberalism overemphasizes the individual to the detriment of the community. Put another way, liberalism is said to focus on an individual with no social context. Liberals argue both that communitarians misrepresent liberalism and that the communitarian alternative destroys liberty.

In this debate, liberals focus on the desirability of developing autonomous individuals who are protected from government by universally applicable rights. Liberals believe that there is a substantial area of private life that should be completely outside the concern of government.

Communitarians focus on the community rather than the individual as the basis for personal and political identity and moral decision making. Much of the communitarian argument developed in opposition to Rawlsian liberalism, but the positive content of communitarianism stems from the contention that all individuals are to some extent created by and embedded in specific communities. Our beliefs, moral systems, our whole sense of ourselves come from the community or communities of which we have been and are a part.

The political conclusions drawn by communitarians from their critique of liberalism and the emergence of the community as a theoretical focus vary across the political spectrum from left to right, although the right has been most clearly identified with communitarianism. Some left-wing communitarians see it as simply an extension of participatory democracy with a greater concern for the community in which the participation takes place. Thus, communitarianism could be seen as a development of the emphasis on community that was found in the New Left,[17] but this is not how most communitarians see it.

Most communitarians are clearly conservatives who believe that the growth of legally enforceable individual rights has gone too far to the detriment of the society as a whole. They believe that there must be a renewed focus on personal, family, and community responsibility. Many liberals do not actually disagree, and many of the differences between liberals and communitarians are fairly technical, but while the desired results are perhaps not very different—fully developed individuals interacting within a healthy society—the differences in the means of getting there are immense. Are individuals responsible to and for themselves or are they the product of the communities of which they are a part and responsible to the community and the community to them?

---

[17]See Lyman Tower Sargent, *New Left Thought: An Introduction* (Homewood, IL: Dorsey Press, 1972).

SUGGESTED READINGS

Conservatism

ABCARIAN, GILBERT. "Political Deviance and Social Stress: The Ideology of the American Radical Right." In *Social Control and Social Change*. Ed. John Paul Scott and Sarah F. Scott. Chicago: University of Chicago Press, 1971: 137–161.

ALLISON, LINCOLN. *Right Principles: A Conservative Philosophy of Politics*. Oxford, England: Basil Blackwell, 1984.

BROMLEY, DAVID G., and ANSON SHARPE, eds. *New Christian Politics*. Mercer, GA: Mercer University Press, 1984.

BRUCE, STEVE. *The Rise and Fall of the New Christian Right: Conservative Protestant Politics in America 1978–1988*. Oxford, England: Clarendon Press, 1988.

BUCHANAN, PATRICK. *Right from the Beginning*. Boston, MA: Little, Brown, 1988.

BUCKLEY, WILLIAM F., JR. *Up from Liberalism*. 25th anniversary ed. New York: Stein and Day, 1984.

BUCKLEY, WILLIAM F., JR. and CHARLES R. KESLER, eds. *Keeping the Tablets: Modern American Conservative Thought*. New York: Harper & Row, 1988.

COOPER, BARRY, ALLAN KORNBERG, and WILLIAM MISHLER, eds. *The Resurgence of Conservatism in Anglo-American Democracies*. Durham, NC: Duke University Press, 1988.

COVELL, CHARLES. *The Redefinition of Conservatism: Politics and Doctrine*. London: Macmillan, 1986.

EAST, JOHN P. *The American Conservative Movement: The Philosophical Founders*. Chicago: Regnery Books, 1986.

FALWELL, JERRY. *Listen America!* Garden City, NY: Doubleday, 1980.

FILLER, LOUIS. *Dictionary of American Conservatism*. New York: Philosophical Library, 1987.

GIRVIN, BRIAN, ed. *The Transformations of Contemporary Conservatism*. London: Sage, 1988.

GOTTFRIED, PAUL, and THOMAS FLEMING. *The Conservative Movement*. Boston: Twayne, 1988.

HARBOUR, WILLIAM R. *The Foundations of Conservative Thought: An Anglo-American Tradition in Perspective*. Notre Dame, IN: University of Notre Dame Press, 1982.

HAYEK, FRIEDRICH A. *The Constitution of Liberty*. London: Routledge & Kegan Paul, 1960.

———. *The Road to Serfdom*. Chicago: University of Chicago Press, 1960.

———. *Studies in Philosophy, Politics and Economics*. Chicago: University of Chicago Press, 1967.

———. *Economic Freedom and Representative Government*. London: Institute of Economic Affairs, 1973.

HIRSCHMAN, ALBERT O. *The Rhetoric of Reaction: Perversity, Futility, Jeopardy*. Cambridge, MA: Belknap Press, 1991.

HOLDEN, MATTHEW, JR., ed. *Varieties of Political Conservatism*. Newbury Park, CA: Sage Publications, 1974.

HONDERICH, TED. *Conservatism*. Boulder, CO: Westview Press, 1990.

HUNTINGTON, SAMUEL P. "Conservatism as an Ideology." *American Political Science Review* 51 (June 1957): 454–473.

KATER, JOHN L., JR. *Christians on the Right: The Moral Majority in Perspective*. New York: Seabury Press, 1982.

KENDALL, WILMOORE. *The Conservative Affirmation*. Chicago: Henry Regnery, 1954.

———, and GEORGE W. CAREY. "Towards a Definition of 'Conservatism.' " *Journal of Politics* 26 (May 1964): 406–422.

KING, DESMOND S. *The New Right*. Belmont, CA: Wadsworth, 1987.

KIRK, RUSSELL. *A Program for Conservatives.* Chicago: Henry Regnery, 1954.

———. *The Intelligent Woman's Guide to Conservatism.* New York: Devin-Adair Co., 1957.

———, ed. *The Portable Conservative Reader,* Harmondsworth, England: Penguin, 1982.

———. *The Conservative Mind from Burke to Eliot.* 7th rev. ed. Chicago: Regnery Books, 1986.

KLATCH, REBECCA E. *Women of the New Right.* Philadelphia: Temple University Press, 1987.

KOLKO, GABRIEL. *The Triumph of Conservatism: A Reinterpretation of American History, 1900–1916.* New York: Free Press, 1963.

KRISTOL, IRVING. *Reflections of a Neoconservative: Looking Back, Looking Ahead.* New York: Basic Books, 1983.

LEVITAS, RUTH, ed. *The Ideology of the New Right.* Cambridge, England: Polity Press, 1986.

MEYER, FRANK S., ed. *What Is Conservatism?* New York: Holt, Rinehart & Winston, 1964.

MEYER, JACK A., ed. *Meeting Human Needs: Toward a New Public Philosophy.* Washington, DC: American Enterprise Institute for Public Policy Research, 1982.

MOEN, MATTHEW C. *The Transformation of the Christian Right.* Tuscaloosa: University of Alabama Press, 1992.

NISBET, ROBERT A. *Conservatism: Dream and Reality.* Minneapolis: University of Minnesota Press, 1986.

NOVAK, MICHAEL. *Freedom with Justice: Catholic Social Thought and Liberal Institutions.* San Francisco: Harper & Row, 1984.

RIBUFFO, LEO P. *The Old Christian Right: The Protestant Far Right from the Great Depression to the Cold War.* Philadelphia: Temple University Press, 1983.

ROSSITER, CLINTON. *Conservatism in America: The Thankless Persuasion.* 2d rev. ed. New York: Knopf, 1966.

ROTHBARD, MURRAY N. *Left and Right: The Prospects for Liberty.* CATO paper no. 1. San Francisco: CATO Institute, 1979.

SARGENT, LYMAN TOWER. *Extremism in America: A Reader.* New York: New York University Press, 1995.

SCHUETTINGER, ROBERT LINDSAY, ed. *The Conservative Tradition in European Thought.* New York: Putnam's, 1970.

SCRUTON, ROGER. *The Meaning of Conservatism.* Harmondsworth, England: Penguin, 1980.

SIGLER, JAY A., ed. *The Conservative Tradition in American Thought.* New York: Capricorn Books, 1969.

STEINFELS, PETER. *The Neoconservatives: The Men Who Are Changing America's Politics.* New York: Simon & Schuster, 1979.

VIERECK, PETER. *Conservatism: From John Adams to Churchill.* Princeton, NJ: Van Nostrand, 1956.

WHITAKER, ROBERT W., ed. *The New Right Papers.* New York: St. Martin's, 1982.

WILL, GEORGE F. *Statecraft as Soulcraft: What Government Does.* New York: Simon & Schuster, 1983.

Liberalism

ABBOTT, PHILIP, and MICHAEL B. LEVY, eds. *The Liberal Future in America: Essays in Renewal.* Westport, CT: Greenwood Press, 1985.

ACKERMAN, BRUCE A. *Social Justice in the Liberal State.* New Haven, CT: Yale University Press, 1980.

ARBLASTER, ANTHONY. *The Rise and Decline of Western Liberalism.* Oxford, England: Basil Blackwell, 1984.

ASHFORD, DOUGLAS E. *The Emergence of the Welfare State.* Oxford, England: Basil Blackwell, 1987.

BARBER, BENJAMIN R. *The Conquest of Politics: Liberal Philosophy in Democratic Times*. Princeton, NJ: Princeton University Press, 1988.

BARRY, NORMAN. *Welfare*. Minneapolis: University of Minnesota Press, 1990.

BLOCK, FRED, RICHARD A. CLOWARD, BARBARA EHRENREICH, and FRANCES FOX PIVEN. *The Mean Season: The Attack on the Welfare State*. New York: Pantheon Books, 1987.

BOBBIO, NORBERTO. *Liberalism and Democracy*. Trans. Martin Ryle and Kate Soper, London: Verso, 1990.

CUMMING, ROBERT DENOON. *Human Nature and History: A Study of the Development of Liberal Thought*. 2 vols. Chicago: University of Chicago Press, 1969.

DAMICO, ALFONSO J., ed. *Liberals on Liberalism*. Totowa, NJ: Rowman & Littlefield, 1986.

DERUGGIERO, GUIDO. *The History of European Liberalism*. Trans. R. G. Collingwood. Boston: Beacon Press, 1959.

FLATHMAN, RICHARD E. *Toward a Liberalism* . . . Ithaca, NY: Cornell University Press, 1989.

FREEDEN, MICHAEL. *The New Liberalism: An Ideology of Social Reform*. Oxford, England: Clarendon Press, 1978.

GALSTON, WILLIAM A. *Liberal Purposes: Goods, Virtues, and Diversity in the Liberal State*. Cambridge, England: Cambridge University Press, 1991.

GAUS, GERALD F. *The Modern Liberal Theory of Man*. London: Croom Helm/New York: St. Martin's, 1983.

———. *Value and Justification: The Foundations of Liberal Theory*. Cambridge, England: Cambridge University Press, 1990.

GRAY, JOHN. *Liberalism*. Minneapolis: University of Minnesota Press, 1986.

GUTMANN, AMY. *Liberal Equality*. Cambridge, England: Cambridge University Press, 1980.

———, ed. *Democracy and the Welfare State*. Princeton, NJ: Princeton University Press, 1988.

HALL, JOHN A. *Liberalism: Politics, Ideology and the Market*. Chapel Hill: University of North Carolina Press, 1988.

LASKI, HAROLD J. *The Rise of European Liberalism: An Essay in Interpretation*. London: George Allen & Unwin, 1936.

LOWI, THEODORE J. *The End of Liberalism: The Second Republic of the United States*. 2d ed. New York: Norton, 1979.

MACEDO, STEPHEN. *Liberal Virtues: Citizenship, Virtue and Community in Liberal Constitutionalism*. Oxford, England: Clarendon Press, 1990.

MANSFIELD, HARVEY C., JR. *The Spirit of Liberalism*. Cambridge, MA: Harvard University Press, 1978.

MASON, RONALD M. *Participatory and Workplace Democracy: A Theoretical Development in Critique of Liberalism*. Carbondale: Southern Illinois University Press, 1982.

MINOGUE, KENNETH. *The Liberal Mind*. New York: Vintage Books, 1963.

PATEMAN, CAROLE. *The Problem of Political Obligation: A Critical Analysis of Liberal Theory*. New York: Wiley, 1979.

RAWLS, JOHN. *Political Liberalism*. New York: Columbia University Press, 1993.

RAZ, JOSEPH. *The Morality of Freedom*. Oxford, England: Clarendon Press, 1986.

The Relevance of Liberalism. Boulder, CO: Westview Press, 1978.

ROSENBLUM, NANCY, ed. *Liberalism and the Moral Life*. Cambridge, MA: Harvard University Press, 1989.

ROTHENBERG, RANDALL. *The Neoliberals: Creating the New American Politics*. New York: Simon & Schuster, 1984.

SANDEL, MICHAEL J., ed. *Liberalism and Its Critics*. New York: New York University Press, 1984.

SCHAPIRO, J. SALWYN. *Liberalism: Its Meaning and History*. Princeton, NJ: Van Nostrand, 1958.

SCRUTON, ROGER. *The Meaning of Liberalism.* Harmondsworth, England: Penguin, 1980.

SIDORSKY, DAVID. *The Liberal Tradition in European Thought.* New York: Putnam's, 1970.

SPITZ, DAVID. *Essays in the Liberal Idea of Freedom.* Tucson: University of Arizona Press, 1964.

VOLKOMER, WALTER E., ed. *The Liberal Tradition in American Thought.* New York: Capricorn Books, 1969.

Communitarianism

AVINERI, SHLOMO, and AVNER DE-SHALIT, eds. *Communitarianism and Liberalism.* Oxford, England: Oxford University Press, 1992.

BELL, DANIEL. *Communitarianism and Its Critics.* Oxford, England: Clarendon Press, 1993.

ETZIONI, AMITAI. *The Spirit of Community: Rights, Responsibilities, and the Communitarian Agenda.* New York: Crown Publishers, 1993.

MULHALL, STEPHEN, and ADAM SWIFT. *Liberals and Communitarians.* Oxford, England: Basil Blackwell, 1992.

PART II

Feminism

6

Feminism

In the past thirty years, one system of beliefs has moved from being a small social and political movement that had split from the New Left,[1] to being an important ideology. That ideology, feminism, now has what still may be called a central core of agreed-on principles and a number of divisions and disagreements, which have become the current focus of attention by writers. Many theorists say that it should now be called *feminisms*, rather than feminism. Because there is clearly still a central core, it is accurate to keep the earlier label; feminism is simply at a point in its growth as a system of thought where the disagreements appear to outweigh the agreements.

Feminism is also continuing to grow as an international movement, a process that helps produce an awareness of differences among feminists. One of the most important continuing effects of feminist scholarship is on understanding human history. The rich and complex history of women in all fields of endeavor that has been discovered by feminist scholars has led to a major reevaluation of the focus of history in a rapidly growing number of countries.

Modern feminism developed from a position of opposition, opposition not to men but to the oppression of women and, first by implication and then

---

[1] On the New Left and the social and political movements of the period, see Lyman Tower Sargent, *New Left Thought: An Introduction* (Homewood, IL: Dorsey Press, 1972), and Jo Freeman, ed., *Social Movements of the Sixties and Seventies* (New York: Longman, 1983).

explicitly, all peoples who are treated as inferior by dominant groups. Feminists learned from the experience of African Americans and applied their understanding of racist oppression to their own experience—sexist oppression. African Americans had argued that racism in the United States had been internalized by blacks as well as whites; African Americans, who had been taught that they were inferior, came to believe in their own inferiority. This made it doubly difficult to break the pattern of oppression.

The resurgence of feminism originated in the West but became an international movement through the United Nations Decade for Women (1975–1985) and the development of networks of contacts among individuals and groups. The development of specific understanding of the ways that women are oppressed in each culture has led to an understanding of both the similarities and differences in women's positions throughout the world. The most significant changes are in the developing nations, but that is also where some of the most significant problems are.

Sexism is the belief that women are inferior to men. Racism is the belief that one group of people is inferior or superior based on factors such as skin color. But sexism and racism are just examples of the much broader point that people are oppressed both individually and as groups by socially constructed patterns of beliefs, attitudes, and practices. Like racism, but to an even greater extent, sexism is pervasive in our languages, art, literature, and religions. More obviously, sexism pervades politics and the economy. Sexism is part of what feminists oppose and hope to eliminate.

OPPRESSION

Language

Eliminating sexism will be extremely difficult since it is, feminists contend, part of all Western languages and part of many dearly held beliefs, including religious beliefs.

Feminists have often been both criticized and laughed at for proposing changes in language use to remove the male bias. But taking the argument seriously and looking at the history of language use, we can see the force of the point. For example, a female first-year university student is called a fresh*man*. Why? Well, at one time, not all that long ago, women could not attend a university, and the term implies that. Of course, language use changes, and most people use *freshman* to refer to both male and female first-year students, but the word is a relic of a past of greater sexual discrimination.[2]

To take another example, when Thomas Jefferson wrote in the Declaration of Independence that "All men are created equal," did he mean all human beings or just male human beings? We don't really know what Jefferson meant, but we do know that for many people at the time the words referred only to white, male human beings. And when we read major thinkers of the past, we

---

[2]See Dale Spender, *Man Made Language*, 2d ed. (London: Routledge & Kegan Paul, 1985).

often simply don't know what the word "man" means; we can read it to mean all human beings, but this may well lead us into simply missing what the author intended us to understand.[3]

A particularly interesting example can be seen in the novel *The Left Hand of Darkness* (1969) by Ursula K. Le Guin (1929–). When *The Left Hand of Darkness* was originally published, there was relatively little awareness of the gendered character of language, and Le Guin called her characters, who changed gender at different points in their lives, "he." The Twenty-Fifth Anniversary Edition (1994) of *The Left Hand of Darkness* addresses the criticism she received for her lack of awareness by providing sample chapters with four different sets of pronouns, one using invented pronouns and genderless personal nouns and titles, one using feminine pronouns and personal nouns rather than the masculine of the original, one using pronouns that reflect the changes her characters go through—neuter and gendered at different life stages, and one using masculine and feminine pronouns for the same character as that person goes through a transition. One's understanding of the text varies remarkably depending on the set of pronouns and personal nouns used, which makes this exercise by Le Guin a striking contribution to the debate on language.

Religion

In her "Introduction" to *The Women's Bible* (1895) Elizabeth Cady Stanton (1815–1902) wrote, "The only points in which I differ from all ecclesiastical teaching is that I do not believe that any man ever saw or talked with God, I do not believe that God inspired the Mosaic code, or told the historians what they say he did about woman, for all the religions on the face of the earth degrade her, and so long as woman accepts the position that they assign her, her emancipation is impossible."[4]

Traditional Judaism makes a rigid division between men and women, with women defined as inferior. Liberal Judaism advocates but does not always practice equality. Women have only recently been allowed to be rabbis in liberal congregations, and the acceptance of women as rabbis is spreading slowly even where it is the policy to allow them.[5]

The same pattern holds true in Christianity even though in the New Testament Christ is presented as treating men and women equally. Almost as soon

---

[3]See the following: Susan Moller Okin, *Women in Western Political Thought* (Princeton, NJ: Princeton University Press, 1979); *The Sexism of Social and Political Theory: Women and Reproduction from Plato to Nietzsche*, ed. Lorenne M. G. Clark and Lynda Lange (Toronto: University of Toronto Press, 1970); Diana H. Coole, *Women in Political Theory: From Ancient Misogyny to Contemporary Feminism* (Brighton, England: Wheatsheaf Books/Boulder, CO: Lynne Rienner, 1988); Jean Bethke Elshtain, *Public Man, Private Woman: Women in Social and Political Thought* (Princeton, NJ: Princeton University Press, 1981); and *Women in Western Political Philosophy: Kant to Nietzsche*, ed. Ellen Kennedy and Susan Mendus (New York: St. Martin's, 1987). A somewhat different perspective is given in Arlene M. Saxonhouse, *Women in the History of Political Thought: Ancient Greece to Machiavelli* (New York: Praeger, 1985).

[4]Elizabeth Cady Stanton, *The Woman's Bible* (New York: European Publishing Co., 1895), p. 12. Reprinted New York: Arno Press, 1972.

[5]See *On Being a Jewish Feminist: A Reader*, ed. Susannah Heschel (New York: Schocken Books, 1983).

as the first Christian churches were organized, women were placed in subordinate roles. In fact, some of the earliest heresies centered on the advocacy of equality for women,[6] and such heresies continued to appear from time to time, particularly around the Reformation7 and again in seventeenth-century England.[8]

Christian churches today are still divided over the role of women. The Episcopalian church in the United States decided, after a long, intense debate, to admit women to the priesthood, and an African American woman has been consecrated as a bishop in the United States. Some Episcopalian churches and priests have left the denomination as a result. The Anglican church has been deeply divided on the same issue. The Roman Catholic Church excludes women from the priesthood. Most Protestant denominations encourage the ordination of women as ministers, but there are still relatively few women ministers in most churches.

These divisions reflect a deep ambivalence about women in Christianity, particularly in the Roman Catholic Church. The conflict can be symbolized by two women, Eve the rebel and temptress and Mary the mother of Christ. Roughly the position has been that to the extent women emulate Mary and remain subordinate to men they are correctly fulfilling their natures; to the extent that they emulate Eve they are dangerous. As a result, many feminists see Eve, the rebel, as a symbol of the real strength of women, but the message that most churches present to women is one of subordination to men.

Socialization

Feminists argue that given the subordination implied in language and religion, it is not surprising that women have been socialized to believe that only certain narrowly defined roles are acceptable for them. As was seen in the first chapter, socialization is the process by which individuals are given the fundamental values of their society. In the case of women this means that they internalize the sense of inferiority that is still the dominant image of women, even in Western society. Feminists are arguing that the process of socialization should not eliminate options for women; women should be allowed to see all the possibilities open to them, not just a few. For example, at one time women could not be secretaries or telephone operators; these jobs were reserved for men both because women were not thought capable of doing them and because women were not expected to have paid employment. But, of course, poor women have always worked in paid employment, and women on farms have always worked along with other family members. And feminist historians have discovered multitudes of women who refused to be limited by stereotypes of acceptable female behavior. This illustrates how the work of recovering the history of

---

[6]See Elaine Pagels, *The Gnostic Gospels* (New York: Random House, 1979).

[7]See Norman Cohn, *The Pursuit of the Millennium: Revolutionary Millenarians and Mystical Anarchists of the Middle Ages* (London: Granada, 1970). ·

[8]For a general study of the period that discusses some of these heresies, see Christopher Hill, *The World Turned Upside Down: Radical Ideas During the English Revolution* (London: Temple Smith, 1972).

women, African Americans, ethnic minorities, and other groups provides psychological support for individuals living today and a basis for the political arguments against discrimination.

Abuse

In addition, feminists argue that women are socialized to accept both physical and mental mistreatment by men. Rape has been considered the most underreported crime in the United States, but the "discovery" of the extent of incest and child abuse indicates that there are a number of rarely reported crimes, almost all of which are crimes against women and children. Feminists argue that these crimes are underreported for a number of reasons. First, women who report rape must generally deal with male police officers who, even if they are—too rarely—sensitive to the woman's trauma, are still men. Second, the legal system has traditionally treated the woman as the offender. Third, women have been taught to accept such abuse from men and to consider it almost normal. For these reasons, women tend not to report the crime of rape. The same socialization process leads women to accept abuse from husbands or companions.

In addition to physical abuse, feminists note that women are subject to almost constant mental abuse. Such abuse, they contend, is pervasive in our culture. It consists, in large part, of treating women as objects or things rather than as individuals or persons. Clearly rape is the most extreme form of treating a person as an object, but many other ways of objectifying women do not involve physical abuse. Pornography, which may or may not include physical abuse, is an obvious case of treating women as objects. This has led many women's groups to mount campaigns against pornography.

Pornography does not directly touch most women, but feminists argue that there is a very fine line between the objectification found in pornography and that encountered by every woman in her daily life. Advertising that sells products using a woman's body as a lure is everywhere. Comments by men about a woman's body as she walks down the street are a form of assault. Women are constantly surrounded by these forms of mental abuse.

Physical and mental abuse are part of the oppression of women, as is the fact that in many jobs women are not paid the same as men for doing the same work; women are frequently sexually harassed at work as well. In addition, while overt political discrimination has been reduced, more subtle forms are still common.

THE DEVELOPMENT OF FEMINISM

Debates over the social roles of men and women go back to classical and biblical times. Both the Old and the New Testaments contain passages that have been used to argue either that women are inferior or that women are equal. Plato's *Republic* has been interpreted as contending both that women should be treated as equals to men and that they are naturally inferior to men.

Such debates are a constant of Western history. For example, in March of 1776 Abigail Adams (1744–1818) wrote to her husband John Adams (1735–1826), then involved in the movement for American independence and later

second president of the United States, entreating him to "Remember the Ladies" in the laws drawn up for the newly independent country. John Adams
responded, "I cannot but laugh," and continued, "We know better than to
repeal our Masculine systems."[9]

At about the same time in England, Mary Wollstonecraft (1759–1797) was
writing the first major work arguing for rights for women. Her *Vindication of the
Rights of Woman* (1792) was part of a European and American movement to
develop a theory of individual human rights. Thomas Paine's *The Rights of Man*
(1791–1792) and the French Declaration of Rights of Man and Citizen (1789)
are other expressions of the movement. But in most cases, these rights were only
for male human beings. Thus Wollstonecraft's book was an early and generally
neglected plea that the radical thinkers of the time should argue for human rights
rather than man's rights.

Earlier, writers like Mary Astell (1668–1731) and Sarah Scott (1723–1795)
had so despaired of being treated as autonomous human beings that they argued
that women should separate themselves from men.[10] And, as we shall see, many
women still argue today that real freedom for women can come only through
separation from men.

In the nineteenth century, the women's movement began as a general
movement for sexual equality and ended dominated by a single issue—the campaign for the vote. In the United States this pattern was repeated in the recent
past with the attempt to pass the Equal Rights Amendment (ERA) as the single
issue. In both cases the general feminist arguments tended to get lost in the
political campaign.

In the first half of the nineteenth century in the United States women like
Angelina Grimké (1805–1879), Sarah Grimké (1792–1873), Margaret Fuller
(1810–1850), and Frances Wright (1795–1852) became involved in the abolitionist movement and, from there, moved into other areas of reform including
the rights of women. As Angelina Grimké put it, "I recognize no rights but
human rights—I know nothing of man's rights and women's rights."[11] Later
Elizabeth Cady Stanton (1815–1902) argued for a wide-ranging emancipation
of women. As she put it in a famous statement to the court on being found
guilty of trying to vote, "You have trampled underfoot every vital principle of
our government. My natural rights, my civil rights, my political rights, are all
alike ignored. Robbed of the fundamental privilege of citizenship, I am degraded from the status of a citizen to that of a subject."[12]

---

[9]*Adams Family Correspondence*, ed. L. H. Butterfield, 4 vols. (Cambridge, MA: The Belknap Press of
Harvard University Press, 1963), 1: pp. 370, 382.

[10][Mary Astell.] *A Serious Proposal to the Ladies: For the Advancement of Their True and Greatest Interest*, by
A Lover of Her Sex (pseud.) (London: Printed for K. Wilkin, 1694), and [Sarah Scott.] *A Description of
Millenium Hall*, by A Gentleman on His Travels (pseud.) (London: Printed for J. Newbury, 1762).

[11]Angelina E. Grimké, *Letters to Catharine Beecher in Reply to an Essay on Slavery and Abolitionism Addressed to A. E. Grimké, Revised by the Author* (Boston: Printed by Isaac Knapp, 1838), p. 118. (Reprinted Arno Press & *The New York Times*, 1965).

[12]*History of Woman Suffrage*, ed. Elizabeth Cady Stanton, Susan B. Anthony, and Martha Joslyn Gage. 3
vols. (New York: Fowler & Wells, 1881), 2: 687. (Reprinted Arno Press & *The New York Times*, 1969).

Women's suffrage parade. The campaign to extend the vote to women was one of the longest-running reform movements in Western democracies. In most countries women did not gain the right to vote until well into the twentieth century. The campaign for the vote included marches, petitions, fasts, violent protests, and demonstrations in which women chained themselves to the doors of public buildings, and involved virtually all the tactics used in later protest movements. The suffrage movement was a single-issue campaign and, as such, many feminists today believe that it detracted from attempts to bring about more radical changes in the condition of women. At the time, many women felt that women with the vote would be able to bring about greater changes. So far this has not been true. (*Culver Pictures, Inc.*)

In 1848 a convention in Seneca Falls, New York, was called "to discuss the social, civil, and religious condition and rights of woman."[13] This convention passed the famous "Declaration of Sentiments" modeled on the U.S. Declaration of Independence. It stated "that it is the duty of the women of this country to secure to themselves their sacred right to the elective franchise."[14] It also stated, much more radically, in words similar to those of Henry David Thoreau's "On the Duty of Civil Disobedience" (1849), that "all laws which prevent women from occupying such a station in society as her conscience shall dictate, or which place her in a position inferior to that of man, are contrary to the great precept of nature, and therefore of no force or authority."[15]

Similar movements existed in most West European countries, and they generally followed the same pattern of radical demands for equality giving way to

[13]Ibid., 1: 67.

[14]Ibid., 1: 72.

[15]Ibid.

the sole demand for the vote. In Britain three works in the nineteenth century were particularly important in establishing the early stages of the women's movement. *Appeal of One-Half of the Human Race, Women, Against the Pretensions of Other Half, Men* (1825) by William Thompson (1775–1833), *The Enfranchisement of Women* (1851) by Harriet Taylor (1808–1858), and *The Subjection of Women* (1869) by John Stuart Mill (1806–1873) all pointed to the mistreatment of women and argued for emancipation. Emmeline Pankhurst (1858–1928) was one of the leaders in the movement for the vote. Her group, the Women's Social and Political Union, used civil disobedience in the campaign. As a result, Pankhurst and many of her followers were repeatedly jailed, thus bringing more attention to the movement. Her daughters Christobel (1880–1958) and Sylvia (1882–1960) were also active. Sylvia attacked marriage and bore a child out of wedlock.

Before World War I the single most important issue for the women's movement besides the vote was birth control. The most prominent figure in the birth control movement was Margaret Sanger (1883–1966), but she was supported by others like the anarchist Emma Goldman (1869–1940), whose broad radical agenda included many issues of particular interest to women. Others who were concerned with more than the vote included Charlotte Perkins Gilman (1860–1935), whose journal *The Forerunner* was a forceful advocate for women, and Jane Addams (1860–1935), who exemplified and argued for an active role for women in improving life in the cities. Gilman's *Women and Economics* (1898) was a widely acclaimed study that argued for the need to restructure social institutions to permit women to work. Her utopian novel *Moving the Mountain* (1911) shows fictionally such a changed society.

When the vote was won there was little noticeable effect on social policy. But with the coming of World War II women were encouraged to join the work force for the war effort and learned to do things that they had been taught were impossible for women.[16] After the war these same women were told to go back home and give up the money and independence that they had come to expect. The publication in France in 1949 of Simone de Beauvoir's *Le Deuxième Sexe* (published in English in 1952 as *The Second Sex*), a study of the treatment of women by various academic disciplines, helped fan the anger at this loss.

Still, it wasn't until the 1960s and the publication of *The Feminine Mystique* (1963) by Betty Friedan (1921–), combined with the rejection of women's issues by the New Left, that a renewed feminist movement began. While this early movement was predominantly white, a number of African American women were also active in the burgeoning feminist movement. Today, the women's movement is acutely aware of the importance of speaking to the needs of minority women and to those of women in the developing nations. And, of course, these women are finding their voices and speaking for themselves.

---

[16]See Susan M. Hartmann, *The Home Front and Beyond: American Women in the 1940s* (Boston: Twayne, 1982), and, for a fictional treatment, Marge Piercy, *Gone to Soldiers* (New York: Summit Books, 1987).

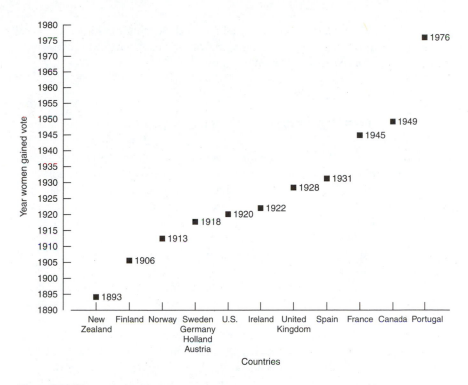

Figure 6-1 Women gain the vote.

All feminists share a concern with freeing women from the tyranny of unwanted childbearing. This concern has been called *reproductive rights* or the right of a woman to control her own body or, more recently, *reproductive freedom* in an attempt to separate it from the narrow, legal conception of rights.[17] For most feminists this means that all methods of birth control should be available and either free or very inexpensive and, since no system of birth control is 100 percent effective, that safe and affordable abortions should be available for all women. For a few feminists this means the end of biological motherhood and the development of artificial means of reproduction, but for most feminists it means the transformation of society that will allow women to fully participate in both reproduction and production. They envision a remodeling of all institutions of socialization so that all human beings can participate fully in all life activities as they freely and independently choose.

There is a difference among feminists on this issue. Some feminists assume that men are capable of the changes needed; others argue that a much more radical transformation of social institutions with a resulting change in men will

[17]See, for example, Alison M. Jaggar, *Feminist Politics and Human Nature* (Totowa, NJ: Rowman & Allanheld/Brighton, England: Harvester Press, 1983), pp. 318–324.

be necessary before men can participate fully in the raising of children.[18] They argue that without this change increased male participation in child rearing will only result in the reduction of women's power.

THE PERSONAL IS THE POLITICAL

In opposing all forms of discrimination against women, feminists have argued that what is political needs to be redefined. If, as some would have it, politics is about power, there is politics between men and women both individually and as groups. There are power relations between friends and lovers and within families. For example, in the family, who makes decisions and how they are made are political questions in this sense, as are questions about who spends how much and on what, who allocates tasks around the house, and the division of labor reflected in such allocation.

An interesting case is housework. This is an important issue because it includes the traditional sexual division of labor in which men work outside the home for a wage and, if a man's wage is high enough for the woman not to work but not high enough to hire servants, the woman works at home without a wage. And, of course, if a woman works outside the home, she still must do the housework. Housework was and is the largest sector of unwaged labor in the economy. Anyone attempting to replace that unpaid labor with paid labor finds that certain aspects of it command substantial wages because, although the work is not well paid, long hours are required. Cooking and child care can be very expensive; regular cleaning is not cheap. Housework is also repetitive and not particularly exciting work. Most people—men and women alike—if given a choice, don't do it.

For these reasons, housework provides an interesting case of work allocation in a modern household. Generally, although there is much awareness of a change toward men helping more (the word *help* implies assistance freely donated, not required) around the house, the traditional pattern remains common with the added factor that the woman works outside the home for a wage as well as doing the same work in the home as before. In other words, the pattern of sexual division of labor that once applied only to the poor has spread to the middle class. Thus both the economics and the internal dynamics of housework illustrate the maxim that the personal is the political. Similar questions affect all relations between women and men.

Another way of putting the situation in which women find themselves can be seen in an expansion of the notion of the personal as the political. If all human relationships are power relationships, whatever else they may also be, women as individuals and as a group have been and are among the powerless. Some

---

[18]See Phyllis Chesler, *Mothers on Trial: The Battle for Children and Custody* (New York: McGraw-Hill, 1986) for a presentation of some of the issues involved.

examples can illustrate the point. When men were telephone operators and secretaries, these positions were adequately paid positions with some prestige; when these positions became "women's work," they changed into low-paid positions with little prestige. When men were the primary white-collar workers, such jobs earned more than blue-collar jobs; now that women are the primary white-collar workers, the pay relationship has reversed.

THE FEMINIST RESPONSES

Feminists agree on some responses to oppression, but they also disagree. Almost all feminists agree that fundamental answers to the problem of women's position in modern society are freedom and equality, but there are disagreements over both the meaning of these terms and how to achieve the desired result. All feminists agree that these changes should not benefit women alone. They oppose racism and homophobia (the belief in the inferiority of homosexuals) as well as sexism, and they argue that any discrimination against any human being is an attack on all human beings. And, they agree, men will also benefit in a free and egalitarian society.

There are a number of ways to classify the feminist responses; none is entirely satisfactory because all group people who have important disagreements and separate people who agree on significant questions. No set of categories is currently acceptable, but it still makes sense to use very general labels—*reform* and *radical,* even though what is "reform" and what is "radical" depend on where one stands—for the two ends of the spectrum. And I have chosen, following Angela Miles, to call the middle group *integrative feminists* because they generally try to recognize and incorporate the concerns of all feminists.

Reform Feminism

Reform feminists argue that the basic pattern of society is generally acceptable but that changes are needed so that women are not put at a disadvantage by their sex. Reform feminists want an equal opportunity to compete with men. Reform feminists propose that means be found, such as improved and expanded day-care facilities and improved parental leave policies, that will more readily allow women to combine paid employment and motherhood. Obviously, these proposals also suggest that men must change their attitude to sharing responsibility for child rearing.

Reform feminists in the United States were particularly supportive of the Equal Rights Amendment, which read:

Section 1. Equality of rights under the law shall not be denied by the United States or by any State on account of sex.

Section 2. The Congress shall have the power to enforce, by appropriate legislation, the provisions of this article.

Section 3. This amendment shall take effect two years after the ratification.

The amendment was defeated by forces that considered it dangerously radical or unnecessary.

Integrative Feminism

Integrative feminists have shown the ways in which men have created a male-centered way of understanding the world that severely limits one's ability to conceptualize human relations that are not hierarchical and patriarchal. The integrative feminist's goal is to break through those mental barriers as well as the political, economic, and cultural barriers that keep all human beings from becoming fully human.[19] For example, Nancy Hartsock has noted that feminists have begun to reconceptualize our notion of power. Power as dominance will give way to power as "energy and competence."[20] All our ways of thinking need to undergo a similar revolution.

Hence, integrative feminists are arguing for a fundamental transformation of not only our political and economic lives but our social, cultural, and personal lives as well. Integrative feminism is truly revolutionary.

Radical Feminism

According to Alison Jaggar, radical feminism, with some exceptions, argues for:

1. Lesbianism—the sexual separation from men, the sexual bonding with women, and the end of the biological family;

2. Development of a woman-centered culture to replace the male-centered culture; and

3. Confrontation with patriarchal institutions.[21]

While not all radical feminists accept all these points and most feminists advocate the second point, radical feminists are building their future world today by practicing all of their principles.

Lesbian communes exist in all Western countries. Shulamith Firestone (1944–) argues for the abandonment of the biological family in *The Dialectic of Sex* (1970), and Marge Piercy (1936–) presents a radical feminist perspective in her novel *Woman on the Edge of Time* (1976). The development of a woman's culture can be seen in the works of Judy Chicago (1939–) and others. And attacks on patriarchal institutions are widespread; the most fundamental such attack can be found in the work of Andrea Dworkin (1946–), particularly her *Intercourse* (1987).

---

[19]See Nancy C. M. Hartsock, *Money, Sex, and Power: Toward a Feminist Historical Materialism* (New York: Longman, 1983); Mary O'Brien, *The Politics of Reproduction* (Boston: Routledge & Kegan Paul, 1981); Angela Miles, "Integrative Feminism," *Fireweed* 19 (1984): 55–81; and Miles's "Feminism, Equality, and Liberation," *Canadian Journal of Women and the Law* 1 (1985): 42–68.

[20]Hartsock, *Money, Sex, and Power*, pp. 224–225.

[21]Jaggar, *Feminist Politics and Human Nature*, pp. 271–286.

CURRENT TRENDS

Feminism is a living ideology and, as a result, a number of changes are taking place. First, feminism is becoming more of a worldwide phenomenon.[22] Second, feminists are developing a relationship with religion that goes beyond the reformist approach of trying to get women accepted as ministers, priests, and rabbis to a reconsideration of theology. In most Western religions God is presented as definitely male, or in more sophisticated versions, with a masculine psychology. Feminists are questioning this version of God, reconsidering the history of male dominance of religion and the resultant male-oriented theologies, and asking the most basic questions possible about the nature of deity.

Third, many feminists are trying to heal a major breach with women who define themselves as wives and mothers. These feminists argue that all the experiences of women are valuable and should be recognized as such. Many feminists are becoming concerned with the need to reconsider what is perceived to be an opposition to the family among feminists. The opposition has been real, but many feminists want to overcome it. Others believe that the family is a serious problem for most women, so the attempt to heal one breach has opened a different one.

Fourth, feminists are divided over pornography. While most feminists consider pornography as a primary example of the subjection of women, they are divided about how to respond to it. Some feminists see pornography as a question of freedom of the press, but the leaders of the feminist opposition to pornography, such as Andrea Dworkin and Catharine A. MacKinnon, argue that freedom of expression is based on the false assumption of general equality. The fact of gender inequality invalidates negative liberty. Thus pornography is not a question of civil liberties but an issue "central to the institutionalization of male dominance."[23] One concern of many feminists who think that Dworkin and MacKinnon are essentially correct is that the antipornography position has been widely supported by the far right, which otherwise is generally opposed to feminist positions. In *The Handmaid's Tale* (1986) the Canadian novelist Margaret Atwood (1939–) presents a future that suppresses women that was brought about by just such a coalition of feminists and the far right; the scenario worries many feminists who are deeply concerned about pornography.

Fifth, feminists are concerned with the division between public and private mentioned in discussing conservatism and liberalism. Traditionally women were expected to lead a private life and not venture into the public sphere. Clearly one of the concerns of feminism has been to change that expectation and move women into public life. This concern is not controversial, but what is becoming controversial is the question of community values versus individual rights. Feminism has a tradition of communitarian values based on the assump-

---

[22]See Barbara J. Nelson and Najma Chowdhury, eds., *Women and Politics Worldwide* (New Haven: Yale University Press, 1994).

[23]See Catharine A. MacKinnon, "Pornography," in her *Feminism Unmodified: Discourses on Life and Law* (Cambridge, MA: Harvard University Press, 1987), p. 146.

tion, among other assumptions, that women will respect the rights of other women. This assumption has, unfortunately, not always been borne out by reality.

Finally, feminism is in the process of changing the focus in the concept of equality from *sameness* to *difference*. While many feminists are concerned with the implications that difference has in possibly supporting the dominance of powerful groups who justify their dominance on the basis of difference, others feel that difference provides such important connections to other women and other subjected or subordinate groups that it can be defended without giving away too much. For some theorists the differences are biologically based, but for most the basis for difference is the shared experience of subordination. This shared experience provides the basis for a new sense of equality that recognizes, accepts, and values diversity without losing the rights that all individuals have as human beings. Thus "difference feminism" is thought of as a way of strengthening equality rather than diminishing it.

Feminism in the Third World

An emerging issue throughout Third World countries is the treatment of women. In many of these countries women have the right to vote and other legally defined rights but are still treated as the property of their fathers and husbands. The so-called dowry murders in India are a major example of the problem, as is the still-common practice of genital mutilation as practiced on women.[24] In addition, in some Islamic countries women are required to wear the *chador*, in which they are covered from head to foot.[25]

At the same time feminism is growing throughout developing countries. Women are insisting on significant changes in their status, and legal gains have been made. It is also true that women have held positions of considerable power in developing countries; there have been and are a number of women prime ministers in these countries, like Benazir Bhutto of Pakistan. Thus the picture is complex. Traditional restrictions on women are strong, but some women have advanced further than in many parts of the West. In addition, some Third World countries like Egypt and India have long-standing, homegrown feminist movements, and Western versions of feminism are beginning to affect women in some countries. Still, women in developing countries have only begun to make significant steps toward the goal of achieving equality in daily life.[26] They are fighting a strong tradition but have on their side the belief among most elites that change is necessary.

---

[24]See Robin Morgan and Gloria Steinem, "The International Crime of Genital Mutilation," in Gloria Steinem, *Outrageous Acts and Everyday Rebellion* (New York: New American Library, 1983), pp. 292–300; and Mary Daly, "African Genital Mutilation: The Unspeakable Atrocities," in her *Gyn/Ecology: The Metaethics of Radical Feminism* (Boston: Beacon Press, 1978), pp. 153–177.

[25]See Azar Tabari and Nahid Yeganeh, *In the Shadow of Islam: The Women's Movement in Iran* (London: Zed Books, 1982) for a discussion of the role of women in Islam.

[26]See Kumari Jayawardena, *Feminism and Nationalism in the Third World* (London: Zed Books, 1986); and Bie Nio Ong, "Women and the Transition to Socialism in Sub-Saharan Africa," in *Africa: Problems in the Transition to Socialism*, ed. Barry Munslow (London: Zed Books, 1986), pp. 72–94.

CONCLUSION

Feminism is developing a critical apparatus for analyzing contemporary society that is challenging all contemporary ideologies. Feminist philosophers and political philosophers are proposing new ways of understanding the world. Feminist economists are analyzing the economic roles of women and suggesting a transformation of economic life.

Specifically, feminists have discovered the central role that women play in the agricultural economies of Third World countries and are arguing that the bias-rooted failure to recognize this fact has undercut all attempts to improve agricultural production in developing countries. Feminist writers and artists are developing a substantial body of literature and art that speaks to different concerns than had been previously addressed.

Feminists are encouraging all human beings to envision the possibility of a society rid of sexism, racism, homophobia, and all the other ways in which human beings have subjugated other human beings. At present feminists are divided over exactly how to go about this transformation, and reform feminists are not convinced that it is either necessary or desirable, but feminism is potentially the most radical of ideologies and the most likely to change the way most of us live today.

SUGGESTED READINGS

BENHABIB, SEYLA, and DRUCILLA CORNELL, eds. *Feminism as Critique: On the Politics of Gender.* Minneapolis: University of Minnesota Press, 1987.

BLEIER, RUTH, ed. *Feminist Approaches to Science.* New York: Pergamon Press, 1986.

BOCK, GISELA, and SUSAN JAMES, eds. *Beyond Equality and Difference: Citizenship, Feminist Politics and Female Subjectivity.* London: Routledge, 1992.

BROWNMILLER, SUSAN. *Against Our Will: Men, Women and Rape.* New York: Simon & Schuster, 1975.

BRYSON, VALERIE. *Feminist Political Theory: An Introduction.* New York: Paragon House, 1992.

CAPLAN, PAT, ed. *The Cultural Construction of Sexuality.* London: Tavistock Publications, 1987.

CARD, CLAUDIA, ed. *Feminist Ethics.* Lawrence: University Press of Kansas, 1991.

CHODOROW, NANCY. *The Reproduction of Mothering: Psychoanalysis and the Sociology of Gender.* Berkeley: University of California Press, 1978.

———. *Feminism and Psychoanalytic Theory.* New Haven, CT: Yale University Press, 1989.

COHEN, JEAN L. "Redescribing Privacy: Identity, Difference, and the Abortion Controversy." *Columbia Journal of Gender and Law* 3, no. 1 (1992): 43–117.

COLLINS, PATRICIA HILL. *Black Feminist Thought: Knowledge, Consciousness, and the Politics of Empowerment.* Boston: Unwin Hyman, 1990.

CONOVER, PAMELA JOHNSTON, and VIRGINIA GRAY. *Feminism and the New Right: Conflict over the American Family.* New York: Praeger, 1983.

DALY, MARY. *Beyond God the Father: Toward a Philosophy of Women's Liberation.* Boston: Beacon Press, 1973.

———. *Gyn/Ecology: The Metaethics of Radical Feminism.* Boston: Beacon Press, 1978.

———. *Pure Lust: Elemental Feminist Philosophy*. Boston: Beacon Press, 1984.

DANN, CHRISTINE. *Up From Under: Women and Liberation in New Zealand, 1970–1985*. Wellington: Allen & Unwin/Port Nicholson Press, 1985.

DAVIS, ANGELA Y. *Women, Race & Class*. New York: Random House, 1981.

DAVIS, FLORA. *Moving the Mountain: The Women's Movement in America Since 1960*. New York: Simon & Schuster, 1991.

DE BEAUVOIR, SIMONE. *The Second Sex*. Trans. and ed. H. M. Parshley. New York: Knopf, 1952.

DI STEFANO CHRISTINE. *Configurations of Masculinity: A Feminist Perspective on Modern Political Theory*. Ithaca: Cornell University Press, 1991.

DURAN, JANE. *Toward a Feminist Epistemology*. Savage, MD: Rowman & Littlefield, 1991.

DWORKIN, ANDREA. *Woman Hating*. New York: Dutton, 1974.

———. *Our Blood: Prophecies and Discourses on Sexual Politics*. New York: Harper & Row, 1976.

———. *Ice and Fire*. New York: Weidenfeld & Nicholson, 1986.

———. *Intercourse*. New York: Free Press, 1987.

EISENSTEIN, ZILLAH R. *The Color of Gender: Reimagining Democracy*. Berkeley: University of California Press, 1994.

EL SAADAWI, NAWAL. *The Hidden Face of Eve: Women in the Arab World*. Trans. and ed. Sherif Hetata. London: Zed Press, 1980.

ELSHTAIN, JEAN BETHKE. *Meditations on Modern Political Thought: Masculine/Feminine Themes from Luther to Arendt*. New York: Praeger, 1986.

———. *Public Man, Private Woman: Women in Social and Political Thought*. Princeton, NJ: Princeton University Press, 1981.

———, ed. *The Family in Political Thought*. Amherst: University of Massachusetts Press, 1982.

———. *Women and War*. New York: Basic Books, 1987.

———. *Power Trips and Other Journeys: Essays in Feminism as Civic Discourse*. Madison: University of Wisconsin Press, 1990.

EVANS, SARA M. *Personal Politics: The Roots of Women's Liberation in the Civil Rights Movement and the New Left*. New York: Knopf, 1979.

FARGAINS, SONDRA. *Situating Feminism: From Thought to Action*. Thousand Oaks, CA: Sage, 1994.

FELDSTEIN, RICHARD, and JUDITH ROOF, eds. *Feminism and Psychoanalysis*. Ithaca, NY: Cornell University Press, 1989.

FERGUSON, ANN. *Sexual Democracy: Women, Oppression, and Revolution*. Boulder, CO: Westview Press, 1991.

FIRESTONE, SHULAMITH. *The Dialectic of Sex: The Case for Feminist Revolution*. New York: Morrow, 1970.

FRANZWAY, SUZANNE, DIANNE COURT, and R. W. CONNELL. *Staking a Claim: Feminism, Bureaucracy and the State*. Sydney, Australia: Allen & Unwin, 1989.

FRASER, NANCY. *Unruly Practices: Power, Discourse, and Gender in Contemporary Social Theory*. Minneapolis: University of Minnesota Press, 1989.

FRIEDAN, BETTY. *The Feminine Mystique*. New York: Norton, 1963.

GILLIGAN, CAROL. *In a Different Voice: Psychological Theory and Women's Development*. Cambridge, MA: Harvard University Press, 1982.

HARTSOCK, NANCY. *Money, Sex, and Power: Toward a Feminist Historical Materialism*. New York: Longman, 1983.

HENNESSY, ROSEMARY. *Materialist Feminism and the Politics of Discourse*. New York: Routledge, 1993.

HESCHEL, SUSANNAH, ed. *On Being a Jewish Feminist: A Reader*. New York: Schocken Books, 1983.

HIRSCH, MARIANNE, and EVELYN FOX KELLER, eds. *Conflicts in Feminism*. New York: Routledge, 1990.

HIRSCHMANN, NANCY J. *Rethinking Obligation: A Feminist Method for Political Theory*. Ithaca: Cornell University Press, 1992.

HOOKS, BELL. *Ain't I a Woman? Black Women and Feminism*. Boston: South End Press, 1981.

JAYAWARDENA, KUMARI. *Feminism and Nationalism in the Third World*. London: Zed Books, 1986.

JONES, KATHLEEN B. *Compassionate Authority: Democracy and the Representation of Women*. New York: Routledge, 1993.

MACKINNON, CATHARINE A. *Sexual Harassment of Working Women: A Case of Sex Discrimination*. New Haven, CT: Yale University Press, 1979.

————. *Feminism Unmodified: Discourses on Life and Law*. Cambridge, MA: Harvard University Press, 1987.

————. *Toward a Feminist Theory of the State*. Cambridge, MA: Harvard University Press, 1989.

————. *Only Words*. Cambridge, MA: Harvard University Press, 1993.

MERCHANT, CAROLYN. *The Death of Nature: Women, Ecology, and the Scientific Revolution*. San Francisco: Harper & Row, 1980.

MERNISSI, FATIMA. *Beyond the Veil: Male-Female Dynamics in a Modern Muslim Society*. Rev. ed. Bloomington: Indiana University Press, 1987.

MILES, ANGELA. "Integrative Feminism." *Fireweed* 19 (1984): 55–81.

————. *Feminist Radicalism in the 1980s*. Montréal: CultureTexts, 1985.

MILLETT, KATE. *Sexual Politics*. Garden City, NY: Doubleday, 1970.

MINOW, MARTHA. *Making All the Difference: Inclusion, Exclusion, and American Law*. Ithaca, NY: Cornell University Press, 1990.

MITCHELL, JULIET. *Women's Estate*. New York: Pantheon, 1971.

MORGAN, ROBIN, ed. *Sisterhood Is Powerful: An Anthology of Writings from the Women's Liberation Movement*. New York: Random House, 1970.

NELSON, BARBARA J., and NAJMA CHOWDHURY, eds. *Women and Politics Worldwide*. New Haven, CT: Yale University Press, 1994.

OAKLEY, ANN. *The Sociology of Housework*. 2d ed. Oxford, England: Harvard University Press, 1985.

O'BRIEN, MARY. *The Politics of Reproduction*. Boston: Routledge & Kegan Paul, 1981.

OKIN, SUSAN MOLLER. *Women in Western Political Thought*. Princeton, NJ: Princeton University Press, 1979.

————. *Justice, Gender, and the Family*. New York: Basic Books, 1989.

————. *Reproducing the World: Essays in Feminist Theory*. Boulder, CO: Westview Press, 1989.

PATEMAN, CAROLE. *The Sexual Contract*. Stanford, CA: Stanford University Press, 1988.

————. *The Disorder of Women: Democracy, Feminism and Political Theory*. Cambridge, England: Polity Press, 1989.

———— and ELIZABETH GROSS, eds. *Feminist Challenges: Social and Political Theory*. Boston: Northeastern University Press, 1987.

PHELAN, SHANE. *Identity Politics: Lesbian Feminism and the Limits of Community*. Philadelphia: Temple University Press, 1989.

PHILLIPS, ANNE. *Engendering Democracy*. University Park: Pennsylvania State University Press, 1991.

————, ed. *Feminism and Equality*. New York: New York University Press, 1987.

REARDON, BETTY A. *Women and Peace: Feminist Visions of Global Security*. Albany: State University of New York Press, 1993.

RING, JENNIFER. *Modern Political Theory and Contemporary Feminism: A Dialectical Analysis*. Albany: State University of New York Press, 1991.

ROTHMAN, BARBARA KATZ. *Recreating Motherhood: Ideology and Technology in Patriarchal Society*. New York: Norton, 1989.

ROWBOTHAM, SHEILA. *Women in the Movement: Feminism and Social Action*. New York: Routledge, 1992.

RUETHER, ROSEMARY RADFORD. *Sexism and God-talk: Toward a Feminist Theology*. Boston: Beacon Press, 1983.

RUSSELL, DIANA E. H. *The Politics of Rape: The Victim's Perspective*. New York: Stein and Day, 1984.

SARGENT, LYDIA, ed. *Women and Revolution: A Discussion of the Unhappy Marriage of Marxism and Feminism*. Boston: South End Press, 1981.

SHAARAWI, HUDA. *Harem Years: The Memoirs of an Egyptian Feminist (1879 – 1924)*. Translated and edited by Margot Badran. New York: The Feminist Press and The City University of New York, 1987.

SHERIDAN, SUSAN, ed. *Grafts: Feminist Cultural Criticism*. London: Verso, 1988.

SPELMAN, ELIZABETH. *Inessential Woman: Problems of Exclusion in Feminist Thought*. Boston: Beacon Press, 1988.

SPENDER, DALE. *Man Made Language*. 2d ed. London: Routledge & Kegan Paul, 1985.

STEINEM, GLORIA. *Outrageous Acts and Everyday Rebellion*. New York: New American Library, 1983.

SUNSTEIN, CASS R., ed. *Feminism & Political Theory*. Chicago: University of Chicago Press, 1990.

"Symposium on Feminism and Political Theory." *Ethics* 99, no. 2 (January 1989): 219–406.

TONG, ROSEMARIE. *Women, Sex, and the Law*. Totowa, NJ: Rowman & Allanheld, 1984.

———. *Feminist Thought: A Comprehensive Introduction*. Boulder, CO: Westview Press, 1989.

TREBLICOT, JOYCE, ed. *Mothering: Essays in Feminist Theory*. Totowa, NJ: Rowman & Allanheld, 1983.

WELCH, SHARON. *Communities of Resistance and Solidarity: A Feminist Theology of Liberation*. Maryknoll, NY: Orbis Books, 1985.

WILLIS, ELLEN. *No More Nice Girls: Countercultural Essays*. Hanover, NH: Wesleyan University Press. Published by University Press of New England, 1992.

PART III

Marxism

7

The Marxist Tradition

Karl Marx (1818–1883) and his followers produced one of the dominant ideologies from World War I into the early 1990s—communism—and a number of variants that have been influential in many parts of the world. Because it has been, and remains, so important, communism is the focus of this chapter. But because some of the confusion surrounding and debates over communism are the result of confusion among various lines of Marxist thought, other forms of Marxism are discussed.

Communism is based on the writings of Marx and Friedrich Engels (1820–1895),[1] and the theoretical structure based on these writings is still widely respected. Interestingly, that respect is today greater in the West than in the East.

Communism was the result of a line of intellectual and political development from Marx and Engels through V. I. Lenin (original name Vladimir Ilyich Ulyanov, 1870–1924) and others that emphasized the authoritarian and centralist aspects of Marx's thought. An alternative Marxist tradition has always been available that stressed decentralist and democratic aspects of Marx's thought, but it has always been a minority position. It is this latter tradition, together with

---

[1] For our purposes Marx and Engels can be treated together. They differ, but their differences on the questions discussed in this chapter are not great. For a complete discussion of Engels, see Friedrich Engels, *Selected Writings*, ed. W. O. Henderson (Baltimore: Penguin, 1967); and Fritz Nova, *Friedrich Engels: His Contributions to Political Theory* (London: Vision Press, 1967). Also see Henrich Gemkow et al. *Friedrich Engels: A Biography* (Dresden, Germany: Verlag Zeit im Bild, 1972).

what are widely recognized as Marx's fundamental insights into social relations in general and the effects of capitalism in particular, that explain Marx's continuing importance. In addition, the collapse of communism has not convinced all Communists that communism has failed. Thus, it is still important to understand various parts of the Marxist tradition.

KARL MARX AND FRIEDRICH ENGELS

To do so, it is essential to look first at the philosophic basis found in the thought of Karl Marx and Friedrich Engels and then to turn to the developments and changes made by others.

Alienation—the Young Marx

In his twenties Marx wrote a number of works that have proven controversial to this day. Most writers now argue that these early writings are central to any understanding of Marx and that the later writings grow out of and develop the themes of the early writings. Those who stress the early writings argue that authoritarian communism lost sight of the human concerns that motivated Marx.

The central concept in these early writings is *alienation*, particularly found in the work known as *The Economic and Philosophic Manuscripts of 1844* (first published in full in 1932). Alienation refers to a relationship between two or more people or parts of oneself in which one is cut off from, a stranger to, or alien to, the other. It has been a major theme in modern literature, with works such as Albert Camus's *The Stranger* (1942), Jean-Paul Sartre's *Nausea* (1938) and *No Exit* (1945), and Samuel Beckett's *Waiting for Godot* (1952), to name four of the best known, depicting various forms of alienation.

For Marx it meant something more specific. He argued that in capitalism, for reasons that will become apparent later, individuals become cut off from— out of tune with—themselves, their families and friends, and their work. They are not and cannot be whole, fully developed human beings in a capitalist society.[2]

For Marx, private property and alienation are intimately linked because the most basic form of alienation is alienated labor, or labor that is sold like an object. Of course, what is being sold is part of a human being. A worker sells her or his strength, effort, skill, and time; so for much of the worker's life someone else has purchased and, thus, has the use of the worker (and in Marx's time this was usually a minimum of twelve to fourteen hours a day, six or seven days a week). Alienated labor produced an alienation of self; no longer whole human beings, workers could not establish full human relationships with others, who were in the same situation. This is the human meaning of capitalism for

---

[2]For extended commentaries, see István Mészáros, *Marx's Theory of Alienation* (London: Merlin Press, 1970); Bertell Ollman, *Alienation*, 2d ed. (Cambridge, England: Cambridge University Press, 1976); and Adam Schaff, "Alienation as a Social and Philosophical Problem," *Social Praxis* 3, nos. 1–2 (1975): 7–26.

Marx: people cut off from self, others, and work. It is this condition that Marx was determined to change; it was the reason for his writings and his revolutionary activity.

Marx's Critique of Capitalism

The Marxian analysis of society and the forces operating in it is a commentary on and condemnation of industrial capitalism. Marx argued both that capitalism was an essential stage in the development to socialism and that capitalism was the most progressive economic system developed so far. Marx attributed most of the ills of contemporary society to the capitalist system. Many evils were inherent in developing industrialism, and Marx was not the only one to point them out. His comments are interesting, though, because they indicate a great deal about Marx and the way he viewed the world. In addition, both Marxian communism and contemporary communism are attempts to solve the problems of industrialism. Much of the appeal of Marxism is found in these criticisms of the industrial system. An understanding of communism is impossible without a careful consideration of these criticisms. For Marx economic relationships are the foundation of the entire social system; therefore, his economic criticisms must be considered first.

For Marx, the most fundamental fact of life is that people must produce goods before they can do anything else. They must also reproduce themselves, but they cannot even do that unless they are capable of feeding themselves. Thus material production or economic relationships are basic to all life.

The primary points in Marxian economics are the *labor theory of value*, the doctrine of *subsistence wages*, and the theory of *surplus value*. Marx used *value* in the sense of real costs in labor. Nothing else was considered. In other words, the value (not the price) of any manufactured object was based on the amount of labor time consumed in producing it.

Marx argued that nothing had value without labor. Neither capital nor land is of any value until labor is added. This is the labor theory of value. An individual has to work a certain number of hours or days to produce enough to provide a living. Marx assumed that the capitalist would pay workers only enough to keep them alive, a subsistence wage. Marx made this assumption because:

1. There was a surplus of laborers, and there was no need to pay more.
2. He could not conceive of the capitalist paying more than absolutely necessary.
3. He assumed that the capitalist would be faced with a series of economic crises that would make it impossible for the capitalist to pay more.

In addition, Marx believed that the profit of the capitalist was taken from the amount produced over and above the wages paid the worker. This is the theory of surplus value and can be used to explain more fully the doctrine of subsistence wages. As capitalists replaced workers with machines (sometimes called dead labor), they would have to reduce wages to keep up their rate of profit since profit came only from surplus value extracted from labor. They would also be able to reduce wages because replacing workers with machines

Karl Marx (1818–1883) was the father of modern communism. His work as a philosopher, political thinker, and economist has made him one of the single most influential
thinkers of all time. Born in Germany, Marx spent much of his life in England studying
contemporary society and actively working for revolution. In association with Friedrich
Engels (1820–1895), he published their famous call for revolution, *Manifesto of the Communist Party*, in 1848. He published the first volume of his study of contemporary economics, *Capital*, in 1867; Engels undertook the publication of the other volumes.
Today, every word that Marx wrote is carefully studied by a wide range of scholars and
revolutionists for clues to his thought. (*Library of Congress*)

produced a pool of unemployed workers who must compete for whatever wages
the capitalists choose to pay. Of course, the real reason that capitalists are constantly pushing down wages is to maximize profits, and Marx was certainly
aware of that fact.

Hence Marx's major economic criticism revolved around the exploitation
of the majority, the proletariat or workers, by the minority, the bourgeoisie or
capitalists. His concern was not purely economic but was also centered on the
extent to which the system kept proletarians from ever fulfilling their potentials
as individuals. It was impossible for them to improve themselves in any way, and
they were denied education and were thereby kept from any real understanding
of their deplorable position.

The state was the tool of the dominant class, the bourgeoisie, and was used
to suppress, violently if necessary, any attempt by the proletariat to better themselves. To Marx and most other radical theorists of the day, the *state* referred to
all those officials, such as the police, the army, bureaucrats, and so forth, who
could be, and were, used to suppress the workers. In addition, Marx contended
that as long as the bourgeoisie was the dominant class, the government would
be its tool and could not be made responsive to the needs of other classes. Marx
always saw the state or the government as the tool of the dominant class, whatever class that might be, and he believed the state would so remain as long as
there was more than one class. For many radicals the state is the epitome of evil,
the symbol of all that is bad about society. This is particularly true among the

anarchists and will be discussed in detail in the chapter on anarchism. This concept is also true of Marx and some of Marx's followers, particularly those prior to Lenin. This notion probably developed because the state, through the bureaucracy, the police, and the army, represents and controls the forces that oppose workers' demands. The history of the labor movement in the United States, for example, reveals the frequent use of the police, the army, and the National Guard to put down strikes, break up demonstrations, and, in general, oppose the labor movement.[3] Thus Marx's ultimate goal, Full Communism, has no state. In this he is similar to the anarchists.

The religious system was also in the hands of the dominant class, the bourgeoisie, and Marx said religion was used to convince the proletariat that if they obeyed the state and their bosses they would be rewarded in another life. This is what Marx meant by his famous statement that religion is the opium of the people. The proletariat was lulled into accepting its way of life by the vision of heaven. This life might well be harsh, but, if the workers stood it for a brief time, they would be rewarded in the next life. Marx believed this kept the workers from actively seeking to change the system. In this way, the religious system was a major focus of Marx's criticisms of contemporary society. He saw religion used by the dominant class, the bourgeoisie, to hold the proletariat in its downtrodden position. As a result, Marx made many scathing attacks on religion and argued that the future society in which the proletariat would rule would have no need for religion. Also, of course, Marx's materialistic position was diametrically opposed to any idea of religion. At the same time, it must be recognized that Marx argued that religion contains the highest expression of the ethical sense of people. The fact that the institution of the church and the beliefs of the masses were used to control people did not mean that Marx rejected all aspects of the content of religious belief.

The state and the religious system were both part of what Marx called the *superstructure*. They were not fundamental economic structures of society; they were a reflection of the relations of production and would change as these relations changed. Thus, as class antagonism was overcome, both the state and religion would begin to disappear.

The capitalist system degraded workers in all of their relationships. Since they had to fight against others of their own class for bare subsistence, they could never hope to establish any sort of valid relationship with another person. For example, Engels wrote bitterly of the effect capitalism had on marriage and the family. To him, the family system of his day was a repetition of the class struggle. The husband symbolized the bourgeoisie and the wife, the proletariat. The contemporary marriage system under capitalism was monogamy supplemented by adultery and prostitution, and it could not change until capitalism ceased to exist. The contemporary marriage system had originated as an institution of private property at about the same time private property in land and goods had originated. It developed in order to ensure that a man's property would be

---

[3]For studies from differing viewpoints, see John R. Commons et al., *History of Labor in the United States*, 4th ed. (New York: Kelly, 1955), and Louis Adamic, *Dynamite: The Story of Class Violence in America*, rev. ed. (New York: Viking Press, 1934).

handed on to his sons. The only way this could be done was to endow the sons of one woman with a particular legal status. This did not limit the man's relationships with other women; it supposedly limited the wife's relationships with other men. In practice, as shown by the incidence of adultery, this latter proscription did not work. It failed because of "individual sex-love." Sometime after the development of monogamous marriage, there developed the tendency to find one sex-love partner and no other. This could, of course, occur after marriage, and it explained the existence of adultery. But, as will be seen later, it also provided the basis for the true monogamous marriage, which Marx believed would develop after the revolution.[4]

It is easy to see how many of Marx's criticisms of capitalism stemmed from the concerns found in his early writings. He was also impressed by Engels's description of the position of industrial workers in *The Condition of the Working Class in England* (1845), which depicted the extreme poverty in which the workers lived and the dehumanizing lives they led as mere extensions of the machines they tended.

Thus both Marx and Engels saw capitalism as destroying the humanity of the workers and the bourgeoisie, since wage slavery was degrading to both buyer and seller. Marx and Engels set out to understand capitalism, to destroy it, and to found a new, better world in its place.

Philosophical Basis—Materialism

For Marx, general theoretical positions must always be related to the concrete, material world and vice versa. Questions of theory are never separated from practice; they are always closely related.

The basis of Marx's philosophy is found in the influence of the conditions of life on people. Although Marx did not develop the basis of this notion thoroughly himself, he once spelled out in capsule form the fundamental thesis, saying it "served as the guiding thread in my studies." Although the jargon is a bit difficult to follow, it is best to have this statement in Marx's own words; it summarizes thoroughly his basic ideas. The meaning will become clearer later.

> In the social production of their means of existence men enter into definite, necessary relations which are independent of their will, productive relationships which correspond to a definite state of development of their material productive forces. The aggregate of these productive relationships constitutes the economic structure of society, the real basis on which a juridical and political superstructure arises, and to which definite forms of social consciousness correspond. The mode of production of the material means of existence conditions the whole process of social, political, and intellectual life. It is not the consciousness of men that determines their existence, but, on the contrary, it is their social condition that

---

[4]Engels discussed the family at length in *The Origin of the Family, Private Property and the State* (Harmondsworth, England: Penguin, 1985). For a modern Marxist commentary, see Juliet Mitchell, *Women's Estate* (Baltimore: Penguin, 1971).

determines their consciousness. At a certain stage of their development the material productive forces of society come into contradiction with the existing productive relationships within which they had moved before. From forms of development of the productive forces these relationships are transformed into their fetters. Then an epoch of social revolution opens. With the change in the economic foundation the whole vast superstructure is more or less rapidly transformed.[5]

The fundamental point, which is a truism today, is that the way people think is greatly affected by the way they live. As was noted in the introduction, the whole process known as socialization is the means by which an individual gains the values of his or her particular society. The point made there was that an individual, by her or his position in life economically, socially, and so forth, and by family and religious background, educational experiences, and such daily influences as the mass media, is presented with a picture or a group of pictures of the world that helps form his or her basic value system. In other words, the way an individual lives does quite clearly affect the way she or he thinks.

But the point generally accepted today is not quite the same as the point Marx was making. Marx argued that the forms taken by the law, religion, politics, aesthetics, philosophy, and so forth, which he called the *superstructure*, are largely determined by the economic structure and processes of society.

Marx is often, with considerable truth, called an economic determinist, and taken at face value, that is the meaning of the phrase "their social condition . . . determines their consciousness." But earlier in the same passage Marx uses the word *conditions* instead of *determines*. In the simplest formulation, Marx can be read as saying there is a cause-and-effect relationship between the economic structure of society and the superstructure. However, Marx thinks of interactions, not simple cause-and-effect relationships. In this case there is a continuing interaction between economic structure and superstructure, where changes in one produce changes in the other back and forth constantly. Marx's analysis is an analysis of a continuing process of change, with all aspects of both the economic structure and the superstructure constantly interacting. The economic structure is the driving force of social and intellectual change, but it is not a simple cause-and-effect relationship, even though Marx can be, has been, and still is read as a simple economic determinist.

The distinction here is a subtle but important one. For Marx, economic relationships are the most important factor determining the social forms produced at any time and place; but these economic relationships interact with some aspects of the superstructure, opening up possibilities for changes in economic relationships that will then produce further changes in the superstructure, and so on. Thus Marx is almost a simple determinist, but not quite.

Today, based in large part on the original insights of Marx, we tend to say

---

[5]Karl Marx, "Preface," in *A Contribution to the Critique of Political Economy*, trans. N. T. Stone (Chicago: Charles H. Kerr, 1913), pp. 11–12.

that economic relationships are among the most important factors influencing the social and intellectual forms produced, but they are not always the most important factors.

In developing his materialistic approach, Marx was attacking a school of German philosophy known as idealism. Its major exponent had been Georg Wilhelm Friedrich Hegel (1770–1831), and it was particularly against Hegel that Marx directed his attack. Hegel's ideas and the diverse influence they had on Marx are a complex subject and cannot be explored thoroughly here. But some attempt at explanation must be made because Hegel's influence on Marx, both in what Marx accepted and what he rejected, was so great. Hegel's basic proposition, from Marx's viewpoint, was the existence of an Absolute Spirit— sometimes Hegel called it God—that gradually revealed more and more of itself as higher and higher stages of human freedom. In Hegel's philosophy the ideal and the material, or concrete, as he called it, were intimately connected, but not as cause and effect. The two were closely bound together, each influencing the other, even though ultimately the ideal was more important than the material.

Marx directed his main attack against Hegel's idealism. As Marx put it, he set Hegel on his feet by emphasizing the material rather than the ideal. Marx, of course, stressed economic relationships in his definition of the material, rather than physical nature or the like. By stressing the material, Marx was able to argue that his position was scientific (Marx's approach is often called *scientific socialism*)[6] because matter, the material, is subject to objective scientific analysis and laws; it behaves in a predictable manner. Marx was one of the first to argue that economics could be treated scientifically, that it followed certain laws. He also contended history followed certain patterns and these patterns could be discovered and projected into the future. Marx did not claim he could predict the future with certainty; he simply argued that, if conditions continued as they were at the present, certain things would probably happen in the future. If conditions changed, which they did (Marx had argued that they probably would not), the future would be different. Since they did change even within his lifetime, some of Marx's positions changed. Finally, it must be noted that Marx believed history was moving not only to a different stage but also to a better one.

Dialectical materialism. The pattern Marx found in history, which he thought was a basic tool of analysis, was the dialectic. Hegel, too, had argued that history was moving to different and better stages; he also used the dialectic as his basic tool of analysis.

Marx's position is sometimes referred to as *dialectical materialism*. The dialectic seems to have originated in ancient Greece as a means of attaining truth through a process of questions and answers. In answer to an original question, such as the meaning of courage, beauty, justice, or the like, a position is stated.

---

[6] The best statement of this argument is still Friedrich Engels, *Socialism: Utopian and Scientific* (1880). Many editions are available.

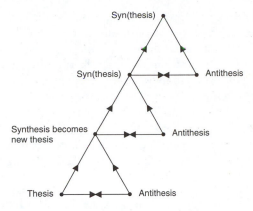

Figure 7-1 The dialectic.

The questioner then criticizes this position through the question-and-answer process until an opposite or significantly different position is taken. Then, by a continuation of the process, an attempt is made to arrive at the truth contained in both positions. The process is then continued until all are satisfied that the correct answer has been reached. The most famous illustrations of this process can be found in the dialogues of Plato, such as the *Republic*.

Marx took the dialectic from Hegel, who argued that all ideas develop through this dialectical process of thesis (first position), antithesis (second position), and synthesis (truth of the opposites), which becomes a new thesis, and, thus, continues the process. Figure 7-1 represents the most common and simple way of picturing the process. This illustration shows us something of what both Hegel and Marx are saying. Starting at the bottom with the original thesis (first position), we see its "opposite" antithesis (second position). This opposition is not one of complete difference; it is produced from the thesis in one of two ways, which are spelled out in the first two laws of the dialectic.

1. *The transformation of quantity into quality.* Changes in degree gradually produce a change in quality or kind. The usual example is the change in water from a solid (ice), to a liquid, to a gas. The changes Hegel had in mind were more basic, say H_2O to H_2O_2. In this process the combination of oxygen and hydrogen first produces H_2O, which is totally different from either hydrogen or oxygen. The continued addition of oxygen produces H_2O_2, which is again different.

2. *Unity or identity of opposites.* Contradictions in the thesis become the antithesis. Thus the opposites are actually similar since they are composed of similar elements. In addition, the thesis and antithesis become unified, differently, in the synthesis. This unification of the thesis and the antithesis is produced through the third law of the dialectic.

3. *Negation of the negation.* Contradictions continue to accumulate until another qualitative change occurs and the synthesis is reached. The synthe-

sis, or the unity of the opposites, is a qualitative change, as was the original step from the thesis to the antithesis. In other words, a new position is reached that is not simply the combination of the thesis and antithesis. In a similar way, chemists sometimes speak of synthesizing a new product from two or more products. Thus water (H_2O) is a synthesis of two parts hydrogen with one part oxygen to produce a product that is significantly different from the original components. The synthesis is then treated as a new product, and the process continues in the same manner. These three laws are often neglected or slighted by students of Marx, but, as will be seen later, they help to provide an understanding of the pattern taken by his analysis of history.

Marx did not attempt to apply the dialectic systematically to the material world. Some of his followers, such as Engels and Lenin, tried to view nature as changing dialectically and spoke vaguely of scientific laws operating dialectically, but these attempts were not very successful.[7]

The general form of the dialectic is the interaction and intermingling of ideas, beliefs, and positions, not the specific form used here as an example of the dialectic. The dialectic is a way of understanding the constant interaction that characterizes the world. For a particularly relevant example, none of the ideologies presented here is, by itself, an accurate reflection of the world, but, on the other hand, each of them has something valuable to contribute to the understanding of how people behave. Ideological positions constantly interact in the world and are changed by that interaction. This very complex constant interaction and change is a more accurate description of the dialectic.

Historical materialism. Marx applied the dialectic to his interpretation of history. Since any change in the economic system is reflected in changes in the entire superstructure, Marx argued that it would be possible to interpret all history from this perspective. He also contended it might be possible to make some general statements about the future on the same basis. Marx did not say he could predict the future. He said there were patterns in history that would in all probability continue into the future. Thus an understanding of history should make it possible to argue that if conditions remain the same, certain things are likely to take place in the future.

Although Marx contended economics is an exact science and is basic to an understanding of his scientific socialism, he nowhere clearly and unambiguously defined the most important element in his economics, the *modes of production*. Most of the time they consist of (1) available natural resources and (2) productive techniques. At times Marx includes the organization of production as a third element, but this is more properly part of the superstructure.

Natural resources become available as we learn how to use them. Human

---

[7]The student who is interested in these attempts should consult the following work: Friedrich Engels, *Dialectics of Nature*, trans. and ed. Clemens Dutt (New York: International Publishers, 1940). For a more recent consideration, see Richard Levins and Richard Lewontin, *The Dialectical Biologist* (Cambridge, MA: Harvard University Press, 1985).

knowledge is basic to both of the modes of production; this illustrates the interactive nature of Marx's materialism. Tools and knowledge grow together, each improvement in tools adding to knowledge and each improvement in knowledge making it possible to improve tools. Through this process more natural resources become available for use, and techniques of production change.

As humans gain knowledge of the uses of natural resources, their modes of production change, and they begin to develop more tools and manufacturing processes. They begin to produce pottery or weave baskets; they learn to form metals into tools and weapons. These changes in turn lead to further changes in both the modes of production and the superstructure.

Changes in productive techniques are brought about because previous changes were made. In other words, each development sets the stage for a further development. Also, major changes in productive techniques, such as the shift from herding to agriculture, produce major changes in the organization of the society and in the belief system of that society. In the case cited, Marx is right. If we look at any civilization where we know the pattern, we can see that the change from herding to agriculture was accompanied by changes in the political, religious, and social system, as different activities became important. Although the change from herding to agriculture is an obvious case where major changes in productive techniques do change the organization of society, and specifically the political system of that society, Marx is probably correct in assuming that any such major change produces a major change in society. It is again obviously true that the change from a predominantly agricultural society to a predominantly industrial society has produced many far-reaching changes in contemporary society, and many argue that similar far-reaching changes will occur as production becomes more and more highly automated.[8]

Part of the superstructure is a set of relations of production, or property relations. These constitute the second key to Marx's theory of history. Property relations in Marx's terminology refer to the ownership of the means of production: land, factories, and so on. These property relations change more slowly than do the modes of production, and thereby a conflict is formed that can be solved only by a change in the property relations. This point is important for an understanding of Marx's analysis of the changes in history and his criticism of contemporary society. Marx argued that property relations evolve more slowly than modes of production, and property relations will not change to meet changing needs. Since his analysis states that property relations are a product of the modes of production, it is clear that it is the property relations that must change to meet the new modes of production rather than the reverse. But, in the meantime, there is a tension between the modes of production and the property relations that is unresolved and cannot be resolved until the more slowly changing property relations have changed.

This tension produces conflict within society and is one of the major reasons for Marx's prediction of a revolution and his certainty that the proletariat will

---

[8]See, for example, Herbert Marcuse, *An Essay on Liberation* (Boston: Beacon Press, 1969).

win the revolution. According to Marx, the owners of property will not be willing to give up their ownership, even though that is dictated by a change in the modes of production. At the same time, they ultimately must give up such ownership because of the change in the modes of production. Thus one can see in operation the three laws of the dialectic mentioned above. There is the transformation of quantity into quality in the changes in the modes of production. There is the unity of opposites in the growing contradiction between the economic foundation and the superstructure. And, finally, there is the negation of the negation in arriving at the new synthesis of modes of production and superstructure.

In addition, Marx uses the dialectic in his concept of progress to higher and higher, or better and better, stages of society. This is an aspect of the idea of progress or the notion that the human race and society are inevitably moving to better things. An extremely popular idea in Marx's time, the idea of progress has fallen into disrepute today. Still, Marx's use of the idea of progress is worthy of some further consideration.

The idea of progress was not simply the notion of the world getting better and better every day in every way. Some believers in progress did think the world was constantly getting better and the human race had nothing to do with it. They argued that the world was moving in a straight line from some primitive state to some ultimate, perfect society in which everything would be good and beautiful; all people had to do was wait and things would get better. But most believers in progress did not accept this simple formulation. They believed that the world, although improving, constantly fell away from the line of progress into some sort of corruption, and then only by great effort, perhaps a revolution, could the world be brought back onto the correct path.

People could affect the path taken by the world in its gradual betterment both for good and evil. Marx seems to have assumed the world would gradually get better in spite of whatever humans did, but he contended that through concerted action people make a tremendous difference in the speed of improvement. Thus humanity's position would improve, but knowledgeable people such as Marx were in a position to recognize the direction that must be taken in order to achieve this.

The Class Struggle

A central part of Marxism is the class struggle, a hypothesis Marx used to explain change. The class struggle is based on the contradiction between the modes of production and the relations of production; this contradiction produces the class struggle. Marx said that in the mid-nineteenth century the means of production were controlled by a class he called the *bourgeoisie*. This class did little if any work but reaped immense profits from its control of the means of production. The actual labor was done by a class Marx called the *proletariat*. The modes of production required the proletariat, but did not, according to Marx, require the bourgeoisie; therefore, a struggle between these two classes resulted. Each wished to control the means of production. For Marx there was no question concerning the result—the proletariat was necessary, the bourgeoisie was not. Although both he and later Marxists applied the theory of the class struggle to all history, Marx argued that the best example of class struggle existed in the mid-nineteenth century, in which society was clearly split into these two classes, the bourgeoisie (capitalists) and the proletariat (workers).

It is important at the outset to be clear regarding the nature of classes and of these two classes in particular. Classes are economic in nature and are groups ordered according to their relationship to the nonhuman powers of production and to each other. The proletariat is the class that makes its living from the sale of its labor power. The bourgeoisie consists of the owners of the productive resources upon which the proletariat works. The bourgeoisie makes its living primarily from profit, interest, and rent, although it may earn some of its income from wages paid for managerial work and for the coordination of risk-taking ventures.

Many other smaller classes existed, but they were generally irrelevant to the unfolding conflict. In addition, Marx had a few problems with the manner in which he included certain groups within the class system. For example, he was always unclear as to exactly where the peasantry fit within his system. He often included the peasantry in a group loosely known as the *petite bourgeoisie* because they were landowners. At other times he split his definition of the peasantry into a variety of groups ranging from the bourgeoisie to the proletariat, but he was never clear exactly where to place the group of peasantry who owned their land and worked it themselves. This problem of classification has plagued Marxist theorists ever since. No one is ever quite certain where to place the peasant. In addition to the peasantry, Marx also added at the bottom of his classification scheme another class called the *lumpenproletariat*, which was composed of the dregs of society, primarily thieves, bums, and the like. Marx never clarified whether it would be possible to include this group within the proletariat itself, but one would assume from his writings that he thought that at some point after the revolution it would be possible to incorporate the lumpenproletariat into the proletariat in the same way the bourgeoisie was to be incorporated.[9] For Marx in the nineteenth century, however, the most important classes were the proletariat and the bourgeoisie.

Revolution

The class struggle would ultimately produce a revolution, and Marx worked for that revolution, arguing that we must move beyond simply understanding society to changing it. Marx was a revolutionary because he believed a revolution was both necessary and inevitable. The revolution was to develop as a result of a series of crises capitalism was to experience. These failed to appear as regularly or as seriously as Marx had expected, and thus the revolution did not

---

[9]For discussion of these problems, see John Plamenatz, *Man and Society: A Critical Examination of Some Important Social and Political Theories from Machiavelli to Marx* (London: Longmans Green, 1963), vol. 2, pp. 293–300, and David Mitrany, *Marx Against the Peasant: A Study in Social Dogmatism* (New York: Collier Books, 1961).

develop. Some contemporary Marxists prefer to say it has not yet developed as anticipated.

In a small book entitled *Imperialism: The Highest Stage of Capitalism* (1916), Lenin attempted to show why these crises failed to occur as predicted. He argued that by colonizing and exploiting underdeveloped countries, the capitalists were temporarily able to stave off the crises. Colonial exploitation made it possible to pay workers slightly better by providing capitalists with:

1. Cheap raw materials;

2. Cheap labor; and

3. Markets for manufactured goods and excess capital.

Lenin believed imperialism merely postponed the revolution; it did not put it off permanently. It lulled the proletariat into believing revolution will not be necessary.[10]

This position is of particular relevance today, and some Marxists argue that Lenin's analysis was correct with the results only now developing. Cheap raw materials were provided for Western factories and higher wages were paid in the West by exporting exploitation to the colonies where very low wages were paid. Today, Third World countries are beginning to control their own resources and are insisting on high prices, in part because of past exploitation. Some contemporary Marxists argue that capitalism will now experience the crises that Marx had predicted and that Lenin argued had been put off temporarily through imperialism. According to this argument the capitalist system will collapse and the revolution will come. So far this has not happened, and in 1986 the price of raw materials dropped dramatically. Marxists argue that this is only temporary and caused by the capitalists, who still control the markets for the raw materials. Many interpret the Gulf War in this light, seeing it as a fight over the control of oil supplies. The popular slogan "No Blood for Oil" reflects this view, as does the commonly expressed feeling that without the oil there would have been no war and Kuwait would now be an integral part of Iraq.

In discussing the Marxian approach to revolution, it is instructive to distinguish between two different types of revolution—the political and the social. The political revolution takes place when political power is seized by the proletariat. The social revolution takes place later, first through changes made in the property relations of society and second as the superstructure adjusts to these changes.

Marx thought the political revolution would be violent, although he did allow for the possibility of peaceful change. The revolution would probably be violent for two reasons. First, Marx argued that achieving the synthesis would always be sudden; thus the gradualness implicit in peaceful change was ruled out by the dialectic. Second, the bourgeoisie would never agree

---

[10]Alfred G. Meyer provides an excellent analysis of Lenin's theory of imperialism and its implications. See Alfred G. Meyer, *Leninism* (New York: Praeger, 1962), chaps. xi and xii. See also the discussion of neocolonialism in chapter 10 of this book.

to its disappearance as a class and would force the proletariat into a violent revolution.

Lenin. Marx was a revolutionary. He believed revolution was necessary and good, and throughout his life he was involved in groups that tried to bring about revolutions in various countries. He was expelled from a number of countries for his activities. But it was his followers, particularly Lenin and Mao, who developed the tactics for and led successful communist revolutions.

Lenin's contribution was the development of the revolutionary party, which was an organizational weapon in the struggle to overthrow capitalism. Lenin argued that such a party was necessary because the proletariat was incapable of recognizing its role as the revolutionary class, whereas the party provided this necessary consciousness. As one scholar stated, "The party is conceived as the organization, incarnation, or institutionalization of class consciousness."[11] The party would be made up of those who had achieved this consciousness and had also become professional revolutionists. In the popular phrase, the party was to be the "vanguard of the proletariat"; it would point the way and lead the proletariat to its goal. The party would bring together the divided masses of workers and would express what they were truly feeling but were unable to express. It would mold them and unify them into a force for change.

Proletarians as individual members of a class would be unlikely to recognize their historic role. In the first place, they would be much too busy attempting to stay alive to be concerned with class questions. Second, very few would ever identify themselves as class members. Thus it would be left up to the few who became aware, the party members, to prepare for the great role the proletariat would play.

The importance of Lenin's party is found in the idea of the professional revolutionary and in the organizational principle of *democratic centralism*. Although the party would be composed of a small conspiratorial group of professional revolutionists, Lenin believed it should develop contacts throughout the society as a whole, since no revolution could be successful without the support of, or at least little direct opposition from, the largest part of the population of the country. This meant that the party members would have to have a variety of organizational skills. They would have to be experts at agitation and propaganda. Since they had to be able to establish and maintain a vast network of "front" organizations throughout the country, they would have to be expert administrators. Ideally, prior to the revolution, the majority of the population should be organized into a variety of these groups that would also provide the basis for organization once the revolution succeeded. In addition, the party members would have to prepare constantly for the revolution, since it would come only when the masses suddenly revolted against their oppressors.

The party might light the spark that set the masses afire, but the spark might come anywhere, anytime, and the party had to be ready to ride the revolution into power. The theory of the spark was important to Lenin. One of his news-

---

[11]Meyer, pp. 31–33.

Vladimir Ilyich Lenin (1870–1924, born Vladimir Ilyich Ulyanov) was a follower of
Karl Marx. He is remembered primarily as the leader of the successful Bolshevik section
of the Communist Party of the Soviet Union and as the first leader of the USSR,
which he headed from the time of the Russian revolution in 1917 to his death. He was
a major theorist of revolution as well as one of its successful practitioners. His books
What Is to Be Done? (1902) and *One Step Forward, Two Steps Back* (1904) presented the
case for a highly disciplined body of revolutionists as the only approach to a successful
revolution. His *Imperialism: The Highest Stage of Capitalism* (1916) and *State and Revolution* (1918) were his major contributions to Marxist theory. (*Library of Congress*)

papers was called *The Spark* (*Iskra*), and he often referred to the necessity of some
incident igniting the masses. In fact, the 1991 coup in the then Soviet Union
fits Lenin's analysis. Lenin believed it was possible for the party to produce the
necessary conditions for a revolution, but he believed it was impossible to be
absolutely sure when the revolution would come. Hence the party had to always
be prepared for the revolution to come at an unexpected time, perhaps even at
a time that was not favorable to the party.

The principle of organization making all this possible is democratic centralism. This principle combines freedom of discussion with centralized control and
responsibility. Before any decision is made by the party, there should be complete freedom to dissent; after the decision is made, it must be accepted unani-
mously. Lenin believed this principle could work because all party members
started from a position of agreement regarding goals. In practice, freedom of
discussion was often forgotten. Democratic centralism would also serve as the
principle of organization in the period immediately following the revolution,
which will be discussed more completely later.

As a technique of revolutionary organization, democratic centralism has important characteristics. In planning a revolution, care must be taken to organize
in order to act at a moment's notice. Everyone must also be able to act in a
completely concerted manner without disagreements or squabbles over what is
to be done now and what is to be done later, or arguments about the correct

techniques of taking over the government or who is to do this or that at a particular moment. It is essential there be complete agreement among the revolutionists over the techniques of the revolution and the organization of society immediately after the successful revolution. Democratic centralism provides this by giving the leaders complete control over the actions of the revolutionists and at the same time allowing all members of the party to participate freely and openly in the process of reaching the appropriate decisions. Again, democratic centralism has usually been used in ways that stressed centralism.

Mao Zedong. Other Marxist theorists have also contributed to the tactics of revolution. For example, Mao Zedong's (1893–1976) theory of guerrilla warfare is also an organizational weapon. Mao's theory can be divided into two parts, the strictly military principles and some political principles derived from one of the military principles. Militarily, Mao developed what are now the commonly recognized principles of guerrilla warfare. These stress a hit-and-run approach, fighting only when fairly certain of victory, and keeping constant pressure on the enemy.[12]

According to Mao, this style of fighting requires a territorial base where the guerrillas will be virtually free from attack so they will be able to rest, train, and so on. In order to achieve this, they must have the positive support of the people in that area. This support is gained by: (1) establishing a peasant government; (2) allowing the peasants to redistribute the land; and (3) helping the peasants in whatever rebuilding activities they undertake. The territorial base will provide food, manpower, and, perhaps most important, experience in organization. The network of tunnels used by the Vietcong during the Vietnam War provided a similar resting place. Thus Mao's theory of guerrilla warfare fulfills the same function as Lenin's theory of the revolutionary party. Mao's tactics are designed with the same purposes in mind as Lenin's strategies.

Dictatorship of the Proletariat

Marx envisioned a brief transitional period after the revolution, known as the *dictatorship of the proletariat*. This stage was to be characterized by the consolidation of the power of the proletariat through the gradual disappearance of the bourgeoisie and the minor classes as they become part of the proletariat.

The bourgeoisie and the other classes would be given jobs that would, over time, change their outlook and make them good members of the proletariat. The dictatorship of the proletariat would be the period in which the superstructure would change to adjust to the socialist mode of production. Loosely, the dictatorship of the proletariat should have the following characteristics:

1. Distribution of income according to labor performed,
2. Gradual disappearance of classes,
3. The state in the hands of the proletariat,

---

[12]Mao Zedong, *Selected Works* (Beijing, China: Foreign Language Press, 1961), vol. 4, pp. 161–162.

4. Increasing productivity,

5. Increasing socialist consciousness—people work with few incentives,

6. Increasing equality,

7. A command economy, and

8. The economy managed by the state.

All of these characteristics were expected to change fairly rapidly, and the dictatorship of the proletariat was to be brief. In practice, no country that has followed Marx's ideas has moved beyond the dictatorship of the proletariat, but a number of countries are in what they call the dictatorship of the proletariat. Contrary to Marx, this "transitional" period does not seem to focus on the economic system. One could almost say the dictatorship of the proletariat as practiced is based on the political system with all else as superstructure rather than being based on the economic system.

Marx refused to make specific predictions about the future. He argued that the new social forms of the future would be created by people who had themselves been shaped by new experiences. Those socialized in the old, bad society could have no notion of what the new, better society would look like except in the most general sense; therefore, Marx never described the dictatorship of the proletariat in any detail. In addition, the dictatorship of the proletariat was to be a short period of transition and would be characterized more by change than by stable institutions. Still, it is possible to say something about the society of the dictatorship of the proletariat because Marx gave enough suggestions to allow some elaboration on the eight points listed previously.

During the dictatorship of the proletariat, the state, as always, will be the tool of the dominant class (in this case the proletariat). The state will be used to achieve a number of related goals. First, the economic system will be reorganized; the means of production must be taken from the capitalists and become the property of the state. The state must also establish a new way of administering the means of production so that the economy is kept running and goods produced, distributed, and consumed. As part of this process, the workers will all become employees of the state (public employees) and will be paid by the state on the basis of the quantity and quality of the work they perform, just as they had been by the previous owners. These previous owners and all other members of the bourgeoisie and the other classes will gradually be absorbed into the proletariat. They will be given jobs, and working for a living will resocialize them into the proletariat's way of thought and belief.

Together these show the operation of a command economy managed by a state in the hands of the proletariat, distribution of income on the basis of work performed, and the gradual disappearance of classes. With the gradual disappearance of classes, there should be greater productivity since there will be more workers available, no unproductive bourgeoisie, and no profit. As a result, equality will increase, and people will become more aware of their roles in society and will require fewer incentives to work.

The dictatorship of the proletariat, it can be seen, represents a unified view of a society in a period of transition. All these factors must be thought of as in change. Some things will change quickly; others will change much more slowly. In practice, of course, a command economy was established that was managed by the state, but in no communist country has the state ever been in the hands of the proletariat, and none of the other changes has occurred. No communist country has even come close to the goals of the dictatorship of the proletariat, let alone the next, and final stage—Full Communism.

Full Communism

The changes in contemporary communism brought about by the fusion of nationalism, the early writings of Marx, and existentialism have given rise to a resurgence of utopian thinking by Marxists. But they have not significantly changed the characteristics of Marx's ideal system, Full or Pure Communism. Full Communism has the following characteristics:

1. Distribution of income according to need, no longer according to labor performed.
2. No classes.
3. The state withers away.
4. Very high productivity, so that there is plenty for all.
5. High socialist consciousness—people work without incentives.
6. More equality but not absolute equality.
7. No money.
8. A command economy.
9. The economy managed by a free and equal association of producers.
10. The differences between occupations disappear, so that there is no social distinction between town and country.
11. Each person does about as much physical as intellectual labor.
12. The system, as Stalin was the first to show, is worldwide.[13]

Full Communism is the goal of the entire system, the utopia or better society toward which all else is aimed. Its general characteristics are not much different from the utopias created by a variety of other socialists throughout the centuries, but some of these characteristics are worth further mention.

The economic aspects of Full Communism are outlined above, and the major similarities and differences between it and the dictatorship of the proletariat are illustrated. The command economy still exists, but it is no longer

---

[13]Adapted slightly and reprinted by permission of the author and the publishers from P. J. D. Wiles, *The Political Economy of Communism* (Cambridge, MA: Harvard University Press, © 1962, by Basic Blackwell & Mott Ltd.), pp. 332–333. See also Howard J. Sherman, "The Economics of Pure Communism," *Soviet Studies* 22 (July 1970); 24–36.

controlled by the state. Marx was primarily concerned with abolishing exploitation, and in Full Communism there are no exploiters, only workers. With the exploiters gone and the people working without incentives, there should be plenty so that all can be rewarded according to need.

The most direct effect of a change to Full Communism would be on the social stratification and mobility systems. Since classes would no longer exist and since no distinction would be made among types of labor, there should be little social stratification. In the classless or single-class society, there would be no basis for any significant distinctions among people. *Significant* for Marx meant economic, and he did not foresee a complete leveling. Individual differences would remain, but they no longer would be detrimental to the individual or the society as they had been under capitalism and all the other socioeconomic systems preceding it. Occupational mobility would be increased greatly, since an individual would be able to move freely among positions.

Marx envisioned other significant changes in the social system. There would, of course, be no religion. There would be education for all. All crime would disappear because there would be no reason for it. With the coming of Full Communism, prostitution and adultery would disappear, and the monogamous family would become a reality. The new family would be based on a love-sex relationship that Marx believed could have only one focus. At the same time, he wanted to free women from housework. A Marxist scholar has suggested that under Full Communism there will be a change from personal housekeeping functions, such as cooking and cleaning, to public or communal services, thus freeing women to choose among occupations in the same way men can.[14]

With the coming of the classless society, the state would no longer be necessary and would disappear. It would be replaced by "the administration of things," which means the economic system would have to be organized and somebody would have to administer it. It would be administered by "a free and equal association of producers" that would have the authority to direct, according to the needs of the people, what should be produced and in what amounts and how it should be distributed. This "free and equal association of producers" could conceivably take a wide variety of forms, depending on the size of the territory and the complexity of the industries within the territory. Most such associations would undoubtedly take some such pattern as follows. A committee would be selected, probably by election, that would collect data on the productive capacity of the region and the needs of the people. It would then establish priorities and goals for the various manufacturing plants, farms, and craft industries. This assumes an economy based on abundance and, thus, would be more concerned with collecting accurate data on needs than with establishing priorities. The process would be continuous, and certainly the composition of the

---

[14]E. G. Balagushkin, "The Building of Communism and the Evolution of Family and Marital Relations," *Soviet Sociology* 1 (Winter 1962/1963): 43. Originally published in 1962 in *Voprosy Filosofii*. For some similar early U.S. plans, see Dolores Hayden, *The Grand Domestic Revolution: A History of Feminist Designs for American Homes, Neighborhoods, and Cities* (Cambridge, MA: MIT Press, 1981).

committee would change periodically. The committee would hold no coercive power, still assuming abundance, and would merely administer the economy.

This is the goal of Marxism. Many Communists today believe Full Communism will never come. Others believe it is still possible. But, whichever position one takes, it illustrates some of the appeal communism has had and will continue to have in the future.

Alternative Marxist Traditions

As mentioned earlier, an alternative tradition within Marxism emphasizes decentralist and humanitarian aspects of Marx's thought. The line of authoritarianism that Lenin developed was only successful after an intellectual and political struggle, and even Lenin regularly expressed reservations about the direction he took. But the centralization of authority that took place under Joseph Stalin (original name Iosif Vissarionovich Dzhugashvili, 1879–1953) became the model for all communist countries and could be justified within the writings of Marx and Lenin. Lenin had rejected Stalin as his successor, but Stalin won the struggle for power after Lenin's death.

Those who lost the early struggle with Lenin, however, remained influential in Western Europe. Revisionists like Eduard Bernstein (1850–1932) argued for an evolutionary rather than a revolutionary Marxism. Rosa Luxemburg (1870–1919) was a revolutionary Marxist who rejected the antidemocratic activities of Lenin.

Other opponents of the emphasis on centralism emerged in various countries. Two of the most important were Antonio Gramsci (1891–1937) of Italy and Anton Pannekoek (1873–1960) of the Netherlands.

Antonio Gramsci. Gramsci was an advocate of democracy within factories. For example, he proposed that each factory be organized into workshops and each workshop into work crews based on similar skills. Each work crew would elect one of their number as delegate. These delegates would meet and elect an executive committee, and, in a federal structure above the individual factories, elected representatives from the various factories in the area would meet in a variety of groupings. This system is democratic centralism with the emphasis on democracy.

Anton Pannekoek and Council Communism. Anton Pannekoek went considerably further than Gramsci. He suggested that what has been called Full Communism be taken seriously and that there be no governing authority. The councils that he proposed would not be able to require obedience from the people. In this Pannekoek was very close to the type of federal communist anarchism described by Pyotr Kropotkin and discussed in the next chapter.

Marxists like Gramsci and Pannekoek provided the basis for the continuation of an alternative Marxist tradition, one that has continued among Western European and American Marxist theoreticians, and, until recently, among Eastern European Marxists.

The Frankfurt School. The Frankfurt Institute for Social Research was founded in 1923, and, under the leadership of Max Horkheimer (1895–1973) and Theodor Adorno (1903–1969), it became the foremost center in the West for Marxist research. The school is most noted for the development of *critical theory*, a general theory that views society from the point of view of the need to change it. Marx saw himself as always being both a social theorist and a revolutionary or someone who believed in the need to transform society. In his famous "Eleventh Thesis on Feuerbach," he even emphasized that change was more important than theory: "The philosophers have only *interpreted* the world in various ways; the point is to *change* it."[15]

Although there was great variety among the members, the Frankfurt School's most influential members have been Herbert Marcuse (1898–1979) and Jürgen Habermas (1929–). Marcuse combined the insights of Marx with those of Sigmund Freud to develop a vision of a nonrepressive society in his *Eros and Civilization* (1955) and *One-Dimensional Man* (1964). He greatly influenced the New Left. Habermas has focused on the concept of rationality as the basis of his theory. He has worked to develop a broad-based concept of rationality as a means of criticizing contemporary culture and as the foundation for positive social change.

Ernst Bloch. Bloch (1885–1977) was a German Marxist philosopher who emphasized the utopian aspects of Marxism. In his magnum opus *Das Prinzip Hoffnung* (*The Principle of Hope*) (1959) and other works, Bloch explored the various manifestations of hope in human history. He argued that the desire for betterment must be brought back to the center of Marxist thought as the real engine of social change. With the recent translation of his works into English, Bloch's writings are beginning to influence contemporary Marxist thought. Earlier Bloch had influenced the development of Liberation Theology.[16]

CURRENT TRENDS

Communism has disappeared as the official ruling force in Eastern Europe and the former Soviet Union. It still exists in China, Cuba, and Vietnam and among numerous parties and groups throughout the world, including dominant parties with new names but the same leaders in parts of Eastern Europe. But, in general, communism as we have known it is coming to an end. Therefore, it seems appropriate to ask, what happened?

The central problem is that the supposedly short-lived dictatorship of the proletariat, during which the various classes of capitalism were to become one

---

[15]Karl Marx, "Theses on Feuerbach," in Karl Marx and Friedrich Engels, *Collected Works* (New York: International Publishers, 1976), 5: 5. Emphasis in the original.

[16]Ernst Bloch, *The Principle of Hope*. Trans. Neville Plaice, Stephen Plaice, and Paul Knight. 3 vols. (Cambridge, MA: MIT Press/Oxford, England: Basil Blackwell, 1986.)

class, became permanent and became a dictatorship in the name of the proletariat but not actually of the proletariat. As Milovan Djilas (1911–1995) pointed out in *The New Class*,[17] communism simply replaced capitalist bosses with bureaucratic bosses who ruled in their own interest rather than in the interest of the proletariat. Some have actually called communism *state capitalism* as a result.

Other problems include the fact that it is almost literally impossible to manage all the details of an economy from the center. As a result, many inefficiencies were built into the Soviet economy, gradually developing into the total breakdown we now see. On the other hand, central planning and control worked in the rebuilding of the Soviet Union after World War II and in their space program. We should not forget that it was the Soviet Union that put the first person into space.

The partial demise of communism does not mean the end of Marxism. In the first place, the demise is partial in part because the inability of capitalism to rapidly overcome the failures of communist regimes has led many people in former communist countries to regret the passing of communism and to vote for the former communists, now under new names. Although no informed person expected capitalism to quickly correct communism's legacy, the fact is that many people believed it would, and self-serving anti-communists oversold capitalism. The required restructuring of the economies involved means that many people are significantly worse off than they were under communism: jobs have been lost; pensions have been radically reduced by inflation; and social services and health care that people relied upon have disappeared. Thus it is no surprise that former communists are being elected to office.

Second, Marxism remains a powerful tool for understanding social relations and social change, and many thinkers still find the Marxist critique of capitalism to contain considerable truth. Social classes largely based on economic power remain even though Marxist and other theoreticians have been arguing for some time that this class analysis needs to be complicated by adding such factors as gender and race. In this and other ways, Marxist thinkers are still contributing significantly to our understanding of the world around us.

SUGGESTED READINGS

Some Classics of Marxism

MARX, KARL. *Capital.*

———. *Economic and Philosophic Manuscripts of 1844.*

——— and ENGELS, FRIEDRICH. *The Communist Manifesto.*

ENGELS, FRIEDRICH. *The Origin of the Family, Private Property and the State.*

———. *Socialism: Utopian and Scientific.*

LENIN, V. I. *Imperialism: The Highest Stage of Capitalism.*

———. *State and Revolution.*

———. *What Is to Be Done?*

---

[17]Milovan Djilas, *The New Class* (New York: Harcourt Brace Jovanovich, 1955).

Works About Marxism

ARNOLD, N. SCOTT. *Marx's Radical Critique of Capitalist Society: A Reconstruction and Critical Evaluation*. New York: Oxford University Press, 1990.

AVINERI, SHLOMO. *The Social and Political Thought of Karl Marx*. Cambridge, England: Cambridge University Press, 1968.

BLACKBURN, ROBIN, ed. *After the Fall: The Failure of Communism and the Future of Socialism*. London: Verso, 1991.

BOGGS, CARL. *Gramsci's Marxism*. London: Pluto Press, 1976.

BOSE, ARUN. *Marx on Exploitation and Inequality*. Oxford, England: Oxford University Press, 1982.

BOTTOMORE, TOM, ed. *Modern Interpretations of Marx*. Oxford, England: Basil Blackwell, 1981.

BRICIANER, SERGE. *Pannekoek and the Workers' Councils*. Trans. Malachy Carroll. St. Louis, MO: Telos Press, 1978.

COHEN, ARTHUR A. *The Communism of Mao Tse-tung*. Chicago: University of Chicago Press, 1964.

COHEN, G. A. *Karl Marx's Theory of History*. Oxford, England: Clarendon Press, 1978.

DAVIDSON, ALASTAIR. *Antonio Gramsci: Towards an Intellectual Biography*. London: Merlin Press/Atlantic Highlands, NJ: Humanities Press, 1977.

DEBRAY, RÉGIS. *Revolution in the Revolution? Armed Struggle and Political Struggle in Latin America*. Trans. Bobbye Ortiz. New York: Monthly Review Press, 1967.

————. *Strategy for Revolution*. Ed. Robin Blackburn. New York: Monthly Review Press, 1970.

————. *Prison Writings*. Trans. Rosemary Sheed. London: A. Lane, 1973.

DJILAS, MILOVAN. *The New Class: An Analysis of the Communist System*. New York: Harcourt Brace Jovanovich, 1955.

————. *Conversations with Stalin*. Trans. Michael B. Petrovich. New York: Harcourt Brace Jovanovich, 1962.

————. *The Unperfect Society: Beyond the New Class*. Trans. Dorian Cooke. New York: Harcourt Brace Jovanovich, 1969.

DUNAYEVSKAYA, RAYA. *Marxism and Freedom from 1776 Until Today*. London: Pluto Press, 1971.

————. *Rosa Luxemburg, Women's Liberation, and Marx's Philosophy of Revolution*. Atlantic Highlands, NJ: Humanities Press, 1982.

ELSTER, JON. *Making Sense of Marx*. Cambridge, England: Cambridge University Press/Paris: Éditions de la Maison des Sciences de l'Homme, 1985.

————. *An Introduction to Karl Marx*. Cambridge, England: Cambridge University Press, 1986.

———— and KARL OVE MOENE, eds. *Alternatives to Capitalism*. Cambridge, England: Cambridge University Press/Paris: Éditions de la Maison des Sciences de l'Homme, 1989.

ENGELS, FRIEDRICH. *Selected Writings*. Ed. W. O. Henderson. Baltimore, MD: Penguin, 1967.

FEHÉR, FERENC, AGNES HELLER, and GYÖRGY MÁRKUS. *Dictatorship over Needs*. New York: St. Martin's, 1983.

FROMM, ERICH. *Marx's Concept of Man*. New York: Frederick Ungar, 1965.

————, ed. *Socialist Humanism: An International Symposium*. Garden City, NY: Anchor Books, 1965.

GEARY, DICK. *Karl Kautsky*. New York: St. Martin's, 1987.

GERAS, NORMAN. *The Legacy of Rosa Luxemburg*. London: NLB, 1976.

GEUSS, RAYMOND. *The Idea of a Critical Theory*. Cambridge, England: Cambridge University Press, 1982.

GILBERT, ALAN. *Marx's Politics: Communists and Citizens*. New Brunswick, NJ: Rutgers University Press, 1981.

GOTTLIEB, ROGER S. *Marxism 1844–1990: Origins, Betrayal, Rebirth*. London: Routledge, 1992.

GRAMSCI, ANTONIO. *The Modern Prince*

and Other Writings. New York: International Publishers, 1957.

———. *Letters from Prison*. Trans. and ed. Lynne Lawner. New York: Harper & Row, 1973.

———. *Selections from Political Writings (1910–1920)*. Ed. Quinton Hoare, trans. John Mathews. London: Lawrence & Wishart, 1977.

———. *Selections from Political Writings (1921–1926)*. Edited by Quinton Hoare. Minneapolis: University of Minnesota Press, 1978.

GRUNDMANN, REINER. *Marxism and Ecology*. Oxford, England: Clarendon Press, 1991.

GUTNOV, ALEXEI, et al. *The Ideal Communist City*. Trans. Renee Neu Watkins. New York: George Braziller, 1968.

HABERMAS, JÜRGEN. *Knowledge and Human Interests*. Trans. Jeremy J. Shapiro. Boston: Beacon Press, 1971.

———. *Theory and Practice*. Trans. John Viertel. Boston: Beacon Press, 1973.

———. *Communications and the Evolution of Society*. Trans. Thomas McCarthy. Boston: Beacon Press, 1979.

HOFFMAN, JOHN. *The Gramscian Challenge: Coercion and Consent in Marxian Political Theory*. Oxford, England: Basil Blackwell, 1984.

HORVAT, BRANKO. *The Political Economy of Socialism: A Marxist Social Theory*. Armonk, NY: M. E. Sharpe, 1982.

———, MIHAILO MARKOVIĆ, and RUDI SUPEK, eds. *Self-Governing Socialism: A Reader*. 2 vols. White Plains, NY: International Arts and Sciences Press, 1975.

HOWE, IRVING, ed. *Essential Works of Socialism*. 3d ed. New Haven, CT: Yale University Press, 1986.

KATZNELSON, IRA. *Marxism and the City*. Oxford, England: Clarendon Press, 1992.

KOLAKOWSKI, LESZEK. *Main Currents of Marxism*. Trans. P. S. Falla. 3 vols. Oxford, England: Clarendon Press, 1978.

———, and STUART HAMPSHIRE, eds.

The Socialist Idea: A Reappraisal. London: Weidenfeld & Nicolson, 1974.

LUXEMBURG, ROSA. *The Accumulation of Capital*. Trans. Agnes Schwarzschild. New York: Monthly Review Press, 1964.

———. *Selected Political Writings*. Ed. Dick Howard. New York: Monthly Review Press, 1971.

MANDEL, ERNEST. *Introduction to Marxism*. Trans. Louisa Sadler. 2d ed. London: Ink Links, 1979.

MARCUSE, HERBERT. *An Essay on Liberation*. Boston: Beacon Press, 1969.

———. *Negations: Essays in Critical Theory*. Trans. Jeremy J. Shapiro. Boston: Beacon Press, 1969.

MARKOVIĆ, MIHAILO. *From Affluence to Praxis: Philosophy and Social Criticism*. Ann Arbor: University of Michigan Press, 1974.

———. *Democratic Socialism: Theory and Practice*. New York: St. Martin's, 1982.

MARX, KARL, and FRIEDRICH ENGELS. *Collected Works*. New York: International Publishers, 1975– . Projected 50 volumes.

MCLELLAN, DAVID. *Karl Marx: His Life and Thought*. New York: Harper & Row, 1973.

MÉSZÁROS, ISTVÁN. *Marx's Theory of Alienation*. London: Merlin Press, 1970.

MEYER, ALFRED G. *Leninism*. New York: Praeger, 1962.

MITRANY, DAVID. *Marx Against the Peasant: A Study in Social Dogmatism*. New York: Collier Books, 1961.

MOORE, STANLEY. *Marx on the Choice Between Socialism and Communism*. Cambridge, MA: Harvard University Press, 1980.

MOUFFE, CHANTAL, ed. *Gramsci and Marxist Theory*. London: Routledge & Kegan Paul, 1979.

MUNCK, RONALDO. *The Difficult Dialogue: Marxism and Nationalism*. London: Zed Books, 1986.

NETTL, J. P. *Rosa Luxemburg*. 2 vols. London: Oxford University Press, 1966.

OLLMAN, BERTELL. *Alienation*. 2d ed.

Cambridge, England: Cambridge University Press, 1976.

———. *Social and Sexual Revolution: Essays on Marx and Reich.* Boston: South End Press, 1979.

O'NEILL, JOHN, ed. *On Critical Theory.* New York: Seabury Press, 1976.

PANNEKOEK, ANTON. *Worker's Councils.* Melbourne, Australia: Southern Advocate for Workers' Councils, 1948.

RAPTIS, MICHEL. *Socialism, Democracy and Self-Management.* Trans. Marie-Jo Serrié and Richard Sissons. London: Allison & Busby, 1980.

RATTANSI, ALI. *Marx and the Division of Labour.* London: Macmillan, 1982.

ROBINSON, CEDRIC J. *Black Marxism: The Making of the Black Radical Tradition.* London: Zed Books, 1983.

ROEMER, JOHN. *Analytic Foundations of Marxian Economic Theory.* New York: Cambridge University Press, 1981.

———. *A General Theory of Exploitation and Class.* Cambridge, MA: Harvard University Press, 1982.

———. *Free to Lose: An Introduction to Marxist Economic Philosophy.* Cambridge, MA: Harvard University Press, 1988.

SCHMITT, RICHARD. *Introduction to Marx and Engels: A Critical Reconstruction.* Boulder, CO: Westview Press, 1987.

SCHRAM, STUART R. *The Thought of Mao Tse-Tung.* Cambridge, England: Cambridge University Press, 1989.

STOJANOVIĆ, SVETOZAR. *Between Ideals and Reality: A Critique of Socialism and Its Future.* Trans. Gerson S. Sher.

New York: Oxford University Press, 1973.

———. *The Search for Democracy in Socialism: History and Party Consciousness.* Trans. Gerson S. Sher. Buffalo, NY: Prometheus Books, 1981.

THOMAS, PAUL. *Karl Marx and the Anarchists.* London: Routledge & Kegan Paul, 1980.

TISMANEAU, VLADIMIR. *The Crisis of Marxist Ideology in Eastern Europe: The Poverty of Utopia.* London: Routledge & Kegan Paul, 1988.

TROTSKY, LEON. *Terrorism and Communism: A Reply to Karl Kautsky.* Ann Arbor: University of Michigan Press, 1961.

———. *The New Course.* Ann Arbor: University of Michigan Press, 1965.

TUCKER, ROBERT C. *Philosophy and Myth in Karl Marx.* Cambridge, England: Cambridge University Press, 1961.

———. *The Marxian Revolutionary Idea.* New York: Norton, 1969.

WIGGERSHAUS, ROLF. *The Frankfurt School: Its History, Theories, and Significance.* Translated by Michael Robertson. Cambridge, MA: MIT Press, 1994.

WILES, P. J. D. *The Political Economy of Communism.* Cambridge, MA: Harvard University Press, 1962.

WILSON, EDMUND. *To the Finland Station: A Study in the Writing and Acting of History.* Garden City, NY: Doubleday & Co., 1940.

PART IV

Traditional Opponents of Marxism and Democracy

8

Anarchism

At one time anarchism was a household word in the United States, but the visibility of anarchism as an ideology has varied throughout the century. Because of the fear with which they were viewed at the beginning of the twentieth century, anarchists became the only group restricted from immigration into the United States on the basis of political beliefs. Later that restriction was extended to communists. At other times, including the period from about 1930 to 1960, little was heard about anarchism, and it was generally thought of as a dead issue.

But anarchism had not disappeared. It reemerged in the 1960s and early 1970s in two forms, generally identified with the left and the right. Anarchism is usually thought of as an ideology of the left, but *libertarianism*, or *minimalism* as it is sometimes called, which is in significant ways similar to anarchism (some libertarians accept the label *anarchist*), is usually identified with the right.

In the 1960s and early 1970s people were probably more aware of anarchism because students in the abortive 1968 revolution in Paris carried the anarchist banner (a black flag), and anarchists were prominent in the New Left and the communal movement and participated in many demonstrations and protests. To many people this form of anarchism will seem to have disappeared again, but it still exists in many countries both as activist groups and individuals and as a theory of social organization.

During the same period libertarianism or minimalism and anarcho-capitalism emerged, first among followers of Ayn Rand (1905–1982), author of *Atlas Shrugged* (1957) and various essays and novels that presented the virtues of an absolutely free market and the evils of any sort of collectivization. Second, followers of Rand became actively involved in the early political career of Ronald Reagan (1911–).[1] Third, the Libertarian party was formed in 1971 and since then has been involved in electoral politics in the United States. Fourth, in 1974 Robert Nozick's *Anarchy, State, and Utopia* was published, giving the minimalist position the support of a professor of philosophy at Harvard and the strongest intellectual justification it has ever had. Today, libertarians are also actively involved in Republican party politics, primarily through influential "think tanks" developing positions on public policy. This influence is almost exclusively in the economic realm because libertarians oppose almost all restrictions on personal moral decision making.

PRINCIPLES OF ANARCHISM

The ideology we call *anarchism* has a variety of forms and includes a number of different ideas. The purpose of this chapter is to explore the principles of anarchism in an effort to understand both the appeal of anarchism and the reaction against it. Most studies of anarchism have focused on a select group of men: Prince Pyotr Kropotkin (1842–1921), Pierre-Joseph Proudhon (1809–1865), Mikhail Bakunin (1814–1876), Count Leo Tolstoi (1828–1910), Max Stirner (1806–1856), William Godwin (1756–1836), and William Morris (1834–1896), who rejected the label, with sometimes a bow in the direction of a few lesser-known figures such as Errico Malatesta (1850–1932), Élisée Réclus (1830–1905), Benjamin Tucker (1854–1939), and Josiah Warren (1798?–1874). Today anarchists and scholars of anarchism recognize the significant contribution made to the anarchist movement and anarchist theory by women. Emma Goldman (1865–1940) is generally recognized as the most important, but women have always been involved in all aspects of anarchism.

This approach, focused on individual anarchists, may produce a valid presentation and analysis of the clusters of ideas that make up anarchism, but it is just as likely to result in a misunderstanding of the important similarities and the equally important differences among anarchists. The best approach, therefore, seems to be to select those parts of the anarchist tradition that are most important today while striving to maintain a balanced presentation.

Kropotkin once defined *anarchism* as

> the name given to a principle or theory of life and conduct under which society is conceived without government—harmony in such a society being obtained, not by submission to law or by obedience to any authority, but by free agreements concluded between the various groups, territorial and professional, freely

---

[1]Jerome Tuccille, *It Usually Began with Ayn Rand* (New York: Stein & Day, 1971).

Pyotr (Peter) Kropotkin (1842–1921) was born into the Russian aristocracy but became the most important anarchist thinker of all time. Kropotkin's ideas originated during a long trip in Siberia as a geographer and naturalist. Intending to demonstrate that there was a "struggle for survival" and "survival of the fittest," he found instead cooperation and what he came to call "mutual aid." He published his findings in a series of essays between 1890 and 1896 and then collected them as *Mutual Aid*. His argument that cooperation rather than competition was the basis of evolution became the foundation for all his thought. From this position he contended that anarchism, not Marxism, was scientific. After escaping from a Russian prison, he spent most of his life in Western Europe, primarily in England, where he published his most famous books, *The Conquest of Bread* (1892), *Memoirs of a Revolutionist* (1898–1899), and *Fields, Factories and Workshops* (1899). He returned to Russia after the revolution in 1917 but quickly came into conflict with Lenin, whom he criticized for centralizing power. *(The Bettmann Archive)*

constituted for the sake of production and consumption, as also for the satisfaction of the infinite variety of needs and aspirations of a civilized being.[2]

Anarchism is, then, a political philosophy that holds that no group in society should be able to coerce anyone. Also, society should contain a wide variety of groups arranged to coordinate social functions. Anarchists differ somewhat on the interrelationships among these groups and on the importance of particular groups in the social system, but they would agree, with some reservations, on this definition. As another anarchist, Alexander Berkman (1870–1936), stated, "Anarchism teaches that we can live in a society where there is no compulsion of any kind. A life without compulsion naturally means liberty; it means free-

[2]Peter Kropotkin, "Anarchism," *Encyclopaedia Britannica*, 11th ed., vol. 1, p. 914.

dom from being forced or coerced, a chance to lead the life that suits you best."[3] This characterization gives a clue to both the appeal of anarchism and the fear of it. Anarchists envision a peaceful, free life without rules and regulations. Such a vision is very appealing, but the anarchist vision also attacks such institutions as the government, church, and family. Anarchism is both hated and feared because many believe anarchism would result in chaos rather than the peaceful, noncoercive society of the vision and, perhaps, because its opponents are afraid that anarchists are right in arguing that the institutions around which most of us have centered our lives are unnecessary or even harmful.

The basic assumption of anarchism is that power exercised by one person or group over another is the cause of most of our contemporary problems. As one anarchist says, "Many people say that government is necessary because some men cannot be trusted to look after themselves, but anarchists say that government is harmful because no man can be trusted to look after anyone else."[4] All anarchists would agree with this statement. They all focus on the corrupting nature of power, and they believe that human beings are capable of organizing their affairs without anyone exercising authority over others. This does not mean there will be no order in society; it means people can cooperatively produce a better system than can be produced by any authority. "Given a common need, a collection of people will, by trial and error, by improvisation and experiment, evolve order out of chaos—this order being more durable than any kind of externally imposed order."[5] This order—this organization—will be better designed for human needs than any imposed system could be because it will be "(1) voluntary, (2) functional, (3) temporary, and (4) small."[6]

Each of these last points is important for an understanding of anarchism. First, basic to all anarchism is the voluntary nature of any association. Second, an association will develop only to fill a fairly specific need and thus will be designed to fill that need alone. Therefore, third, it will disappear after the need is met. Finally, it must be small enough so people can control it rather than be controlled by it. This type of organization can be found in the consumer cooperatives existing in most Western countries today. They are voluntary, provide higher quality goods than are otherwise available and do so at lower prices, last only as long as needed, and are small enough to be controlled by the members without a hierarchy of officers. They are a good example of how anarchists wish to organize society.

Rejection of authority and the belief that it is possible to replace a coercive society with voluntary cooperation is about the only thing anarchists agree upon, and there are undoubtedly a few who would want to modify this state-

---

[3]Alexander Berkman, *ABC of Anarchism*, 3d ed. (London: Freedom Press, 1964), p. 10.

[4]Nicolas Walter, *About Anarchism* (London: Freedom Press, 1969), p. 6. Originally published as *Anarchy 100*, vol. 9 (June 1969).

[5]Colin Ward, "Anarchism as a Theory of Organization," *Anarchy 62*, vol. 6 (April 1966): 103.

[6]Ward, "Anarchism," p. 101. See also Terry Phillips, "Organization—The Way Forward," *Freedom* 31 (August 22, 1970): 3.

ment. But "the essence of anarchism, the one thing without which it is not anarchism, is the negation of authority over anyone by anyone."[7]

Beyond this, anarchism divides loosely into two categories: (1) collectivist, with emphasis on the individual within a voluntary association of individuals; and (2) individualist, with emphasis on the individual separate from any association. The former is sometimes divided into communist anarchism and anarcho-syndicalism; the latter is usually divided into individualist anarchism and anarcho-capitalism, also known as minimalism or libertarianism. In each case, though, the similarities are more important than the differences.

Collectivist Anarchism

Communist anarchism, traditionally associated primarily with Kropotkin, is the most developed and comprehensive anarchist theory. It starts, as does all anarchism, with the assumption that coercion in any form is bad. It suggests, as the solution to the problem of order in a society without a government, the establishment of a series of small, voluntary communes or collectives. These communes would join together into a federation to deal with any common problems. As George Woodcock (1912–1995) wrote, "The village would appoint delegates to the regional federations, which in their turn would appoint delegates to the national federations. No delegate would have the power to speak for anything but the decisions of the workers who elected him and would be subject to recall at any time."[8] He goes on to say that the delegates would be elected for a short period of time, and although expenses might be paid, the delegate would receive exactly the same salary as if still working at his or her regular job.[9] In this way, the anarchist delegate is a very restricted representative.

Anarcho-syndicalists take essentially the same approach, except that they refer specifically to the work situation, particularly industrial work. The basic principles are as follows:

1. Each industry is organized into a federation of independent communes.
2. Each industry is controlled by the workers in that industry.
3. Policy questions and questions of intercommune relations are handled by a coordinating council.

The key to understanding anarcho-syndicalism is its industrial base. The central element of anarcho-syndicalism is workers' control.[10] Society is organized on the basis of the control of each industry by the workers in that industry. The word *industry* is normally defined broadly to include such activities as the

---

[7]Walter, *About Anarchism*, p. 8.

[8]George Woodcock, *New Life to the Land* (London: Freedom Press, 1942), p. 26.

[9]On this point, see also P.S., "Anarcho-Syndicalism—The Workers' Next Step," *Freedom* 26 (January 30, 1965): 4.

[10] There is a vast literature on workers' control. For a sampling see *Workers' Control*, ed. Ken Coates and Tony Topham (London: Panther Books, 1970), and *Anarchy 2*, vol. 1 (April 1961).

building industry, which then would be controlled by all the different workers who participate in building any structure. These individuals meet to resolve the particular problems of that industry. Then representatives of each industry assemble to administer the economic life of the entire country. The key word here is *administer*.

This is the same thing as Engels's statement that in the final stage of communism, the government of people will become the administration of things. People will no longer be governed. They will be free from government, but they will participate in administering the economic life of the country. The contention is that there need be no such thing as a political decision. The administration of things should be, according to anarcho-syndicalism, a fairly simple and mechanical operation not giving rise to many conflicts. When conflicts do arise because of, for example, problems of allocating scarce goods, the workers will be in the best position to know what is most important, what can be produced least expensively, and how to improve production. Therefore, these workers rather than managers who are not in contact with the actual work should be making such decisions. The anarcho-syndicalist also argues that putting the workers in control will enable them to produce more, thus lessening the problem of the allocation of scarce goods. The anarcho-syndicalist argues that workers' control acts as a work incentive.

Some anarcho-syndicalists have argued that the basis for the new society is to be found in the organization of the present trade unions, but most anarcho-syndicalists view trade unions as conservative. Although the idea of syndicalism originated as part of the trade union movement in France, anarcho-syndicalism has moved away from the union movement. Modern anarcho-syndicalists oppose the existing union movement and argue that it fails to support workers against management and government.

The differences between communist anarchism and anarcho-syndicalism are not great. Anarcho-syndicalism is more directly concerned with the organization of industry than is communist anarchism, but both arrive at fundamentally the same conclusions. Both accept the notion that the people in a given area should administer that area for the benefit of the society as a whole (whether it be a commune as in communist anarchism or an industry as in anarcho-syndicalism). It is assumed in both cases that the entire population will be workers in that everyone will participate to some degree in the economic life of the society. Both believe that by removing coercion a viable society can develop. The primary difference is found in the emphasis in anarcho-syndicalism on the operation of the industrial system.

Anarcho-syndicalism and communist anarchism developed a secondary level of organization that is important for understanding the course of anarchist thought. Both stress the need for some way of developing cooperation among communes or industries as well as within the commune or industry. Although the focus of most studies of anarchist thought has been on individual freedom, anarchists have always argued that it is not possible to stop there. The primary focus of collectivist anarchism is not the isolated individual. The focus is an individual within a noncoercive society. The emphasis is on producing a society that will allow individual freedom. Most anarchists recognize that the small commune or industry is not sufficient for individuals in contemporary society. Some cooperation among communes and industries is necessary to produce enough goods in sufficient diversity for each individual.

This idea is most clearly recognized in anarcho-syndicalism because its basic form of organization—the industry—is specialized. Therefore, in order to give each individual the goods necessary for life, there must be a high degree of cooperation among industries to provide an efficient distribution system for the goods produced by the individual industries. The only way to handle this is through cooperation by the workers within the various industries. To some extent, what is looked for here is simply a form of enlightened self-interest, because each worker in a particular industry needs the products of a wide variety of industries. Therefore, the individual workers will cooperate with workers from many other industries since they all need the products of each and every industry. Anarcho-syndicalists believe this cooperation can be developed readily once coercion disappears.

In order to get to that point, all coercion must be abolished. This means government and, for the collective anarchist, capitalism must go. Getting rid of them raises the question of violence. Anarchists believe no established authority will simply give up without a fight; therefore, revolution is likely to be the means of change.[11] The abolition of capitalism is a central concern for most anarchists because they believe workers are exploited by the capitalist in about the same ways Marx believed. Collectivist anarchists argue for common ownership of the means of production and the distribution of goods according to need. Anarcho-capitalists, discussed shortly, believe that this system would exploit the best workers. Collectivist anarchists respond that capitalism exploits all workers. It may be that this disagreement is incapable of being solved, but to put it in perspective, let us look at the individualist position.

Individualist Anarchism

The individualist anarchist recognizes nothing above his ego and rebels against all discipline and all authority, divine or human. He accepts no morality and when he gives himself to the feelings of love, friendship, or sociability, he does so because it is a personal need, an egoistic satisfaction—because it pleases him to do it.[12]

Individualist anarchism is traditionally associated with Max Stirner. Essentially the position is as stated above; individuals determine for themselves, out of their own needs and desires, what is right for them. Stirner even applies this to murder.[13]

---

[11]For a recent discussion, see Vernon Richards, ed. *Violence & Anarchism: A Polemic* (London: Freedom Press, 1993).

[12]Enzo Martucci, "Individualist Amoralism," *Minus One*, no. 16 (November/December 1966); 5, trans. J.-P.S. from *L'Unique*, no. 37.

[13]See Max Stirner (pseud.), *The Ego and His Own: The Case of the Individual Against Authority*, trans. Steven T. Byington and ed. James J. Martin (New York: Libertarian Book Club, 1963), p. 190.

Individualist anarchists do not completely reject cooperation. They argue that cooperation is essential for the fulfillment of some needs. But they contend that only the individualist of their own definition is capable of genuinely forming a voluntary association with others. In addition, they never see this association as an end in itself but merely as useful for a temporary purpose. It must be the servant of the members, not dominate the members.

Individualist anarchists argue against the collective ownership of goods, but not all are convinced the capitalist system is any better. Here, one finds a major split in the ranks of individualist anarchists. On one hand, there are those who reject both capitalism and socialism and argue that they are not convinced that either system is valid. On the other hand, there are anarcho-capitalists, who contend the only form of economic life compatible with individualism is capitalism. Usually their approach is connected with a view of life similar to that of the Social Darwinist. They see life as a struggle for survival and hold that a socialist economic system supports those who do not deserve to survive. Anarcho-capitalists take the position that all essential social services can be better operated privately for profit than by any government or commune; this includes the police, education, the military, and so forth.

LIBERTARIANISM

Closely related to anarcho-capitalism, but generally not considered as extreme, is libertarianism, which is sometimes called *minimalism* because it stresses minimal government. In *Anarchy, State, and Utopia* Robert Nozick argues for a minimal government based upon the preeminent right of private property. His ideal system would consist of a number of small communities in which the members have collectively agreed upon a way of life; many differing communities mean that many ways of life would be available.

The libertarianism that is currently playing a significant role in American politics is not that extreme, although the emphasis on private property is central to both Nozick's scheme and libertarianism. Libertarianism assumes that the free market almost always provides a better way of organizing social life than any system developed by government, and all libertarians are committed to severely reducing government.

In the United States, one of the forms taken by libertarianism is the Libertarian party, a political party supporting candidates for office who are pledged to severely reduce government. The first two paragraphs of the Libertarian party platform state, "We, the members of the Libertarian Party, challenge the cult of the omnipotent state and defend the rights of the individual. We hold that all individuals have the right to exercise sole dominion over their own lives, and have the right to live in whatever manner they choose, so long as they do not forcibly interfere with the equal right of others to live in whatever manner they choose."[14] The platform includes a wide variety of points stressing the freedom of the individual but is particularly concerned with economic questions.

> There is no conflict between property rights and human rights. Indeed, property rights are the rights of humans with respect to property and, as such, are entitled to the same respect and protection as all other human rights.

Moreover, all human rights are property rights, too. Such rights as the freedom from involuntary servitude as well as the freedom of speech and the freedom of press are based on self-ownership. Our bodies are our property every bit as much as is justly acquired land or material objects.

> We further hold that the owners of property have the full rights to control, use, dispose of, or in any manner enjoy their property without interference, until and unless the exercise of their control infringes the valid rights of others.[15]

As far as the economy is concerned Libertarians are virtually, but not quite, anarchists. They advocate the unfettered free market and argue that the only role for government "in the economic realm is to protect property rights, adjudicate disputes, and provide a legal framework in which voluntary trade is protected."[16] Libertarians also see a role for government in the protection of person and property from crime and in defense.

In other areas of social policy, the Libertarian party generally opposes government interference in individual decision making. They oppose laws outlawing drugs or requiring prescriptions to obtain medication and any laws that restrict sexual activity such as prostitution. They oppose, for example, restrictions on abortion, the sale of alcohol, the sale of sexually explicit material, gambling, and suicide. The Libertarian party is not large or strong, but it represents an important variant of anarchism, one with a long tradition in the United States. It appears destined to be a long-term addition to American third parties.

ANARCHIST SOCIAL THOUGHT

All of anarchism, whether communist, anarcho-syndicalist, or individualist, is concerned with the freedom of the individual. Anarchism rejects control by any group, but particularly by the organized group we call the state or government. Anarchists argue that people are capable of both freedom and cooperation. They believe human beings are willing and able to help each other. They believe the human being's best instincts are destroyed by the present organization of society. They believe, as did Marx, that true love between individuals is impossible, or virtually impossible, under contemporary conditions. They believe a morality

---

[14]1992 Libertarian Party Platform.

[15]Ibid.

[16]Ibid.

system that rejects physical relationships without the sanction of church and state destroys the possibility of developing what Marx called the love-sex relationship. The anarchist does not insist on or reject the simple monogamous marriage relationship. Individuals, they contend, must decide about what kind of relationship they want. It is their life; they must be free to live it as they choose.

The anarchist also contends that parents have a real responsibility to ensure freedom for their children. Anarchists believe the contemporary educational system is destructive of freedom, creativity, and learning. They believe there must be an educational system directed to the individual child, whatever her or his needs. Education directed to the individual child cannot be found, they contend, in the highly organized, overly complex system we have today. It can be found in the small group concerned with educating for freedom. Anarchists believe a child, given the freedom to choose and the encouragement to follow his or her own bent, will gradually find distinct interests and, getting interested, will apply to those interests the tremendous energies children can develop. Children will learn more this way than by traditional methods.

Much of what we are taught in our schools, the anarchist believes, is irrelevant to our lives; we waste many years in attempting to learn things that will never interest us or be of any use to us. A child should be encouraged to look at the world and interpret it on her or his own rather than being given answers. This approach to education puts a tremendous burden on parents and teachers. Teachers must develop a close relationship with the child in order to be able to understand the child's changing interests and to suggest ways in which the child might best fulfill them. This must be done without too much direction. Parents must be capable of giving the child freedom. Parents must not control children too much. Anarchist theories of child rearing and education have been some of the most innovative, instructive, and successful of any of the anarchist approaches to contemporary life.[17]

There is no anarchist proscription or support of religion. Within anarchist circles, considerable debate takes place over the question of religious affiliation. Many argue that such affiliation is incompatible with anarchism; others argue that it depends on the type of organization or church.

Still others, including Catholic anarchists such as Dorothy Day (1897–1980) and Ammon Hennacy (1893–1970) (who left the church shortly before he died), argued that faith in the doctrines of the church did not affect them as anarchists. They held that the church speaks only on matters of faith and morals; it did not deal with the rest of their lives. Outside of the areas of faith and morals, Catholic anarchists consider themselves free of the church. The Catholic anar-

---

[17]See, for example, Herbert Read, *The Education of Free Men* (London: Freedom Press, 1944); A. S. Neill, *Summerhill: A Radical Approach to Child Rearing* (New York: Hart Publication, 1960); Neill, *A Dominie's Log* (London: The Hogarth Press, 1986. Originally published London: Herbert Jenkins, 1915); Ivan D. Illich, *Deschooling Society* (London: Calder/New York: Harper & Row, 1971); and *Education Without Schools*, ed. Peter Buckman (London: Souvenir Press, 1973).

chist is merely a special case of contemporary anarchism. Individuals such as Day and Hennacy who accepted an authoritarian religion and at the same time considered themselves anarchists were merely taking one part of their life, that part dealing with questions of religious faith, and there accepting the dictates of the church. As long as this acceptance is restricted to religious and, perhaps, moral questions, it does not necessarily affect the social and political positions of the anarchist.

Anarchist theory has developed mostly as a series of commentaries on specific areas of life believed to be coercive and that could be improved by providing a free atmosphere. The ultimate goal is a truly free life in a commune that weaves together the various ways of being free.[18]

Anarchism will probably always remain a minor ideology. It is unlikely that anarchism will ever succeed in this world, but anarchism is a belief in the human being. Anarchism is the ideology that has the most faith in people. It believes, more than any other ideology does, that people are capable of freedom and cooperation.

CURRENT TRENDS

A number of recent or continuing developments must be noted. First, as discussed earlier, anarcho-capitalism, libertarianism, and minimalism are continuing to grow and gain recognition by established political parties. Second, various forms of anarchism have been discovered by popular writers, particularly writers of science fiction. The most noteworthy of these writers are Poul Anderson (1926–), who has written many works from the perspective of anarcho-capitalism, and Ursula K. Le Guin (1929–), who wrote a novel, *The Dispossessed: An Ambiguous Utopia* (1974), that depicts in detail and with sympathy the struggles of a successful anarchist society to hold true to its principles.

Third, there has been a controversy among anarchists over whether a new anarchism that developed in the 1960s was essentially different from anarchism as it previously existed. Some of the differences relate to the social composition, age, class background, and so forth of the "new" as opposed to the "old" anarchism. Other differences related to questions of tactics, such as violence versus nonviolence, which have always been controversial.

While a survey of the literature of the "new" anarchism reveals significant stylistic differences, it is at least debatable whether there are significant differences in content. In most cases, analysis shows such differences do not exist, but at the same time there is an emphasis on spontaneity and a rejection of reasoned argument in the "new" anarchism that does not appear in the "old" anarchism.

---

[18]See, for example, W. David Wills, *Throw Away Thy Rod: Living with Difficult Children* (London: Victor Gollancz, 1960); Wills, *The Barns Experiment* (London: George Allen & Unwin, 1945); Alex Comfort, *Delinquency* (London: Freedom Press, 1951); John Hewetson, *Ill-Health, Poverty and the State* (London: Freedom Press, 1942); and George Woodcock, *Railways and Society* (London: Freedom Press, 1943).

Emma Goldman (1869–1940) was known as "Red Emma" and was a leading anarchist, lecturer, popularizer of the arts, and agitator for birth control, women's rights, and free speech. Born in Russia, she emigrated to the United States in 1885. In 1889 she moved from Rochester, N.Y., to New York City, where she met Johann Most (1846–1906) and Alexander Berkman (1870–1936) and became active with them in anarchist circles. In 1892 she and Berkman attempted to assassinate the industrial leader Henry Clay Frick. She edited the journal *Mother Earth* (1906–1917) and wrote a number of books including *Anarchism and Other Essays* (1911), *The Social Significance of Modern Drama* (1914), and *Living My Life* (1931). She was involved in most radical activities in the United States until she was deported as an undesirable alien in 1919. After she was deported she traveled in the Soviet Union and wrote *My Disillusionment with Russia* (1923) and *My Further Disillusionment with Russia* (1924), both of which discussed the authoritarian nature of the Soviet government. After leaving Russia she continued her career as a radical agitator through involvement in the Spanish Civil War. (*Library of Congress*)

Fourth, there is a considerable growth of feminist theory within the context of anarchism, sometimes called anarcha-feminism. Feminism has had a long tradition within anarchism, and there have been a number of important female anarchists, including Emma Goldman (1869–1940), Voltairine de Cleyre (1866–1912), and Dorothy Day in the United States, and Marie Louise Berneri (1918–1949) in England.

Finally, a number of creative anarchist thinkers have published innovative applications of anarchist theory to current issues of public policy. The most important of these writers is Colin Ward (1924–), a freelance writer who has been particularly concerned with transportation policy, housing and town planning, and environmental policy. Better known than Ward, and discussed further in Chapter 13, is Murray Bookchin (1921–), a critic of contemporary technology and a major theorist of social ecology. Alex Comfort (1920–) is best known for his writings arguing for a freed sexuality, but he has contributed substantially to anarchist theory in the area of aging.

Anarchist theory is still being created by these and other thinkers, and it is particularly being extended into ecological theory. In Chapter 13 some of these specific developments are discussed further.

SUGGESTED READINGS

ARMAND, EMILE (pseud.). *Anarchism and Individualism: Three Essays.* Trans. D. T. W. London: S. E. Parker, n.d.

————. *What Individualist-Anarchists Want.* Trans. Mark William Kramrisch. Adapt. S. E. Parker. London: S. E. Parker, n.d.

AVRICH, PAUL. *Bakunin & Nechaev.* London: Freedom Press, 1974.

————. *The Modern School Movement: Anarchism and Education in the United States.* Princeton, NJ: Princeton University Press, 1980.

————. *Anarchist Portraits.* Princeton, NJ: Princeton University Press, 1988.

BAKUNIN, MIKHAIL. *God and the State.* New York: Dover, 1970.

————. *Bakunin on Anarchy: Selected Works by the Activist-Founder of World Anarchism.* Ed. and trans. Sam Dolgoff. New York: Knopf, 1971.

BALDELLI, GIOVANNI. *Social Anarchism.* Chicago: Aldine-Atherton, 1971.

BARRETT, GEORGE (pseud. George Powell Ballard). *The First Person.* London: Freedom Press, 1963.

BERKMAN, ALEXANDER. *ABC of Anarchism.* 3d ed. London: Freedom Press, 1964.

BERNERI, CAMILLO. *Peter Kropotkin: His Federalist Ideas.* London: Freedom Press, 1942.

BOOKCHIN, MURRAY. *Post-Scarcity Anarchism.* Berkeley, CA: Ramparts Press, 1971.

BOSE, ATINDRANATH. *A History of Anarchism.* Calcutta, India: World Press Private, 1967.

BRAILSFORD, H. N. *Shelley, Godwin, and Their Circle.* New York: Henry Holt, n.d.

BROOKS, FRANK H., ed. *The Individual Anarchists: An Anthology of "Liberty" (1881–1908).* New Brunswick, NJ: Transaction, 1994.

CAHM, CAROLINE. *Kropotkin and the Rise of Revolutionary Anarchism 1872–1886.* Cambridge, England: Cambridge University Press, 1989.

CARR, E. G. *Michael Bakunin.* New York: Vintage Books, 1937.

CARTER, APRIL. *The Political Theory of Anarchism.* London: Routledge & Kegan Paul, 1971.

CHRISTIE, STUART, and MELTZER, ALBERT. *The Floodgates of Anarchy.* London: Kahn & Averill, 1970.

CROWDER, GEORGE. *Classical Anarchism: The Political Thought of Godwin, Proudhon, Bakunin, and Kropotkin.* Oxford, England: Clarendon Press, 1991.

DE CLEYRE, VOLTAIRINE. *Selected Works of Voltairine de Cleyre.* Ed. Alexander Berkman. New York: Mother Earth Publishing, 1914.

DELEON, DAVID. *The American as Anarchist: Reflections on Indigenous Radicalism.* Baltimore, MD: Johns Hopkins University Press, 1978.

DE LUBAC, HENRI, S. J. *The Un-Marxian Socialist: A Study of Proudhon.* Trans.

R. E. Schantlebury. New York: Sheed & Ward, 1948.

DOLGOFF, SAM, ed. *The Anarchist Collectives: Workers' Self-Management in the Spanish Revolution 1936–1939*. New York: Free Life Editions, 1974.

ELTZBACHER, PAUL. *Anarchism: Exponents of the Anarchist Philosophy*. Ed. James J. Martin. Trans. Steven T. Byington. London: Freedom Press, 1960.

FALK, CANDACE. *Love, Anarchy, and Emma Goldman: A Biography*. New York: Holt, Rinehart & Winston, 1984.

FLEMING, MARIE. *The Anarchist Way to Socialism*. London: Croom Helm, 1979.

FREIRE, PAULO. *Pedagogy of the Oppressed*. Trans. Myra Bergman Ramos. New York: Seabury Press, 1970.

———. *The Politics of Education: Culture, Power, and Liberation*. Trans. Donaldo Macedo. South Hadley, MA: Bergin & Garvey, 1985.

GIBSON, TONY. *Love, Sex & Power in Later Life: A Libertarian Perspective*. London: Freedom Press, 1992.

GLADSTEIN, MIMI REISEL. *The Ayn Rand Companion*. Westport, CT: Greenwood Press, 1984.

GODWIN, WILLIAM. *Enquiry Concerning Political Justice and Its Influence on Morals and Happiness*. Ed. R. E. L. Priestley. 3 vols. Toronto: University of Toronto Press, 1946.

GOLDMAN, EMMA. *Anarchism and Other Essays*. New York: Dover, 1970.

———. *Living My Life*. 2 vols. New York: Dover, 1970.

GUÉRIN, DANIEL. *Anarchism from Theory to Practice*. Trans. Mary Klopper. New York: Monthly Review Press, 1970.

HALL, DAVID L. *Eros and Irony: A Prelude to Philosophical Anarchism*. Albany: State University of New York Press, 1982.

HENNACY, AMMON. *The Book of Ammon*. The author, 1965.

———. *The One-Man Revolution in America*. Salt Lake City, UT: Ammon Hennacy Publications, 1970.

HOLTERMAN, THOM, and VAN

MAARSEVEEN, HENC, eds. *Law in Anarchism*. Rotterdam, The Netherlands: Erasmus University, 1980.

HOSPERS, JOHN. *Libertarianism: A Political Philosophy for Tomorrow*. Santa Barbara, CA: Reason Press, 1971.

HYAMS, EDWARD. *Pierre-Joseph Proudhon: His Revolutionary Life, Mind and Works*. London: John Murray, 1979.

ILLICH, IVAN D. *Celebrating Awareness: A Call for Institutional Revolution*. London: Calder & Boyars, 1971.

———. *Deschooling Society*. New York: Harper & Row, 1971.

———. *Tools for Conviviality*. London: Calder & Boyars, 1973.

———. *The Right to Useful Unemployment and Its Professional Enemies*. London: Marion Boyars, 1978.

JACKER, CORRINE. *The Black Flag of Anarchy: Antistatism in the United States*. New York: Scribner's, 1968.

JOLL, JAMES. *The Anarchists*. 2d ed. London: Methuen, 1979.

KELLY, AILEEN. *Mikhail Bakunin: A Study in the Psychology and Politics of Utopianism*. Oxford, England: Clarendon Press, 1982.

KNABB, KEN, ed. *Situationist International Anthology*. Trans. Ken Knabb with Nadine Block and Joel Cornault. Berkeley, CA: Bureau of Public Streets, 1981.

KORNBLUTH, JOYCE L., ed. *Rebel Voices: An I.W.W. Anthology*. Ann Arbor: University of Michigan Press, 1968.

KRIMERMAN, LEONARD I., and LEWIS PERRY, eds. *Patterns of Anarchy: A Collection of Writings on the Anarchist Tradition*. Garden City, NY: Doubleday, 1966.

KROPOTKIN, PETER. *The Conquest of Bread*. New York: Putnam's, 1907.

———. *The Great French Revolution 1789–1793*. 2 vols. Trans. N. F. Dryhurst. New York: Vanguard Press, 1909.

———. *Ethics: Origin and Development*. Trans. Louis S. Friedland and Joseph R. Piroshnikoff. New York: Tudor, 1924.

———. *Mutual Aid: A Factor of Evolution*.

Boston: Extending Horizons Books, 1955.

———. *Memoirs of a Revolutionist.* Ed. James Allen Rogers. Garden City, NY: Doubleday, 1962.

———. *Fields, Factories and Workshops.* New York: Benjamin Blom, 1968.

———. *Kropotkin's Revolutionary Pamphlets.* Ed. Roger N. Baldwin. New York: Dover, 1970.

———. *Fields, Factories and Workshops Tomorrow.* Ed. Colin Ward. London: George Allen & Unwin, 1974.

———. *Act for Yourselves: Articles from Freedom 1886–1907.* Ed. Nicolas Walter and Heiner Becker. London: Freedom Press, 1988.

LABADIE, LAURENCE. *Selected Essays.* Colorado Springs, CO: Ralph Myles, 1978.

LOCKE, DON. *A Fantasy of Reason: The Life and Thought of William Godwin.* London: Routledge & Kegan Paul, 1980.

MACHAN, TIBOR R. *Individuals and Their Rights.* La Salle, IL: Open Court, 1989.

MALATESTA, ERRICO. *Anarchy.* 8th ed. London: Freedom Press, 1949.

MARSH, MARGARET S. *Anarchist Women 1870–1920.* Philadelphia: Temple University Press, 1981.

MARSHALL, PETER. *Demanding the Impossible: A History of Anarchism.* London: HarperCollins, 1992.

MARSHALL, PETER M. *William Godwin.* New Haven, CT: Yale University Press, 1984.

MARTIN, JAMES J. *Men Against the State: The Expositors of Individualist Anarchism in America, 1827–1908.* Colorado Springs, CO: Ralph Myles, 1970.

MILLER, DAVID. *Anarchism.* London: J. M. Dent & Sons, 1984.

MILLER, MARTIN A. *Kropotkin.* Chicago: University of Chicago Press, 1976.

NARVESON, JAN. *The Libertarian Idea.* Philadelphia: Temple University Press, 1988.

NOZICK, ROBERT. *Anarchy, State, and Utopia.* New York: Basic Books, 1974.

NURSEY-BRAY, PAUL, with the assistance of JIM JOSE and ROBYN WILLIAMS. *Anarchist Thinkers and Thought: An Annotated Bibliography.* Westport: Greenwood Press, 1992.

OSOFSKY, STEPHEN. *Peter Kropotkin.* Boston: Twayne, 1979.

PARKER, S. E. *Individualist Anarchism: An Outline.* London: S. E. Parker, 1965.

PENNOCK, J. ROLAND, and JOHN W. CHAPMAN, eds. *Anarchism: Nomos XIX.* New York: New York University Press, 1978.

PERKINS, RICHARD, and ERNESTINE PERKINS. *Precondition for Peace and Prosperity: Rational Anarchy.* St. Thomas, Ontario, Canada: Authors, 1971.

PERLIN, TERRY N., ed. *Contemporary Anarchism.* New Brunswick, NJ: Transaction Books, 1979.

PETERS, VICTOR. *Nestor Makhno: The Life of an Anarchist.* Winnipeg, Manitoba, Canada: Echo Books, 1970.

PIEHL, MEL. *Breaking Bread: The Catholic Worker and the Origin of Catholic Radicalism in America.* Philadelphia: Temple University Press, 1982.

PROUDHON, PIERRE-JOSEPH. *General Idea of the Revolution in the Nineteenth Century.* Trans. John Beverley Robinson. London: Freedom Press, 1923.

———. *Selected Writings of P.-J. Proudhon.* Ed. Stewart Edwards. Trans. Elizabeth Fraser. Garden City, NY: Anchor Books, 1969.

———. *The Principle of Federation.* Trans. Richard Vernon. Toronto, Ontario, Canada: University of Toronto Press, 1979.

———. *What Is Property? An Inquiry into the Principle of Right and of Government.* 2 vols. in 1. Trans. Benjamin R. Tucker. London: William Reeves, n.d.

PYZIUR, EUGENE. *The Doctrine of Anarchism of Michael A. Bakunin.* Chicago: Henry Regnery, 1965.

QUAIL, JOHN. *The Slow Burning Fuse [The Lost History of British Anarchists].* London: Paladin, 1978.

READ, HERBERT. *The Philosophy of Anarchism.* London: Freedom Press, 1940.

————. *The Education of Free Men*. London: Freedom Press, 1944.

————. *Poetry and Anarchism*. 2d ed. London: Freedom Press, 1947.

————. *Anarchy and Order: Essays in Politics*. London: Faber & Faber, 1954.

READ, LEONARD E. *Elements of Libertarian Leadership: Notes on the Theory, Methods, and Practice of Freedom*. Irvington-on-Hudson, NY: Foundation for Economic Education, 1962.

REICHERT, WILLIAM O. *Partisans of Freedom: A Study in American Anarchism*. Bowling Green, OH: Bowling Green University Popular Press, 1976.

RICHARDS, VERNON, comp. and ed. *Errico Malatesta: His Life and Ideas*. London: Freedom Press, 1965.

————. *The Impossibilities of Social Democracy*. London: Freedom Press, 1978.

————, ed. *Violence & Anarchism: A Polemic*. London: Freedom Press, 1993.

RITTER, ALAN. *Anarchism: A Theoretical Analysis*. Cambridge, England: Cambridge University Press, 1980.

ROBERTS, NANCY J. *Dorothy Day and the "Catholic Worker."* Albany: State University of New York Press, 1984.

ROCKER, RUDOLF. *Nationalism and Culture*. Trans. Ray E. Chase. Los Angeles, CA: Rocker Publications Committee, 1937.

ROOUM, DONALD. *What Is Anarchism? An Introduction*. London: Freedom Press, 1992.

ROTHBARD, MURRAY N. *Power & Market: Government and the Economy*. Menlo Park, CA: Institute for Humane Studies, 1970.

————. *For a New Liberty*. New York: Macmillan, 1973.

————. *The Ethics of Liberty*. Atlantic Highlands, NJ: Humanities Press, 1982.

ROUSSOPOULOS, DIMITRIOS I., ed. *The Anarchist Papers*. 3 vols. Montréal, Québec, Canada: Black Rose Books, 1986–1990.

SCHUSTER, EUNICE MINETTE. *Native American Anarchism: A Study of Left-Wing American Individualism*. New York: Da Capo Press, 1970. Originally published 1932.

SEGARS, MARY C. "Equality and Christian Anarchism: The Political and Social Ideas of the Catholic Worker Movement." *Review of Politics* 40, no. 2 (April 1978): 196–230.

SMITH, MICHAEL P. *The Libertarians and Education*. London: George Allen & Unwin, 1983.

SONN, RICHARD D. *Anarchism*. New York: Twayne, 1992.

STIRNER, MAX (pseud.). *The Ego and His Own: The Case of the Individual Against Authority*. Ed. James J. Martin. Trans. Steven T. Byington. New York: Libertarian Book Club, 1963.

————. *The False Principle of Our Education or Humanism and Realism*. Ed. James J. Martin. Trans. Robert H. Beebe. Colorado Springs, CO: Ralph Myles, 1967.

TAYLOR, MICHAEL. *Anarchy and Cooperation*. New York: Wiley, 1976.

————. *Community, Anarchy and Liberty*. Cambridge, England: Cambridge University Press, 1982.

THOMAS, JOAN. *The Years of Grief and Laughter: A "Biography" of Ammon Hennacy*. Phoenix, AZ: Hennacy Press, 1974.

TIFFT, LARRY, and DENNIS SULLIVAN. *The Struggle to Be Human: Crime, Criminology, and Anarchism*. Over the Water, Sanday, Orkney: Cienfuegos Press, 1980.

TOLSTOY, LEO. *The Law of Love and the Law of Violence*. Trans. Mary Koutouzow Tolstoy. London: Anthony Blond, 1970.

————. *What Then Must We Do?* Trans. Aylmer Maude. Bideford, Devon, England: Green Books, 1991. Translation originally published 1925.

TUCKER, BENJAMIN R. *Individual Liberty: Selections from the Writings of Benjamin R. Tucker*. Ed. C. L. S. New York: Vanguard Press, 1926.

TULLOCK, GORDON, ed. *Explorations in the Theory of Anarchy*. Blacksburg, VA: Center for the Study of Public

Choice, Virginia Polytechnic Institute and State University, 1972.

———. *Further Explorations in the Theory of Anarchy*. Blacksburg, VA: University Publications, 1974.

WARD, COLIN. *Housing: An Anarchist Approach*. London: Freedom Press, 1976.

———. *Anarchy in Action*. 2d ed. London: Freedom Press, 1982.

———. *Welcome, Thinner City: Urban Survival in the 1990s*. London: Bedford Square Press, 1989.

———. *The Child in the City*. London: Architectural Press, 1978. Reprinted without illustrations London: Bedford Square Press, 1990.

———. *The Child in the Country*. London: Robert Hale, 1988. Reprinted London: Bedford Square Press, 1990.

———. *Freedom to Go: After the Motor Age*. London: Freedom Press, 1991.

WEXLER, ALICE. *Emma Goldman: An Intimate Life*. New York: Pantheon, 1984.

WOODCOCK, GEORGE. *Anarchy or Chaos*. London: Freedom Press, 1944.

———. *William Godwin: A Biographical Study*. London: Porcupine Press, 1946.

———. *Pierre-Joseph Proudhon: A Biography*. London: Routledge & Kegan Paul, 1956.

———. *Anarchism: A History of Libertarian Ideas and Movements*. Cleveland, OH: World Publishing, 1962.

———, ed. *The Anarchist Reader*. London: Fontana Books, 1977.

———. *Anarchism and Anarchists*. Kingston, Ontario, Canada: Quarry Press, 1992.

———, and IVAN AVAKUMOVIC. *The Anarchist Prince: A Biographical Study of Peter Kropotkin*. London: T. V. Broadman, 1950.

WOOLF, ROBERT PAUL. *In Defense of Anarchism*. New York: Harper & Row, 1970.

9

❦

Fascism and National Socialism

For the generation that lived through World War II, the words *fascism, national socialism,* and *nazism* raise indescribably horrible pictures of brutality and inhumanity. For those who have grown up since the end of the war, the horror associated with the concentration camps has faded. For many years now the word *fascist* has been used loosely to refer to various countries and individuals. Sometimes the label is accurate, but frequently it is simply a stronger word for authoritarian. Using the word loosely like this tends to hide the fact that fascism and national socialism still exist as small but active movements in many countries and in the ideologies of many individuals.

Fascism and national socialism are similar enough to be called one ideology. There are differences, but national socialism is more accurately seen as one of a number of varieties of fascism rather than different in kind. We identify national socialism with Adolf Hitler (1889–1945), which tends to isolate it in time and space; but national socialism continues without Hitler, even though he is one of its heroes. Fascism as an ideology developed early in this century in France and Italy, and the first successful fascist movement was in Italy in the 1920s.

The discussion here focuses on the major movements in Germany and Italy prior to World War II, but fascism and national socialism are not dead. Small groups exist in many countries and are getting stronger both in the countries of their origin and in many others around the world.

THE THEORETICAL BASE

Any discussion of fascism and national socialism must stress seven basic ideas. Although the emphasis varies, these ideas are almost always found in fascist and national socialist writing. They are:

1. Irrationalism;

2. Social Darwinism;

3. Nationalism;

4. Glorification of the state;

5. The leadership principle;

6. Racism (more important in national socialism than in fascism); and

7. Anticommunism.

The first two are basic themes that are rarely explicitly stated. All seven concepts are interrelated but can be separated for analysis.

Irrationalism

Irrationalism permeates the approach of fascism and national socialism but by its very nature is difficult to analyze. Irrationalism rejects the idea that reason or science can solve social problems. In the nineteenth and early twentieth centuries, reason and science were the central tenets of liberal and Marxist approaches to social change, and irrationalism specifically rejects those approaches. In opposition to this approach, fascism and national socialism reject the application of reason and science to social problems and use myth, emotion, and hate as tools of manipulation. The basic assumption is that humans are not rational beings. They need not and cannot be reasoned with; they can only be led and manipulated. Other ideologies take note of the irrational aspects of human psychology and behavior, and some stress the positive aspects of the irrational. But only fascism and national socialism emphasize the irrational and treat it as a central part of the ideology.

The emphasis in national socialism is on myths of blood (racism) and soil (nationalism) and on violence as a constant part of life. Violence is not only directed at the national and racial enemies but is a normal aspect of political life. Germans who did not fit Hitler's image of racial purity were executed along with Jews, homosexuals, and the physically and mentally disabled.

Paradoxically racial hatred and intense nationalism are part of the appeal of fascism and national socialism. If you are insecure—financially, socially, or emotionally—an appeal based on racial hatred and intense nationalism, which promotes a feeling of worth in you as a member of a superior race or nation and which identifies people who are said to be inferior, can be very effective. Fascism and national socialism give a sense of belonging, superiority, and security to those who feel cut off, inferior, or insecure. It does this in such a way that the feeling need not be questioned. This is very clear in contemporary racist fascism in the United States.

Social Darwinism

Social Darwinism is the name generally given to social theories viewing life as a struggle for survival within each species as well as between species. In Charles Darwin's *On the Origin of Species by Means of Natural Selection* (1859), he stated that life evolved through a struggle for survival *between* species, although Darwin (1809–1882) did not use the phrase *struggle for survival*. That phrase was first coined by Herbert Spencer (1820–1903), the real father of Social Darwinism. The Social Darwinists took this idea and applied it to each species. In other words, rather than seeing a struggle for survival *between* species, they saw a struggle for survival *within* each species.

Pyotr Kropotkin (1842–1921) argued in his book *Mutual Aid* (1902) that there is considerable evidence for cooperation within a species. In contrast, Fascists and National Socialists applied Social Darwinism to their theories of nationalism and racism, and we will return to it in that context.[1] Not all Social Darwinists are racists. Social Darwinism is a general theory that the Fascists and National Socialists applied to their theories.

Nationalism

By far the most important theme, as illustrated in the phrase *national socialism*, is nationalism. In chapter 2 we looked at the basic characteristics of nationalism. Here we will see what they mean to the Fascist. In fascism and national socialism, nationalism takes on a different meaning, to the extent that some scholars call it by a modified name, such as "integral" nationalism.[2]

The nation is the key unit to which the Fascist relates. For the National Socialist, this position is most often taken by race, with the nation as a secondary concern. For the Fascist, individuals are first and foremost members of the nation to which they give all of their loyalty, dedication, and love. The individual does not exist apart from his or her existence in the nation. There is almost no such thing as an individual within fascist ideology. An individual is one small part of the nation. The individual and the nation are inseparable. Individuals should not be able to conceive of themselves as distinct entities, separate from existence in the nation. People should be completely wrapped up in the nation. Although not all citizens of fascist countries felt this strongly, this was the fascist ideal. Fascist citizens would think this way if they completely fit the mold of the ideology. Certainly, very few individuals will completely fit that mold; but one must remember again the underlying motif of the irrational in fascist ideology,

---

[1]For further analysis of the role of Social Darwinism in national socialism, see Hajo Holborn, "Origins and Political Character of Nazi Ideology," *Political Science Quarterly* 74 (December 1964): 542–554.

[2]See, for example, Carlton J. H. Hayes. *The Historical Evolution of Modern Nationalism* (New York: Macmillan, 1931), pp. 164–231.

Adolf Hitler (1889–1945) was founder and leader of the National Socialist German
Workers' Party, chancellor (1933–1945), and head of state (1934–1945) of Germany.
He was the leading figure of the Nazi movement and is still venerated as such by Nazis
everywhere. He was violently nationalist and anti-Semitic. He was the author of one of
the classic texts of national socialism, *Mein Kampf* (1925–1927). The swastika on his
uniform is the symbol of national socialism. Standing next to him is Benito Mussolini
(1883–1945). In this picture he is giving the Nazi salute. Mussolini, known as Il Duce
(the Leader), ruled Italy from 1922 until shortly before his death. (*Culver Pictures, Inc.*)

particularly since this love of nation was consciously used by the leadership to
mold the citizens as close to the model as possible. The Fascists believed the
nation was the key to this molding. The National Socialists thought it was race,
but it was race closely connected with nation.

For the National Socialist, nationalism was usually so closely connected with
racism that it formed one concept rather than two. For example, among the
basic principles on which the National Socialists intend to reform the legal
system, race is considered the most important:

> The legal protection of the race, which has created a new concept of nationality
> [*Volkszugehörigkeit*], is consciously put in first place, for the most significant histor-
> ical principle which has been established by the victory of National Socialism is
> that of the necessity for keeping race and blood pure. All human mistakes and er-
> rors can be corrected except one: "the error regarding the importance of main-
> taining the basic values of a nation."

The purpose of this legal protection of the basic value of *race* must be the prevention for all time of a further mixture of German blood with foreign blood, as well as the prevention of continued procreation of racially unworthy and undesirable members of the people.[3]

For most Fascists, racism is not closely connected to nationalism. In fact, racism, although part of their fascist outlook, played a fairly minor role in both ideology and practice in a number of countries, such as Italy. In other countries with fascist groups today, racism is an important part of small groups that are either National Socialist or Fascist and racist.

Nonracist fascism holds a strongly nationalist position usually presented in connection with the concept of the state. The following statement by Benito Mussolini (1883–1945) is a good example: "The keystone of the Fascist doctrine is the conception of the State, of its essence, of its functions, its aims. For Fascism the State is absolute, individuals and groups relative."[4] Mussolini continued in the same vein, contending that the state is the carrier of the culture and spirit of the people or nation; that it is the past, present, and future; that it represents the "immanent conscience of the nation"; and that it educates the citizens in all the virtues.[5] Here is the connection between the state and nationalism in fascist ideology. The state is seen as the physical embodiment of the spirit of the nation. The state brings together the ideas and ideals that form the basis of nationalism. Nationalism and the state cannot be easily separated for the Fascist. The state, as Mussolini said, is the carrier of the culture and spirit of the people, the driving force that welds the people together. The state is capable of focusing the spirit of the people and the nationalism of the country. The state, therefore, must be strong; it must have the power necessary to achieve these goals.

Glorification of the State

The state is the vehicle through which the attributes of the nation, the nationality, or the race are expressed, but the state, at least as seen by Hitler, is a "rigid formal organization," and the nation or the people is a "living organism" that must replace the state.[6] In other words, the people or the nation is the locus of emotion and the state is the structure through which that emotion is expressed.

---

[3]Otto Gauweiler, *Rechtseinrichtungen und Rechtsaufgaben der Bewegung* (Munich: Zentralverlag der NSDAP, Franz Eher, Nachfolger, 1939); trans. in *National Socialism: Basic Principles. Their Application by the Nazi Party's Foreign Organization, and the Use of Germans Abroad for Nazi Aims*. Prepared in the Special Unit of the Division of European Affairs by Raymond E. Murphy, Francis B. Stevens, Howard Trivers, and Joseph M. Roland (Washington, DC: GPO, 1943), pp. 208–209.

[4]Benito Mussolini, "The Doctrine of Fascism," in Mussolini, *Fascism: Doctrine and Institutions* (New York: Howard Fertig, 1968), p. 27.

[5]Ibid., pp. 27–28.

[6]Adolf Hitler, *The Speeches of Adolf Hitler, April 1922–August 1939*, ed. Norman H. Baynes (London: Oxford University Press, 1942), vol. 1, p. 178. Speech of September 1930.

The theory of the state as actually presented by Fascists and National Socialists combines these two notions into the idea of an organic or corporate state.[7]

This conception of the state stresses the continuity of the entire society over generations. In this context, the word *organic* means "social groups as fractions of the species receive thereby a life and scope which transcends the scope and life of the individuals identifying themselves with the history and finalities of the uninterrupted series of generations."[8] Put somewhat differently, this means society, represented by the state, is a separate entity having a life or existence at once different from, and more than, the life of any individual within that society. This also means the life of the individual is less important than the life of the society.

This point is best illustrated by the idea of the folkish state which we find expressed by Hitler in *Mein Kampf:* "Thus, the highest purpose of a *folkish* state is concern for the preservation of those original racial elements which bestow culture and create the beauty and dignity of a higher humanity."[9] The folkish state is the best symbol for the full idea of the identification of the individual with the mass. Here, the ideas of blood and soil are intermingled in a way that illustrates why they are so important to national socialism. The folkish state is a racial state. It is a state in which only the members of the true Aryan race may participate, but they participate only in the sense of giving of themselves to the state. They do not govern. The folkish state, then, is a state based on racial purity, and it is a state based on ideas of soil—myths of racial content connected with the particular history of the German nation. Here race and nationalism, blood and soil, combine in the folkish state. An understanding of national socialism as it developed in Germany cannot be separated from an understanding of race and nationalism and the combination of the two in a folkish state.

There is a difference of emphasis between fascist and national socialist conceptions of the state. For example, Mussolini specifically rejected Hitler's position that the nation is prior to the state. He did this simply by arguing that the nation cannot exist without the state to weld together the disparate masses into a nation. Mussolini said the state is the source of the life of the people of all generations that compose it.[10] The state is owed supreme loyalty by the individuals who live in it, but the state is also something more than what these somewhat mechanical notions imply. It is also a "spiritual" unit, but this "spiritual" side is closely related to the authority controlling the

---

[7]Some Fascists reject the idea that they are presenting the "organic theory of the state." See, for example, Alfredo Rocco, "The Political Doctrine of Fascism," trans. D. Bigongiari, *International Conciliation* no. 223 (October 1926): 393–415.

[8]Ibid.

[9]Adolf Hitler, *Mein Kampf*, trans. Ralph Manheim (Boston: Houghton Mifflin, 1943), p. 394. Emphasis in the original.

[10]Mussolini, "The Doctrine of Fascism," pp. 11–12.

state. The state "enforces discipline and uses authority, entering into the soul and ruling with undisputed sway."[11] It does this through the leadership principle.

The Leadership Principle

The state is the mechanism for enforcing fascist beliefs, and the state is run on the *leadership* or *Führer principle*, under which each subordinate owes absolute obedience to his or her immediate superior, with everyone ultimately subordinate to the absolute leader, the *Führer*, which was Hitler's title. Mussolini's title was *Il Duce*, which also means "the leader." This hierarchy of leaders with a single, absolute leader at the top is an important chracteristic of fascism and national socialism. The underlying theory is that the *Führer* is not absolute, but the only limit on the leader's power is that the *Führer* must reflect the collective will of the people. This does not limit power because the leader's will is, by definition, the same as the collective will. "His will is not the subjective individual will of a single man, but the collective national will."[12] The leader's authority is absolute. In practice these leaders have also tended to be what we call charismatic leaders, those who are able to attract people by sheer force of personality. Therefore, few fascist movements have survived the death of the leader.

    The *Führer* principle on which Hitler based his power and organization seems, on the surface, to be complicated. But it is similar to the notion of a representative as embodying the will of the constituency. Hitler, as leader, was the representative of the German nation and the Aryan race in that he embodied within himself all the aspirations of the people. This does not mean that Hitler followed the will of the people, but that he, by embodying their will, was capable of *rightly* interpreting it. This is the key to the whole *Führer* principle—the *Führer* is the only one capable of rightly interpreting the will of the people. When the *Führer* speaks, he represents what the people truly want. In this sense he is virtually infallible, and this is clearly how Hitler viewed himself. Hitler as *Führer* could do no wrong.

    But no one person, even a *Führer*, can rule an entire country; even an absolute ruler needs some apparatus to enforce rules. This apparatus is the party. Party members are separate from and above the rest of the population. They are usually identified by some clearly recognizable sign, such as a uniform. Finally, there is an elite corps within this elite to check on the rest of the party. The two groups that served this function within the National Socialist German Workers' Party (the official name of Hitler's party) were the SA (*Sturmabteilung*) and the SS (*Schutzstaffel*). Hitler defined the task of the SA as follows: "The SA on behalf of our German people must educate the young German in mind and

---

[11]Mussolini, p. 14.

[12]Ernst Rudolf Huber, *Verfassungsrecht des grossdeutschen Reiches* (Hamburg, 1939), p. 195; trans. and quoted in *Readings on Fascism and National Socialism* (Denver, CO: Alan Swallow, n.d.), p. 75.

body so that he becomes a man hard as steel and ready to fight. Out of hundreds of thousands of individuals it must forge one united, disciplined, mighty organization."[13] The party was the effective ruling mechanism. But as Hitler said, "Every member of the Party has to do what the leader orders."[14]

In fascism and national socialism the party plays a role similar to that of the Communist party in Lenin's thought. The party is the vanguard of the nation or the race rather than the proletariat, but the general notion is the same. The party is the forerunner of the new order to come. The National Socialist believes the new order is based on race.

Racism

Probably the single, best-known part of national socialism is its racism. Hitler based racism originally on the right of the stronger,[15] and he believed that from the very beginning the Aryan, or Nordic, or white, or sometimes German, race dominated all others. He contended this domination was good for all because it was natural and founded on reason, and it would also ultimately be accepted by the dominated races.[16]

Here, clearly stated, is the thesis of the struggle for survival among races. Hitler believed racial domination by the Aryans would gladly be accepted by the dominated races, but the Social Darwinian struggle for survival as interpreted by the National Socialists does not include the survival of the dominated races. The logic of the position is that the inferior races will be eliminated, not merely dominated.

For national socialism, racism (1) represents the underlying current of Social Darwinism and (2) is a mechanism of social control, negatively by destroying the Jews and others identified by the regime—primarily Gypsies and homosexuals—and thus instilling fear in the Germans, and positively by instilling a pride in the Germans in their so-called racial heritage. Nazi policy stressed what was known as both negative and positive eugenics. Negative eugenics was aimed at keeping those perceived to be unfit from having children. Positive eugenics was aimed at encouraging the fit to have children.

The racial policies of Hitler were not limited to extermination and breeding. They included the belief that all that is good in culture stems from the Aryan race and that, therefore, the Germans as the representative of the Aryans had the best cultural heritage of the Western world and would have an even better culture in the future. In the chapter on nationalism it was noted that one of Hitler's great loves was Wagner. This is because Wagner's operas were in some ways operas of the folkish state. They represented the myths of blood and soil that were so important to Hitler. In particular, they represented what he saw as

---

[13]Adolf Hitler, "Introduction to the Service-Order of the SA," quoted in Hitler, *Speeches*, vol. 1, p. 169.

[14]Ibid., p. 459, Speech of May 21, 1930.

[15]Ibid., p. 465, Speech of January 15, 1936.

[16]Ibid., pp. 465–466.

a high point in German culture—an illustration that the Germans did have a great culture and particularly that Wagner, as a representative of German culture, seemed to agree with some of the ideas put forth by Hitler. Therefore, Hitler was able to present national socialism as a logical outgrowth of German culture and the German nation.

The relationship of the state to racism is seen in *Mein Kampf* where Hitler wrote, "The state is a means to an end. Its end lies in the preservation and advancement of a community of physically and psychically homogenous creatures."[17]

The effect of racism on other aspects of the society is fairly obvious. For example, social stratification would be based on racial purity and party membership. Other things that would be taken into account would be positive support for the regime and contributions to the country. In addition, the racist ideology would indicate the control of marriage, and the desire to control the minds of the children would dictate control of the family system. Along these lines, German women were encouraged to have many children; that is, if they were of the correct racial type. As Goebbels put it, "The mission of woman is to be beautiful and to bring children into the world."[18] She was also supposed to be athletic and refrain from wearing makeup or from such things as smoking in public. But, above all, she was to have children. We have seen the way in which the educational system was used to develop the correct values in children. The family and religion were used in the same way. Parents were to teach their children the true national socialist ideas from birth. National socialism also contended it was supported by God; thus, religion was used for the same purpose.

Anticommunism

One of the aspects of the ideologies of fascism and national socialism that made them acceptable to many was their anticommunist stance. As one scholar of fascism put it, "Before all else, it was anticommunist. It lived and throve on anticommunism."[19] This was an aspect of fascism's antirationalist approach, and its general rejection of the modern world, but it became a significant element in the appeal of fascism.[20]

Communists argue that anticommunism is the only defining characteristic of fascism and that it should not be considered an ideology at all, but merely a reaction to the events of the early twentieth century, particularly the develop-

---

[17]Hitler, *Mein Kampf*, p. 393.

[18]Joseph Goebbels, quoted in Mosse, *Nazi Culture*, p. 41. A good introduction to the socialization process is [Fritz Brennecke,] *The Nazi Primer: Official Handbook for Schooling the Hitler Youth*. Translated by Harwood L. Childs. New York: Harper & Brothers, 1938. Reprinted New York: AMS Press, 1972.

[19]H. R. Trevor-Roper, "The Phenomenon of Fascism," in S. J. Woolf, ed., *European Fascism* (New York: Vintage Books, 1969), p. 24.

[20]See, for example, Alastair Hamilton, *The Appeal of Fascism: A Study of Intellectuals and Fascism 1919–1945* (New York: Macmillan, 1971).

ment of an organized working class. While this interpretation has its merits, it misses the complexity of fascism and national socialism.

Fascism and national socialism were not only anticommunist, but also anti-intellectual, antirational, and antimodern because they glorified the past with myths of blood and soil. As the Communists argue, much of the ideologies of fascism and national socialism developed first as practice and was never tightly tied together by theory. But the very lack of rational coherence can be seen as an integral part of the ideologies and part of the rejection of what was seen as the overly intellectual, overly rational approach of communism.

THE ECONOMIC SYSTEM

The economic theory of fascism and national socialism was never developed very systematically, and there were marked differences in the countries involved. Even though socialism is part of the name national socialism and Mussolini was originally a socialist, neither fascism nor national socialism was actually socialist. National socialism began from that position, but it quickly changed as it gained the support of capitalists.[21] Probably the best statement of the general economic theory of national socialism is, "All property is common property. The owner is bound by the people and the Reich [government] to the responsible management of his goods. His legal position is only justified when he satisfies this responsibility to the community."[22] Thus property under national socialism was held in private hands, but it had to be used as the government dictated or it would be confiscated. Here again is the idea of the people as a whole acting for the best interests of the state.

A major concern in the economic theory is to establish economic self-sufficiency. For fascism and national socialism to achieve their goals, the countries involved must be self-sufficient; they must not depend on other countries for supplies.[23] All the stress on the nation, the state, the race, and the people would lose considerable force if these entities were dependent on other nations, states, races, and peoples.

The economic system of national socialism clearly states that, even though an individual may have temporary control of some economic good, be it land, capital, or whatever, this control must serve the interests of the collectivity as interpreted by the *Führer*, or the control must be terminated.

The economic system of fascism as distinct from that of national socialism includes the idea of state-controlled syndicates. The state creates all economic organizations, as the Labour Charter of April 21, 1927, says:

---

[21]On this point see Martin Broszat, *German National Socialism 1919–1945*, trans. Kurt Rosenbaum and Inge Pauli Boehm (Santa Barbara, CA: CLIO Press, 1966), pp. 22–24.

[22]Huber, *Verfassungsrecht*, pp. 372–373, quoted in *Readings on Fascism*, p. 91.

[23]See the discussion in Paul M. Hayes, *Fascism* (London: George Allen & Unwin, 1973), pp. 89–105.

> Work in all its forms—intellectual, technical and manual—both organizing or executive, is a social duty. On this score and only on this score, it is protected by the State.
>
> From the national standpoint the mass of production represents a single unit; it has a single object, namely, the well-being of individuals and the development of national power.[24]

All economic organization under fascism is ultimately controlled by the state. All economic organizations under fascism are designed to include both workers and employers in the same organization so that all of the economy can be directly controlled from above; this is called *corporatism* or the *corporate economy*. In this way, the state is made superior to every part of the economy. The syndicates are designed to ensure that production continues as long as the state requires it. The right to strike is taken away from the workers, but at the same time the syndicate, operating as an arm of the state, usually has the power to set wages; thus the syndicate acts as a policy-making arm of the state in economic affairs. It should be clear that, as in Germany, the Fascist party in Italy with Mussolini at the head had ultimate power. In many ways, the syndicates were merely administrative arms of the Fascist party and of Mussolini rather than having any real power to make decisions. The leadership principle was not abrogated in Italy. It was maintained, and the syndicates acted as lower-level leaders following the dictates of the leader.

CURRENT TRENDS

In the past few years fascism and national socialism have been revived in a number of countries, including Germany, Italy, and the United States. In Italy parties associated with fascism have made substantial electoral gains. In Germany direct reference to national socialism is rare, but opposition to immigration has produced groups that are quite similar to early national socialism. This is particularly true in the former East Germany where the unification of Germany has produced substantial unemployment and poverty in contrast to the obvious wealth of the former West Germany. In the United States quite a number of groups, mostly fairly small, either identify with national socialism through the use of its traditional symbols (mostly the swastika) or support social and political traditions closely associated with national socialism.

One example of a racist and anti-Semitic program can be found in the novel *The Turner Diaries* (2d ed. 1980), which a number of far-right groups in the United States treat as a blueprint for a future race war. Probably the best-known of the contemporary United States groups is the Aryan Nation, which is led by Richard Girnt Butler and operates from an enclosed compound in Hayden

---

[24]"The Labour Charter," in Benito Mussolini, *Four Speeches on the Corporate State* (Rome: "Laboremus," 1935), p. 53.

Lake, Idaho. All these groups are very small, but most of them are bigger than Hitler's initial political party.[25]

SUGGESTED READINGS

BARKUN, MICHAEL. *Religion and the Racist Right: The Origins of the Christian Identity Movement.* Chapel Hill: University of North Carolina Press, 1994.

BELL, LELAND. *In Hitler's Shadow: The Anatomy of American Nazism.* Port Washington, NY: Kennikat Press, 1973.

BEYME, KLAUS VON, ed. *Right-Wing Extremism in Western Europe.* London: Frank Cass, 1988.

BLINKHORN, MARTIN, ed. *Fascists and Conservatives: The Radical Right and the Establishment in Twentieth-Century Europe.* London: Unwin Hyman, 1990.

[BRENNECKE, FRITZ.] *The Nazi Primer: Official Handbook for Schooling the Hitler Youth.* Trans. Harwood L. Childs. New York: Harper & Brothers, 1938. Reprinted. New York: AMS Press, 1972.

CAROCCI, GIAMPIERO. *Italian Fascism.* Trans. Isabel Quigly. Harmondsworth, England: Penguin, 1974.

CARSTEN, F. L. *The Rise of Fascism.* Berkeley: University of California Press, 1967.

CHELES, LUCIANO, RONNIE FERGUSON, and MICHALINA VAUGHAN, eds. *Neo-Fascism in Europe.* New York: Longman, 1991.

DEFELICE, RENZO. *Interpretations of Fascism.* Trans. Brenda Huff Everett. Cambridge, MA: Harvard University Press, 1977.

FEST, JOACHIM C. *The Face of the Third Reich: Portraits of the Nazi Leadership.* Trans. Michael Bullock. New York: Pantheon Books, 1970.

———. *Hitler.* Trans. Richard and Clara Winston. New York: Harcourt Brace Jovanovich, 1974.

FORMAN, JAMES D. *Fascism: The Meaning and Experience of Reactionary Revolution.* New York: New Viewpoints, 1974.

GLASER, HERMANN. *The Cultural Roots of National Socialism.* Trans. Ernest A. Menze. Austin: University of Texas Press, 1978.

GREGOR, A. JAMES. *The Ideology of Fascism: The Rationale of Totalitarianism.* New York: Free Press, 1969.

———. *Fascism: The Classic Interpretations of the Interwar Period.* Morristown, NJ: General Learning Press, 1973.

———. *Fascism: The Contemporary Interpretations.* Morristown, NJ: General Learning Press, 1973.

———. *Italian Fascism and Developmental Dictatorship.* Princeton, NJ: Princeton University Press, 1979.

———. *Young Mussolini and the Intellectual Origins of Fascism.* Berkeley: University of California Press, 1979.

GRIFFIN, ROGER. *The Nature of Fascism.* New York: St. Martin's, 1991.

HAMILTON, ALASTAIR. *The Appeal of Fascism: A Study of Intellectuals and Fascism, 1919–1945.* New York: Macmillan, 1971.

HARRISON, HENRY SILTON. *The Social Philosophy of Giovanni Gentile.* Urbana: University of Illinois Press, 1960.

HITLER, ADOLF. *My New Order.* New York: Reynal & Hitchcock, 1941.

———. *The Speeches of Adolf Hitler, April 1922–August 1939.* Ed. Norman H. Baynes, 2 vols. London: Oxford University Press, 1942.

———. *Mein Kampf.* Trans. Ralph

---

[25]For more on these groups, see Lyman Tower Sargent, ed. *Extremism in America: A Reader* (New York: New York University Press, 1995). For a history, see Michael Barkun, *Religion and the Racist Right: The Origins of the Christian Identity Movement* (Chapel Hill: University of North Carolina Press, 1994.)

Manheim. Boston: Houghton Mifflin, 1943.

KAMENETSKY, CHRISTA. *Children's Literature in Hitler's Germany: The Cultural Policy of National Socialism.* Athens: Ohio University Press, 1984.

KÜHL, STEFAN. *The Nazi Connection: Eugenics, American Racism, and German National Socialism.* New York: Oxford University Press, 1994.

LAQUEUR, WALTER, ed. *Fascism: A Reader's Guide.* Berkeley: University of California Press, 1976.

LARSEN, STEIN UGELVIK, BERNT HAGTVET, and JAN PETTER MYKLEBUST. *Who Were the Fascists? Social Roots of European Fascism.* Oslo, Norway: Universitetsforlaget, 1982.

LYTTELTON, ADRIAN, ed. *Italian Fascisms: From Pareto to Gentile.* Trans. Douglas Parmee. London: Jonathan Cape, 1973.

MOSSE, GEORGE L. *The Crisis of German Ideology: Intellectual Origins of the Third Reich.* New York: Grosset & Dunlap, 1964.

———. *Nazi Culture: Intellectual, Cultural and Social Life in the Third Reich.* New York: Grosset & Dunlap, 1966.

———. *Masses and Man: Nationalist and Fascist Perceptions of Reality.* New York: Howard Fertig, 1980.

MUSSOLINI, BENITO. *My Autobiography.* New York: Scribner's, 1928.

———. *Four Speeches on the Corporate State.* Rome: "Laboremus," 1935.

———. *The Corporate State.* Florence, Italy: Vallecchi, 1936.

———. *Fascism: Doctrine and Institutions.* New York: Howard Fertig, 1968.

NEUMANN, FRANZ. *Behemoth: The Structure and Practice of National Socialism.* 2d ed. New York: Octagon Books, 1963.

NOLTE, ERNST. *Three Faces of Fascism: Action Francaise, Italian Fascism, National Socialism.* Trans. Leila Vennewitz. New York: Holt, Rinehart & Winston, 1965.

PAYNE, STANLEY G. *Fascism: Comparison and Definition.* Madison: University of Wisconsin Press, 1980.

POIS, ROBERT A. *National Socialism and the Religion of Nature.* New York: St. Martin's, 1986.

Readings on Fascism and National Socialism. Denver, CO: Alan Swallow, n.d.

REICH, WILHELM. *The Mass Psychology of Fascism.* Trans. Vincent R. Carfagno. New York: Farrar, Strauss & Giroux, 1970.

ROCCO, ALFREDO. "The Political Doctrine of Fascism." Trans. D. Bigongiari. *International Conciliation* no. 223 (October 1926): 393–415.

ROSENBERG, ALFRED. *Race and Race History.* Ed. Robert Pois. New York: Harper & Row, 1970. Published in the U.K. as *Selected Writings.* London: Jonathan Cape, 1970.

———. *The Myth of the Twentieth Century: An Evaluation of the Spiritual-Intellectual Confrontations of Our Age.* Trans. Vivian Bird. Torrance, CA: Noontide Press, 1982.

SARGENT, LYMAN TOWER, ed. *Extremism in America: A Reader.* New York: New York University Press, 1995.

SPEER, ALBERT. *Inside the Third Reich: Memoirs.* Trans. Richard Winston and Clara Winston. New York: Macmillan, 1970.

STEPHENSON, JILL. *Women in Nazi Society.* London: Croom Helm, 1975.

STERNHELL, ZEEV with MARIO SZNAJDER and MAIA ASHERI. *The Birth of Fascist Ideology: From Cultural Rebellion to Political Revolution.* Translated by David Maisel. Princeton, NJ: Princeton University Press, 1994.

"Theories of Fascism." *Journal of Contemporary History* 11 (October 1976).

VIERECK, PETER. *Metapolitics: The Roots of the Nazi Mind.* Rev. ed. New York: Capricorn Books, 1961.

WELSH, DAVID, ed. *Nazi Propaganda: The Power and the Limitations.* London: Croom Helm, 1983.

WILKINSON, PAUL. *The New Fascists.* London: Grant McIntyre, 1981.

PART V

The Third World

10

Third World Ideologies

This chapter provides an overview of the various ideologies that have developed in the so-called Third World and serves as an introduction to the two of those ideologies that are of major significance today—Liberation Theology and Islam. The latter is, of course, one of the major world religions and its theology is discussed only to the extent needed to understand its social and political aspects.

The phrase "the Third World" was first used in 1952 by Alfred Sauvy, a French demographer, and refers to all those countries that were trying to find a "third" way between capitalism and communism. With the partial demise of communism, the phrase has lost much of its meaning, but no other of the commonly used labels fits very well either. "Developing nations" ignores the highly developed countries like Singapore and Saudi Arabia that identify with the Third World. "The South" ignores Australia, New Zealand, and South Africa, which are not part of the Third World.

Thus, the label Third World will be used here because it fits the situation as well as most, and better than some, of the other labels. Although there are both capitalist and communist countries in the Third World, most of the countries that identify with the Third World are still looking for an economic system that is neither capitalist nor communist. Capitalism is rejected because capitalists were the colonial rulers or had dominated the economies. Communism is rejected because it is authoritarian and because many Third World leaders reject a central communist concept, the class struggle. Both capitalism and commu-

nism are rejected because Third World countries want to develop their economies free from outside control and without the exploitation found in both capitalism and communism.

Third World countries have some differences and some similarities; the most
obvious similarity of the Third World countries is that most suffer from overwhelming poverty—poverty of a degree almost unimaginable in the West. In
most Third World countries this poverty is combined with the presence of a
wealthy elite. Their fragile economies are still largely dependent on the industrial North. This has made the problem of *neocolonialism* (economic dependence)
worse.

In many Third World countries there exists a small, generally Western-
educated elite combined with a largely illiterate population. The rich and the
educated are generally the same people, hold political power, and do not intend
to lose either power or money.

MOVEMENTS FOR NATIONAL LIBERATION

While virtually no generalization can be made about the histories of Third
World countries to which there will be no exceptions, certain similarities exist
in these histories. Most Third World countries have gone through a series of
stages in the process of development from the colonial period to independence.
The colonial experience was the first stage, followed, not necessarily in this
order, by the development of a movement for independence, the revitalization
of the indigenous culture, political independence, neocolonialism, one-party
rule with internal conflict, and, often, a military takeover. Few Third World
countries have achieved stable political institutions.

The Colonial Experience

The one experience that all Third World countries share is having been colonies. Although Western countries like the United States, Canada, Australia, and
New Zealand were also colonies (of Britain) at one time, generally the experience is sufficiently in the past so there is little awareness of what it means politically, economically, and psychologically. For most countries of the Third
World the colonial experience is still part of the recent past.

Politically, being a colony meant simply that all decisions were made by
others for their own benefit. Major decisions were not even made in the colony
but in Europe; other decisions were made by a colonial bureaucracy composed
of people sent from Europe. Politically a colony was just a minor concern in the
overall policy of the European power.

Economically, the colony was there to provide raw materials for the
"home" country, a market for its goods, and cheap labor. For most colonies
economic relations with their masters were simple in the extreme—exploitation. Also, most colonies were required to limit their economies to one or two

cash crops and were not allowed to diversify. This policy has produced long-term economic damage. Most colonies originally provided agricultural goods; later those colonies with mineral resources were mined. But virtually never was more than minimal processing done in the colony; that would have required trained workers, and training workers might raise their expectations and pose problems. Ultimately, such predictions were proven correct; training workers for skilled jobs did raise expectations and produced leaders of the independence movement.

Even more dangerous was education. Most colonial powers did not educate the indigenous population, although Christian missionaries provided schools and, in fact, educated many of the leaders of the later independence movements. The fact that most of the education was provided by Christian missionaries illustrates another fact about the colonial experience—the attack on the indigenous culture. This process of deculturation proved traumatic for many people, but it also provided the tools that made independence possible. On one hand, the imposition of an alien culture stripped many people of their sense of self. Their religions were suppressed; their languages were replaced; their customs were denigrated; even their clothes and hairstyles were replaced by Western styles. Everything indigenous was treated as inferior and this attitude was taught in schools.

On the other hand, the acceptance, at least temporarily, of Western culture provided both the intellectual and physical tools needed for independence. And at least some colonial rulers found it more difficult to treat as inferior someone who dressed and spoke as they did and who had been educated at the same schools and universities. The Western traditions of liberty and equality provided the vocabulary needed for an independence movement. And technical training provided the ability to replace the colonial rulers in running the government and the economy.

The Independence Movement

The most common scenario for an independence movement was years of covert and overt opposition. Most, if not all, independence leaders spent time in prison for their activities; in fact, in many countries some years in prison became a requirement for gaining acceptance, respect, and credibility.

In most cases independence was actually won through violent revolution or long years of a war for independence. India was the major exception; although there were violent incidents, its independence leaders, Mohandas K. Gandhi (1869–1948) and Jawaharlal Nehru (1889–1964), used nonviolent techniques to win independence.

The struggle for independence provided a focus for the development or redevelopment of a national identity. It also became the basis for a national · culture. In almost all cases, the independence movements attempt to ensure that their supporters worked solely for the benefit of the people as a whole rather than for their own benefit. A good example of this approach is found in the "Rules of Discipline" announced by Kwame Nkrumah (1909–1972), the leader of the independence movement in what was the British colony the Gold Coast, which became Ghana on independence in 1957. In his "Rules of Discipline," Nkrumah says, among other rules, that those involved in the revolution should "not take a single needle or piece of thread from the masses"; "not take liberties with women"; "always guide and protect the children"; and "always be the servant of the people."[1] Julius K. Nyerere (1922–), the leader of the independence movement in Tanganyika (later Tanzania), went even further in the Arusha Declaration, declaring that no member of government or leader in a political party should "hold shares in any company"; "hold directorships in any privately owned enterprise"; "receive two or more salaries"; or "own houses which he rents to others." He states explicitly that the prohibition extends to spouses.[2] Until independence and for a while afterward, such programs usually worked, but after a time, many leaders of liberation movements used their new power to line their own pockets rather than to help develop the country as a whole. There were, of course, exceptions. Nyerere was one of the exceptions.

The Revitalization of Indigenous Culture

The indigenous cultures had been damaged but not destroyed, and the development of a national identity required that the culture be revived.[3] Language, literature, and the arts, together with religion and music, were all rediscovered, encouraged, and, with independence, taught in a refashioned educational system. In places where the traditional culture had been most nearly destroyed, notably sub-Saharan Africa, the process of revitalization has been slow, but it is still taking place and does provide more and more people a recovered sense of self. Still, the continued Westernization and urbanization that have followed independence have added to the difficulty of establishing a national culture. Independence is not the solution to all problems that it had seemed to many.

For most Third World countries political independence, which had been the sole goal, suddenly became a step to goals of economic independence, political stability, and decent lives for their citizens. The first step toward all these goals was to take effective control of the economy, but this proved difficult.

Neocolonialism

After formal independence is achieved, there is the problem of economic ties with the ex-colonial power that may resemble continued control. This is

---

[1]Kwame Nkrumah, *Handbook of Revolutionary Warfare: A Guide to the Armed Phase of the African Revolution* (New York: International Publishers, 1969), p. vii.

[2]Julius K. Nyerere, *Ujamaa—Essays on Socialism* (Dar es Salaam, Tanzania: Oxford University Press, 1968), p. 36.

[3]See, for example, Sékou Touré, "A Dialectical Approach to Culture," in *Pan-Africanism*, ed. Robert Chrisman and Nathan Hare (Indianapolis, IN: Bobbs-Merrill, 1974), pp. 52–73; Amilcar Cabral, "National Liberation and Culture," trans. Maureen Webster, in his *Return to the Source: Selected Speeches* (New York: Monthly Review Press, 1973), pp. 39–56; and Cabral, "The Role of Culture in the Battle for Independence," *UNESCO Courier* (November 1973): 12–16, 20.

known as *neocolonialism*. Most of the new countries develop some sort of rapprochement with the former colonists, usually to mutual advantage. The problem of neocolonialism is a complex one. It is essential for rapid economic development that the new nation be able to trade with older, more established nations. Often the only thing the new nation has to trade is raw materials. The colonial power had exploited the nation by taking its raw materials and giving little in exchange. It is hard for the new leaders to see their raw materials going to a more highly developed country, even though they are getting something in return, such as manufactured goods or even industries. The problem stems from the fact that raw materials sell on the world market at a much lower price than do manufactured goods. Therefore, the new nation feels it is being exploited by selling a commodity that is relatively inexpensive in order to purchase one that is relatively expensive.

Such attitudes make neocolonialism an extremely important and difficult issue for the new nation. It must deal with older, more developed countries, often including its previous colonial ruler, in order to survive, but it feels it is being exploited in virtually the same way it was while still a colony. Therefore, many new countries have insisted that the processing of the raw materials take place at home, thus producing an industry, employing people, and giving them some sense that they are not being exploited.

Political Instability

After independence usually one political party dominated, and it often allowed no significant opposition to develop. One-party rule, it was argued, was necessary to provide the unity and stability needed to forge a new nation. Frequently one-party rule has resulted in military coups because the military was the only alternative center of power. This pattern has left many Third World countries struggling for political and economic survival and searching for an identify that allows them independence from East, West, and North.

DEVELOPMENTAL SOCIALISM

One way of appearing independent was to create an economic system neither capitalist nor communist. The most original such creation has been called *African socialism* and *communitarian socialism* but is best known as *developmental socialism*. It was developed by Julius K. Nyerere (Tanzania), Léopold Senghor (1906–) (Senegal), U Nu (1907–1995) (Myanmar, formerly Burma), and Vinoba Bhave (1895–1982) (India), and it stresses social solidarity and cooperation as the means of developing the economy. Developmental socialism has also emphasized the establishment of a network of close social and economic ties to help form national identity. So far, world economic and political realities have brought failure to developmental socialism.

A good illustration of the basic idea of developmental socialism is found in the Swahili word Nyerere uses for socialism, *ujamaa*—familyhood. As he put it,

Julius K. Nyerere (1922–) was president of the United Republic of Tanzania (formed by uniting Tanganyika and Zanzibar) from 1964 to 1985. He is one of the few leaders of an African independence movement not to be overthrown (a few attempts were made) and to retire from office. He was president of the Tanganyika African National Union (TANU), the political party to bring independence to Tanganyika, from 1954 on. He is known for his advocacy of African socialism and what he called *ujamaa* (a Swahili word that he translates as "familyhood") as the basis for developing Third World economies. (*Courtesy of the Embassy of Tanzania*)

"The foundation, and the objective, of African socialism is the extended family."[4] The extended family—consisting of a wide range of relatives who work cooperatively and share all family resources—is the model for village and tribal socialism. All members of the village are fed, clothed, and housed as well as the group can afford. The aged and the ill are supported. Developmental socialism explicitly rejects the class divisions of communism. All are workers; there is little or no tradition of an indigenous exploiting class.

In Nyerere's socialism all people must recognize that they are part of a single group working together to achieve a common end. This end is designed to achieve economic security and human dignity by changing the distribution system. "There must be something wrong in a society where one man, however hardworking or clever he may be, can acquire as great a 'reward' as a thousand of his fellows can acquire between them."[5] A cardinal principle in Nyerere's socialism reflects the fact that in traditional African society, as in the societies of the Native American, land could not be owned, only used.

---

[4]Nyerere, "Ujamaa—The Basis of African Socialism" (1962), in *Ujamaa*, p. 11.

[5]Ibid., p. 3.

These lofty goals have been unmet or only partially met, with a future that looks grim at best. External forces such as the world economy produced conditions that might have made success impossible even if everything had gone perfectly within the countries.

Internally, all Third World countries face a multitude of problems. Among the worst problems are rampant corruption, extreme differences of wealth, the threat of military takeover, and tribal and religious conflict. As a result, no Third World country has been in a position to put developmental socialism into practice even had external factors been perfect.

COMMUNISM IN THE THIRD WORLD

Although communism has not been adopted often by the Third World countries, it has served as a model, particularly for Western revolutionaries. Cambodia, China, Vietnam, North Korea, and Cuba are communist.[6] In other countries, communism is represented by communist political parties or national liberation movements; so far they have been generally unsuccessful. This lack of success has a variety of causes, and assigning specific causes to specific cases would be foolhardy without a detailed analysis of all the factors involved. However, it seems clear that one of the major reasons is the rejection of the Marxist-Leninist approach by most leaders of the developing nations.

One of the peculiarities of the Third World nations that causes problems for the Marxist theorist is the lack of a proletariat. This problem was first faced by Lenin in Russia. It was true also of China at the time of the communist revolution there, and Mao based his revolutionary techniques on the peasants as a revolutionary class rather than the proletariat. Nevertheless, it is usually argued that the proletariat is the most revolutionary class, even in the developing countries where the proletariat is either nonexistent or exists only in very small numbers. If a revolution is successful without a proletariat, as it was in China, much effort is put into developing a proletarian class immediately after the revolution. This, of course, is necessary anywhere in the modern world because industrialization is impossible without a large laboring class. Therefore, a dictatorship of the proletariat is introduced, even where the proletariat is virtually nonexistent.

The lack of a proletariat in many Third World nations, or at least of a proletariat in the industrial sense as Marx usually used the term, causes serious problems for the Marxist theorist who is attempting to discuss the developing nations. The problem is not so much in the period of the revolution, although supposedly the proletariat should lead the revolution. It is partly a theoretical and partly a practical problem after the revolution. The Third World nations,

---

[6]A good brief discussion of Afro-Marxism can be found in Crawford Young, *Ideology and Development in Africa* (New Haven, CT: Yale University Press, 1982), pp. 25–32.

without exception, wish to industrialize. They cannot industrialize without the development of an industrial proletariat. Therefore, for the theoretical reasons of the Marxian ideology that requires a proletariat, and the very practical reason of the desire and need for industrialization, one of the first steps any Marxist leader in a developing country takes is to develop or attempt to develop a proletariat.

At the same time, a number of Third World countries are led by people who call themselves Marxists even though it would be stretching the term too much to call them communist (some will disagree with this assessment and want to label these countries communist). Zimbabwe (formerly Southern Rhodesia and then Rhodesia) came under majority rule in 1980 and is led by Robert Mugabe (1924–), who describes himself as a Marxist but not a Communist.

But there are strong reasons for general rejection of communism in the Third World. The destruction wreaked on Cambodia by the communist regime led by Pol Pot (1925/28–) has certainly reinforced the rejection of communism. The invasion of one communist country (Vietnam) by another (China), the later invasion of Cambodia by Vietnam, the conflict between China and the USSR, and the Soviet invasion of Afghanistan all reinforced this rejection. The collapse of communism in Eastern Europe and the Soviet Union has added to the reasons for the general rejection of communism, but most Third World countries are still at best ambivalent about capitalism.

CAPITALISM IN THE THIRD WORLD

Although capitalism is rejected by much of the Third World, it is practiced in other parts. South Korea, Singapore, and Chile are examples of capitalist Third World countries.[7] Many other Third World countries, particularly in Latin and South America, have capitalist economies but with a number of important nationalized industries.

Singapore and South Korea are the greatest economic success stories in the Third World. Their economies are developing rapidly in large part because they have been able to attract industries from more developed countries by offering low wages for both skilled and unskilled labor and a nonunion, tractable work force. In addition, companies are interested in many Third World countries because they have few environmental or safety regulations and cheap labor is abundantly available. Third World countries, in turn, are interested in companies with money to invest. Therefore, capitalism clearly has a future in the Third World, particularly if it can be shorn of its past association with colonialism and neocolonialism.

---

[7]A good brief discussion of African capitalism can be found in Crawford Young, *Ideology and Development in Africa* (New Haven, CT: Yale University Press, 1982), pp. 185–190.

CURRENT TRENDS

The past few years in the Third World have been a continuation and intensification of the turmoil of the previous decades. The picture is not a pleasant one. Whether one is primarily concerned with the human cost in lives lost to war, disease, and famine or the potential for one or more of the conflicts to spread and thus precipitate World War III, it is impossible to find much to be positive about in the Third World today.

The Economic Problems

The disastrous economic situation in which many countries in the Third World find themselves is not likely to get better without more help from the developed countries. In 1980 the Independent Commission on International Development Issues (better known as the Brandt Commission) issued a report that was hailed in the Third World as a major step toward the understanding of their economic problems and a basis for a possible solution.[8]

The Brandt Commission recommended that immediate steps be taken to alleviate hunger, improve the energy situation in the Third World, and reform the international economic system. It argued that the position of the Third World was so desperate that action must be taken at once. Nothing much has happened.

Democratization

A majority of the countries in Asia and Africa that became independent after World War II and a majority of the Latin American countries that were military dictatorships into the 1970s currently have governments that were elected by majority rule. Although a wide variety of restrictions dictate who can vote in some of these countries, procedural democracy has been established and generally accepted within a relatively short period of time in the Third World.

At the same time, democracy in many of these countries is very fragile and frequently does not extend beyond what I have called *procedural democracy* to any significant degree of regular citizen participation. Still, some Third World countries, like India, have a substantially higher voter turnout than developed countries, like the United States, even though they may have even fewer citizens regularly participating in political activities.

Thus while democratization has become an important subject because of the changes taking place in Eastern Europe and the former Soviet Union, the Third World does not provide a clear model to emulate. Many democracies have been established in the Third World, but it is not yet clear that a democratic outlook on life has become ingrained in either citizens or leaders.

---

[8]Independent Commission on International Development Issues, *North–South: A Programme for Survival* (Cambridge, MA: MIT Press, 1980).

If we take the various elements considered as part of democracy in chapter 3, the Third World is clearly still in a period of aspiring to full democratic citizenship rather than having achieved it. Citizens vote and their votes are mostly counted on the basis of "one person (sometimes still just man), one vote," but there is frequently little freedom or other forms of equality, the rule of law is still developing, and education for citizenship is frequently lacking. At the same time, given the length of time it took developed countries to establish their democracies and develop fairly high degrees of equality and liberty, the Third World has done a great deal in a short period of time.

The Fourth World

In addition to the Third World, there is a Fourth World of indigenous peoples—populations like the Native Americans. The United Nations has developed a "Draft Declaration of Principles for Indigenous Rights," which asserts among its twenty points that

> All indigenous nations and peoples have the right to self-determination, by virtue of which they have the right to whatever degree of autonomy or self-government they choose. This includes the right to freely determine their political status, freely pursue their own economic, social, religious and cultural development, and determine their membership and/or citizenship, without external interference.

No settler country in the world recognizes this right to any significant extent.

Only recently are indigenous people becoming aware that others are in similar positions in other parts of the world and attempting to develop a network of concerned supporters to publicize their plight.[9] It is not yet clear that they share an ideological commonality, but in general they appear to have at least a shared awareness of the earth and its fragility.

The situation in both the Third and Fourth Worlds is dangerous. A very delicate balancing act is being performed in many countries in attempts to stave off economic collapse and avoid revolution.

SUGGESTED READINGS

AKE, CLAUDE. *Revolutionary Pressures in Africa*. London: Zed Press, 1987.

ALBRIGHT, DAVID E., ed. *Communism in Africa*. Bloomington: Indiana University Press, 1980.

ARAT, ZEHRA F. *Democracy and Human Rights in Developing Countries*. Boulder, CO: Lynne Rienner, 1991.

BÂ, SYLVIA WASHINGTON. *The Concept of Negritude in the Poetry of Léopold Sédar Senghor*. Princeton, NJ: Princeton University Press, 1973.

---

[9]See *Fourth World Bulletin* begun in June of 1988 and published by the Department of Political Science of the University of Colorado at Denver.

BAUZON, KENNETH E., ed. *Development and Democratization in the Third World: Myths, Hopes, and Realities*. Washington, DC: Crane Russak, 1992.

BERGER, PETER L., ed. *Capitalism and Equality in the Third World*. Lanham, MD: Hamilton Press and the Institute for Educational Affairs, 1987.

BIKO, STEVE. *I Write What I Like*. London: Bowerdean Press, 1978.

BISHOP, MAURICE. *Maurice Bishop Speaks. The Grenada Revolution 1979–83*. New York: Pathfinder Press, 1983.

BOESAK, ALLAN. *If This Is Treason, I Am Guilty*. Grand Rapids, MI: Eerdmans/Trenton, NJ: Africa World Press, 1987.

BRAGANÇA, AGUINO DE, and IMMANUEL WALLERSTEIN, eds. *The African Liberation Reader*. 3 vols. London: Zed Press, 1982.

BURNELL, PETER J. *Economic Nationalism in the Third World*. Boulder, CO: Westview Press, 1986.

BUVINIĆ, MAYRA, MARGARET A. LYCETTE, and WILLIAM PAUL MCGREEVEY, eds. *Women and Poverty in the Third World*. Baltimore, MD: The Johns Hopkins University Press, 1983.

CABRAL, AMILCAR. *Revolution in Guinea*. Trans. and ed. Richard Handyside. New York: Monthly Review Press, 1969.

————. *Unity and Struggle: Speeches and Writings*. Trans. Michael Wolfers. London: Heinemann, 1980.

DEBRAY, RÉGIS. *Prison Writings*. Trans. Rosemary Sheed. New York: Random House, 1973.

DIAMOND, LARRY, JUAN J. LINEZ, and SEYMOUR MARTIN LIPSET, eds. *Democracy in Developing Countries*. Vol. 2., *Africa*. Boulder, CO: Lynne Rienner, 1988.

FANON, FRANTZ. *The Wretched of the Earth*. Trans. Constance Farrington. New York: Grove Press, 1963.

————. *A Dying Colonialism*. Trans. Haakon Chevalier. New York: Grove Press, 1965.

————. *Toward the African Revolution (Political Essays)*. Trans. Haakon Chevalier. New York: Grove Press, 1967.

GORDON, DAVID C. *Images of the West: Third World Perspectives*. N.p.: Rowman & Littlefield, 1989.

GUEVARA, ERNESTO CHE. *Reminiscences of the Cuban Revolutionary War*. Trans. Victoria Ortiz. New York: Monthly Review Press, 1968.

————. *Socialism and Man*. New York: Young Socialist Alliance, 1969.

ILIFFE, JOHN. *The Emergence of African Capitalism. The Anstey Memorial Lectures in the University of Kent at Canterbury 10 – 13 May 1982*. Minneapolis: University of Minnesota Press, 1983.

IYOB, RUTH. *The Eritrean Struggle for Independence: Domination, Resistance, Nationalism, 1941–1993*. Cambridge, England: Cambridge University Press, 1995.

JAYAWARDENA, KUMARI. *Feminism and Nationalism in the Third World*. London: Zed Books, 1986.

KARPAT, KEMAL H., ed. *Political and Social Thought in the Contemporary Middle East*. Rev. and enlarged ed. New York: Praeger, 1982.

KELLER, EDMOND J., and DONALD ROTHCHILD. *Afro-Marxist Regimes: Ideology and Public Policy*. Boulder, CO: Lynne Rienner, 1987.

KENNEDY, PAUL. *African Capitalism: The Struggle for Ascendency*. Cambridge, England: Cambridge University Press, 1988.

LANGLEY, J. AYO. *Ideologies of Liberation in Black Africa 1856–1970: Documents on Modern African Political Thought from Colonial Times to the Present*. London: Rex Collings, 1979.

LEWIS, I. M., ed. *Nationalism and Self Determination in the Horn of Africa*. London: Ithaca Press, 1983.

MANDELA, NELSON. *Long Walk to Freedom*. Boston: Little, Brown, 1994.

MAZRUI, ALI A., and MICHAEL TIDY. *Nationalism and New States in Africa from About 1935 to the Present*. London: Heinemann, 1984.

MCCULLOCH, JOCK. *In the Twilight of Rev-

olution: The Political Theory of Amilcar Cabral. London: Routledge & Kegan Paul, 1983.

MUNSLOW, BARRY. *Mozambique: The Revolution and Its Origins.* London: Longman, 1983.

———, ed. *Samora Machel: An African Revolutionary. Selected Speeches and Writings.* Trans. Michel Wolfers. London: Zed Books, 1985.

MYRDAL, GUNNAR. *Asian Drama: An Inquiry into the Poverty of Nations.* 3 vol. New York: The Twentieth Century Fund, 1968.

———. *The Challenge of World Poverty: A World Anti-Poverty Program in Outline.* New York: Pantheon, 1970.

NASSAR, GAMAL ABDEL. *The Philosophy of the Revolution.* Buffalo, NY: Smith, Keynes & Marshall, 1959.

NKRUMAH, KWAME. *The Autobiography of Kwame Nkrumah.* Edinburgh, Scotland: Thomas Nelson and Sons, 1957.

———. *I Speak of Freedom: A Statement of African Ideology.* New York: Praeger, 1961.

———. *Neo-Colonialism: The Last Stage of Imperialism.* New York: International Publishers, 1966.

———. *Consciencism: Philosophy and Ideology for De-Colonization.* Rev. ed. New York: Monthly Review Press, 1970.

———. *Revolutionary Path.* New York: International Publishers, 1973.

NYERERE, JULIUS K. *Freedom and Socialism: Uhuru na Ujamaa, A Selection from Writings and Speeches 1965–1970.* Dar es Salaam, Tanzania: Oxford University Press, 1968.

———. *Freedom and Development: Uhuru na Maendelo, A Selection of Writings and Speeches 1968–1973.* Dar es Salaam, Tanzania: Oxford University Press, 1973.

OBOTE, A. MILTON. *The Common Man's Charter.* Entebbe, Uganda: Government Printer, 1970.

OSTERGAARD, GEOFFREY, and MELVILLE CURRELL. *The Gentle Anarchists: A Study of the Sarvodaya Movement for Non-Violent Revolution in India.* Oxford, England: Clarendon Press, 1971.

OTTAWAY, DAVID, and MARINA OTTAWAY. *Afrocommunism.* New York: Africana Publishing, 1981.

PINKNEY, ROBERT. *Democracy in the Third World.* Boulder, CO: Lynne Rienner, 1994.

ROBERTSON, CLAIRE, and IRIS BERGER. *Women and Class in Africa.* New York: Africana Publishing, 1986.

SENGHOR, LÉOPOLD SÉDAR. *On African Socialism.* New York: Praeger, 1964.

SMITH, ANTHONY D. *State and Nation in the Third World: The Western State and African Nationalism.* New York: St. Martin's, 1983.

SUKARNO. *An Autobiography. As Told to Cindy Adams.* Indianapolis, IN: Bobbs-Merrill, 1965.

WRIGHT, MOORHEAD, ed. *Rights and Obligations in North–South Relations: Ethical Dimensions of Global Problems.* New York: St. Martin's, 1986.

YOUNG, CRAWFORD. *Ideology and Development in Africa.* New Haven, CT: Yale University Press, 1982.

11

Liberation Theology

A fairly recent addition to the list of important ideologies is Liberation Theology. With European and Latin American theological and political origins, but reaching its peak in Latin America, Liberation Theology has spread north, to affect the United States, and back across the Atlantic, where indigenous movements such as Irish Liberation Theology have developed. As a result of the sustained opposition of Pope John Paul II, Liberation Theology appears not to be spreading as rapidly as it had been, but it is firmly rooted in Latin American theology and politics.

Liberation Theology developed as a response to the poverty found in Latin America together with the fact that the Roman Catholic Church, the dominant church in the area, was identified with the rich and powerful. The Church was having difficulty providing priests for rural areas where most of the poor lived. As a result, those who were concerned with these problems began, first in Brazil as early as the late 1950s, to encourage community-based organizations, later to be called Basic Christian Communities, to provide for their own religious needs. This led, quite rapidly, to these same groups identifying social, economic, and political needs and organizing themselves to try to meet those needs also.

As the movement developed, intellectuals began to look for theological and theoretical justification. They found the French worker-priest movement, and they found Western Marxism with its concern for the poor. The worker-priest movement helped them encourage priests to work in communities as equals with the people. Marxism, but particularly the so-called Marxist-Christian dialogue of the late 1960s, provided a theory that could be integrated with the theological movements that had produced the Ecumenical Council of 1962–1965, generally known as Vatican II, with its emphasis on modernizing the church and making it more responsive to laypeople. Vatican II also stressed collective responsibility in the Church, which fitted nicely with the community organizations that Liberation Theology was developing.

THE MARXIST-CHRISTIAN DIALOGUE

Much of the Marxism found in Liberation Theology came through Ernst Bloch (1885–1977), who was discussed in chapter 7.[1] Bloch's emphasis on hope provides some of the radical thrust of Liberation Theology, and Bloch found the basis for hope in Western civilization in Christianity. Thus Bloch, a Marxist who chose to spend much of his life in what was then East Germany, argued for the radical potential of Christianity. And theologians within Liberation Theology found that Marx's emphasis on the poor resonated with their concerns and the needs of their people.

In 1965 the French Marxist Roger Garaudy (1913–) published a book entitled *From Anathema to Dialogue: The Challenge of Marxist-Christian Cooperation*. The publication of this book began a long-lasting debate on the degree to which Marxists and Christians could learn from each other or even actively cooperate. The basis of the developing dialogue was the writings of the young Marx, which focus on human alienation and the dehumanizing effects of capitalist society. These writings attracted theologians with similar concerns, and some Marxists have found in Christianity, particularly early Christianity, a deep concern with the oppressed and a message of hope for the future in this life. Therefore, both Marxists and Christians began to consider what they could say to each other without losing the essential characteristics of their beliefs.

However, Liberation Theologians see Marx as limited by his rejection of God. Thus "Marx (like any other Marxist) can be a companion on the way . . . but he can never be *the* guide, because 'You have only one teacher, the Christ' (Matt. 23:10)."[2] In addition to Marx, one of the most important non-theological sources of Liberation Theology is the work of the Brazilian Paulo Freire (1921–), particularly his *Pedagogy of the Oppressed* (1970). Freire advocates what he calls *conscientization* or consciousness-raising, a process in which the oppressed become aware of their oppression through participation in group discussion. Anarchists also claim Freire as an important theorist.

As this dialogue developed, theologians from the Third World, particularly Latin America, became interested because the issues of poverty and political and

---

[1] See Tom Moylan, "Bloch Against Bloch: The Theological Reception of *Das Prinzip Hoffnung* and the Liberation of the Utopian Function," *Utopian Studies* 1, no. 2 (1990): 27–51.

[2] Leonardo Boff and Clodovis Boff, *Introducing Liberation Theology*, trans. Paul Burns (Maryknoll, NY: Orbis Books, 1987), p. 28.

economic repression that so concerned both Marx and the early Christians were central issues of daily life for many of their church members. Since most of Latin America is Roman Catholic, the effect of the dialogue has been felt mostly, but not entirely, in the Roman Catholic Church.

Out of the dialogue has arisen a major new approach to theology, known as *Liberation Theology*, which has divided the Roman Catholic Church in Latin America and in Europe. "Liberation theology was born when faith confronted the injustice done to the poor."[3] Although the current pope condemned Liberation Theology in the past, he subsequently accepted some of its basic positions. Most conservatives within the Roman Catholic Church still reject most of Liberation Theology.

In broad outline the position of Liberation Theology is as follows:

1. The church should be concerned with poverty.

2. The church should be concerned with political repression.

3. The church should be concerned with economic repression.

4. Priests should become actively involved in trying to solve these problems.

5. Priests should move beyond general activity to
   a. Direct political action, and, possibly,
   b. Direct involvement in attempts to change political and economic systems, even by actual participation in revolutionary activity.

6. The establishment of base communities or communities including religious (priests and nuns) and laypeople in communes or communities that are political and economic units, thus overcoming the division between religious and laypeople.

The Roman Catholic Church specifically rejects item five and is not sure about item three. The pope had previously rejected item six but has accepted it in some circumstances.

One of the early theorists of Liberation Theology was Gustavo Gutiérrez (1928–) of Chile. His *Theology of Liberation* (1971, English translation 1973) was the first work to bring together the elements of Liberation Theology. Gutiérrez argued, based on Freire and Ernst Bloch, that the Church must recognize the positive function of the idea of utopia. Utopia includes the condemnation of the evils of the present and an affirmation of the possibilities of the future. As Gutiérrez put it,

> The theology of liberation attempts to reflect on the experience and meaning of the faith based on the commitment to abolish injustice and to build a new society; this theology must be verified by the practice of that commitment, by active, effective participation in the struggle which the exploited social classes have undertaken against their oppressors. Liberation from every form of exploitation, the

---

[3] Boff and Boff, p. 3.

possibility of a more human and more dignified life, the creation of a new man—all pass through this struggle.[4]

Today the best known theorist of Liberation Theology is Leonardo Boff (1938–). He argues that Liberation Theology developed as and where it did because Latin Americans are both poor and Christian. The Church was generally supportive of the rich and powerful, and many both inside and outside the Church found this fact morally repugnant. As Boff and Clodovis Boff (1944–) wrote, "How are we to be Christian in a world of destitution and injustice? There can only be one answer: we can be followers of Jesus and true Christians only by making common cause with the poor and working out the gospel of liberation."[5]

That gospel is a political one. The oppressed must organize both for immediate reform—"better wages, working conditions, health care, education, housing, and so forth"—and for a "new society characterized by widespread participation, a better and more just balance among social classes and more worthy ways of life."[6] Thus Liberation Theology is part of the radical movements that developed in the 1960s and 1970s, stressing consciousness-raising, participatory forms, and socialism.

Liberation Theology is different from these radical movements both in that it, like feminism, is still around and in that it is a theology. While it is beyond the scope of this book to explore the theology of Liberation Theology, it must always be remembered that it is a theology and bases its political and economic message on an understanding of the Bible and, particularly, the mission of Christ. " . . . Liberation theology deals with two principal tasks: first, to point out the theological relevance of freedom movements. . . . Second, the theology of liberation deals with emphasizing the liberating aspects that are present in the Gospel in the life and praxis of Jesus, and in the great tradition of the Church."[7]

Like many radical theologians and spiritual leaders of the past, the leading thinkers of Liberation Theology see the Christian message as directed particularly to the poor and oppressed. One of the earlier spiritual leaders to whom the Liberation Theologians look is St. Francis of Assisi who, it should be remembered, insisted on the absolute poverty of his followers. St. Francis was too radical for the church of his day, as is Liberation Theology today.

A central political-theological tenet of Liberation Theology is the idea of the poor. "Objectively, the poor are poor because, the way society is organized, since they have the strength to work but not the capital, they are placed on the

---

[4]Gustavo Gutiérrez, *A Theology of Liberation: History, Politics and Salvation*, 15th anniv. ed., trans. and ed. Sister Caridad Inda and John Eagleson (Maryknoll, NY: Orbis Books, 1988), p. 174.

[5]Boff and Boff, p. 7.

[6]Ibid., p. 5.

[7]Leonardo Boff, *Saint Francis: A Model for Human Liberation*, trans. John W. Diercksmeier (New York: Crossroad Press, 1982), pp. 84–85.

Leonardo Boff (1938–) is a Franciscan priest and Professor of Systematic Theology at the Institute for Philosophy and Theology in Petrópolis, Brazil. He is one of the best-known theologians of Liberation Theology. He was "silenced" (meaning he could not publish) by the Vatican for one year in response to his writings on Liberation Theology. (*Claus Meyer/Black Star*)

margin."[8] But the Boffs argue that the idea of the poor must be expanded to include all the oppressed—specifically, blacks, indigenous peoples, and women.[9] The poor are, for the Boffs, "the Disfigured Son of God."[10] In this way the idea of the poor and oppressed, while not losing its relationship to oppressed people in actual situations, is "opened up to the Infinite"[11] and connected to eternal life and also to the transformation of both the spiritual and actual lives of all peoples.

> The holy city, the new Jerusalem that comes down from heaven (Rev. 21:2), can be established on earth only when men and women filled with faith and passion for the gospel, united with each other, and hungry and thirsty for justice, create the human dispositions and material conditions for it. But the earth will not then be the same earth, neither will the heavens be the same heavens; they will be a *new* heaven and a *new* earth. The old earth with its oppressions will have passed away. The new earth will be a gift of God and the fruit of human effort. What

---

[8]Ibid., p. 86.

[9]Boff and Boff, p. 29.

[10]Ibid., p. 31.

[11]Ibid.

was begun in history will continue in eternity: the kingdom of the freed, living as brothers and sisters in the great house of the Father.[12]

ACTION—BASE COMMUNITIES

"More important than to see and to judge is to *act*. . . ."[13] In Liberation Theology the most basic form of action is the establishment of base communities or base ecclesial communities.

> From its own identity in faith, the Church organizes the people in Christian communities, those in which the lowly meet, meditate on the Word of God, and, enlightened by that Word, discuss their problems and find ways of solution. These base communities have an immediate and direct religious value, but they also achieve social importance because they are places for the formation of social conscience, responsibility, and the desire for change.[14]

In 1979 Latin American bishops meeting at Puebla, Mexico, recognized the base communities as an important new form of both evangelizing and liberating the poor and oppressed. " . . . We have found that small communities, especially the CEBs [Base-level Ecclesial Communities], create more personal interrelations, acceptance of God's Word, re-examination of one's life, and reflection on the reality of the Gospel. They accentuate committed involvement in the family, one's work, the neighborhood, and the local community."[15]

In Liberation Theology, communitarianism rather than individualism is considered the way forward. Ever since Vatican II (1962–1965) there has been a movement in the Roman Catholic Church to involve the laity more fully in the Church. The development of base communities is one of the responses to this movement.

Boff describes a typical community as follows:

> The base ecclesial community is generally made up of fifteen to twenty families. They get together once or twice a week to hear the Word of God, to share their problems in common, and to solve those problems through the inspiration of the Gospel. They share their comments on the biblical passages, create their own prayers, and decide as a group what their tasks should be. After centuries of silence, the People of God are beginning to speak. They are no longer just parishioners in their parish; they have their own ecclesiological value; they are recreating the Church of God.[16]

---

[12]Ibid., p. 95.

[13]Boff, p. 87.

[14]Ibid.

[15]*Puebla and Beyond: Documentation and Commentary*, ed. John Eagleson and Philip Scharper (Maryknoll, NY: Orbis Books, 1979), p. 211.

The sense of participation that is encouraged is a radical departure for the Roman Catholic Church, which has traditionally been hierarchical and authoritarian. Many in the Church have difficulty accepting the empowerment of the laity and the degree of control over their own forms of worship that are being demanded.

In some ways Liberation Theology is as much an outgrowth of the New Left as is feminism, and both of these ideologies are slowly transforming the worlds that they affect.

CURRENT TRENDS

Liberation Theology is in a somewhat difficult and complex position today. On one hand, it is still successful in Latin America and has gained supporters around the world. On the other hand, it is still under pressure from the Vatican to conform to the generally conservative theology of the current pope. In addition, many of its supporters are beginning to recognize that there are problems within Liberation Theology that need to be addressed. Much of the questioning is coming from the developed North and reflects issues of concern there, but as Liberation Theology has spread it has had to face issues that it did not face in Latin America.

The main criticisms center on the question of equality. Although Liberation Theology tried to deal with the question of equality between clergy and laypeople, it did not deal with questions of gender and race. Given the position of women in the Roman Catholic Church, the former failure is hardly a surprise. And given that most of the clergy are European, European-trained, or of European ethnic origin, the latter problem should not be too surprising either. But critics from the left who support the activities and goals of Liberation Theology contend that it must come to terms with these issues also. A few wish to add sexual preference to the list. The argument is that a generally radical social analysis must have some way of dealing with these questions or it will fail.

Another failure identified that might seem to fall outside the purview of Liberation Theology is the failure to be involved with ecological issues. Some critics, again mostly from the developed North, contend that ecological issues are central to any radical critique today, and Latin America is a focus of such critiques.

A more general criticism is that Liberation Theology has not rejected strongly enough the conservatism of the current pope. Contemporary Church dogma as promulgated by the Vatican has rejected many of the initiatives of

[16]Leonardo Boff, *Church, Charism, Power: Liberation Theology and the Institutional Church*, trans. John W. Diercksmeier (New York: Crossroad Press, 1985), pp. 125–126. From *Church, Charism and Power: Liberation Theology and the Institutional Church* by Leonardo Boff, trans. John W. Diercksmeier. Reprinted by permission of The Crossroad Publishing Company.

Vatican II, and appointments to the Church hierarchy are normally given to those who oppose change and reject movements like Liberation Theology.

In general, supporters of Liberation Theology accept that its understanding of gender and racial issues has been weak and are beginning to support ecological initiatives (although some contend that conservation benefits only the already well-to-do). They tend to argue that in order to survive within the Church, some accommodation must be made with the Vatican. They argue that as a movement Liberation Theology is succeeding with the poor where it is most important and that it can outlast the current conservatism.

SUGGESTED READINGS

BERRYMAN, PHILLIP. *The Religious Roots of Rebellion: Christians in Central American Revolutions.* Maryknoll, NY: Orbis Books, 1984.

————. *Liberation Theology: Essential Facts About the Revolutionary Movement in Latin America and Beyond.* Philadelphia: Temple University Press, 1987.

BOFF, CLODOVIS, O. S. M. *Feet on the Ground Theology: A Brazilian Journey.* Trans. Phillip Berryman. Maryknoll, NY: Orbis Books, 1987.

————. *Theology and Praxis: Epistemological Foundations.* Trans. Robert R. Barr. Maryknoll, NY: Orbis Books, 1987.

BOFF, LEONARDO. *Jesus Christ Liberator: A Critical Christology for Our Time.* Trans. Patrick Hughes. Maryknoll, NY: Orbis Books, 1978.

————. *Liberating Grace.* Trans. John Drury. Maryknoll, NY: Orbis Books, 1981.

————. *Saint Francis: A Model for Human Liberation.* Trans. John W. Diercksmeier. New York: Crossroad Press, 1982.

————. *Way of the Cross—Way of Justice.* Trans. John Drury. Maryknoll, NY: Orbis Books, 1982.

————. *The Lord's Prayer: The Prayer of Integral Liberation.* Trans. Theodore Morrow. Maryknoll, NY: Orbis Books, 1983.

————. *Church, Charism and Power: Liberation Theology and the Institutional Church.* Trans. John W. Diercksmeier. New York: Crossroad Press, 1985.

————. *Ecclesiogenesis: The Base Communities Reinvent the Church.* Trans. Robert R. Barr. Maryknoll, NY: Orbis Books, 1986.

————. *Trinity and Society.* Trans. Paul Burns. Maryknoll, NY: Orbis Books, 1988.

————, and CLODOVIS BOFF. *Salvation and Liberation: In Search of a Balance Between Faith and Politics.* Trans. Robert R. Barr. Maryknoll, NY: Orbis Books/Melbourne, Australia: Dove Communications, 1984.

————. *Introducing Liberation Theology.* Trans. Paul Burns. Maryknoll, NY: Orbis Books, 1987.

————, and VIRGIL ELIZONDO, eds. *The People of God Amidst the Poor.* Edinburgh, Scotland: T. & T. Clark, 1984.

————. *Convergences and Differences.* Edinburgh, Scotland: T. & T. Clark, 1988.

BROWN, ROBERT MCAFEE. *Gustavo Gutiérrez: An Introduction to Liberation Theology.* Maryknoll, NY: Orbis Books, 1990.

CHOPP, REBECCA S. *The Praxis of Suffering: An Interpretation of Liberation and Political Theologies.* Maryknoll, NY: Orbis Books, 1986.

DORRIEN, GARY J. *Reconstructing the Common Good: Theology and the Social Order.* Maryknoll, NY: Orbis Books, 1990.

DUSSEL, ENRIQUE. *History and Theology of Liberation: A Latin American Perspective.* Trans. John Drury. Maryknoll, NY: Orbis Books, 1975.

———. *Philosophy of Liberation.* Trans. Aquilina Martinez and Christine Morkowsky. Maryknoll, NY: Orbis Books, 1985.

———. *Ethics and Community.* Trans. Robert R. Barr. Maryknoll, NY: Orbis Books, 1988.

ELLUL, JACQUES. *Jesus and Marx: From Gospel to Ideology.* Trans. Joyce Main Hanks. Grand Rapids, MI: William B. Eerdmans, 1988.

FENN, DEANE WILLIAM, ed. *Third World Liberation Theologies: An Introductory Survey.* Maryknoll, NY: Orbis Books, 1986.

———. *Third World Liberation Theologies: A Reader.* Maryknoll, NY: Orbis Books, 1986.

GARCÍA, ISMAEL. *Justice in Latin American Theology of Liberation.* Atlanta, GA: John Knox Press, 1987.

GUTIÉRREZ, GUSTAVO. *The Power of the Poor in History.* Trans. Robert R. Barr. Maryknoll, NY: Orbis Books, 1983.

———. *We Drink from Our Own Wells: The Spiritual Journey of a People.* Trans. Matthew J. O'Connell. Maryknoll, NY: Orbis Books/Melbourne, Australia: Dove Communications, 1984.

———. *On Job: God-Talk and the Suffering of the Innocent.* Trans. Matthew J. O'Connell. Maryknoll, NY: Orbis Books, 1987.

———. *A Theology of Liberation: History, Politics and Salvation.* 15th anniv. ed. Trans. and ed. Sister Caridad Inda and John Eagleson. Maryknoll, NY: Orbis Books, 1988.

HAIGHT, ROGER, S. J. *An Alternative Vision: An Interpretation of Liberation Theology.* Mahwah, NJ: Paulist Press, 1985.

HENNELLY, ALFRED T., S. J., ed. *Liberation Theology: A Documentary History.* Maryknoll, NY: Orbis Books, 1990.

HEWITT, W. E. *Base Christian Communities and Social Change in Brazil.* Lincoln: University of Nebraska Press, 1991.

HINKELAMMERT, FRANZ J. *The Ideological Weapons of Death: A Theological Critique of Capitalism.* Trans. Phillip Berryman. Maryknoll, NY: Orbis Books, 1986.

LAMB, MATTHEW L. *Solidarity with Victims: Toward a Theology of Social Transformation.* New York: Crossroad Press, 1982.

McGOVERN, ARTHUR F. *Liberation Theology and Its Critics: Toward an Assessment.* Maryknoll, NY: Orbis Books, 1989.

MÍGUEZ BONINO, JOSÉ. *Doing Theology in a Revolutionary Situation.* Philadelphia: Fortress Press, 1975. Published in the United Kingdom as *Revolutionary Theology Comes of Age.* London: SPCK, 1975.

———. *Toward a Christian Political Ethics.* Philadelphia: Fortress Press, 1983.

MIRANDA, JOSÉ PORFIRIO. *Marx and the Bible: A Critique of the Philosophy of Oppression.* Trans. John Eagleson. Maryknoll, NY: Orbis Books, 1974.

———. *Being and the Messiah: The Message of St. John.* Trans. John Eagleson. Maryknoll, NY: Orbis Books, 1977.

———. *Marx Against the Marxists: The Christian Humanism of Karl Marx.* Trans. John Drury. Maryknoll, NY: Orbis Books, 1978.

———. *Communism in the Bible.* Trans. Robert R. Barr. Maryknoll, NY: Orbis Books, 1982.

MOYLAN, TOM. "Denunciation/Annunciation: The Radical Methodology of Liberation Theology." *Cultural Critique* 20 (Winter 1991–1992): 33–64.

———. *Rereading Religion: Ernst Bloch, Gustavo Gutiérrez, and the Post-Modern Strategy of Liberation Theology.* Milwaukee: Center for Twentieth Century Studies, University of Wisconsin-Milwaukee. Working Paper No. 2, Fall 1988.

NASH, RONALD, ed. *Liberation Theology.* Milford, MI: Mott Media, 1984.

NOVAK, MICHAEL. *Will It Liberate? Questions About Liberation Theology.* New York: Paulist Press, 1986.

PIXLEY, JORGE, and CLODOVIS BOFF. *The Bible, the Church and the Poor: Biblical, Theological and Pastoral Aspects of the Option for the Poor.* Trans. Paul Burns. Tunbridge Wells, Kent, England: Burns & Oates, 1989.

POTTENGER, JOHN R. *The Political Theory of Liberation Theology: Toward a Convergence of Social Values and Social Science.* Albany: State University of New York Press, 1989.

QUADE, QUENTIN L., ed. *The Pope and Revolution: John Paul II Confronts Liberation Theology.* Washington, DC: Ethics and Public Policy Center, 1982.

ROBERTSON, ROLAND. "Liberation Theology in Latin America: Sociological Problems of Interpretation and Explanation." In *Prophetic Religions and Politics: Religion and the Political Order,* edited by Jeffrey K. Hadden and Anson Shupe, pp. 73–102. New York: Paragon House, 1986.

————. "Latin America and Liberation Theology." In *Church-State Relations: Tensions and Transitions,* edited by Thomas Robbins and Roland Robertson, pp. 205–220. Rutgers, NJ: Transaction Books, 1987.

RODES, ROBERT E. *Law and Liberation.*

Notre Dame, IN: University of Notre Dame Press, 1986.

ROELOFS, H. MARK. "Liberation Theology: The Recovery of Biblical Radicalism." *American Political Science Review* 82, no. 2 (June 1988): 549–566.

SEGUNDO, JUAN LUIS. *Liberation of Theology.* Trans. John Drury. Maryknoll, NY: Orbis Books, 1976.

————. *Theology and the Church: A Response to Cardinal Ratzinger and a Warning to the Whole Church.* Trans. John W. Diercksmeier. Minneapolis, MN: Winston Press/London: Geoffrey Chapman, 1985.

SHAULL, RICHARD. *Heralds of a New Reformation: The Poor of South and North America.* Maryknoll, NY: Orbis Books, 1984.

SIGMUND, PAUL E. *Liberation Theology at the Crossroads: Democracy or Revolution?* New York: Oxford University Press, 1990.

TABB, WILLIAM K. *Churches in Struggle: Liberation Theologies and Social Change in North America.* New York: Monthly Review Press, 1986.

TAMEZ, ELSA. *Bible of the Oppressed.* Trans. Matthew J. O'Connell. Maryknoll, NY: Orbis Books, 1982.

12

Islam

Islam is a religion that has become a major political force in the contemporary world.[1] It is also widely misunderstood in the West. Islam is the second largest world religion, after Christianity, with about a billion adherents. They live mostly in a wide belt from Senegal on the west coast of Africa, east to Indonesia on the western edge of the Pacific Ocean, and reaching south into sub-Saharan Africa and north into the southern part of the former Soviet Union. This area contains forty-four countries that are predominantly Islamic; in addition, there are growing Muslim communities throughout the rest of the world.

For most of this century Islam has not been a significant political force in world affairs. Most Islamic countries were attempting to modernize and join the

---

[1] Islamic political thought has not yet been studied very much in the West. The following sources in English include works both for the beginner and for someone wanting some depth. A good place for the complete neophyte to start is Aziz Al-Azmeh, "Islamic Political Thought," in *The Blackwell Encyclopedia of Political Thought*, ed. David Miller (Oxford, England: Blackwell Reference, 1987), pp. 249–253. Other works to consult include Hamid Enayat, *Modern Islamic Political Thought: The Response of the Shi'i and Sunni Muslims to the Twentieth Century* (London: Macmillan, 1982); Abdulrahman Abdulkadir Kurdi, *The Islamic State: A Study Based on the Islamic Holy Constitution* (London: Mansell, 1984); Bernard Lewis, *The Political Language of Islam* (Chicago: University of Chicago Press, 1988); E. I. J. Rosenthal, *Political Thought in Medieval Islam: An Introductory Outline* (Cambridge, England: Cambridge University Press, 1962); and W. Montgomery Watt, *Islamic Political Thought: The Basic Concepts* (Edinburgh, Scotland: Edinburgh University Press, 1968). Some texts can be found in "Political Philosophy in Islam," ed. Muhsin Mahdi, in *Medieval Political Philosophy: A Sourcebook*, ed. Ralph Lerner and Muhsin Mahdi (New York: Free Press, 1963), pp. 22–186, and Kemal H. Karpat, ed. *Political and Social Thought in the Contemporary Middle East*, rev. and enlarged edition (New York: Praeger, 1982).

ranks of the developed world and therefore were relatively uninvolved. Three things changed this. First, the establishment of the state of Israel in 1948 on land then occupied by Palestinians united Islamic countries that had been previously divided. Second, the rapid rise in the price of oil meant that some poor countries were suddenly rich. Third, the Iranian revolution, combined with Iranian attempts to foment revolution in other Islamic countries, has led to a much greater focus on Islamic thought both in the Middle East and elsewhere. As a result Islam has become an important political force, but one that many Westerners identify with terrorism and violence.

The conflicts are the reflection of deep divisions within Islam together with the rejection by many Muslims of the modernization and Westernization that had characterized many Islamic countries. This rejection is best labeled Islamic revivalism, although in the West it is commonly called Islamic fundamentalism. The label *Islamic fundamentalism* is not used here because it suggests a misleading parallel with movements within contemporary Protestantism in the United States. The label *Islamic revivalism* is not completely satisfactory, but it avoids the more important problems with the word *fundamentalism*.

BELIEFS

Although it is neither possible nor relevant to discuss Islamic theology here, a few points of religious belief are necessary as background to help understand what the splits within Islam are all about. Islam is unified by its faith in God (Allah in Arabic), the holy book the Quran, and the teachings of its great prophet, Muhammad. Islam sprang from the same roots and the same geographic area as Judaism and Christianity, and Islam accepts the Jewish prophets and Jesus as great religious teachers who were forerunners to Muhammad. Islam, like both Judaism and Christianity, is monotheistic. Jews, Christians, and Muslims are all thought of as "People of the Book."

There are five "pillars" of Islam that every pious Muslim must perform:

1. In a lifetime the believer must at least once say, "There is no god but God and Muhammad is the messenger of God," in full understanding and acceptance.

2. The believer must pray five times a day (at dawn, noon, mid-afternoon, dusk, and after dark).

3. The believer must give alms generously.

4. The believer must keep the fast of Ramadan (the ninth month of the Muslim year).

5. The believer must once make the pilgrimage (*hajj*) to Mecca.

A sixth pillar is sometimes included, the *jihad*, usually thought of in the West as denoting "holy war" but actually meaning "to struggle" and signifying that believers must struggle with themselves and their communities to be good Muslims and to proselytize to enlarge the Muslim community.[2] At times and for certain sects *jihad* does also mean "holy war."

Beyond these basic beliefs and duties, the believer refers for guidance to the *Sharia* (path or way), the religious law.[3] Islamic law gives both legal and moral guidance and has provided an additional point of reference for the widely divergent cultures represented by the many Islamic countries. Of course, any law requires interpreters, and who is to interpret the law is, the basis for certain disagreements within Islam.

Islamic law is derived from the Quran, the Sunna of the Prophet (the life of Muhammad), legal reasoning, and the consensus of the community.[4] It is more like a set of moral and ethical principles than what Westerners today think of as law, and it was, and in many Muslim countries is, interpreted and applied by a variety of courts and officials.

In addition, in most countries the *Sharia* was gradually supplemented and, in the eyes of some, supplanted by laws emerging from political authorities that were designed to deal with changing economic and political conditions and, later, the impact of the West. As a result, one of the most common demands of Islamic revivalists is the reestablishment of the *Sharia* as the primary law. This demand is made by members of both the major divisions (Sunni and Shiite) within Islam.

Islamic countries have traditionally been theocratic (*theo* = God, *kratos* = rule), or societies where religious and political life have been tightly bound together, but with politics subordinate to religion. Part of Islamic revivalism is the result of the political leaders in some countries changing or trying to change that relationship.

HISTORY

It is impossible to understand the current situation in Islam without a little history. Muhammad lived from about 570 to 632, and the major division in Islam relates to his succession. Most Islamic groups accept that the first four Caliphs (successors) were correctly chosen. The dispute involves the line of succession after the fourth Caliph. The main Shiite sect, the Twelvers (believers in the Twelfth Imam), believe that the correct succession was through his descendants by his wife Fatima, Muhammad's daughter, through a line of infallible Imams, beginning with Ali ben Abi Tabib, the fourth Caliph, and his two sons and extending through nine others until the Twelfth Imam, who disappeared

---

[2]John L. Esposito, *Islam: The Straight Path*, expanded ed. (New York: Oxford University Press, 1991), p. 93.

[3]Ibid., pp. 75–76.

[4]Ibid., pp. 79–85.

The Great Mosque, or Haran, at Mecca, Saudi Arabia, is the spiritual center of Islam.
At the center of the mosque is the Kaaba or Caaba, the most sacred sanctuary in Islam.
Mecca and the mosque is the destination of the *hajj*, or the pilgrimage that every
Muslim is required to make in their lifetime. The towers are minarets, and from them
the faithful are called to prayer five times a day by a muezzin. (*UPI/Bettmann*)

while still a boy. The Twelvers believe that the Twelfth Imam is waiting for the
right time to return, at which time he will bring justice to the earth and overthrow oppression. The Sunni, on the other hand, believe that the Caliphs that
followed Ali were correctly chosen. They also accept a different basis for the
choice—consensus—whereas the Shiites believe in divine appointment.

Another division that has affected both Sunni and Shiites has been the development of Sufiism. Sufiism is a mystical sect within Islam that has gained
considerable popularity in the West. Although significant numbers of Muslims
are Sufi, they are not important politically.

The next great division within Islam that is relevant to the contemporary
political situation was brought about by the impact of the West. As with most
other colonized areas, the Islamic countries went through a process of combined
acceptance and rejection of Western values and practices. While it was clear that
Western technology, which allowed the colonization to take place, was useful,
perhaps even necessary, there was a deep division over the acceptance of Western values, particularly those related to individual freedom and equality.

Islamic thought has no concept of individual freedom or rights.[5] The emphasis is on the community of believers rather than the individual. An Islamic government is expected to provide the internal and external security that will allow the believer to worship and to earn a living. But these are not rights that an individual can claim against a government. The process of government is dependent upon the *Sharia*, which means that religious teachers and interpreters are very powerful, as the Imam Khomeini (1900–1989) in Iran was during his lifetime.

The ideas of freedom, rights, and equality proved appealing to some believers, however, and groups of Westernizers, Islamic liberals, Islamic socialists, and advocates of women's rights began to appear in the nineteenth and early twentieth centuries. Thus in practice the ideals of Islam have been challenged and compromised, particularly through contact with the West and its emphasis on individual liberty, the rights of the individual against the state, and the equality of women and men.

ISLAM TODAY

Today Islam is divided into the two major historical divisions, the Sunni making up about 85 percent of all Muslims and the Shiites composing the other 15 percent. In addition, the Shiites currently include one major sect within their ranks, the Ismailis, and the Druse split off from the Ismailis. In the past, a number of other sects have existed among the Shiites.

Islamic Liberalism

In the nineteenth and early twentieth centuries Islam went through a lengthy liberal period during which Islamic thought experienced a transformation similar to the changes Christianity experienced in the seventeenth through nineteenth centuries. Specifically, Islamic liberal thinkers accepted the notion of historical change and, in particular, the idea that Islamic texts could be reinterpreted to meet changing conditions. These thinkers also argued for the reconciliation of reason and faith, the need for educational reform to take advantage of Western science and technology, and the desirability of greater equality for women.[6] For quite some time and in many countries, Islamic liberalism was dominant, but in the second quarter of the twentieth century a shift began to take place, based on the experience of colonialism, that rejected Islamic liberalism as too Western. The identification of Islamic liberalism with the West and colonialism provided the ideological basis for the emergence of Islamic revivalism.

---

[5] Watt, *Islamic Political Thought*, p. 96.

[6] See Nader Saiedi, "What is Islamic Fundamentalism?" In *Prophetic Religions and Politics: Religion and the Political Order*, ed. Anson Shupe and Jeffrey K. Hadden (New York: Paragon House, 1986), pp. 179–182.

Islamic liberalism survives today in movements that stem from it but have made compromises with Islamic revivalism. In Egypt the movement started by Gamal Abd al Nasser (1918–1970) still exists but is of much less importance than it once was, even though the current leaders of Egypt see themselves as the heirs of Nasser. Nasserism was essentially secular but used Islamic symbols. In Libya, Colonel Muammur Qadahafi (1942–) has established a highly idiosyncratic version of Islam that hides a dictatorship behind most of the policies of Islamic liberalism. In Syria the Baath party, which was founded in 1940 by Michel Aflaq (1910–), a Christian, and Salah al-Din Baytar (1911–1980), a Muslim, is essentially secular while using Islamic symbols. It rejects both capitalism and communism because both are based on materialism; economically the Baath party is socialist. Its greatest emphasis, though, is on Arab nationalism and the desirability of a single Arab nation; the party finds Islamic origins for this position.

Politically the most important disagreement of Islamic liberalism is between those who reject and those who accept Westernization, primarily meaning secularization and modernization, particularly in social relations. The most striking political example of Islamic modernization was the election of Benazir Bhutto (1953–) as prime minister of Pakistan. The election of a woman as prime minister was a remarkable development, but her first term was very short, in large part because of opposition from more traditional groups.

Revivalism

The Sunni make up the overwhelming majority of Muslims today, but there are divisions within the Sunni centering on the acceptance or rejection of modernization, Westernization, or both. Many Muslims who reject Westernization because they see it as undermining Islam accept modernization because they see it as improving the lives of the people. Others wholly reject both Westernization and modernization and characterize both as evil.

In the West revivalism is usually associated with the Shiites, but while there are significant differences between Sunni and Shiite revivalists, there are also major agreements. All revivalists want the reestablishment of the *Sharia*, which they believe will result in an Islamic theocracy and the full realization of the ideal Islamic community.

The Muslim Brotherhood. The fact that revivalism can combine modernization with a rejection of Westernization is demonstrated best by the Muslim Brotherhood (al-Ikhwan al-Muslimun), the first major revivalist movement, founded in 1928 in Egypt by Hasan al-Banna (1906–1949). The Brotherhood, which became one of the most powerful movements ever to exist within Islam and still exists today, emphasizes both a return to Islamic traditions and scientific and technical education. The Muslim Brotherhood also argues for major social and economic reforms within the framework of Islam. In addition, the Brotherhood seeks the unification of all Muslims.

Politics. For Muslims, Allah is the only legislator; any earthly ruler is only to ensure that God's laws are practiced. The ruler is an administrator, not a law-giver. Sunni and Shiite revivalists disagree on who should rule. The most extreme Sunni believe that a Caliph (successor) should administer the Divine Law. Shiite Islam requires the presence of the *Mahdi*, or Twelfth or Hidden Imam, for the correct government to be established. In his absence a monarch or sultan who rules with the consent of the *ulama*—religious teachers or those who are learned in the divine law—is the best possible solution.

As was seen in Iran under Ayatollah Khomeini, a legislature composed of the *ulama* operating with the advice of an Imam (leader) can replace the monarch or sultan. But that legislature is still subordinate to the *Sharia*. Khomeini believed that the clergy were the appropriate rulers. He also argued that the most preeminent among the clergy—that is, the most learned, just, and pious—should hold the highest office, that of deputy to the Hidden or Twelfth Imam. Khomeini saw himself in that role and was accepted as such.

Economics. On the whole, the economic theory of Islam supports private property, but it imposes a duty of almsgiving and charity. The *Sharia* mentions specific taxes, forbids usury (charging interest), and opposes extreme concentrations of wealth. In general, the position is that if social justice can be provided for privately, it should be. But if social justice as defined by the *Sharia* cannot be established by private means, the government should intervene to ensure its establishment.

Social Organization. The family is at the center of the Islamic community. The traditional Islamic family is patriarchal, with the man as its head. However, the Quran gives women specific rights. Most important, women can hold and inherit property, although these rights have been frequently violated and some revivalists would like them limited. But women are to function only in the private sphere; only men are to act publicly.

In traditional Islam, which the revivalists want to see reestablished, equality between women and men is impossible—the concept is meaningless. According to one scholar's interpretation, the functions of men and women could be divided into privileges and duties. Men have the privileges of social authority and mobility and the duty of economic responsibility.[7] A Muslim man may have four wives as long as he can support them. Women have three privileges:

1. "A woman in traditional Islamic society does not have to worry about earning a living."

2. "A women does not have to find a husband for herself."

3. A woman "is spared direct military and political responsibility." Her

---

[7]Seyyad Hossein Nasr, *Ideals and Realities of Islam*, 2d ed. (London: George Allen & Unwin, 1975), p. 112..

primary duty "is to provide a home for her family and to bring up her children properly."[8]

In the West, the best-known aspect of women's position in revivalist (and other) Islamic communities is probably dress. Veiling—which ranges from a scarf covering the hair to clothing that fully covers the woman from head to toe—is not found in the Quran but developed over the long history of Islamic countries. Another aspect of the position of women in Islam is that under the law the testimony of two women is equal to that of one man.

CURRENT TRENDS

In December 1994 a group of Islamic militants hijacked an Air France plane in Algeria, apparently planning to blow it up over Paris, killing themselves, the people on the plane, and hundreds, possibly thousands, in Paris. When they were killed as the hostages were freed, other Islamic militants from the same group killed four priests in Algeria—three French and one Belgian. At a time when relations between Islam, Christianity, and Judaism seemed to be improving, this event is a useful reminder that Islam is itself deeply divided.

Groups like the Algerian militants exist in all Islamic countries and within Islamic communities in other countries. While these groups are mostly small minorities, they have the potential to become powerful in many countries. In Algeria, for example, militant Islamic political parties were thought to be likely to win a national election; the government in power canceled the election. In Egypt, which is trying to improve relations with Israel, the government is under constant threat by militant groups, who are currently attacking tourists in an attempt to undermine this mainstay of the Egyptian economy. On the whole, militant Islamic groups flourish in places where there is widespread poverty or where young people who have managed to get an education that should lead to professional employment are unable to find a job.

The divisions between liberal and militant Islam are likely to continue for the foreseeable future, and some countries are likely to be taken over by militant forces. At the same time, the movement to improve relations among the three major religions in the Middle East is likely to continue and bear fruit.

SUGGESTED READINGS

ABRAHAMIAN, ERVAND. *Khomeinism: Essays on the Islamic Republic.* Berkeley: University of California Press, 1993.

AHMAD, JALAL AL-E. *Gharbzadegi* [*Weststruckness*]. Trans. John Green and Ahmad Alizadeh. Lexington, KY: Mazdâ Publishers, 1982.

———. *Iranian Society: An Anthology of Writings.* Comp. and ed. Michael C. Hillmann. Lexington, KY: Mazdâ Publishers, 1982.

AHMED, LEILA. *Women and Gender in Islam: Historical Roots of a Modern Debate.* New Haven, CT: Yale University Press, 1992.

[8]Ibid., pp. 112–113.

BANISADR, ABOLHASSAN. *The Fundamental Principles and Precepts of Islamic Government.* Trans. Mohammad R. Ghanoonparvar. Lexington, KY: Mazdâ Publishers, 1981.

BINA, CYRUS, and HAMID ZANGENEH, eds. *Modern Capitalism and Islamic Ideology in Iran.* New York: St. Martin's, 1992.

CHOUEIRI, YOUSSEF M. *Islamic Fundamentalism.* Boston, MA: Twayne, 1990.

COHN-SHERBOK, DAN, ed. *Islam in a World of Diverse Faiths.* London: Macmillan, 1991.

DAFTARY, FARHAD. *The Isma'ilis: Their History and Doctrines.* Cambridge, England: Cambridge University Press, 1990.

DEKMEJIAN, R. HRAIR. *Islam in Revolution: Fundamentalism in the Arab World.* Syracuse, NY: Syracuse University Press, 1985.

DONOHUE, JOHN J., and JOHN L. ESPOSITO, eds. *Islam in Transition: Muslim Perspectives.* New York: Oxford University Press, 1982.

EL SAADAWI, NAWAL. *The Hidden Face of Eve: Women in the Arab World.* Trans. and ed. Sherif Hetata. London: Zed Press, 1980.

ENAYAT, HAMID. *Modern Islamic Political Thought: The Response of the Shi'i and Sunni Muslims to the Twentieth Century.* London: Macmillan, 1982.

ESPOSITO, JOHN L., ed. *Voices of Resurgent Islam.* New York: Oxford University Press, 1983.

————. "Modern Islamic Sociopolitical Thought." In *Prophetic Religions and Politics: Religion and the Political Order,* ed. Anson Shupe and Jeffrey K. Hadden (New York: Paragon House, 1986), pp. 153–172.

————. *Islam and Politics,* 2d rev. ed. Syracuse, NY: Syracuse University Press, 1987.

————. *Islam: The Straight Path.* Expanded ed. New York: Oxford University Press, 1991.

GOLDZIHER, IGNAZ. *Introduction to Islamic Theology and Law.* Trans. Andras Hamori and Ruth Hamori. Princeton, NJ: Princeton University Press, 1981.

HALM, HEINZ. *Shiism.* Trans. Janet Watson. Edinburgh, Scotland: Edinburgh University Press, 1991.

HEPER, METIN, and RAPHAELI ISRAELI, eds. *Islam and Politics in the Modern World.* New York: St. Martin's, 1984.

KELLY, MARJORIE, ed. *Islam: The Religious and Political Life of a World Community.* New York: Praeger, 1984.

KHOMEINI, AYATOLLAH SAYYED RUHOLLAH MOUSAVI. *Islamic Government.* Trans. Joint Publications Research Service. New York: Manor Books, 1979.

————. *Sayings of the Ayatollah Khomeini: Political, Philosophical, Social, and Religious.* Trans. Harold J. Salemson. Ed. Tony Hendra. New York: Bantam, 1980.

————. *Islam and Revolution.* Trans. Hamid Algar. Berkeley, CA: Mizan Press, 1981.

————. *A Clarification of Questions.* Trans. J. Borujeroi. Boulder, CO: Westview Press, 1984.

KURDI, ABDULRAHMAN ABDULKADIR. *The Islamic State: A Study Based on the Islamic Holy Constitution.* London: Mansell, 1984.

LEWIS, BERNARD. *The Political Language of Islam.* Chicago: University of Chicago Press, 1988.

MERNISSI, FATIMA. *Beyond the Veil: Male–Female Dynamics in Modern Muslim Society.* Rev. ed. Bloomington: Indiana University Press, 1987.

MUTALIB, HUSSIN, and TAJ ul-ISLAM HASHMI, eds. *Islam, Muslims and the Modern State: Case-Studies of Muslims in Thirteen Countries.* London: Macmillan/New York: St. Martin's Press, 1994.

NAKASH, YITZHAK. *The Shi'is of Iraq.* Princeton, NJ: Princeton University Press, 1994.

SAIEDI, NADER. "What Is Islamic Fundamentalism?" In *Prophetic Religions and Politics: Religion and the Political Order,* ed. Anson Shupe and Jeffrey K.

Hadden (New York: Paragon House, 1986), pp. 173–195.

SIVAN, EMMANUEL. *Radical Islam: Medieval Theology and Modern Politics*. Enlarged ed. New Haven, CT: Yale University Press, 1990.

TALEQANI, SEYYED MAHMOOD. *Islam and Ownership*. Trans. Ahmad Jabbari and Farhang Rajaee. Lexington, KY: Mazdâ Publishers, 1983.

VATIKIOTIS, P. J. *Islam and the State*. London: Croom Helms, 1987.

VOLL, JOHN OBERT. *Islam: Continuity and Change in the Modern World*. Boulder, CO: Westview Press, 1982.

WATT, W. MONTGOMERY. *Islamic Political Thought: The Basic Concepts*. Edinburgh, Scotland: Edinburgh University Press, 1968.

ZUBAIDA, SAMI. *Islam, the People and the State: Essays on Political Ideas and Movements in the Middle East*. London: Routledge, 1989.

PART VI

An Emerging Ideology

13

The Green Movement and the Emerging Ideology of Environmentalism

Even though it does not yet have an agreed-upon name, a new ideology is clearly emerging and taking on more and more definite outlines. This chapter briefly examines the origins and development of what is variously called *ecologism, environmentalism, Green politics,* or *Green political thought.* Here it is simply called the *Green Movement* because this label illustrates the way recent ideological developments appear to have come from social and political movements and because people disagree on the right name for the ideology. In the United States the ideology is most often called *environmentalism,* but in Europe, where the movement is more developed, the word *environmentalism* reflects a fairly conservative approach, rather like the word *conservationism* does in the United States. Thus European thinkers tend more toward words like *ecologism,* which has not caught on in the United States.

In Europe many countries have Green political parties that have elected members to various local and regional legislative bodies and a number that have elected members to national legislative bodies. Representatives of Green parties have also been elected to the European Parliament of the European Union. Few such parties exist in North America. Of course, as we shall see, there are radical groups in North America. In fact, environmental radicalism appears to have originated in North America with Greenpeace in Canada, although Greenpeace is now an international organization and has reduced its direct action.

The Green Movement is overwhelmingly a movement of the developed North (including Australia and New Zealand in the South but generally excluding Japan) and is only beginning to be felt in the rest of the world. Thus, if a new ideology is emerging, it is emerging in the developed world. Many thinkers in the Third World nations argue that while they would like to encourage environmentally sound policies, they can't afford to; they see the Green Movement as a luxury that only the developed world can afford. The Green Movement has not yet convinced them that environmentalism is good economic policy.

Some writers see the Green Movement as a new ideology. Other writers reject that label, arguing that the Green Movement has no coherent belief system. The position taken in this chapter is that such a coherent belief system is emerging, but it is too early to conclude that any lasting new ideology has developed.

ORIGINS

If a new ideology is developing, where does it come from? A number of routes have coalesced in the development of the Green Movement. One route is the conservationism, or environmentalism narrowly conceived, that developed in the United States out of such works as *Silent Spring* (1962) by Rachel Carson (1907–1964) and out of concern about the effects of overpopulation stemming from works like *The Population Bomb* (1968) by Paul Ehrlich (1932–). The other main route goes back to the immediate origins of the movement and gives the movement its belief system. This route is fairly easy to trace because it is possible to follow the careers and writings of major figures back to the ferment of the 1960s. In North America the Vietnam era antiwar, anti–nuclear weapons, and anti–nuclear power movements produced a broadening awareness of the way these issues interact with issues related to political power and social conflict.

There was a strong concern with self-sufficiency and a "back-to-the-land" component to some of the movements of the 1960s and 1970s. In the United States, the immensely successful series *The Whole Earth Catalog* (1968–1981) and the related *CoEvolution Quarterly* (1974–1984) are evidence of this. The fact that a new edition of *The Whole Earth Catalog* was published in 1994 and that the *CoEvolution Quarterly* continues as the *Whole Earth Review* suggests that these movements did not end with the end of the earlier social movements. Related activities exist in Europe, Canada, Australia, and New Zealand based on similar earlier activities.

In Europe, the development of the movement was similar, but the failed revolutions of 1968 were of central importance, followed by the campaign against nuclear weapons, a growing recognition of the cross-national effects of pollution, and an early awareness that political and economic systems were centrally involved in the existing environmental problems as well as in any possible solutions.

A slightly different path involving the same issues can be traced in the writings of major theorists of the Green Movement such as André Gorz (1924–), Ivan Illich (1926–), and Murray Bookchin (1921–). These theorists usually started from a position of general radicalism and then focused more and more on ecological issues.

Photographs of earth from space—like the one above—make the point that all human beings are inhabitants of a single place. These photographs struck a chord in many people and encouraged them to become aware of themselves as part of an international community. In addition, the earth from space has a fragile beauty that has helped fuel the recognition that ecological and environmental concerns cross all national borders. (*NASA*)

It is also important to remember that the Green Movement has more remote origins that are more difficult to define precisely. In North America these origins can be found in the writings of early environmentalists like John Muir (1838–1914), who was a campaigner for forest reserves and is now a patron saint of the radical environmentalists, or Henry David Thoreau (1817–1862), a writer whose *A Week on the Concord and Merrimack Rivers* (1849) and, especially, *Walden, or Life in the Woods* (1854) are imbued with a sensuous love of nature and a political rebelliousness that are echoed in many contemporary works.

Ecotopia

In 1975 Ernest Callenbach (1929–) self-published a novel that was to become the classic ecological utopia, particularly after it was republished in 1977 in a mass-market edition.[1] *Ecotopia* also produced a small industry in the publishing of related materials.[2]

---

[1] Ernest Callenbach, *Ecotopia: The Notebooks and Reports of William Weston* (Berkeley, CA: Banyan Tree Books, 1975). Part first published as "First Days in Ecotopia," *American Review* 19 (January 1974): 79–102; part later published as "Ecotopia," *Oregon Times* (October–November 1975): 22–23, 32–36; and as "Journey to Ecotopia: The Notebooks and Reports of William Weston," *Harper's Weekly* 65 (May 17, 1976): 11–18; reprint (New York: Bantam Books, 1977).

[2] See Ernest Callenbach, *Ecotopia Emerging*, (Berkeley, CA: Banyan Tree Books, 1981); and Ernest Callenbach, *The Ecotopian Encyclopedia for the 80s: A Survival Guide for the Age of Inflation*. (Berkeley, CA: And/Or, 1980). See also Judith Clancy, *The Ecotopian Sketchbook: A Book for Drawing, Writing, Collaging, Designing, Thinking About and Creating a New World Based on the Novel Ecotopia by Ernest Callenbach.* (Berkeley, CA: Banyan Tree Books, 1981).

Ecotopia is a country formed out of what used to be the Northwest of the United States (Washington, Oregon, and Northern California). The story of the revolution that led to this successful secession is told in Callenbach's *Ecotopia Emerging* (1981) and need not detain us here. In 1999, when *Ecotopia* is set, a reporter is visiting Ecotopia for the first time since the 1980 secession. Although Ecotopia has a decentralized economic system, it also has a strong political system. There is more political power at the local level than in the United States, but Ecotopia does have a Chief of State (a concept that would be anathema in most of the other ecological utopias). It also is as law- and lawyer-ridden as the United States. Much of the content of Ecotopian law is different from that of U.S. law, but the laws are there.

Another interesting point about Ecotopian society is that the 1960s' belief in "letting it all hang out" leads to frequent minor violence between friends and acquaintances. The intensity of casual relationships colors life in Ecotopia, and the incidence of violence would suggest a degree of social instability. Callenbach's point is, of course, just the opposite: the expression of feeling acts as a safety valve.

The description of the train in *Ecotopia* is one of the best examples of what the Green Movement hopes to achieve.

> I went down to my train. It looked more like a wingless airplane than a train. At first I thought I had gotten into an unfinished car—there were no seats: The floor was covered with thick spongy carpet, and divided into compartments by knee-high partitions; a few passengers were sprawled on large baglike leather cushions that lay scattered about. One elderly man had taken a blanket from a pile at one end of the car, and laid down for a nap. Some of the others, realizing from my confusion that I was a foreigner, showed me where to stow my bag and told me how to obtain refreshments from the steward in the next car. I sat down on one of the pillows, realizing that there would be a good view from the huge windows that came down to about six inches from the floor. My companions lit up some cigarettes, which I recognized as marijuana from the odor, and began to pass them around. As my first gesture of international good will, I took a few puffs myself, and soon we were all sociably chatting away.
>
> Their sentimentality about nature has even led the Ecotopians to bring greenery into their trains, which are full of hanging ferns and small plants I could not identify. (My companions however reeled off their botanical names with assurance.) At the end of the car stood containers rather like trash bins, each with a large letter—M, G, and P. These, I was told, were "recycle bins." It may seem unlikely to Americans, but I observed that during our trip my fellow travelers did without exception dispose of all metal, glass, or paper and plastic refuse in the appropriate bin. That they did so without the embarrassment Americans would experience was my first introduction to the rigid practices of recycling and re-use upon which Ecotopians are said to pride themselves so fiercely.[3]

The principles behind Callenbach's description and the rest of the utopia he presents in *Ecotopia* are not just the recycling mentality that comes through in

---

[3]Callenbach, *Ecotopia*, pp. 9–10.

Ivan Illich (1926–) is the Austrian-born co-founder of the Center for Intercultural Documentation (CIDOC) in Cuernavaca, Mexico. He is a radical priest who has written extensively about contemporary society. He is most noted for his books arguing for the need to reexamine all social institutions, such as *Deschooling Society* (1969), *Tools for Conviviality* (1973), and *The Right to Useful Unemployment* (1978). His *Energy and Equity* (1974) was one of the earlier attacks on the way we waste our energy resources. (*Barbara Pfeffer/Black Star*)

this passage. Even on the train the people are close to nature, with plants inside the train and the windows placed so that inside and outside are brought together. Also, the Ecotopians are knowledgeable about the natural world, as shown by their ability to name the plants.

THE PRINCIPLES

Other writers have explicitly spelled out what they see as the fundamental principles of the Green Movement. Lester W. Milbrath (1925–) has argued that environmentalism is a new ideology. He says that there is a "new environmental paradigm" with the following characteristics:

I. High valuation on nature
    A. Nature for its own sake (worshipful love of nature)
    B. Humans harmonious with nature
    C. Environmental protection over economic growth

  II. Generalized compassion toward:
  - A. Other species
  - B. Other peoples
  - C. Other generations

 III. Carefully plan and act to avoid risk
  - A. Science and technology not always good
  - B. Stop further development of nuclear power
  - C. Develop and use soft technology
  - D. Use regulation to protect nature and humans—government responsibility

 IV. Limits to growth
  - A. Resource shortages
  - B. Population explosion—limits needed
  - C. Conservation

  V. Completely new society needed (new paradigm)
  - A. Humans seriously damaging nature and themselves
  - B. Openness and participation
  - C. Emphasis on public goods
  - D. Cooperation
  - E. Postmaterialism
  - F. Simple lifestyles
  - G. Emphasis on worker satisfaction in jobs

 VI. New politics
  - A. Consultative and participatory
  - B. Partisan dispute over human relationship to nature
  - C. Willingness to use direct action
  - D. Emphasis on foresight and planning[4]

It will become clear that not all people connected with the Green Movement agree with all these principles, but they make a good starting point because Milbrath establishes a middle ground, where others in the movement would generally differ only in degree.

Elsewhere Milbrath has expanded on these characteristics with proposals that are more radical while rejecting any sort of right/left political dichotomy. In a later work, he insists on the necessity of eliminating the whole concept of dominance over nature; but much more important is his argument that we must both reduce the population in the world and lower the standard of living in the West.[5] While many in the Green Movement agree with this position, it is not frequently stated because there is a fear that it will frighten people away from the movement.

---

[4]Lester W. Milbrath, "Environmental Beliefs and Values," in *Political Psychology* (San Francisco: Jossey-Bass, 1986), p. 100.

[5]See his argument in *Envisioning a Sustainable Society: Learning Our Way Out* (Albany: State University of New York Press, 1989).

Another author who has outlined the basic principles of what he calls *environmentalism* is Robert C. Paehlke. His list of "the central value assertions of environmentalism" is as follows:

1. An appreciation of all life forms and a view that the complexities of the ecological web of life are politically salient.

2. A sense of humility regarding the human species in relation to other species and to the global ecosystem.

3. A concern with the quality of human life and health, including an emphasis on the importance of preventative medicine, diet, and exercise to the maintenance and enhancement of human health.

4. A global rather than a nationalist or isolationist view.

5. Some preference for political and/or population decentralization.

6. An extended time horizon—a concern about the long-term future of the world and its life.

7. A sense of urgency regarding the survival of life on earth, both long-term and short-term.

8. A belief that human societies ought to be reestablished on a more sustainable technical and physical basis. An appreciation that many aspects of our present way of life are fundamentally transitory.

9. A revulsion toward waste in the face of human need (in more extreme forms, this may appear as asceticism).

10. A love of simplicity, although this does not include rejection of technology or "modernity."

11. An aesthetic appreciation for season, setting, climate, and natural materials.

12. A measurement of esteem, including self-esteem and social merit, in terms of such nonmaterial values as skill, artistry, effort, or integrity.

13. An attraction to autonomy and self-management in human endeavors and, generally, an inclination to more democratic and participatory political processes and administrative structures.[6]

A third list derives from a leaflet put out by the Denver Region Greens in 1989:

1. Ecological Wisdom

2. Grassroots Democracy

3. Personal and Social Responsibility

4. Nonviolence

5. Decentralization

---

[6]Robert C. Paehlke. *Environmentalism and the Future of Progressive Politics* (New Haven, CT: Yale University Press, 1989), pp. 144–145.

6.   Community-based Economics

7.   Postpatriarchal Values

8.   Respect for Diversity

9.   Global Responsibility

10. Future Focus[7]

These three lists show the similarities and differences among those trying to define a Green ideology. In addition, the fact that the lists have such basic similarities begins to make the case for the actual existence of a coherent Green ideology. At the same time, some differing positions within the Green Movement are reflected in some of the differences found in these lists. Here we will look briefly at three of these different positions—ecosocialism, ecofeminism, and Deep Ecology.

ECOSOCIALISM

André Gorz

André Gorz argues that "*the ecological movement is not an end in itself but a stage in the larger struggle.*"[8] That larger struggle is the one against capitalism. Gorz is a Marxist who rejects the centralism of the dominant Marxist tradition and uses Marx's philosophy to argue for a way of life that is no longer dominated by work. He wants a simpler lifestyle for all based on the production only of socially necessary goods. Everyone would work, but people would work less and at more satisfying jobs. To the extent possible, necessary but repetitive work would be replaced by automated machinery, a position that many in the Green Movement reject, as they would reject the high-technology train in *Ecotopia*.

Gorz also contends that ecology cannot produce an ethic, another argument that is widely rejected in the Green Movement. With the existence of journals like *Environmental Ethics*, it would seem that Gorz has lost part of the argument. Gorz contends that ecology should be seen as "a purely scientific discipline" that "does not necessarily imply the rejection of authoritarian technological solutions."[9]

Most people in the Green Movement argue that ecology does produce an ethic, one that requires the rejection of "authoritarian technological solutions." But Gorz's argument is based on the fact that many environmentalists accept the possibility of using highly technological means to solve some of the world's pollution problems. Thus, while the left wing of the Green Movement rejects

---

[7]"Green Values" (Denver: Denver Region Greens, 1989).

[8]André Gorz, *Ecology as Politics*, trans. Patsy Vigderman and Jonathan Cloud (Boston: South End Press, 1980), p. 3. Emphasis in the original.

[9]Ibid., p. 17.

his position and argues for an ethic that is antitechnological, those to Gorz's right generally accept his conclusion and support the use of technology to solve problems brought about by technology.

Murray Bookchin

Murray Bookchin (1921–) is best described as an anarchist, but he also fits under the label of ecosocialism. Bookchin described what he calls "an ecological society" in the following terms: "An ecological society would fully recognize that the human animal is biologically structured to live with its kind, and to care for and love its own kind within a broadly and freely defined social group."[10] In the last part of his *The Ecology of Freedom* (1982) and in his *Toward an Ecological Society* (1980), Bookchin describes a society that seems to be based on many of the principles outlined by Milbrath, Paehlke, and the Denver Greens. It is radically decentralized, participatory, and has overcome hierarchy, replacing it with a society that respects each individual and the planet on which we live.

ECOFEMINISM

The set of ideas called *ecofeminism* is a combination of feminism, the peace movement, and the Green Movement.[11] It springs mostly from the part of feminism that views women as more in tune with nature than men, but it begins with the assertion that our ecological problems stem from the male notion of dominance as applied to nature and other human beings. Thus, it explicitly rejects the sort of technological solution accepted by Gorz. An interesting example of this sensibility can be found in Ursula K. Le Guin's short story "She Unnames Them," in which Eve is depicted as freeing the animals from Adam's domination by unnaming them—that is, giving them back their own identity rather than the identity imposed on them through Adam's names.

Ecofeminism tends to accept what is called the *Gaia hypothesis* and thus sees the earth as a living being that must be nourished and protected rather than exploited. Many ecofeminists see this as part of a revived belief in what they call the Goddess, an old/new religion that in some ways is close to nature worship. It should be noted that not all self-described ecofeminists are women and that parts of their beliefs, like the Gaia hypothesis, are widely accepted in the Green Movement.

Ecofeminists are thus using age-old traditions combined with new understandings contributed by feminism and environmentalism to give birth to a different way of viewing the relationship between the human race and the rest of the natural world. They argue that technological solutions to environmental

---

[10]Murray Bookchin, *The Ecology of Freedom: The Emergence and Dissolution of Hierarchy* (Palo Alto, CA: Cheshire Books, 1982), p. 318.

[11]The best statement of ecofeminism is *Reweaving the World: The Emergence of Ecofeminism*, ed. Irene Diamond and Gloria Feman Orenstein (San Francisco: Sierra Club Books, 1990).

problems are male solutions that simply cause different problems in the future without correcting the current ones. Ecofeminists are close to the most controversial movement found in the Green Movement, Deep Ecology; but they contend that Deep Ecology has missed the point that our problems stem from the masculine worldview of domination rather than the more general human-centeredness that Deep Ecology identifies as the source of our environmental problems.[12]

DEEP ECOLOGY

The single most controversial movement found within environmentalism today is Deep Ecology, sometimes called *biocentrism*. It is controversial because it places the rest of nature above humans. In other words, human interests and even human beings can be damaged if nature can be protected. One of its popularizers, Dave Foreman (1946–), the founder of Earth First!, puts it as follows: "This philosophy states simply and essentially that all living creatures and communities possess intrinsic value, inherent worth. Natural things live for their own sake, which is another way of saying they have value. Other beings (both animal and plant) and even so-called 'inanimate' objects such as rivers and mountains are not placed here for the convenience of human beings."[13]

The "deepness" of Deep Ecology is found in its rejection of the emphasis on human beings that it finds in most of the Green Movement. There are "deeper" values that emphasize the entire biosphere, as opposed to just human beings. For Deep Ecology nature is not for human use; it has value in and of itself. Nature has rights that need to be protected against human beings. Nature is the standard, and human beings are the problem.

Clearly such a position is not acceptable to many in the Green Movement. Murray Bookchin, for example, has attacked Deep Ecology in his *Remaking Society* (1989). Bookchin argues that the whole approach of biocentrism is wrongheaded. He contends that it simply reverses the domination of nature by humanity to the domination of humanity by nature. He says that the goal should be balance, not domination.

CURRENT TRENDS

The Problem of Animal Rights

Closely related to Deep Ecology is a problem that has interested both philosophers and activists, the question of the rights of animals. The first question is, of course, do animals have rights? The second question is, if so, what are they?

---

[12]See Rik Scarce, *Eco-Warriors: Understanding the Radical Environmental Movement* (Chicago: Noble Press, 1990), p. 39.

[13]Dave Foreman, *Confessions of an Eco-Warrior* (New York: Harmony Books, 1991), pp. 26–27.

On the whole, people in the Green Movement accept the notion that animals have rights at roughly the same level as human beings—that is, at a minimum they have the right to be treated in the way that humans call humane. Others argue that animals have more rights, including the right to not be exploited by human beings. This position translates into vegetarianism and the rejection of the use of animals in scientific experimentation.

But animal rights are clearly rejected by most Western societies, and the belief in animal rights is one of those positions that leads many people to reject the Green Movement. Thus it is a position that many in the Green Movement try to play down. On the other hand, there is a substantial minority that wishes to protect animals and uses civil disobedience to do so.

Monkeywrenching

In the Green Movement in the United States, civil disobedience or direct action is frequently called *monkeywrenching* after Edward Abbey's (1927–1990) novels *The Monkey Wrench Gang* (1975) and *Hayduke Lives!* (1990), which describe a group of environmental activists who destroy things that they believe are damaging the environment. The Deep Ecology group called Earth First! follows the precepts of Abbey's novels, as do those who free animals from experiments or from battery farms (farms where animals are kept closely penned for life).

The people who are now being called *ecowarriors* contend that they are trying to break down the wall between the human and the nonhuman. They see it as their aim to protect biodiversity through direct action, particularly direct action that will play well to the media. There is no real central organization in any of the groups that practice monkeywrenching; monkeywrenchers act either individually or in small groups. As a means of indicating that they practice what they preach, many ecowarriors live in voluntary poverty.[14] Many in the Green Movement respect the ecowarriors and monkeywrenching while not believing it to be a good tactic politically.

CONCLUSION

Is there a new ideology? If there is one, it is not yet a *political* ideology, or is so only in a limited sense. The Green Movement does not have specific responses to many of the questions outlined in chapter 1 or a systematic vision of a new society, although Lester Milbrath has begun the development of one in his *Envisioning a Sustainable Society* (1989). The Green Movement shares a belief in participatory democracy with the more radical exponents of democracy; it shares an awareness of domination with feminism. And within the Green Movement there are major disagreements over both strategy and tactics.

What the Green Movement does have in its most radical aspects is the be-

---

[14]See Scarce, *Eco-Warriors*, pp. 5–6.

ginning, only just emerging, of an entirely new way of conceptualizing the world, a way that moves human beings off center stage and puts the biosphere, of which humanity is only a small part, at the center.

SUGGESTED READINGS

ABBEY, EDWARD. *The Monkeywrench Gang.* Philadelphia: Lippincott, 1975.

———. *Hayduke Lives!* Boston: Little, Brown, 1990.

ATTFIELD, ROBIN. *The Ethics of Environmental Concern.* New York: Columbia University Press, 1983.

BAHRO, RUDOLF. *Socialism and Survival (Articles, Essays and Talks 1979 – 1982).* London: Heretic Books, 1982.

BERRY, WENDELL. *Home Economics: Fourteen Essays.* San Francisco: North Point Press, 1987.

BOOKCHIN, MURRAY. *The Limits of the City.* New York: Harper & Row, 1974.

———. *Toward an Ecological Society.* Montréal: Black Rose Books, 1980.

———. *The Ecology of Freedom: The Emergence and Dissolution of Hierarchy.* Palo Alto, CA: Cheshire Books, 1982.

———. *Remaking Society.* Montréal, Québec, Canada: Black Rose Books, 1989.

———. *Urbanization Without Cities: The Rise and Decline of Citizenship.* Montréal, Québec, Canada: Black Rose Books, 1992.

CALDECOTT, LÉONIE, and STEPHANIE LELAND, eds. *Reclaim the Earth: Women Speak Out for Life on Earth.* London: The Women's Press, 1983.

CALLENBACH, ERNEST. *Ecotopia: The Notebooks and Reports of William Weston.* Berkeley, CA: Banyan Tree Books, 1975.

———. *Ecotopia Emerging.* Berkeley, CA: Banyan Tree Books, 1981.

CALLICOTT, J. BAIRD, and ROGER T. AMES, ed. *In Defense of the Land Ethic: Essays in Environmental Philosophy.* Albany: State University of New York Press, 1989.

———. *Nature in Asian Traditions of Thought: Essays in Environmental Philosophy.* Albany: State University of New York Press, 1989.

CARSON, RACHEL. *Silent Spring.* Boston: Houghton Mifflin, 1962.

CAVALIERI, PAOLA, and PETER SINGER, eds. *The Great Ape Project: Equality Beyond Humanity.* New York: St. Martin's, 1994.

CLARK, JOHN, ed. *Renewing the Earth: The Promise of Social Ecology. A Celebration of the Work of Murray Bookchin.* London: Green Print, 1990.

CLUB OF ROME. *The Limits to Growth.* New York: Universe Books, 1972.

COMMONER, BARRY. *The Closing Circle: Nature, Man, and Technology.* New York: Alfred A. Knopf, 1971.

DAVIS, JOHN, ed. *The Earth First! Reader: Ten Years of Environmental Radicalism.* Salt Lake City, UT: Gibbs Smith, 1991.

Deep Ecology & Anarchism: A Polemic with Contributions from Murray Bookchin, Brian Morris, Rodney Aitchtey, Graham Purchase, Robert Hart, Chris Wilbert. London: Freedom Press, 1993.

Defending the Earth: A Debate Between Murray Bookchin and Dave Foreman. Montréal, Québec, Canada: Black Rose Books, 1991.

DEVALL, BILL, and GEORGE SESSIONS. *Deep Ecology.* Salt Lake City, UT: Peregrine Smith Books, 1985.

DIAMOND, IRENE, and GLORIA FEMAN ORENSTEIN, eds. *Reweaving the World: The Emergence of Ecofeminism.* San Francisco: Sierra Club Books, 1990.

DOBSON, ANDREW. *Green Political Thought: An Introduction.* London: Unwin Hyman, 1990.

ECKERSLEY, ROBYN. *Environmentalism*

and Political Theory: Toward an Ecocentric Approach. Albany: State University of New York Press, 1992.

EHRLICH, PAUL. *The Population Bomb*. New York: Ballantine, 1968.

FOREMAN, DAVE. *Confessions of an Eco-Warrior*. New York: Harmony Books, 1991.

FUKUOKA, MASANOBU. *The Road Back to Nature: Regaining the Paradise Lost*. Trans. Frederic P. Metreaud. Tokyo: Japan Publications, 1987.

GAARD, GRETA, ed. *Ecofeminism: Women, Animals, Nature*. Philadelphia: Temple University Press, 1993.

GOLDSMITH, EDWARD. *The Way: An Ecological World View*. London: Rider, 1992. Reprinted Boston: Shambhala, 1993.

GORZ, ANDRÉ. *Ecology as Politics*. Trans. Patsy Vigderman and Jonathan Cloud. Boston: South End Press, 1980.

————. *Farewell to the Working Class: An Essay on Post-Industrial Socialism*. Trans. Michael Sonenscher. London: Pluto Press, 1982.

————. *Paths to Paradise: On the Liberation from Work*. Trans. Malcolm Imrie. London: Pluto Press, 1985.

————. *Capitalism, Socialism, Ecology*. Trans. Chris Turner. London: Verso, 1994.

GRANBERG–MICHAELSON, WESLEY. *A Worldly Spirituality: The Call to Redeem Life on Earth*. San Francisco: Harper & Row, 1984.

ILLICH, IVAN. *Energy and Equity*. London: Calder & Boyars, 1974.

KELLY, PETRA. *Fighting for Hope*. Trans. Marianne Howarth. London: Chatto & Windus/The Hogarth Press, 1984.

MANES, CHRISTOPHER. *Green Rage: Radical Environmentalism and the Unmaking of Civilization*. Boston: Little, Brown, 1990.

MARTINEZ–ALIER, JUAN. *Ecological Economics: Energy, Environment and Society*. Oxford, England: Basil Blackwell, 1987.

McCLOSKEY, H. J. *Ecological Ethics and Pol-itics*. Totowa, NJ: Rowman and Littlefield, 1983.

MELLOS, KOULA. *Perspectives on Ecology: A Critical Essay*. New York: St. Martin's, 1988.

MILBRATH, LESTER W. *Envisioning a Sustainable Society: Learning Our Way Out*. Albany: State University of New York Press, 1989.

MUIR, JOHN. *The Velvet Monkey Wrench*. Santa Fe, NM: John Muir Publications, 1973.

NAESS, ARNE. *Ecology, Community and Lifestyle: Outline of an Ecosophy*. Cambridge, England: Cambridge University Press, 1989.

NASH, RODERICK FRAZIER. *The Rights of Nature: A History of Environmental Ethics*. Madison: University of Wisconsin Press, 1989.

OATES, DAVID. *Earth Rising: Ecological Belief in an Age of Science*. Corvallis: Oregon State University Press, 1989.

OELSCHLAEGER, MAX. *The Idea of Wilderness: From Prehistory to the Age of Ecology*. New Haven, CT: Yale University Press, 1991.

PAEHLKE, ROBERT C. *Environmentalism and the Future of Progressive Politics*. New Haven, CT: Yale University Press, 1989.

REGAN, TOM. *All That Dwell Therein: Animal Rights and Environmental Ethics*. Berkeley: University of California Press, 1982.

————. *The Struggle for Animal Rights*. Clarks Summit, PA: International Society for Animal Rights, Inc., 1987.

RODD, ROSEMARY. *Biology, Ethics, and Animals*. Oxford, England: Clarendon Press, 1990.

ROLSTON, HOLMES, III. *Philosophy Gone Wild: Essays in Environmental Ethics*. Buffalo, NY: Prometheus Books, 1986.

RUBIN, CHARLES T. *The Green Crusade: Rethinking the Roots of Environmentalism*. New York: Free Press, 1994.

SCARCE, RIK. *Eco-Warriors: Understanding the Radical Environmental Movement*. Chicago: Noble Press, 1990.

SCHEFFER, VICTOR B. *The Shaping of Environmentalism in America.* Seattle: University of Washington Press, 1991.

SINGER, PETER, ed. *In Defense of Animals.* Oxford, England: Basil Blackwell, 1985.

———. *Animal Liberation.* 2d ed. New York: New York Review of Books, 1990.

SKOLIMOWSKI, HENRYK. *Eco-Philosophy: Designing New Tactics for Living.* Boston: Marion Boyars, 1981.

TAYLOR, PAUL W. *Respect for Nature: A Theory of Environmental Ethics.* Princeton, NJ: Princeton University Press, 1986.

TOBIAS, MICHAEL, ed. *Deep Ecology.* San Diego, CA: Avant Books, 1984.

———. *After Eden: History, Ecology and Conscience.* San Diego, CA: Avant Books, 1985.

TRAINER, F. E. *Abandon Affluence!* London: Zed Books, 1985.

WALL, DEREK. *Green History: A Reader in Environmental Literature, Philosophy and Politics.* London: Routledge, 1994.

WARD, BARBARA, and RENE DUBOS. *Only One Earth: The Care and Maintenance of a Small Planet.* New York: Norton, 1972.

WARREN, KAREN J. "The Power and the Promise of Ecological Feminism." *Environmental Ethics* 12, no. 2 (Summer 1990): 125–146.

ZIMMERMAN, MICHAEL E. *Contesting Earth's Future: Radical Ecology and Postmodernity.* Berkeley: University of California Press, 1994.

PART VII

Conclusion

14

Conclusion

A number of sets of ideologies have been discussed in this book. Each is a set of ideologies and not a monolithic position free of disagreements. Major disagreements and differences of opinion have been indicated in connection with all of them. Here, these ideologies are compared with regard to questions of political philosophy (see the questions in chapter 1) and with various parts of the social system. Any comparison has to be general, while attempting to avoid being too broad and therefore meaningless. A number of points will be relevant only to certain ideologies.

HUMAN NATURE

The first question concerns human nature; thus we ask: (1) What are the basic characteristics of human beings as human beings? and (2) What effect does human nature have on the political system? The first question is answered in surprisingly similar ways by all the ideologies with the exception of fascism and national socialism. In Marxism, democracy, anarchism, and feminism we find the position that human beings are capable of a high degree of community spirit and good feeling toward other humans. Hate and fear are stressed in fascism and national socialism. Also underlying much of Marxism, democracy, and anarchism is a belief that humans are fundamentally rational. This is not found in nationalism, fascism, and national socialism; instead our irrational side is stressed. Feminism attempts to recognize both sides. Liberation Theology is also balanced because it recognizes the Christian assumption of original sin but stresses the liberating nature of Christ's message. Both Islam and the Green Movement have a mixed view of human nature; people are capable of both great good and great evil.

The second question—What effect does human nature have on the political system?—is not answered directly or conclusively by most of the ideologies. In Marxism, fascism, national socialism, anarchism, feminism, Liberation Theology, and Islam, the concern is with the effect changes in the political system have on people. This is most obvious in anarchism—the development of a noncoercive society will allow the growth of a better, more sociable human being. Democracy has perhaps the most sophisticated approach. The whole complex of ideas focusing on freedom with limits, representation with regular checks by voters, and general equality is based on the position that each individual is capable of both high-minded self-sacrifice and corruption, that the human being is an extremely complex creature who cannot be encompassed by a unidimensional system.

ORIGINS

The second set of questions—the origin of society and government or the state—are, on the whole, ignored. I have indicated that both traditional Marxism and certain arguments for democracy include discussions about these origins, but contemporary political ideologies are not often concerned with such questions for the simple reason that most people view them as irrelevant. People everywhere find themselves in society and ruled by government; therefore, the question of how this happened does not seem very important.

Anarchist thinkers, because they reject the notion of government and the state, do deal with their origins. Generally, the conclusion is that humans at some time or other formed a society for protection. Some anarchists argue that government was also formed out of society for protection or security. Others argue that government came about simply by usurpation on the part of some group within society. Each argument accepts society as a necessary form of cooperation, whereas government is rejected. It can and should be done away with because it stifles our ability to cooperate.

OBLIGATION

Questions in the third set, centering on political obligation, are answered by all the ideologies except feminism, Liberation Theology, and the Green Movement but in some ideologies, such as democracy, the answers are so diverse and varied that it is difficult even to summarize them. Why do or should people obey the government or, in order to include anarchism, should they at all? Anarchism gives the simplest answer: there is no reason why anyone should obey government.

For Fascists and National Socialists government must be obeyed because it is the government—because the system of leadership demands obedience. People must obey because it is their role to obey. Marxists argue that the dictatorship of the proletariat should be obeyed because it provides security and economic benefits in the period of transition from bourgeois society to a Full Communist society. At the same time, Marxists contend that the individual living under capitalism has no specific obligation to obey; on the contrary, the proletariat has an obligation to attempt to overthrow capitalism.

Democracy is a much more complicated problem because of the wide variety of reasons given for justifying obedience, some of which are similar to the reasons given in other ideologies. These reasons may be summarized as follows: (1) security, (2) other benefits, (3) requirement by the community justifying obedience, and (4) the ability of citizens to change the entire system while still obeying. Democracy raises other problems with regard to revolution and the possibility of disobedience. Contemporary democratic theory is beginning to accept the idea of disobedience without revolution (this was discussed in chapter 3). Most democratic ideology rejects revolution within a democracy, for the fourth reason for obedience given above. Islam is a theocracy with God's will interpreted by the ruler; therefore, the citizen clearly must obey.

LIBERTY

The fourth set of questions concerns liberty. Marxists argue that under Full Communism the individual is given complete liberty. Under the dictatorship of the proletariat, the individual must have sharply curtailed liberty in order to achieve the transition. Fascists and National Socialists consider the question of liberty irrelevant. The individual's freedom, such as it is, is found entirely in giving himself or herself up to the state. Anarchism, since there is no government, has a system of complete liberty. Liberation Theology stresses the need to develop liberty as a means of helping the oppressed.

Democracy again is the most complicated of the ideologies since it provides limited liberty within the system. The problem for democracy is to maintain a system in which the people of the country are willing and able to limit themselves, both individually and through the legal system, so the liberty of one individual does not infringe upon the liberty of another.

Almost equally complex is feminism. Reform feminists argue that freedom is all that is really needed, but most feminists are ambivalent. Shouldn't pornography be eliminated? Is advertising that exploits women acceptable? Hence most feminists, while arguing for the basic freedoms, feel that some limitations may be necessary, particularly to overcome the mental abuse that women suffer. There is no concept of freedom in Islam.

EQUALITY

The fifth set of questions concerns equality. Clearly, Fascists and National Socialists reject any form of equality. In anarchism all individuals should be equal. There is considerable debate among anarchists whether economic equality is a worthwhile goal. Marxists stress social equality and include political equality in the ideal of Full Communism. In the period of the dictatorship of the proletariat, social equality would exist, but political equality would not, because of the need for strong power at the top. Limited economic equality is a goal of Marxism. Marxists argue for overcoming the extremes of economic inequality. This last point would hold true equally well for many democratic theories, including both democratic capitalism and democratic socialism, with the differences between the two being those of means rather than of ends. In democracy political and legal equality and equality of opportunity are emphasized; economic equality is of less interest. Feminists generally argue for all forms of equality. Reform feminists would exclude economic equality but stress equality of opportunity. Liberation Theology stresses the need to overcome inequality. Islam assumes a hierarchical society; people are equal in the eyes of God but not in society.

COMMUNITY

The sixth set of questions concerns the problem of community, which is reemerging as a central concern of some ideologies. In nationalism, developmental socialism, and Islam, community is and always has been a major component of the belief systems. In fascism and national socialism, the idea of the nation has elements of community as does the vision of community-based authority in Full Communism, but the usual way that many of the other ideologies formerly presented themselves tended to downplay community and stress individual fulfillment. But today, as a result of the debate between liberals and communitarians and the sense of a community of interest among the oppressed while recognizing and valuing difference in feminism, there is a new attempt to focus on ties among human beings rather than the areas of conflict among them.

POWER

The seventh set of questions relates to power. Power for the Marxist ideology varies depending on whether one is concerned with the dictatorship of the proletariat or Full Communism. In Full Communism, power would be widely diversified among all individuals. In the dictatorship of the proletariat, power rests in the hands of a few at the very top of the Communist party. Some contend power resides in the party as such, but it is more accurate to see it in the hands of a few. Fascists and National Socialists also invest power in the hands of the very few or one individual at the very top. Supporters of democracy argue that power is spread among all citizens. It is more accurate to see power in the hands of those actively concerned with the governmental process and working within it. There is no focus on power in anarchism; power is found in each individual. Many feminists argue for the empowerment of women as a means of balancing male power, but others argue for a transformation of our whole notion of power. Liberation Theologians argue for the empowerment of the poor and oppressed. They want power in the sense of domination replaced with a concept of social or communal power. In Islam there is no single attitude about power. Islamic liberals and revivalists differ as do Sunnis and Shiites.

JUSTICE

The next two sets of questions, justice and the end of society or government, may be conveniently collapsed together because in each ideology justice will be found by achieving the end of the ideology or the ends of the society or government. In Marxism, justice is found in the proletariat owning the means of production and distribution. For the democrat, justice is found in the individual citizen controlling his or her own destiny through the political system. For the Fascist and National Socialist, justice is found in the individual giving up himself or herself willingly and thoroughly to the state. For the anarchist, justice is found in the end of government and the achievement of a society based on the individual. For the feminist and Liberation Theologian, justice is found in a truly free and equal society. In Islam most believers find justice in the application of the *Sharia* or Islamic law.

STRUCTURE

The final set of questions concerns the structural characteristics of government. Clearly this is almost irrelevant in nationalism, anarchism, Full Communism, feminism, and the Green Movement. The other ideologies do include answers to the questions but not in any way that makes valid generalization possible.

In the answers to these questions, we are able to see the variety of positions taken on fundamental political questions. The answers vary considerably from ideology to ideology, but the answers are also sometimes quite divergent within a given ideology. This overview gives us some basis for comparing the political aspects of the ideologies. In order to understand fully the value system in each ideology, we must look at certain other social institutions. Therefore, a second stage of comparing the ideologies must look at these other subsystems of the social system.

SOCIAL STRATIFICATION

The first is the social stratification and mobility system. Marxists argue that there will be no social stratification and hence no social mobility system within Full Communism. Under the dictatorship of the proletariat, the only stratification system would be that between the proletariat and the remnants of the bourgeoisie and the peasantry. The only form of mobility would be for the bourgeoisie and the peasantry to move into the proletariat. In fact, the dictatorship of the proletariat has produced a new social stratification system that establishes a class of technocrats who operate the government, the Communist party, and the various important institutions of the country.

The democratic social stratification and mobility system is based primarily on money and education. The primary means of mobility in the democratic system is education. In fascism and national socialism, stratification is based on race, indications of loyalty to the nation, and service in the party and to the state. Mobility is based on the same standards. In anarchism, there should be no social stratification and hence no mobility system. Feminists are mostly concerned with removing sexual, racial, and sexual orientation barriers from the operation of the social mobility system. Liberation Theology is directed at removing barriers to social advancement. Islam has a highly structured social stratification system based on birth, wealth, and learning.

SOCIALIZATION

The socialization system is made up of various institutions in society that help to give an individual the values of that society. The primary institutions of socialization are the family, the education system, the religious system, and in modern societies, the mass media. Children gain ideas about life before they are capable of articulating those ideas themselves. They hear their parents give positive or negative connotations to certain words and phrases the children can identify but for which they have no meaning. For example, a child in the United States might acquire a positive connotation with the word *democratic* and a negative connotation with the word *republican* from parents who were strongly in favor of the Democratic party. Throughout life we hear words given particular connotations. Again, using the United States as an example, the child might hear the word *communism* as denoting something bad. Therefore, before the individual is capable of understanding what communism is about, she or he is convinced that it is bad, and this conviction will be difficult to change. Institutions of socialization are thus extremely important, and it is instructive to look at some of the attitudes of these ideologies toward the major institutions of socialization.

It is noteworthy, first, that Marxists, Fascists, and National Socialists, almost without exception, hold that the mass media must be carefully controlled so it will present a positive picture of the system. Anarchists tend to argue for completely unlimited mass media. Democracy comes very close to this, limiting the media only in cases of libel and then only in relatively rare cases. Democracies have found a greater problem, though, in connection with the unwillingness of governmental officials to give the mass media complete information, thus attempting to control it.

One would think Marxism, fascism, and national socialism would also include control of the other institutions of socialization, and in some cases they do. Marxists argue for control of religion because it is seen as a direct threat to the ideology. Fascists and National Socialists tend, on the other hand, to view religion as a positive support of the nationalism that was so important to the ideology, and in many cases, the religious system did support fascism and national socialism or did not actually oppose them. In anarchism and democracy, there is little concern with controlling religion, although in anarchism one often finds an antipathy toward religion. Many anarchists believe religion consistently supports the state and thus is opposed to the anarchist philosophy. Most, but not all, democratic ideologies and democratic systems include a separation between the religious sytem and the political system. At the same time, in democracy religion is often a support for the political system.

In every ideology the educational system is used to directly support the ideology. For all the ideologies, education is the most potent force of socialization; therefore, the educational system must be used to support the values of the society or the ideology. On the other hand, only feminism and, to a lesser extent, anarchism include much about changing the family system. It is probably better policy to attempt to imbue parents with the values one wishes to have passed on to the children; if the parents accept the values, they will be automatically passed on to the children. Therefore, it is not really necessary to tamper with the family system. Clearly the greatest concern of Liberation Theology is changing the church as a means of socialization. It also wants to change other mechanisms of socialization, but the church is its primary target.

Most feminists feel a need for a completely transformed socialization system. Education, the family, religion, and the mass media must not merely be open to women, but must be changed so that no one will be socialized into submission. In this sense feminism is potentially the most radical of contemporary ideologies.

In Islam the family is the center of society; socialization takes place there first. Education and, of course, the mosque also play central roles. Socialization is designed to give the person the values of the religion.

THE ECONOMIC SYSTEM

In each of the ideologies we have discussed, a considerable amount of time has been spent analyzing the last aspect of the social system, the economic system. It is not necessary here to repeat those arguments, but only to say that each of the ideologies differs regarding the economic system. Marxism combines a state socialist economic system with an authoritarian political system. Democracy combines either a capitalist or a socialist economic system with its political system. Fascism and national socialism have authoritarian political systems combined with modified capitalist systems. Developmental socialism is connected to a wide variety of political systems. Anarchists are unclear concerning the appropriate system. Feminists are deeply divided on economic questions. Liberation Theology is primarily concerned with the results of the economic system, not the means, but it is accurate to say that it leans heavily toward socialism. Islam encourages private property with a religious duty of charity.

It is noteworthy that the Green Movement has few positions that fit the categories used here. This fact suggests that the Green Movement is still developing the attributes of an ideology.

These comments have been very general, but they provide some basis for comparing the ideologies. It is important for a student of contemporary political ideologies to understand both the similarities and the differences among these ideologies. We do not know what the future holds for any of them, but it is important for us to understand what each of these ideologies accepts so we will be able to evaluate them objectively.

In conclusion, I hope the reader will reflect carefully on the challenges that the variety of belief systems poses for his or her own beliefs. What can be expected of humanity in the future? Are we rational, capable of determining a desirable future and working for it, or are we irrational, incapable of so choosing or unwilling to work for our goal? Must humans be coerced or can we cooperate without coercion? Can humanity achieve a meaningful equality or is equality of any sort an impossible dream? Can humans be free or is freedom a dangerous fantasy? All these questions and many others will be answered in the near future. We must reflect on the society in which we want to live. We must ask ourselves: In what ways are we affected by ideologies? Do we have an ideology? What are its elements? How does it affect us? How do the ideologies held by others affect us? The answers to all these questions will affect the way we spend our lives.

Glossary

This glossary provides a short definition of certain terms used in the text to help the reader better understand the discussion. Many of the terms are discussed at some length in the text; the reader is referred to the index to locate that discussion. An asterisk identifies these terms. Since some words have different meanings in different ideologies, it is important, in using the index, to follow the word throughout the text.

Alienation Estrangement or being cut off.
★**Anarchism** A system of social order achieved without government.
Aristocracy Originally meaning rule by the few best, it now means rule by the few, usually with the implication of a hereditary few.
Authority Legitimate power (*see* Power).
Ayatollah A Shiite title meaning sign of God.
Biocentrism A theory that argues that the biosphere should be the focus of value as opposed to human beings as the focus (anthropocentrism).
Bourgeoisie In Marxism refers to the owners of the means of production contrasted to the proletariat (*see* Proletariat), who have only their labor power to sell. More generally used to refer to the property-owning middle class.
Bureaucracy The set of dominant nonelected officials in any political system.
Caliph Successor (Sunni).
★**Capitalism** Private ownership of the means of production and the organization of production for profit.
Caste An exclusive, hereditary class. Most often refers to the system found

in Hinduism in which people who are members of specific occupations are separated from other occupations through rigid social divisions that prohibit any kind of contact.

Chador A dress that covers a woman from head to foot.

Charismatic leader A person who is able to gain followers through the force of her or his personality.

Civil disobedience The belief that disobedience to the law (*see* Law) is an appropriate means of forcing a political system to change the law.

Class A way of ranking or ordering society. In Marxism the ranking is based on the relationship to the means of production. Other ideologies rank on the basis of wealth, education, racial purity, service to the state, or some other criterion.

★Class struggle In Marxism used to describe the fundamental relationship between or among classes and the driving force of social change.

Co-housing A modern version of cooperative housing in which a group of people own individual houses or apartments and collectively own the land and common buildings.

Colonialism A system in which one state (*see* State) controls another state for the benefit of the former (*see also* Neocolonialism).

★Communism A social and economic system characterized by an authoritarian political system and a state socialist economic system. Originally meant community of goods or goods publicly held (*see also* Full Communism).

Communitarianism Focus on the community rather than on the individual.

★Community A sense of common interest.

★Conservatism The belief that social change should take place slowly with a due account taken of tradition.

Cooperation An economic theory in which people join together to form an economic unit from which they will all benefit.

★Corporatism Sometimes called *neo-corporatism*. The arrangement of political and economic relationships so that power groups in society are actively involved with government in making public policy.

Critical theory A general theory that views society from the point of view of the need to change it.

Decentralization A system in which power is moved from a central organization to regional centers or from a large group to small groups composing it.

Deep Ecology A movement that stresses the importance of the entire biosphere as opposed to human beings.

★Democracy A political system characterized by direct or indirect rule by the people (*see also* Participatory democracy *and* Representation).

Democratic centralism A system developed by V. I. Lenin in which discussion within an organization is completely free until a decision is made, at which time all must support the decision.

Democratization The process of developing democratic institutions in societies in which they did not previously exist.

Developmental socialism A theory that proposes to use socialist economic policies to assist the economic development of a country.

*Dictatorship of the proletariat In Marxism, the transitional stage after a successful revolution in which society is gradually transformed.

Direct democracy Democracy by citizens rather than by representatives.

Ecofeminism A movement that argues that women are closer to nature than men are and that the Green Movement fails to recognize the male bias of environmentalism.

Economic democracy A theory that suggests that some portion of the economy, ranging from individual firms to the entire economy, should be run democratically.

Ecosocialism A movement that combines environmentalism and socialism.

Elitism The belief that society is and/or should be ruled by a small group of powerful people.

*Equality Sameness in some defined way.

*Equality of opportunity The situation that exists when an individual has the possibility of succeeding or failing on the basis of his or her own ability and effort with no artificial barriers to that success or failure.

Essentially contested concepts Concepts over which there is a fundamental, unreconcilable difference.

Ethnic group A group of people united by race or national origin.

Eurocommunism The belief that Communist parties in the West should compete for election on the same basis as other political parties and accept defeat if they lose.

False consciousness A phrase within Marxism referring to the results of the class-based socialization process in which an individual gains an incorrect view of the world. Similar to the concept of ideology (*see* Ideology).

*Fascism Originally referring to the principles of the 1922 Italian anti-Communist revolution. Now a general term referring to authoritarian political systems characterized by extreme nationalism (*see also* National socialism).

Federalism The division of political power between a central government and governments representing defined territories within the country. These latter units, called states in the United States, may be further divided into smaller units, but these do not have the same standing as the other two levels of government.

*Feminism An ideology centered on eliminating oppression of all human beings.

Fourth World There are two very different meanings in use today. In this book the phrase refers to indigenous peoples; it is also sometimes used to refer to the poorest of the developing countries.

Frankfurt School The school of Marxist thought that developed critical theory (*see* Critical theory).

*Freedom The ability to act without constraint (*see also* Liberty *and* Rights).

Führer German word for leader. Used in national socialism.

*Full Communism The final stage of the Marxist theory of history.

General strike A strike in which all workers engage at the same time. Generally believed to be a major tactic in a revolution or to put pressure on a government.

Government *See* Political system.

Hajj The annual pilgrimage to Mecca required at least once from every Muslim.

Hegemony A word used by Antonio Gramsci and others to refer to the intellectual and cultural dominance of a class. Similar to the concept of ideology (*see* Ideology).

*Human nature The essential characteristics of all human beings.

Ideologue A true believer or one who has an extremely limited view of the world based on an ideology. An unusually strong believer in an ideology.

*Ideology A value system or belief system accepted as fact or truth by some group. It is composed of sets of attitudes toward the various institutions and processes of society. It provides the believer with a picture of the world both as it is and as it should be, and, in doing so, it organizes the tremendous complexity of the world into something fairly simple and understandable.

Imam Leader (Shiite)

Impeachment A method of removing a public official from office that involves a hearing of charges before a body of public officials, most often a legislature.

Initiative A method of bringing a proposed piece of legislation to a vote of the citizenry through a petition signed by citizens.

Internationalism A belief in the need to unify the entire world in some way. A love of the world.

Intifada The word used to describe the recent Palestinian uprising in Israel.

Jihad The struggle to follow Islam. Holy war.

*Justice Fairness.

*Law A rule established through an accepted procedure within a community that permits or prohibits certain actions. The system of rules so established.

*Liberalism A general tendency to accept the ability of human beings to use their reason to reform the social system. A general tendency accepting change as inevitable but controllable. The advocacy of liberty.

*Liberation Theology The combination of Marxism and Roman Catholic theology in opposition to oppression.

*Libertarianism An ideology related to anarchism (*see* Anarchism) that advocates a radically reduced role for government. Also known as *minimalism*.

*Liberty Freedom (*see* Freedom). Generally used to refer to legally established freedoms (civil liberty) (*see also* Rights).

Lumpenproletariat The lowest class in the Marxist class analysis composed of thieves, bums, and the like.

Majority rule An electoral system in which 50 percent +1 or more of those voting win.

Market socialism Socialism that accepts some aspects of the free market.

*Materialism The belief that matter or the material (as opposed to spirit, the spiritual, or the ideal) is the determining factor in human life.

Minimalism *See* Libertarianism.

Monetarism The belief that the control of the money supply is the most important tool for manipulating a national economy and avoiding inflation.

Monkeywrenching Direct action or civil disobedience to protect the biosphere.

Monopoly An organization that controls trade in some commodity or a sector of the economy of a country.

Nation A people or race with common descent, language, history, and/or political institutions.

*

Nationalism An ideology based on love for the nation (*see* Nation) or patriotism (*see* Patriotism) together with demands for action to enhance the power and prestige of the nation.

Nationalization of industries Taking industries into public ownership.

*****National socialism** An ideology developed in Germany under the leadership of Adolf Hitler emphasizing an authoritarian political system, extreme nationalism, and racism (*see also* Fascism).

Naturalization A process by which a citizen of one country becomes a citizen of another country.

Negative liberty Liberty achieved by limitations on government activity.

*****Neocolonialism** A system of economic dominance of an ex-colony by an industrialized nation (*see also* Colonialism).

*****Neoconservatism** The position held by ex-liberals in the United States who have become fiscal and foreign policy conservatives.

Neo-corporatism *See* Corporatism.

*****Neoliberalism** The position taken by liberals in the United States who have tried to modify the welfare-state image of liberalism.

Neutralism *See* Nonalignment.

*****New Right** The extreme conservative wing in U.S. politics.

Nonalignment A stance taken in the Third World in which Third World nations refuse to identify themselves with either of the two major power blocs—hence the name Third World.

Ombudsman A Swedish word that has been adopted into English to refer to a public official whose duties are to protect the rights (*see* Rights) of citizens against government, particularly bureaucracies.

Participation In democracy, to be actively involved in the political system.

*****Participatory democracy** A form of democracy in which individuals who are to be affected by a decision make the decision collectively.

*****Patriotism** Love of country (*see also* Nationalism).

Petite bourgeoisie In Marxist class analysis, the class of small shopkeepers, artisans, and the like who are being pushed down into the proletariat (*see* Proletariat).

*****Political obligation** The duty to obey the dictates of the political system (*see* Political system).

*****Political system** Those parts of the social system that have the ability to make authoritative or binding decisions for a territory.

Positive liberty Liberty achieved through government support.

*****Power** The ability to compel others to act in the way one wishes (*see also* Authority).

PR *See* Proportional representation.

Privatization The movement of activities from public control to private control.

*****Proletariat** That class in Marxism that has only its labor power to sell (*see also* Bourgeoisie).

Property Something owned or possessed. Private property: something owned by an individual. Public property: something owned collectively.

Proportional representation A system of election in which individuals are elected on the basis of the proportion of the votes received rather than the majority as under majority rule (*see* Majority rule).

Quran The holy book for Muslims.

Ramadan The ninth month of the Muslim year. A month of fasting.

Reapportionment The process of realigning the boundaries of electoral districts to bring them more in balance in population.

Recall A mechanism by which an elected official may be removed from office during his or her term through a vote of the electors in the area he or she represents.

Referendum A process of deciding political questions by the direct vote of the electorate.

Regionalism The tendency that exists in a number of parts of the world to form economic and sometimes political agreements among states (*see* State) to form larger and more powerful units.

★Representation A system in which voters choose other individuals to act in their place in making political decisions.

Republic A state (*see* State) in which political decisions are made by elected representatives.

Reverse discrimination The argument that policy to overcome discrimination against one group discriminates against another group.

★Revolution The process of bringing about radical political and social change, usually violently.

★Rights Legally defined and enforceable freedoms (*see* Freedom). More generally, something to which a person is entitled. Traditionally divided into natural rights or rights that are due a person just because of his or her existence as a human being and civil rights or rights that are guaranteed by government (*see also* Liberty).

Self-governing socialism *See* Self-management.

★Self-management A type of socialism (*see* Socialism) sometimes known as self-governing socialism in which workers' control (*see* Workers' control) operates in industry and decentralized democracy works in government.

Sharia Islamic law.

Social construction of reality A phrase used in Marxism to refer to the socialization process. It means that an individual gains a view of the world based on her or his place in society.

Social Darwinism The belief that relations among human beings are characterized by a struggle for survival.

★Socialism Public ownership of the means of production and distribution. May be highly centralized as in communism (*see* Communism) or very decentralized as in self-management (*see* Self-management).

★Socialization The process by which a society transmits its values from generation to generation.

★Social mobility The process by which individuals move up or down in a society's social stratification system (*see* Social stratification).

★Social stratification The system by which a society ranks the people within it (*see also* Caste, Class, Equality of opportunity, *and* Social mobility).

★State An organized community (*see* Community) with its own political system (*see* Political system) and law (*see* Law).

Sunna Exemplary behavior of Muhammad.

★Superstructure In Marxism, all those parts of life that are produced by the basic economic relations of society.

*Surplus value In Marxism, the value of goods produced above and beyond that needed to support labor.

Syndicalism A system in which the means of production and distribution are under the control of a federation of trade unions.

Theocracy Literally, rule by God. Usually refers to a government in which religious leaders rule directly or indirectly based on their claim of divine authority.

Toleration The recognition and acceptance of differing belief systems, particularly the acceptance of beliefs believed to be wrong.

Tribe A group of people who usually regard themselves as having a common ancestor and acknowledge the authority of a chief. Any group of people who identify themselves as a group.

Ulama Muslim religious scholar.

Welfare The system of contributory and noncontributory pension, health, unemployment, and other benefits and social services funded and regulated by government.

Workers' control Power (*see* Power) in the workplace in the hands of workers rather than management. The industrial system produced by such an arrangement.

Workplace democracy Democracy within the working environment.

Biographical Notes

ABBEY, EDWARD (1927–1990), is revered by radical environmentalists for his fictional portrayals of environmental direct action.

ADAMS, ABIGAIL (1744–1818), was an early advocate of women's rights in the United States and wife of John Adams, the second president.

ADAMS, JOHN (1735–1826), was the second president of the United States.

ADDAMS, JANE (1860–1935), was a social settlement worker and peace advocate. She ran Hull House in Chicago from 1889 to 1935. She was awarded the Nobel Peace Prize in 1931.

ADORNO, THEODOR (1903–1969), was one of the founders of the Frankfurt School.

AFLAQ, MICHEL (1910–), was a founder of the Baath party in Syria.

AL-BANNA, HASAN (1906–1949), was the founder of the Muslim Brotherhood.

ANDERSON, POUL (1926–), is a science fiction writer whose novels often reflect anarcho-capitalism.

ANTHONY, SUSAN B. (1820–1906), was one of the leaders of the women's suffrage movement.

ARAFAT, YASIR (1929–), is the leader of the PLO (Palestinian Liberation Organization).

ASTELL, MARY (1668–1731), was an English author who proposed a separate community of women in her *A Serious Proposal to the Ladies* (1694).

ATWOOD, MARGARET (1939–), is the author of *The Handmaid's Tale* (1986), a picture of a future that suppresses women.

BAKUNIN, MIKHAIL (1814–1876), was a leading Russian anarchist theorist who spent most of his life in Western Europe.

BAYTAR, SALAH AL-DIN (1911–1980), was a founder of the Baath party in Syria.

BEAUVOIR, SIMONE DE (1908–1986), was a French author best known for her reflections on the status of women, *La Deuxième Sexe* (1949, in English as *The Second Sex* in 1952).

BECKETT, SAMUEL (1906–1989), was an Irish playwright who lived and wrote mostly in France.

BELLAMY, EDWARD (1850–1898), a U.S. author, is remembered for his best-selling utopian novel, *Looking Backward 2000–1887* (Boston: Ticknor, 1888). A movement for social change was founded to promote Bellamy's ideas and was influential both in the United States and abroad.

BENTHAM, JEREMY (1748–1832), was the chief advocate of utilitarianism.

BERKMAN, ALEXANDER (1870–1936), was a friend of Emma Goldman and an activist in the American anarchist movement who spent many years in prison in the United States.

BERLIN, ISAIAH, is a British historian of ideas and a social theorist.

BERNERI, MARIE LOUISE (1918–1949), was an Italian-born British anarchist.

BERNSTEIN, EDUARD (1850–1932), was a follower of Marx who rejected revolutionary socialism. He was a major Marxist revisionist arguing for evolutionary socialism and political activity.

BHAVE, VINOBA (1895–1982), was an Indian spiritual leader.

BHUTTO, BENAZIR (1953–), is prime minister of Pakistan.

BLOCH, ERNST (1885–1977), was a German Marxist philosopher best known for his book *Das Prinzip Hoffnung (The Principle of Hope)* (1959).

BOFF, CLODOVIS (1944–), is a Servite priest and a professor of theology at the Catholic University of Sao Paulo. He is the brother of Leonardo Boff.

BOFF, LEONARDO (1938–). See page 219.

BOOKCHIN, MURRAY (1921–), is a major anarchist theorist who has recently been a major contributor to environmentalism in the United States.

BOSANQUET, BERNARD (1848–1923), was an English conservative philosopher.

BRANDT, WILLY (1913–1992), was active in German politics throughout the postwar period. He was best known for his period as Governing Mayor of Berlin (1957–1966) and as Chancellor of the Federal Republic of Germany.

BURKE, EDMUND. See page 107.

BUTLER, RICHARD GIRNT, is the leader of Aryan Nation.

CABET, ÉTIENNE (1798–1856), was a French utopian socialist who established a series of communities in the United States.

CABRAL, AMILCAR (1921–1973), was the leader of the independence movement in Guinea-Bissau (formerly Portuguese Guinée) but was murdered before independence.

CALLENBACH, ERNEST (1929–), is the author of a series of books describing a fictional society emphasizing ecology.

CAMUS, ALBERT (1913–1960), was a French novelist who won the Nobel Prize in Literature in 1957.

CARSON, RACHEL (1907–1964), was an early writer on environmental issues.

CHICAGO, JUDY (1939–), is a feminist artist.

COMFORT, ALEX (1920–), is best known for his books on sexual technique, but his career has ranged through fiction, poetry, anarchist theory, and geriatric psychology.

DAHL, ROBERT A. (1915–), is professor of political science at Yale University.

DARWIN, CHARLES (1809–1882), was a famous English naturalist who put forth a number of important theses regarding evolution.

DAY, DOROTHY (1897–1980), was a leader of the anarchist Catholic Worker Movement.

DE CLEYRE, VOLTAIRINE (1866–1912), was an American anarchist.

DJILAS, MILOVAN (1911–1995), was a supporter of Tito in Yugoslavia, who broke with him and developed a theory of communist society which he saw as violating basic Marxist principles.

DWORKIN, ANDREA (1946–), is a feminist writer.

DWORKIN, RONALD (1931–), is a legal philosopher.

EHRLICH, PAUL (1932–), was one of the first writers on the problems of overpopulation.

EISENHOWER, DWIGHT DAVID (1890–1969), was president of the United States from 1953 to 1961. Previously he had been commander in chief of the Allied forces in World War II.

EMERSON, RALPH WALDO (1803–1882), was the most famous essayist and lecturer of the nineteenth century.

ENGELS, FRIEDRICH (1820–1895), was a friend and co-author of Karl Marx.

FIRESTONE, SHULAMITH (1944–), is a feminist writer.

FLATHMAN, RICHARD (1934–), is professor of political science at Johns Hopkins University.

FOREMAN, DAVE (1946–), is an active environmentalist and founder of Earth First!

FOURIER, CHARLES (1772–1837), was a French utopian socialist.

FRANCIS OF ASSISI (born Giovanni Francesco Bernardone, 1182–1226) was the radical founder of the Franciscan movement and is now recognized in Libertation Theology as an early advocate of the poor.

FREIRE, PAULO (1921–), is a Brazilian social theorist best known for his book *The Pedagogy of the Oppressed* (1972).

FREUD, SIGMUND (1856–1939), was the Austrian founder of psychoanalysis.

FRIEDAN, BETTY (1921–), is a feminist author and lecturer.

FRIEDMAN, MILTON (1912–), won the Nobel Prize in Economics for his work in monetary theory. He is the best-known conservative economist in the United States. He taught economics at the University of Chicago for many years.

FULLER, MARGARET (1810–1850), was a teacher and writer struggling against the limited roles allowed women during her lifetime.

GANDHI, MOHANDAS K. (1869–1948), was a leader of the anticolonial movement in India who used nonviolence as a means of bringing about social change. He had been influenced by Henry David Thoreau and influenced Martin Luther King, Jr.

GARAUDY, ROGER (1913–), is a French Marxist philosopher.

GEERTZ, CLIFFORD (1926–), is a professor in the school of social science at the Institute for Advanced Study, Princeton.

GEORGE, HENRY (1839–1897), was an American economic theorist who developed a theory based on land taxation, known as the single tax, as a means of redistributing wealth.

GILMAN, CHARLOTTE PERKINS (1860–1935), was a feminist writer.

GODWIN, WILLIAM (1756–1836), was the earliest British anarchist theorist.

GOEBBELS, JOSEPH (1897–1945), was Minister for Propaganda and National Enlightenment under Hitler.

GOLDMAN, EMMA. See page 182.

GOLDWATER, BARRY (1909–), was U.S. Senator from Arizona (1952–1964, 1969–1987). He was the Republican candidate for president in 1964.

GORZ, ANDRÉ (1924–), is a French social theorist.

GRAMSCI, ANTONIO (1891–1937), was an Italian social theorist and is considered one of the most original Marxist theorists after Marx. He was one of the founders of the Italian Communist party.

GREEN, THOMAS H. (1836–1882), was a professor of philosophy at Oxford University.

GRIMKÉ, ANGELINA E. (1805–1879), was an abolitionist and women's rights pioneer.

GRIMKÉ, SARAH MOORE (1792–1873), was an abolitionist and women's rights pioneer.

GUTIÉRREZ, GUSTAVO (1928–), is a Peruvian theologian and professor of theology at the Catholic University of Lima.

HABERMAS, JÜRGEN (1929–), is one of the most important contemporary thinkers influenced by Marxism and the Frankfurt School.

HARRINGTON, MICHAEL. See page 92.

HARTSOCK, NANCY C. M. (1943–), is professor of political science and women's studies, Washington University, Seattle.

HAYEK, F. A. (1899–1992), was one of the most important conservative thinkers of the twentieth century.

HEGEL, GEORG WILHELM FRIEDRICH (1770–1831), was a German philosopher who influenced most of the major streams of modern political theory.

HENNACY, AMMON (1893–1970), was an important American anarchist.

HERDER, JOHANN GOTTFRIED VON (1744–1803), was a German philosopher and writer. He is considered the founder of cultural history.

HILL, JAMES J. (1838–1916), was a U.S. industrialist and railroad magnate.

HITLER, ADOLF. See page 191.

HORKHEIMER, MAX (1895–1973), was one of the founders of the Frankfurt School.

HUMPHREY, HUBERT H. (1911–1978), was a leading liberal thinker in the United States, senator from Minnesota (1948–1965, 1970–1978), and vice president (1965–1969).

ILLICH, IVAN (1926–). See page 241.

JEFFERSON, THOMAS. See page 60.

JOHN PAUL II (1920–) has been pope of the Roman Catholic Church since 1978.

JOHNSON, LYNDON BAINES (1908–1973), president of the United States from 1963 to 1969, presided over a period of great change in U.S. social policy, particularly the beginnings of the extension of civil rights to African Americans and the establishment of many social welfare programs. He is perhaps still best known for his failure to solve the Vietnam crisis.

KEYNES, JOHN MAYNARD (1883–1946), was an English economist. His major works were *The Economic Consequences of the Peace* (1919), *A Treatise on Money* (1930), and *The General Theory of Employment, Interest and Money* (1936).

KHOMEINI, AYATOLLAH (1900–1989), was the religious leader of Iran after the Shiite overthrow of the Shah.

KIRK, RUSSELL (1918–1994), was an important twentieth-century conservative thinker.

KROPOTKIN, PYOTR. See page 173.

LE GUIN, URSULA K. (1929–), is a major science fiction, fantasy, and children's author whose novel *The Dispossessed* (1974) is a contribution to anarchist theory.

LENIN, VLADIMIR ILYICH (born Vladimir Ilyich Ulyanov, 1870–1924), was the leader of the Russian revolution of 1917 and ruled the Soviet Union after the revolution until his death.

THE LEVELLERS were a seventeenth-century British movement favoring political equality.

LINCOLN, ABRAHAM (1808–1865), was the sixteenth president of the United States.

LOCKE, JOHN. See page 61.

LUXEMBURG, ROSA (1870–1919), was a Polish Marxist revolutionary who opposed both Lenin's centralizing tendencies and Bernstein's gradualism.

MACKINNON, CATHARINE A. (1946–), is the most important contemporary feminist legal theorist.

MADISON, JAMES. See page 54.

MALATESTA, ERRICO (1850–1932), was a leading Italian anarchist theorist.

MANDELA, NELSON (1918–), is President of the Republic of South Africa.

MANNHEIM, KARL (1893–1947), was a Hungarian-born sociologist active in Germany until he fled the Nazis in 1933. He is best known as the major theorist of the sociology of knowledge.

MAO ZEDONG (1893–1976), was longtime leader of the Peoples' Republic of China.

MARCUSE, HERBERT (1898–1979), was a member of the Frankfurt School who stayed in the United States after it returned to Germany following World War II. Marcuse was a major influence on the New Left.

MARX, KARL (1818–1883). See page 146.

MILBRATH, LESTER W. (1925–), is the Director of the Research Program in Environment and Society and professor of political science at the State University of New York at Buffalo.

MILES, ANGELA (1946–), is in the Department of Adult Education at the Ontario Institute for Studies in Education, Toronto.

MILL, JOHN STUART. See page 110.

MILLER, DAVID (1946–), is Official Fellow of Nuffield College, Oxford, England.

MORGAN, J. P., (1837–1913), was a U.S. financier.

MORRIS, WILLIAM (1834–1896), was the leader of the British arts and crafts movement who some label as an anarchist theorist. He considered himself a Marxist.

MUGABE, ROBERT (1924–), is the Marxist leader of Zimbabwe.

MUHAMMAD (570–632) was the founder of Islam.

MUIR, JOHN (1838–1914), was an American naturalist who was a conservationist and a crusader for national parks. He is revered as one of the founders of the Green Movement.

MUSSOLINI, BENITO (1883–1945), was the founder of the fascist movement and head of the Fascist party in Italy.

NASSER, GAMAL ABD AL (1918–1970), was the leader of the Egyptian revolution and head of the country for many years.

NEHRU, JAWAHARLAL (1889–1964), was a leader of the anticolonial movement in India and prime minister of India after independence.

NIXON, RICHARD MILHOUS (1913–1994), president of the United States from 1969 to 1974, was the only president forced to resign from office by the threat of imminent impeachment. He presided over the largest expansion of social welfare programs in U.S. history, ended the war in Vietnam, and reestablished political relations with the Peoples' Republic of China.

NKRUMAH, KWAME (1909–1972), was the leader of Ghana from independence until 1966.

NOZICK, ROBERT (1938–), is a professor of philosophy at Harvard University and author of *Anarchy, State, and Utopia* (1974), the best exposition of modern anarcho-capitalism.

NU, U (1907–1995), was a leader of Burmese independence, Secretary General of the United Nations, and one of the advocates of developmental socialism.

NYERERE, JULIUS K. (1922–), was the first president of Tanganyika and then of Tanzania after it was formed through the amalgamation of Tanganyika and Zanzibar. He is one of the theorists of African socialism.

OWEN, ROBERT (1771–1858), was a British utopian socialist.

PAEHLKE, ROBERT C., is a writer on environmental issues.

PAINE, THOMAS (1737–1809), was a political agitator, revolutionist, and political theorist.

PALME, OLOF (1927–1986), was a leader of European democratic socialists.

PANKHURST, CHRISTOBEL (1880–1958), was the daughter of Emmeline Pankhurst and active in the British suffrage movement.

PANKHURST, EMMELINE (1858–1928), was a leader of the British suffrage movement.

PANKHURST, SYLVIA (1882–1928), was the daughter of Emmeline Pankhurst and active in the British suffrage movement.

PANNEKOEK, ANTON (1873–1960), was the Dutch founder of Council Communism.

PIERCY, MARGE (1936–), is a contemporary novelist whose novel *Woman on the Edge of Time* (1976) is a major feminist utopia.

POT, POL (1925/28–), is leader of the Khmer Rouge guerrillas in Cambodia and responsible for genocide against the citizens of Cambodia.

PROUDHON, PIERRE-JOSEPH (1809–1865), was a leading French anarchist theorist.

QADAHAFI, MUAMMUR (1942–), is the leader of Libya.

RAINSBOROUGH, THOMAS (d. 1648), was one of the leaders of the army that sided with the Levellers in the English civil war. He gave a famous speech in support of electoral equality.

RAND, AYN (1905–1982), was a novelist, lecturer, and essayist who influenced the growth of libertarianism and minimalism in the United States.

RAWLS, JOHN (1921–), is a professor of philosophy at Harvard University and has been the major liberal theorist of the twentieth century.

REAGAN, RONALD (1911–), was the fortieth president of the United States.

RÉCLUS, ÉLISÉE, (1830–1905), was a Belgian geographer known also as an anarchist theorist.

ROCKEFELLER, JOHN D., (1839–1937), was a U.S. financier.

ROUSSEAU, JEAN-JACQUES. See page 49.

SAINT-SIMON, HENRI (1760–1825), was a French engineer and utopian socialist.

SANGER, MARGARET (1883–1966), was an early advocate of birth control and women's rights.

SARTRE, JEAN-PAUL (1905–1980), was a French novelist and philosopher.

SCOTT, SARAH (1723–1795), was a British writer, who is now most remembered for her book *Millennium Hall* (1762), in which she depicted a community of women.

SENGHOR, LÉOPOLD (1906–), was a leader of the anticolonial movement in Senegal, a leader of the country after independence, and a significant French poet.

SMITH, ADAM. See page 84.

SOREL, GEORGES (1847–1922), was a French journalist and political theorist.

SPENCER, HERBERT (1820–1903), was an English philosopher and the major proponent of Social Darwinism.

STALIN, JOSEPH (born Iosif Vissarionovich Dzhugashvili, 1879–1953), was the leader of the USSR after Lenin.

STANTON, ELIZABETH CADY (1815–1902), was one of the founders of the first women's rights conventions in Seneca Falls, New York, in 1848 and a leader of the nineteenth-century women's rights movement.

STIRNER, MAX (pseud. for Casper Schmidt, 1806–1856), was the founder of individualist anarchism.

TAYLOR, HARRIET (1808–1858), wrote on women's rights. She was the wife of John Stuart Mill and influenced him to write on women's rights.

THOMPSON, WILLIAM (1775–1833), wrote on women's rights.

THOREAU, HENRY DAVID (1817–1862), was a naturalist and writer. He published his famous *Walden* in 1854. An advocate of civil disobedience, he influenced Mahatma Gandhi and Martin Luther King, Jr.

TOLSTOI, LEO (1828–1910), was a famous Russian novelist who is also known as an anarchist theorist.

TOURÉ, SÉKOU (1922–), was the leader of the independence movement and first president of Guinea.

TUCKER, BENJAMIN (1854–1939), was one of the most important American anarchist theorists.

WAGNER, WILHELM RICHARD (1813–1883), is best known for his operas expressing Teutonic mythology.

WALTER, NICHOLAS (1934–), is a major British anarchist theorist.

WARD, COLIN (1924–), is a freelance writer who was editor of the British journal *Anarchy*.

WARREN, JOSIAH (1798?–1874), was an early American anarchist theorist.

WOLLSTONECRAFT, MARY (1759–1797), was one of the earliest feminist theorists.

WOODCOCK, GEORGE (1912–1995), was a British anarchist theorist who settled in Canada and became one of the most important scholars of anarchism.

WRIGHT, FRANCES (1795–1852), was a lecturer and writer concerned with women's rights, slavery, and the plight of workers, among other issues. She founded the Nashoba Community as a means of freeing slaves.

Index

Credits

This page constitutes an extension of the copyright page. We have made every effort to trace the ownership of all copyrighted material and to secure permission from copyright owners. In the event of any question arising as to the use of any material, we will be pleased to make the necessary corrections in future printings. Thanks are due to the following authors, publishers, publications, and agents for permission to use the material indicated.

Chapter 7: 161, excerpt from *The Political Economy of Communism,* by P. J. D. Wiles. Copyright 1962 by Basil Blackwell Ltd. & Mott Ltd. Reprinted by permission of Basil Blackwell Ltd. & Mott Ltd., Harvard University Press, and the author.

Chapter 11: 217–218, excerpt from *A Theology of Liberation,* by Gustavo Gutiérrez. Revised edition copyright 1988 by SCM Press. 15th Anniversary Edition copyright 1988 by Orbis Books. Reprinted by permission. **219, 220,** excerpts from *Introducing Liberation Theology,* by Leonardo and Clodovis Boff. Translated by Paul Burns. Copyright 1987 by Orbis Books. Reprinted by permission. Also reprinted by permission of Burns & Oates Ltd. **220, 221,** excerpt from *Church, Charism, Power: Liberation Theology and the Institutional Church* by Leonardo Boff. English translation © 1985 by T.C.P.C. Reprinted by permission of The Crossroad Publishing Company.

Chapter 13: 240, excerpt from *Ecotopia: The Notebooks and Reports of William Weston,* by Ernest Callenbach. Copyright 1975 Banyan Tree Books. Reprinted with permission. **241–242,** excerpt from "Environmental Beliefs and Values," by L. W. Milbrath. In M. G. Hermann (Ed.), *Political Psychology: Contemporary Problems and Issues.* Copyright © 1986 by Jossey-Bass, Inc. Reprinted by permission. **243,** excerpt from *Environmentalism and the Future of Progressive Politics,* by R. C. Paehlke. Copyright 1989 by Yale University Press. Reprinted by permission.